T0355001

'Poland' in Hebrew, according to a Middle Ages rabbinic saying:
"'Poh Lin'; here we shall rest."

Rabbi Dov Ber Meisels (1863):
"We should love the Polish nation more than any other, because the Poles have been our brothers for centuries."

Cardinal August Hlond (1936):
"It is an actual fact that the Jews fight against the Catholic Church, they are freethinkers, and constitute the vanguard of atheism, bolshevism and revolution. The Jewish influence upon morals is fatal, and the publishers spread pornographic literature. It is also true that the Jews are committing frauds, practicing usury, and dealing in white slavery. ... Not all Jews are like that... It is not permissible to hate anyone. Not even Jews."

Zofia Kossak-Szczucka, creator of Żegota that helped many Jews (1942):
"The slaughter of millions of defenseless people is being carried out amid general sinister silence... Whoever is silent witnessing murder, becomes a partner to the murder. ...Our feelings toward the Jews have not changed. We continue to deem them political, economic, and ideological enemies of Poland...Today the Jews face extermination.... I must save them. ... After the war ... I will tell the Jews: 'I saved you, sheltered you when you were persecuted. To keep you alive I risked my own life and the lives of those who were dear to me. Now nothing threatens you. .... Now I am depriving you of my home. Go and settle somewhere else."

German billboard poster, Przemyśl, November 19, 1942:
"Any Pole that admits a Jew with him or affords him shelter, accommodation or hiding, will be shot. Any Pole who aids a Jew in any way, found outside his residential district [ghetto], will be shot. Any Pole who even attempts to carry out these aforementioned acts, will be shot."

Władysław Kowalski, rescuer of a large group of Jews in Warsaw:
"I did nothing special and I don't consider myself a hero. I only fulfilled my human obligation towards the persecuted and suffering ones... I sought no compensation for what I did... In summary, I should like to re-emphasize that all I did was to help 49 Jews survive the Holocaust. That's all."

Irena Sendlerowa helped save hundreds of children from the Warsaw Ghetto:
"As long as I live and as long as I have the strength I shall always say that the most important thing in the world and in life is Goodness."

POLAND, THE JEWS AND THE HOLOCAUST

Promised Beginnings and Troubled Past

MORDECAI PALDIEL

This book is a work of non-fiction.

Archway Publishing books may be ordered through booksellers or by contacting:

Archway Publishing
1663 Liberty Drive
Bloomington, IN 47403
www.archwaypublishing.com
844-669-3957

ISBN: 978-1-6657-1972-8 (sc)
ISBN: 978-1-6657-1973-5 (e)

Library of Congress Control Number: 2022904044

Print information available on the last page.

Archway Publishing rev. date: 04/13/2022

CONTENTS

Introduction vii

Chapter 1   Polish-Jewish Relations Up to World War I 1
Chapter 2   The Interwar Period (1918-1939) 39
Chapter 3   World War II: Germans, Poles and Jews 65
Chapter 4   Polish-Jewish Relations During the War Years 97
Chapter 5   On the Aryan Side 117
Chapter 6   Rescuers of Jews 145
Chapter 7   Organizational and Diplomatic Assistance 179
Chapter 8   The Polish Government-in-Exile and the
             Underground 201
Chapter 9   Postwar Situation 237

Conclusion 257
Notes 261
Bibliography 315
Index 335

INTRODUCTION

*"There is no history of Poland without the history of the Jews,
and no history of the Jews without the history of Poland."*
Jacob Goldberg[1]

In 1939, Poland was the center of the European Jewish world. It had the largest Jewish population in Europe, who were heirs to a highly developed social and religious community, rooted for nearly a thousand years on Polish soil. Many Jewish leaders came from Poland and its fringe lands; including those in the Zionist movement, such as Chaim Weizmann, David Ben Gurion, Menachem Begin, Levi Eshkol, Moshe Sharet, and the fathers of Moshe Dayan, Ariel Sharon, and Benjamin Netanyahu.[2] It was also the home of many luminaries in Jewish religious thought (the list is too long to recite), a center of Hasidism (presently reestablished in Israel, New York, London and elsewhere), and of various secular movements, such as the Jewish socialist Bund. In short, the mainstay of Jewish cultural and religious creativity. One of the ironies of this age-long Polish Jewish heritage is that many of the renewed and enlarged ultra-Orthodox Hasidic communities, and their rabbinic leaders, still call themselves after places in Poland, Lithuania and Ukraine; such as: Gur (Góra Kalwaria), Kock, Belz, Lubavitch, Slonim, Tzanz (Nowy Sącz), Bobov (Bobowa), Nadwórna, Bratslav; cities and towns where there are hardly any Jews left.[3] This is a phenomenon not known in earlier Jewish history. One hardly remembers the cities where Rashi and Maimonides, Jewish spiritual giants, penned their timeless and enduring religious writings. Yet, Eliyahu ben Solomon is still commonly known, not by his birth name, but as the Vilna Gaon; a city where the conquering Germans and local Lithuanians butchered the entire Jewish population during World War II. This, too, is a testimony to the enduring impact that places such as these had in Jewish religious and cultural history.

All of this is gone, as the destruction of the Jews of Poland accounted for more than half of all the victims of the Holocaust. Equally painful, here most of the ghettos were established, and here the German-constructed death camps stood. Here the railroad tracks converged, bringing hundreds of thousand Jews from the remotest corners of Europe to feed the Nazi death machine. Non-Jewish Poles found themselves witnesses to this horrific spectacle, from beginning to end, a full five years. In the words of Michael Steinlauf, to witness murder on such a scale, at such close range, for such a long time, cannot lead to simple responses.[4]

I was born in Belgium from parents who arrived there from Poland, during the 1920s and 1930s, hoping to seek a better life; my father originated in Miechów; my mother in Uhnów (today in Ukraine). I remember that at home, whenever Poles were mentioned, it was mostly on how they disliked the Jews. Poland, my parents made clear, was a place where Jews felt it better to leave, in spite of the hundreds of years of residence there. I always wondered whether throughout the long history of Jewish habitation in that country that, paradoxically, began with the Polish monarchs inviting the Jews to come there, anti-Jewish feelings predominated, or were the exception. From all my reading on this subject, it seems to me that over many centuries Jews felt very secure amidst the non-Jewish population of Poland; at least until the late 19th century, and especially until the rebirth of Poland as an independent nation at the end of World War I.

When the Germans marched into Soviet held Polish lands, on June 22, 1941 (much of Poland had already been conquered and occupied by Germany in early September 1939), local enthusiastic collaborators (especially Ukrainians and Lithuanians, and some Poles as well, such as in Jedwabne) greeted them by staging pogroms and killing raids on local Jews. This continued into 1942, when the Germans, with their special liquidation troops, known as Einsatzgruppen, aided by local collaborators, continued the slaughter of Jews by mass shootings. This is now known as Holocaust by Bullets. In German-occupied Poland, the situation was different. No mass scale killing sprees took place there until the summer months of 1942, when the ghettos where most of Polish Jews were imprisoned until then, were forcibly emptied of their Jewish inhabitants, and they were exterminated, via poisoning in specially constructed German death camps, on Polish soil: such as, Chełmno, Treblinka, Sobibór, Majdanek, Bełżec, and the largest of them all, Auschwitz-Birkenau.

Starting especially in mid-1942, some tens of thousands of Jews (perhaps as many as close to 200,000) sought succor by fleeing the ghettos and labor camps into non-Jewish inhabited cities and towns, or throughout the many villages that dotted the Polish countryside, or again, deep into forest lairs, hoping to remain invisible. Many were hunted down by German security units, who were aided by the Polish so-called Blue Police and, with increasing incidence, by a growing number of Poles, while many other Poles, at great risks to themselves, saved Jews from the Germans. This killing spree increased in ferocity during the closing days of the war, and spilled over into the post-war years, as Jews returning to their homes were waylaid and killed by vigilant antisemites, and this led to a panicky stampede out of the country of most surviving Jews. Then, in 1968, the remnant few Jews (many of them holding professional government positions) were targeted by the communist regime as anti-Polish, expelled from their jobs and told to leave the country; and this, finally put a cap on the centuries-old Jewish presence in Poland.

Historians have since grappled with various theories to explain the presence of antisemitism among broad masses of the population, at a time when Poland itself was suffering from a terrible German occupation (one of the worst in German-occupied Europe), which claimed hundreds of thousands of innocent Polish lives. The search for answers is still ongoing, accompanied at times with acrimonious and accusatory debates between opposing sides.

At the same time, while fellow Poles facilitated the German roundup of Jews either actively or in other ways, other Poles took it upon themselves to save Jews from death, by mostly sheltering them in their homes, or obtaining for them new and false credentials, or helping them cross into safer regions, and finally, initiating the rescue of thousands of children, who were also slated for destruction by the Germans. These heroic humanitarian acts were done in the face of dangers to the life of the rescuers, and some Poles, indeed, paid with their lives (the approximate numbers are still highly debatable). Most others, however, took great precautions to keep their rescue a secret not only from the Germans, but also from their own kinsfolk and relatives – many of whom held to antisemitic tropes – so as not to be betrayed to the authorities. This book is an attempt to portray both sides of Polish behavior toward the many Jews that inhabited Poland for over nine centuries, in numbers larger than in any other European country, for the greater part of Polish history.

One of the reasons that prompted me to write this book are the stories of Polish rescuers of Jews, that I came across during the 24 years that I headed the Righteous Among the Nations Department at the Yad Vashem Holocaust institute, in Jerusalem. The courage and humanitarianism displayed by these persons inspired me to uphold my belief in the perseverance of universal human values, as demonstrated by these courageous people, who acted under duress; under the harshest conditions imaginable – the threat of losing their own lives, in light of the German warning of the death penalty to anyone aiding Jews to avoid detection and arrest. During the period that I presided over the work of the Righteous, I pride myself that some 18,000 names of non-Jewish rescuers from many, mostly European countries, were added to the Righteous honor list, for risking their lives to save Jews from the Nazis and their collaborators, and thousands of Poles are prominently included among these rescuers. I admit, however, that while studying the testimonies and historical material that landed on my desk, it told not only of help to Jews to survive through the help of compassionate Poles, but a different and darker side story – of an ongoing antisemitism among wide strata of the Polish population, that may have facilitated the German-orchestrated Final Solution of the Jews. All this, while as a conquered nation, non-Jewish Poles themselves underwent terrible sufferings at the hands of the Germans.

This book is an attempt to explain the paradox of a country that originally invited the Jews to settle there, and created conditions that allowed them to develop diversified religious and cultural systems; then, of late, the country's leaders urged these long-centuries numerous guests to leave and find another place for themselves. At the same time, I am careful not to correlate anti-Jewish feelings of one sort or another with active participation of harm to Jews, for the simple reason that many who participated in the hunt of Jews were also driven by an uncontrollable lust of robbery and plunder, in a country where, during the harsh German occupation, moral and humanitarian values took a back seat, rather than solely due any ideological beliefs that many may have held about the Jews.

I say this, because while surveying the long history of Jews in Poland, one finds only a handful of antisemitic outbreaks against the Jews by Poles in pre-modern timesl and none of the expulsion of Jews in the scope that was common in other European countries, situated close to Poland. The 1648-49 pogroms of Jews on Polish soil were staged by Ukrainians and led by the non-Pole, Bohdan Khmelnytsky. During the Middle Ages, and sometimes later, in German lands, Jews were expelled many times from this and that city and province; several times from most of France, twice from Austria, once from Hungary, and once from England (a ban which lasted 365 years). In Tsarist Russia, Jews were restricted to a Pale of Settlement – whereas, not once did Jews in Poland, who originally numbered in the tens of thousands, then in the hundreds of thousands, face total expulsion from Poland proper, or were restricted in their habitations. The sole exception was very late in the modern period – at the very end of the Jewish presence in that country – when in 1968 the last pitiful and dismal remnant 50,000 Jews were expelled by a communist regime, in which some Jews had earlier played a prominent part. This is quite an unusual phenomenon when compared with Jewish vicissitudes in other European countries.

Another issue worth pondering is that while France flirted with antisemitism during the Dreyfus Affair, in the 19th century, many years after their emancipation by the French Revolution (see the example Edouard Drumont's *La France Juive*), and Germany gave birth to modern antisemitism, a term coined by Wilhelm Marr, and taken up by Richard Wagner, and Houston Chamberlain – in the same century in Poland, it came only somewhat later, toward the end of the 19th century, and picked up steam in the 20th century. On the flip side, one must also mention that while in France and Germany, Jews underwent a growing process of acculturation, in Poland most Jews still stuck close to themselves and their own indigenous folk culture. They were consequently perceived by non-Jews as outsiders and an alien element. They were especially marked – different and visible in dress, culture, religion, language (Yiddish) and national aspirations than the non-Jewish population.

A strong current of antisemitism rose in Poland after it re-emerged as a nation at the end of World War I, after a 123 years hiatus as a country divided among three powerful neighbors. The new-born independent country was fused in bloody confrontations with other ethnic groups: Ukrainians, Russians, Lithuanians and Germans. This led to a determination by Polish leaders to forcefully Polonize those minorities susceptible to assimilation – primarily the Ukrainians and Byelorussians, and induce those not susceptible to Polonization to have them leave the country – foremost, the Jews. In line with this policy, Polish authorities pressured Jews to leave through a whole series of discriminatory laws, but not extermination.

During the German occupation of Poland, it was the Germans, not the Poles, who for primarily racial and antisemitic reasons decided to exterminate all living Jews, whether in Poland or elsewhere, coupled with threats to Poles of the death penalty for anyone affording help to Jews to avoid this onslaught on their lives. In this study, all these conflicting themes in the saga of Polish-Jewish relations are mentioned so as to give a balanced picture, as much as possible, of the composite relationship between Jews and non-Jews in a country that began with the Polish kings inviting the Jews to come and settle there – and leading up to the Holocaust. Also, the troubling aftereffects in Poland of the Holocaust legacy, and the recent attempts to restore a modicum of Jewish life in a country that centuries ago had such a promising beginning.

When dealing with such a subject, that is not only controversial but also mired in divisive passionate debates, one cannot merely restrict oneself to Polish-Jewish relations in the 20th century, but one must trace the roots of this relationship back in history, covering many centuries, in order to analyze and combine the promised beginnings with the dismal and tragic endings of this togetherness of two diverse socio-religious cultures – at times cordial and harmonious, and at other times, discordant, unfriendly, and even hostile. I find that all studies of this relationship during the Holocaust period, shorten their analysis only from the rebirth of Polish independence in the wake of World War I, while remaining oblivious to the long history of Polish-Jewish relations over the hundreds of years before the 20th century. I find this a serious shortcoming, hindering a better understanding of the nature of this relationship, and I, thereby, begin Chapter 1 with tracing and summarizing the generally tolerable and peaceful relationship over the eight centuries that preceded the Polish rebirth after World War I.

It should not be surprising that nearly every issue that will be examined in the following pages may be open to controversy and disagreements. I am sure that some will claim I was too lenient; others too harsh on the Poles; that I suffer from naivete, or the opposite – prejudice. Also, that I missed mentioning this and that author in support of whatever I wrote. To all these critics, learned or not, I can only thank them for their contribution to an ongoing debate, although at times bitter and painful, that undoubtedly will last for many more years.

CHAPTER 1

Polish-Jewish Relations
Up to World War I

Origins. In no other European country had Jews lived in such considerable numbers for so long a time as in Poland.[1] Jewish traders are mentioned in chronicles dating back before 963 CE, when the oldest Polish state, that of the Piast kings, first appeared on the scene. The Jewish connection to Poland is therefore as old as Polish history, primarily since Jews continued to be invited by Polish kings and princes to settle there in the following years, in order to help build up commerce and trade.[2] Some have attributed the early Jewish immigration to the Khazar people, an ethnic Turkic tribe, that lived in the area between the Caspian and Black Seas, and created a large kingdom. In the latter part of the 9th century CE, the Khazar king and many of his subjects converted to Judaism. However, Khazar rule did not last long, and it collapsed in the early 10th century, and some claimed that Khazar persons dispersed and migrated westward into Polish lands. But this is hard to sustain, except perhaps in a few cases only, in light of the use of Yiddish, as the vernacular language of Polish Jews. This, rather, points to their migration coming primarily from German-speaking areas west of Poland, not the east.[3]

Jews arrived mostly from western and southwestern Europe, from the Rhine and Danube river provinces, as they fled persecutions since the early Middle Ages, principally in German lands and Bohemia-Moravia, such as the persecutions attending the First Crusade that caused many

Jews to move to Poland in 1098.[4] From this point onward, undisputed and datable information on Jews living in Poland begins to appear. Under the tolerant rule of king Bolesław III (1102–1139), Jews settled throughout the vast regions of Poland, including over the border into Lithuanian territory and eastward as far as Kjiv, in today's Ukraine. From 1241 onward, the Mongol invasions caused heavy losses in life and destruction to property in Poland; yet, subsequent kings of Poland eagerly sought Jewish immigrants from the west, and afforded them assistance to settle in the villages and towns. Many more headed there in the fourteenth and fifteenth centuries, when persecution drove thousands of Jews eastwards from northeastern France and Germany. The Jews brought with them a well-developed culture and religious practice, and helped to promote the already spoken Yiddish by Polish Jews – a popular vernacular Germanic original language.[5]

In the 14th century, Jews are mentioned as residing in Plock, Kalisz, Kraków, Lwów, Sandomierz, Poznań, Liuboml, Brest-Litovsk, Grodno and Troki, and other places, and they numbered between 20,000 and 30,000.[6] For the most part they were an urban element, but many also lived in villages and small towns, where they served as middlemen, leaseholders and managers of the noblemen's new properties. These smaller towns, which Jews called *shtetlech* (singular, *shtetl*), were particularly widespread throughout Poland, and remained the characteristic form of Jewish settlement until late in the nineteenth century, when the large cities again began to attract great numbers of Jews.[7]

In the years of the Black Death plague, during the 14th century, ravaging all of Europe, outbreaks against Jews, who were held guilty for this plague, also occurred in Kalish, Kraków, Glogau, and other cities.[8] However, Jews continued to be generally well treated, such as not compelled to wear ignominious badges as in many other places in western Europe. Jewish fortunes ebbed and improved under successive kings, who had to counter the anti-Jewish demands of the clergy, the city-dwelling burghers, the guilds, and German merchants inside Poland who envied the competitive Jewish traders. The strongest supporters, however, of the Polish Jews were the Polish nobility, who held high official posts, and

Polish kings usually dovetailed decisions in close consultation with them; the occasional laws against Jews, therefore, remained a dead letter, to the vexation of the clergy, the guilds and burghers.[9]

At all events, the Jews of Poland fared far better than those in many other places in Europe. Jews also continued to enjoy a wide range of civic, economic and religious privileges under the 12-year reign of Stefan Bathory (1575-1586), while at the same time period, they already had been expelled from Spain and Portugal, some 70 to 80 years earlier, and continued to suffer indignities elsewhere in Europe. These pro-Jewish policies continued in the long reign of Bathory's successor, Sigismund III (1587-1632), although ceding to ecclesiastical demands, he ordained that the permission of the clergy had to be gained to build new synagogues. What's important to emphasize is that in no part of Christian Europe did Jews enjoy such a sense of security as in those years in Poland, and they never faced the threat of wholesale expulsion from the country, as prevailed elsewhere. Their rights were constantly renewed and issued by the king with the assent of the Polish nobility, the real power behind the throne.[10]

In 1589, the Kingdom of Poland and the Grand Duchy of Lithuania were united into the Polish-Lithuanian Commonwealth, and consequently it remained for a long time one of the largest and most powerful states in Europe.[11] During the several hundred years of its existence, the Polish-Lithuanian Commonwealth was a multi-national and multi-religious state. It included within its borders not only Poles but also Germans, Lithuanians, Byelorussians, Ukrainians, Jews, Armenians and many other national groups, as well as a large number of religious groupings – each adhering to their own cultural, religious, and linguistic differences.[12]

Starting 1572, Polish monarchs were elected by the country's most powerful nobles (known as *szlachta*) and magnates, and this gradually led to the weakening of the king's authority, but did not paralyze it entirely, at least not immediately. Yet, between the sixteenth and eighteenth centuries, the political structure of the Commonwealth shifted from a strong monarchy to a state ruled by powerful nobles.[13] The monarchy felt weak in administering the vast domains of the state and failed to create a bureaucracy which could carry out these functions. That bolstered the nobility, who enjoyed a monopoly of political power, which they exercised through the legislature, (the *Sejm*), or local councils. One outcome of this weakening of the central government was the kingdom's toleration of the various ethnic groups constituting the Commonwealth.[14] According to historian Theodore Weeks, during the late Middle Ages, mostly Catholic Poland remained one of the most tolerant states in Europe, benefiting the religious minorities, especially the Jews, the Russian Orthodox, and for a time the Protestants.[15]

Jewish privileges. The legal position of the Jews in Poland has its origin in the charter issued by Prince Bolesław V, the Pious, of Kalisz in 1264, the so-called Statute of Kalisz. This document put the Jews in the category of *servi camerae regis* (servants belonging to the king's treasury); they were under the sovereign's protection and had a wide-range of permitted economic activities and the right to practice their religion. Jewish places of worship and cemeteries were tax free.[16] Half a century later, in 1334, King Casimir-Kazimierz III the Great (ruled 1333–1370), who was especially friendly to the Jews, extended these privileges and protected them from demands of forced baptism and other anti-Jewish accusations by the Catholic bishops. Overriding canonical laws established by the churches, he granted a charter to the Jews, in which he placed the rights enjoyed by Jews on equal terms with Christians. Furthermore, to protect Jews from the blood libel charge, the king decreed that if a Christian charged an individual Jew with using Christian blood for ritual purpose, and the Christian accuser was not in a position to substantiate his charge by credible testimony, he was to be punished, even with death.[17]

Of great importance were matters involving judicial rulings. Some of them established that minor civil cases between Jews were to be judged by the Jewish community's jurisdiction. Moreover, in certain court cases, all lawsuits involving a Jew whether as a plaintiff or defendant, it was to adjudicated by a Jewish court, especially when it involved city-dwelling burghers.[18] When occasioned in noble-owned towns, the powers of the Jewish judiciary were slightly reduced. Until the end of the Polish Commonwealth at the close of the eighteenth century, no law was passed diminishing the authority of the Jewish courts of justice that had been earlier authorized.[19] In the first half of the seventeenth century, the noted Polish writer Szymon Starowolski emphasized, perhaps with some dismay, that "justice was meted out more quickly to the Jews than to anyone else who had committed a wicked act, and that the Jews got away more easily without a fine than anyone else." No wonder that representatives of the burghers and clergy repeatedly demanded the curtailment of the rights contained in the privileges granted to the Jews.[20] Poland, therefore, in the words of historian Heinrich Graetz, had become a second Babylon for the Jews, in which on the whole they were protected from bloody persecutions, and where they were allowed to develop their religious and social lives without the humiliating restraints imposed on their brethren elsewhere in Europe.[21]

Council of Four Lands. The period from 1580 to 1648 is considered the Golden Age in Poland, as well as for its Jewish population.[22] It was a time when, in the combined Polish-Lithuanian Commonwealth, Jews obtained a degree of self-government which went considerably beyond that enjoyed by their co-religionists elsewhere in Europe. Jews were enabled to create a particularly autonomous system of self-governance unprecedented in other parts of the Diaspora: a hierarchy of regional and provincial councils overseen by a supreme deliberative and judicial body, that constituted a kind of autonomous Jewish government.[23] The basic unit of the self-governing structure was the local community, *kehilla* or *kahal*; *kehillot* in the plural.

The executives of the *kehillah*, at the lower level, represented the Jews before non-Jewish authorities and administrative and judicial bodies.[24] The lower *kehillot* were integrated into a larger body, established in 1580 – an autonomous institution that came to direct Jewish life in Poland, and known as the Council of the Four Lands (*Vaad Arba Aratsot*). The four lands referred to the constituent parts of the Polish Kingdom – Great Poland (Poznań and Kalisz), Little Poland (Kraków and Sandomierz), today's Ukraine (including Lwów), and Volhynia

(Ostróg, Łuck, Włodzimierz and Przemieniec). There was also a separate council for Lithuania.[25] As the head of Jewish self-government from 1580 until its abolition in 1764, the Council of the Four Lands (henceforth, Council) was the main representative body of the Jewish population in matters pertaining to tax assessment, secular legislation and intervention with the appropriate state authorities.[26] Among its functions was maintaining the community organizational structure and various services, such as paying the rabbis who it hired, and operating its own courts for Jews involved in disputes with one another. It also raised the taxes to be paid to the king (a head tax to the king's treasury was imposed on Jews in 1552). According to historian Shmul Ettinger, taxation was the main factor that led into the permanent structure of the Council, as the government handed over responsibility for collecting the tax to the Jews, who had to apportion the amount among themselves at their assemblies.[27]

The Council, which generally met twice a year during the Lublin and Jarosław fairs, represented the Jews' internal leadership, and dealt with their problems and vital issues. This centrally elected Jewish autonomous leadership was known in Polish as the Jewish parliament (*Sejm Żydowski*).[28] The local *kehillot* would send delegates, learned men of proved excellence, to the Council meetings, who in turn chose a president, who directed the agenda of issues, and drew up a report of the session. The elective president (*Parnas di Arba Aratsot*) stood at the head, and conducted public affairs. Disputes in the communities, questions of taxation, religious and social regulations, the averting of threatened dangers, and help to brethren in distress, were the main points treated by the Council synods, and settled peacefully. The communities and rabbis had civil, and to a certain extent criminal jurisdiction, at least against informers and traitors.[29]

The Council also sat in judgment as a high religious court (*Bet Din*) on lawsuits between Jews from various communities. The Council also took measures for the strengthening of religious life, such as ordinances relating to the proper observance of the Sabbath. It also exempted Torah scholars from liability to tax and passed ordinances requiring the *kehillot* to establish Talmudic academic (*yeshivot*) and provide for the subsistence of the students and their teachers.[30] It also dealt with the conduct of business and the performance of work by non-Jews in those areas when complete estates or branches of estates were leased to Jews by the nobility. Finally, the Council also elected several office-bearers – *parnasim* and *shtadlanim* – as trustees, who upheld the continuity of the Council's activities and maintained contact with the authorities to defend Jewish interests between periods of the Council assemblies, especially during times of trouble.

At times, the Council also intervened in disputes in Jewish communities far outside the borders of Poland, as it did in the affairs of the *kehillot* of Frankfurt-am-Main and Amsterdam. Additionally, it played a part in raising money to benefit Jews in Palestine-Eretz Israel.[31] The Council was continuously active over a period of about 200 years (from the sixteenth to the eighteenth centuries) and was recognized by the authorities as the Jewish representative body until its official disbandment in 1764.

According to Jacob Goldberg, historian of Polish Jewry, the Council constituted a parliamentary representation sui generis of the biggest and liveliest center of world Jewry.[32] Historian Graetz, living in nearby Germany, goes a step further and terms the Council situation as consisting as close to an independent state within a larger state; a situation unequalled elsewhere in the world where Jews lived.[33] No wonder, that the Council was regarded as the greatest expression of Jewish aspirations towards self-rule since the institution of the Gaonate came to an end, in earlier times, in distant Babylonia.[34]

The Council system was abolished in 1764, by King Stanislaus August Poniatowski; a weak ruler, whose reign also coincided with the loss of Polish independence that began eight years after the Council's abolishment, and lasted 123 years. With the abolition of the Council, the whole operation of Jewish self-government was transferred to the local level, to the individual communities headed by their elders.[35] The golden years of Polish Jewry seemed to have come to an end, but, surprisingly, Jewish life continued to pulsate and produce a major new form of religious devoutness, that swept through Poland, Ukraine, and beyond—Hasidism (that will later be further mentioned).[36]

Yeshivot and religious center. Over the years, due to the religious freedom enjoyed by Jews in Poland, the country also became the chief home of Talmud study and the nursery of Talmudic students and rabbis. The Talmudical schools in Poland became the most celebrated throughout the whole of European Judaism. All who sought sound religious learning betook themselves there. The fame of the rabbinical schools of Poland was during a certain time due to three men: Shalom Shachna; his pupil, Moses Isserles (1520-1572), better known as the Remah; and Solomon Luria (the Maharshal).[37] The study of the Talmud in Poland, established by these three men, reached a pitch attained at no previous time, nor in any other country. This included the system of Pilpul (literally, pepper) or "theological hair-splitting."[38] Moses Isserles in Kraków, achieved renown among the Jews as the co-author of the Code of Jewish Law (*Shulchan Aruch*).[39] These Talmudic scholars laid the foundation of the extraordinary erudition of Polish Jews. Any complicated or generally interesting religious question, or passionate disputes, arising elsewhere in Europe or Turkey, was submitted to them, especially to Isserles, for final decisions. This rabbinical triumvirate founded a kind of supremacy in religious matters over the Jews of Europe, acknowledged on all sides, and the Polish rabbis maintained their position as leaders even after the disappearance of Poland as an independent nation, as the yeshivot (Talmudic academies) in many Polish cities (as well as in nearby Lithuania) achieved fame throughout Europe.[40] Magnificent synagogue buildings were erected as early as the 16th century, including the printing of many religious works.[41] Poland thus became a principal center of Jewish religious studies, rarely seen elsewhere in Europe, and remained so until the Holocaust.

Here we shall rest. It was not for nothing that the enemies of the Jews at that time jeered that Poland was a paradise for Jews ("*clarum regnum Polonorum est paradisum Judaeorum*").[42] The reasons for that was as stated by the long Alsatian-French resident of Poland, J.L. de la Fontaine, that, "nowhere else do they enjoy such open freedoms and security as here" (*"nirgends geniesst er so viel öffentlichen Freyheiten und Sicherheit als hier."*)[43] The Jewish side agreed with these assessments at already an earlier period, as voiced in the 16th century by the famed earlier mentioned rabbinic leader, Moses Isserles, of Poland as "this land of refuge." And three hundred years later, rabbi Dov Ber Meisels, a patriot of Polish national aspirations, referred to Isserles in the following words: "Our greatest religious authority, Moses Isserles, on whose rulings the whole house of Israel is based, showed us in his decisions regarding the relations of Jews to nations of other religions, that we should love the Polish nation more than any other, because the Poles have been our brothers for centuries."[44]

Through the late Middle Ages, Poland remained the most tolerant country in Europe for Jews, in comparison to other European countries. Not surprisingly, for many Jews, the Hebrew word for Poland, *Polin*, was broken down into two parts and read in Hebrew as: *po* ("here") *lin* ("[you shall] dwell") As also shown by another favorite Hebrew pun, *Polania* (another appellation of the country in Hebrew) could also be read as *Poh-lan-ya* ("God rests here"). These attributes have no parallel in any other European country. The message was clear; Poland was a good place for the Jews.[45] No wonder that during that phase of Polish history, stretching hundreds of years, up to the end of the 18th century, Jews did not emigrate from Poland but, on the contrary, immigrated to it, especially in large numbers – a phenomenon not replicated elsewhere in Europe.[46]

Nobles and Jews. Another striking historical novum in Polish-Jewish relations, not prevalent anywhere else in Europe, was the non-formal but solid alliance over the centuries between the Jews and the nobility, the *szlachta*, the real power behind the throne. The noble aristocracy had acquired the veto power, that included the right of every individual noble in the Sejm to frustrate the passage of any resolution not to its liking.[47] Additional rules tied the king further to them, such as limiting his right to impose new taxes without their approval, and in foreign affairs, by forcing him to seek their approval, especially in matters of war and peace, so much that Poland was often referred to as the Republic of the

Nobles. Most important, it stipulated that, should the king violate any of these rules, the nobles had the right to renounce allegiance to him, as they did several times over several centuries. The Polish-Lithuanian state had become a confederation of principalities controlled by individual magnates, including control of most of the land in the hands of a powerful few, especially during the expansion of the kingdom in the newly acquired eastern regions. The workings of this feudal system were one of the reasons for the backwardness of the Polish economy as compared with other European countries.[48]

The nobles encouraged migration and settlement in their newly acquired large estates, known as latifundia. Jews also benefited from this process, and increasingly moved eastward. By settling in these underpopulated, noble-owned lands, Jews became ever more central to the economy of the nobles, as the latter in the 16th century granted extensive privileges to the Jewish communities living in towns on their estates. Jews made themselves indispensable as agents of the great feudal lords, and they played an important role as merchants, middlemen, leaseholders and estate agents for Polish noble landowners.[49] As leaseholders and employers of Christians, Jews were often in a position of authority over lower-class Christians.[50] Over half of the Jewish population of Poland-Lithuania lived on such private estates, where, in the 16th century, they were under the sole jurisdiction of the noble owners.[51]

The resulting weakness of royal power meant that the Jews were increasingly dependent on the goodwill of the great magnate families. A solidarity based on community interests grew between the state's ruling circles and the wealthiest Jewish merchants and businessmen. If, at the beginning of their settlement in Poland, Jews forged a strong relationship with the monarchs, who issued privileges and assured the Jews' protection, when the balance of power shifted from a strong monarchy to a decentralized nobles' ruling system, the Jewish relationship with the king was transformed into a symbiotic relationship with the powerful nobles, and Jews' reliance on royal protection was transferred to reliance on the nobles.[52] It was not without reason that this relationship was reflected in the wide currency of observation, such as "every nobleman his Jew," and "Poland is heaven for the Jews, paradise for the nobles and hell for the serfs."[53] Thus, whenever Jews were inclined to hold Poles in esteem, it involved primarily only one segment of society – the nobility.[54]

Jewish trades. Other than the nobles' economic connection, Jews also dealt in various trades, such as hides, wax, honey and many oriental goods, such as fabrics and Turkish carpets. On the whole, Jews were far more common in small workshops and retail trade, as well as tailors and tavern keepers. During the early period, Jews also dealt in gold medal minting bearing the Polish sovereign's name in Hebrew letters, together with the names of the minters.[55] Towards the end of the 18th century, about 70 percent of Jewish craftsmen worked in the textiles and haberdashery trades and 17 percent in food; the rest comprised goldsmiths, glaziers, coppersmiths, soap-makers and other trades.[56] In the late 19th century thousands of Jews began to concentrate in large cities, where slowly, but surely, Jews began to assume the role of a middle class. Still, at the dawn of the 20th century, over one-third of Polish Jews were blue-collar workers in various factories and workshops.[57]

Guilds and Burghers. It was not always smooth sailing for the Jews in Poland, as one may conclude from the previous reading, and at times they had to contend with others, mostly due to commercial competition; especially, against those belonging to guilds who tried to restrict the business privileges of Jewish merchants, and prevent them from having their own guilds. The townspeople, in many instances, regarded the Jews as their principal competitors, and their spokesmen voiced sharply anti-Jewish allegations.[58] In 1612, for instance, the city authorities in Warsaw reintroduced a 1523 ruling forbidding Jews to import products into the city, for sale.[59] Jews, nevertheless, began to have their own guilds in 1613. At least nine Jewish guilds were started in Poland between 1613 and 1648; in Kazimierz near Kraków and in Lwów, there was one each by tailors, goldsmiths, barber-surgeons, trimmers and peddlers. Despite these early creations, in many towns, especially the larger royal ones, anti-Jewish guild laws were in force, so that Jewish trade masters had to compromise and come to an agreement with the town guilds, such as the mixed Christian-Jewish guilds that appeared in Nowy Sącz, Gniezno,

Tarnogród, Jarosław, Rzeszów, Lubartów and other towns in the Polish Commonwealth.[60] At the same time, Jewish entrepreneurs succeeded in creating a total of 105 separate Jewish guilds between 1613 and 1795. Of the single-profession guilds, the tailors were the most numerous – formed in 44 towns and one village. Next came the guilds of the haberdashers (five towns), bakers (four towns) and goldsmiths (three towns). Then, there were guilds for capmakers, barber-surgeons, musicians, trimmers, brewers, armorers, weavers, tanners, locksmiths, embroiderers and hosiery workers.[61]

The municipalities of Kraków and nearby Kazimierz intervened 15 times in favor of Jews and 17 times in trying to limit their privileges. But it was mostly Polish kings who took up the defense of Jewish economic interests by supporting their wishes to create independent guilds, against the attempts by city burghers to curtail their rights. In 1567, for instance, King Zygmunt August, granted the Jews of Wiślica the same rights as those enjoyed by the burghers in trade, crafts and the possession of immovable property. The king intervened seven times in favor of the Jews in Poznań, to freely buy and sell real estate and do business. On only two occasions did he favor the complaints of the burghers against Jewish privileges. In 1667, the reigning monarch rejected the claims of the tailors in Kraków against Jewish competition, and forbade them to restrict Jewish business activities in the city. In total, in Kraków, the king intervened 37 times, of which on 23 occasions it was in favor of the Jews, although in some of these cases, Jews had to pay a substantial sum to the royal treasury for these favorable results. Everywhere else, Polish kings were more inclined to favor the Jewish side in protecting their rights, in contrast to the city elders, who under pressure of the guilds, more often tried to restrict the commercial rights of Jews.[62]

One of the classes. The special status enjoyed by Jews in the Polish-Lithuanian Commonwealth has led some to view the Jewish population as one of the constituent classes of the country – alongside the nobility, the clergy, the burghers and the peasantry. Ludwik Gumplowicz, the descendant of a well-known Jewish family, in an 1867 study, asserted that: "In Poland, Jews were a class within the nation, of which they were integral members, like the nobles, peasants, burghers... Among those classes of the nation, Jews were by no means the lowest, as they stood equal with the burghers." The fact that from the second half of the thirteenth century Jews had separate courts, in which they applied their own laws (at least partly), is an important aspect of their special status.[63] Clearly, the Jews were for all intents and purposes a separate estate, lived according to its own duties and privileges. Only with the coming of modern ideologies of democratic, homogeneous national so-cieties – ideologies that filtered eastward in the nineteenth century – did the separate corporate existence of the Jewish community Poland begin to be widely seen as a problem in and of itself.[64]

Jewish population. Jews, not too large at the start, continued to grow in the late seventeenth and eighteenth centuries and do not seem to have suffered lasting effects caused by the massacres of the Cossacks, during the Khmelnytsky rebellion, beginning 1648. At any rate, by 1648, Antony Polonsky gives the number of Jews in Poland (excepting Lithuania) as 170,000, while Shmul Ettinger raises the figure a bit higher – to 300,000. Salo Baron goes even a step further – to 450,000.[65] Maria Bogucka quotes one source that numbers the Jews in 1648 as 500,000 in the Commonwealth, and another source mentions 749,968 persons at a later period, in 1764 (to which one must 201,000 in the Grand Duchy of Lithuania). Based on another estimate, about 411,500 Jews lived in the towns of central Poland at the end of the 18th century; that is, about 50 percent of the total urban population of this area."[66] To put it differently, from a strict Jewish perspective, by the mid seven-teenth century, 30 percent of world Jewry lived in Poland, and rising to almost 45 percent at the start of the eighteenth century – this, in spite of the ravages suffered during the Cossack rebellion of 1648. By the mid-eighteenth century, perhaps half of the world's Jewish population lived within the Polish-Lithuanian Commonwealth.[67]

Compared with fellow Jews in the rest of Europe, those in Poland considered themselves relatively well-off and secure, before they were sav-aged by the non-Polish Cossack massacres of 1648. In Polish historiogra-phy, the century and a half from 1500 to 1648 is known as the Golden

Age. It was a period when Polish kings ruled a vast Polish-Lithuanian Commonwealth that stretched from the Oder River, in the west, to the Dnieper River, in the east, and from the Baltic Sea, in the north, to the Black Sea, in the south. This Commonwealth was a land of great ethnic and religious diversity, multiple centers of authority, and comparative stability, and Jews felt safer there than anywhere else in Europe.[68]

Khmelnytsky and the Cossacks. All this seemed to have suffered a serious setback in 1648, during the Cossack upheaval led by Bohdan Khmelnytsky, that brought great misery to the Jewish population, mostly those in present-day Ukraine. The Khmelnytsky rising led to mass murders of Jews, the flight of tens of thousands of refugees and a serious undermining of Jewish economic activity. This was followed with Polish wars against Sweden, Russia and Turkey that lasted until 1660.[69] During these upheavals, the country lost over a third of its population (some three million people). Jewish losses were unprecedented, mainly at the hands of the Cossacks. Viewed from the context of Jewish-Gentile relations, the significance of this disaster is that all other previous mass deadly attacks against Jews in various parts of Europe were prompted by various charges against Jews, but never because of any perceived close association of the Jews with the country's ruling elite. The Khmelnytsky case was different. Here, Jews were targeted for their link and close relationship with the Polish masters of the country, especially the role of Jews as collectors of fees, and thus were perceived as part of the oppressive system. This is added proof of the tranquility and peaceful condition of Jewish life in Polish and the harmonious relationship with the country's rulers up to that moment.

It is estimated that Jews suffered 20% losses of its population, coupled with the destruction of entire Jewish communities in the eastern and southern parts of the country (today's Ukraine).[70] Many chose to emigrate from Poland.[71] About 6,000 Jews were put to the sword in one city alone, Nemirov. Thousands of defenseless Jews were also slaughtered in other towns; and more than 300 communities suffered full or partial depredations.[72] The Polish Commonwealth never fully recovered from this devastating episode in its history. In these wars, especially during

the struggle against a combination of other countries, cities were decimated; the power of the king declined still further, and all these led to
a growing foreign interference in the Polish political life, which led to a
further decline of the country's standing and power.[73]

However, surprisingly, the Jewish community recovered speedily,
and these traumatic events did little to arrest the continuous development of Jewish communal life. Jewish merchants moved to lumber
and furs, while shopkeepers and artisans developed new products and
services. While the Jewish population of Poland had decreased, it still
outnumbered Jewish settlements in western Europe, and Poland continued to be the spiritual center of Judaism. By 1764, the Jewish population
had risen to close to 600,000 Jews in the Polish–Lithuanian kingdom,
while the worldwide Jewish population at that time was estimated at
1,2 million; and in 1775 the Jewish population in both regions had increased to 750,000, according to some sources; about 550,000 of them
in Poland proper and close to 200,000 in Lithuania.[74] On the eve of
country's disappearance as an independent nation, the Jews numbered
about 800,000, spread over the vast territory of the Polish-Lithuanian
kingdom; in summary, many more multiple numbers of Jews in that
single country than in any other country, elsewhere.[75]

The Church's anti-Judaism. Poland is also known for its faithful
adherence to the Roman Catholic religion, and Protestantism did not
succeed in making permanent inroads. Over the centuries, Catholic
church elders rankled at the special privileges enjoyed by Jews, which
they considered a flagrant violation of the church's traditional theological
position in which Jews were to be in "perpetual servitude" to Christians,
not the other way around. What some found especially galling were the
occasions when, first the king, then the nobles, placed Jews in positions
of authority over Christians.[76] A resolution of a synod in Chełm, in 1604,
condemned the "the shameful" situation in Poland, of the dominance
"of the godless persons who had shed the Lord's blood over those who
have been graciously redeemed by it."[77] In 1737, Bishop Josaphat Michał
Karp, of Samognita, was dismayed that Poles had no qualms about
subjecting "free sons" (i.e., Christians) to "the sons of Hagar the maid,"

a phrase sometimes applied to Jews by church leaders and taken from Paul's critique of the Jews, in Epistle to the Galatians (4:21-26).[78]

Some jobs Christians took on under Jewish employers were seen as more humiliating and problematic than others. The episcopal prohibitions against Christians working for Jews singled out some of these. Bishop Szembek, in 1752, pronounced: "We prohibit the commoners and all faithful who are loving members in Christ, to hire themselves out to Jews as coach-drivers, as farmhands, guards, helpers, or bath-house assistants to Jews; whereas we prohibit the women from hiring themselves as maids, laundresses, wet nurses, nannies of Jewish children, innkeepers or from taking up any work for Jews on a yearly contract." A year earlier, Bishop Józef Andrzej Załuski prohibited Christians from serving Jews on Jewish holidays, and in particular from trimming candles on Yom Kippur or serving in whatever capacity in synagogues.[79] However, these injunctions were mostly honored by disregard than obedience.

In 1718, Father Stefan Żuchowski, of Santomierz, argued that when Christians lease their properties, mills and inns to the Jews, the latter use this to lure Christian women to steal the Eucharist, "to give Christian children away for slaughter and they [also] use them for obscenities." He added that "what is [most] annoying is that they [the nobles] defend the Jews but they attack the clergy."[80] Polish bishops took it a step further and complained to the Vatican, in Rome, about Jewish authority over Christians. Bishop Sierakowski of Przemyśl, in his 1743 report to the Vatican wrote: "Not only do they [the Jews] hold breweries and taverns everywhere on annual or three-year contracts from lords of whatever status, but they also cultivate fields and they obtain whole villages with full jurisdiction in them." In 1751, frustrated Polish bishops obtained an encyclical, A Quo Primum, from Pope Benedict, in which he expressed concern over the number of Jews in Poland who held authority over Christians.[81] Paradoxically, all these fulminations are also added testimony to the close communal, trade and commercial relations between Jews and non-Jews, to a level unknown in most other European countries.

The Blood Libel. An accusation prevalent in many European countries during the Middle Ages was the belief that the Jews constantly pierced stolen Hosts (sanctified bread representing the body of Jesus) or murdered innocent Christian children.[82]

The principal use to which Jews were believed through the ages to put this blood to use was its addition to the unleavened bread (*Matza*) which was prepared for Passover. As late as the 20th century, small children who misbehaved would be threatened that Jews would seize them for their matzoh-baking.[83] The previously-mentioned Father Żuchowski, in an extensive work of nearly 400 pages, in 1700 or several years later, listed all the Polish victims of "Jewish cruelty." He counted as many as 68 (or 85) ritual murders in the course of three centuries (1407-1710), a rate that proportionately was much higher, according to Żuchowski, than in other European countries, due to the greater number of Jews living in the Polish-Lithuanian Commonwealth, who consequently put forward proportionately larger demands for Christian blood. Bishop Załuski, in the mid 18th century, asserted that, in Sochaczew alone, "Jews have killed more children than there are houses."[84] While, during the 17th and 18th centuries, trials of persons accused of child murder gradually came to an end in other European countries, it showed an increase in the Polish Commonwealth.[85] There were as many as 53 pogroms of Jews and 86 trials for ritual murder and profanation of the Host in the 16th to 18th century Poland. Since most of these trials, which sometimes included several persons, ended with convictions, it can be assumed that between two and three hundred Jews were executed for ritual murders.[86] At the same time, in contrast to other places in Europe, Jews in Poland were never forced to convert or face *auto da fe* style burnings at the stake, as many of their co-religionists elsewhere.[87]

Isolation and Restrictions. The idea of a geographic segregation of Jews from Christians first appeared in 1267 when, in the early years of Jewish settlement in the Polish lands, the Church Council of Breslau (Wrocław) in Silesia sought to establish physical segregation between Jews and Christians, as existed in some other European countries, but few of these orders and prohibitions found their way into Polish life. The Breslau synod also ordered Jews to wear a pointed hat so that they could be easily identified as other than Christians, and in 1538, in Piotrków, an attempt was made to require Jews to wear distinctive garments, on top of a pointed yellow hat. But in practice, these regulations were never put into effect.[88] King Sigismund I, in 1534, rejected the demands that Jews wear any distinguishing mark on their clothing, as was common in certain other European regions.[89]

Alcohol and taverns. The other accusation most often levelled against Jews was that as innkeepers they induced the peasants to drink heavily and thus reduced them to incoherent behavior. Bishop Krzysztof Szembek, in 1776, charged that "what is it which has most fundamentally impoverished the serfs and made them indolent and economically negligent if not these Jewish taverns, which have driven the peasantry to drunkenness and ravaged their population, so that they lack food and comfort."[90]

Jews were largely involved in alcohol production and innkeepers, in tandem with the nobility, in the eighteenth century, solely as an economic source of income. This originated when the European decline in the price of grain and the decreased demand for exports made the producers of grain, that was mainly in the hands of the nobles and the magnates, look for other ways of making money from grain. They settled above all in producing alcohol (mainly vodka, but beer as well), and selling it to their subjects in their own inns, as a way of raising revenues in the feudal economy of the country. The nobles chose Jews as innkeepers, since this job had to be run by canny persons, who knew about trade and had some general education (that is, were literate and numerate), and Jews were felt better able to fulfil such functions than the local peasants. Moreover, Jews often did not drink alcohol themselves, or were moderate drinkers, thus remaining sober when managing the inns, which the nobles feared would probably not have been the case if innkeepers had been chosen from the local peasantry. Thus, the greater demand for Jews as innkeepers, especially in the eastern part of the Polish Commonwealth, where Jews tended to congregate in greater numbers.[91]

Consequently, Jews gradually acted as extra agents in the nobles' tavern monopoly. They ran the inns and often held a monopoly to sell liquor.[92] Some church elders tried to limit the Jewish participation in this business. Bishop Andrzej Stanisław Załuski, in his *Edictum contra Iudaeos*, of 1751, forbade Jews to "brew beer and liquor" and to keep their taverns open on Catholic holidays until the church service ended.[93] A century later, in 1881, with a major part of Poland under Russian domination, the Jewish assimilation journal Izraelita took to task those who condemned Jewish innkeepers for supposedly encouraging drunkenness among the peasantry. Izraelita asked rhetorically whether peasants drank less or behaved more decently in the Russian interior, where there were no Jewish inns.[94]

Church loans to Jewish communities. In light of the Church's continuing anti-Jewish fulminations and charges, it is most surprising if not shocking (from a Middle Ages Christian perspective), the phenomenon of churchmen engaging in widespread business relations with Jews, as confirmed by Jewish sources. The minutes of the Council of Four Lands that listed communal expenses, included payments of debts owed by Jews for loans by the Jesuits and Dominicans. Catholic clergymen welcomed Jews living on church lands, and this explains why many synods found it necessary to rule against the custom of leasing church properties to Jews. Internal church correspondence, furthermore, reflects irritation at ongoing economic ties between some church institutions and Jews, but it nevertheless went on, indicating that economic interests outweighed theological considerations to the contrary.[95]

From the outset, the Catholic church formed a main source of loans at interest to Jewish public bodies. In fact, about 75-80 percent of loans taken by Jewish communities and councils were from Church held financial sources. The question remains why the church lent money to Jews, while discouraging non-church institutions from such financial ties? It should also be noted that this strengthening of economic ties between the Church and the Jews (not only in the field of loans, but also in leases of church property) took place during the hardening of attitudes towards Jews. The desire for a dependable income, frequently led these creditors to lend money in the form of *wyderkauffs*. This mode of lending is where the lender receives an annual interest in perpetuity on the loan, without the principal ever having to be repaid. Since the interest was perpetual, rates were low. In Lublin, for example, church documents demonstrate that the interest on *wyderkauff* loans could be as low as 3 percent, while the interest on a regular loan might be 20 percent or higher.[96]

To exemplify – a loan agreement between the Jewish community of Włodzisław and the priest Stanisław Górski, in 1680, stated that the sole reason for taking the loan was to build a new synagogue, which itself was to serve as security for this loan. In the face of synagogues and cemeteries as collateral in the possession of the ecclesiastical creditors, and at times the communal leaders in debtors' prison, Jewish communities decided to try to raise funds abroad. By the turn of the 18th century, for instance, the Lublin *kahal* (Jewish community leadership at a local level) was deeply in debt, particularly to various ecclesiastical institutions. In 1706 the Lublin Jesuit College sued the *kahal* for arrears totaling 127,443 złoty. The court decided that the *kahal* was to repay the money in ten annual installments of 12,744 złoty each.[97]

During the period of 1661-1786, Lublin *kahal* creditors were as follows: Clergy (10 names); Church institutions: Augustine Order, Bazylian Order, Brigyta Order, Carmelite Order, Dominical Order, St. Dutch Hospital, Franciscan Order, Jesuit Order, Kolegiat Church, Lublin Church, St. Michał Chapter, Trinitarian Order, and St. Wojciech Hospital. In the seventeen-year period between 1692 and 1708, the Lublin *kahal* borrowed some 400,000 złoty; of this, almost half came from church institutions.[98]

This contradiction between church ideology and practice found expression in numerous orders issued by the church hierarchy, instructing clergy not to grant loans to Jews nor to lease them church property. In a letter of 1740, Bishop Josaphat Michał Karp of Samognita bewailed to his elders the practice of church loans to Jews. His demands must have gone unheeded because a year later he wrote again, "not without sorrow did I receive the news that my demands made so many times to remove Jews from some ecclesiastical properties have been in vain, ... as these Jews are stubbornly tolerated in ecclesiastical properties by some chapters priests."[99] The Bishop of Przemyśl, in 1744, also added his voice to the protests of his colleagues, and there were others as well. Due to the very fact that these protests were repeated time and again, as well as the existence of documentary evidence of large Jewish debts to the church, it is clear that these contrary injunctions were never observed.[100] This goes further to demonstrate that in spite of the church's traditional theological fulminations against the Jews, in practice church clerics and institutions in Poland allowed themselves to liberally transact business deals with Jews, thus benefitting both sides. In summary, Poland at large remained a safe haven for Jews, especially when compared to the condition of Jews in many other European countries, before the dawn of the modern age.

Partition and Jewish participation in Polish rebellions. Starting 1772 and following the next thirteen years, Poland gradually ceased to be an independent nation, as it was partitioned and gobbled up among its three neighboring powerful countries. Prussia took the western areas, Austria the southern province called Galicia, while the lion's share, central Poland along with most of the eastern borderlands, went to Russia.[101] Jews were most numerous in the territories that fell under the control of Austria and Russia. Except for a short period (1807-1813) when Poland was under French protection during Napoleon's rule, this lack of independence prevailed until the end of World War I. As a result of the elimination of a previously independent and robust Poland, romantic poets, above all the national bard Adam Mickiewicz, began to view Poland as the mythic victimized nation representing the universal struggle for freedom.[102] This victimization myth would later also fuel a strong Polish nationalism.[103]

There were several attempts to regain a modicum of Polish sovereignty with Jewish participation. During the 1794 Polish rebellion led by Tadeusz Kościuszko, the Jewish Dov Ber (Berek) Joselewicz joined in by forming a 500-man Jewish cavalry regiment that fought the Russians, and he became a legendary figure for generations among the small group of assimilated Jews. Following in his footsteps, a small number of Jews also fought beside their Polish comrades in the insurrections of 1831 and 1863. In 1831, in an act symbolizing Polish-Jewish cooperation, Ber Meisels, the orthodox chief rabbi of Warsaw, preached support for the Polish uprising and formed a Jewish militia to assist in the defense of Warsaw, mostly from well-to-do Warsaw families.[104] The apogee of Polish-Jewish friendship was reached in 1861, when leaders of the Polish patriotic movement placed the emancipation of Jews on their agenda. Warsaw rabbis supported the initiative, inviting their co-religionists to collaborate with the Poles and to support their national claims. Polish anthems were sung in synagogues, while a growing number of Jews began to refer to themselves as "Poles of Mosaic denomination." The service for the dead of the current uprising, held in March 1861, in Warsaw, and led by the Lublin Bishop Wincenty Pieńkowski, was also attended by Rabbi Meisels and a sizeable Jewish congregation.[105] Several hundred Jews were among those wounded, arrested, exiled, and executed by the Russians for participation in the uprising. On the other hand, the Orthodox and especially the Hasidic community, did not support the uprising, for fear of Russian retribution.[106]

The Great, or Four-year *Sejm* (Parliament). After the first partition of Poland in 1772, an effort was made to stem further partitions by making major and innovative structural changes in the country's composition and the rights of its citizens, Jews included – unfortunately without much success. Some civic leaders, influenced by ideas of the Enlightenment philosophers in Western Europe, made various proposals to the state authorities and the *Sejm* to transform the self-sustaining Jewish population into a more Polish integrated community, through changes in the Jewish educational system. One such spokesman, the nobleman deputy, M. Butrymowicz, attached the widest liberal views in his pamphlet, "A way of turning Polish Jews into citizens useful to the state," published in 1789. He introduced a bill for the granting of greater rights to the Jews. Józef Pawlikowski expressed similar views in an anonymously published pamphlet.[107] Stanisław Staszic proposed that Jewish education be transferred into Polish hands, and Jews be educated in Polish instead of "a broken German" – Yiddish. Jews were to be integrated into Polish society and culture, and in return shed their separate corporate institutions and "mentality;" briefly, Jewish "separatism" was to be eliminated. Another writer, Tadeusz Czack, added that after a few years all Jews would be obliged to discard "Jewish attire" and dress according to their social class in Polish society.[108] But these ideas did not go very far even among non-Jewish civic leaders.

On June 4, 1791, representatives of the Jewish community submitted a claims petition to the still existing *Sejm* which included a request for wealthy Jews to be granted municipal rights in all free towns, but this was rejected. To buttress their demands, Jewish representatives of several hundred Jewish communities claimed that that despite their separate religious and social and national status, as inhabitants of Poland for centuries, they, in fact, formed an integral part of the larger society, and wished this to remain so, including retaining the special privileges associated with their separate status.[109] Soon thereafter, in 1792, came the second partition of Poland, followed three years later with the final and complete partition of the Polish Commonwealth. Poland, that a century earlier was one of the great European powers, had ceased to exist as an independent political nation – to last for the next 123 years.

Religious and cultural innovations. These last-ditch efforts to modernize Jewish life and bring it into harmony with the culture of the host nation, as prevailed in other west European countries, came to an abrupt halt. Instead, coinciding with the partition of Poland, a new form of religious practice came to birth in Jewish religious life, known as Hasidism, which had a profound impact on the Jewish population and emerged as the dominant form of Judaism in most of Poland, and in some contiguous countries beyond.[110] Led originally by the charismatic Israel Baal Shem Tov (1700-1760), a.k.a. the Besht, Hasidism proclaimed faith and emotional expression of religious practice to be equal, if not above, plain learning and erudition. Joy and ecstasy were to transform religious worship into an escape from the dreariness and fears of everyday life. The Besht's followers, Hasidic leaders known as Tsaddikim (Righteous), or simply Rebbes, or Admorim, established separate centers to propagate the new teaching; such as Elimelech of Lizhensk (Leżajsk), and others who created centers in their hometowns after which they remained known: Góra Kalwarja (a.k.a. Ger), Kock, Belz, Chabad-Lubavitch, Bobowa (Bobov), and other Hasidic courts of various sizes, named after the residence of the Admorim. Those opposed to this new populist teaching of Judaism were known as Misnagdim (Opponents), and they were centered in northeastern Poland and Lithuania. They remained known for their rigorous Talmudic studies, such as the yeshivot in Volozhin, and Mir, near Grodno (both cities today in Belarus).[111] These religious institutions exerted an influence far and wide over Jewish communities throughout the world.

Side by side with Hasidism, Enlightenment ideas in western Europe succeeded in making some inroads. It was known among Jews as Haskalah, and their followers as Maskilim. Haskalah stressed secular ideas and values, and pushed for a greater integration into non-Jewish societies. Its disciples gained many adherents, and in many Jewish schools modern secular courses were added to the religious instructions, and this gave rise to assimilationist tendencies, but only among small groups of Jews, since unlike west European countries, Jewish religious tradition retained a strong hold on most Jews in Polish lands.[112]

Russian rule and the Pale. Official Russian policy for Polish Jews under its rule would eventually prove to be substantially harsher than Austrian and Prussian policies in their parts of divided Poland. Russian Empress, Catherine II restricted Jewish residence to a Pale of Settlement which covered most regions of former Poland, as well as Lithuania, Ukraine, and today's Belarus and Moldova. By the late 19th century, over four million Jews lived in that region, known as the Pale.[113] In 1804, Tsar Alexander I of Russia issued a Statute Concerning Jews, meant to accelerate the process of assimilation of the empire's Jewish population. Polish Jews were allowed to establish schools with Russian, German or Polish curricula, and they were permitted to own land in some of the annexed Polish lands. But, their living conditions in the Pale began to dramatically worsen under the rule of Alexander's successor, Nicholas I. In 1827, he made Jews subject to general military recruitment laws that required Jewish communities to provide 7 recruits, between the ages of 12 and 25, per each 1,000 persons, every 4 years, for long-term service in the Russian military. It was hoped that under the pressure of their new environment, these youngsters would abandon Judaism and assimilate through conversion into full-fledged Russians.

Polish pro-Jewish pronouncements. It is worth repeating that up to around the 1870s, Polish liberal thinkers generally supported the idea of Jewish assimilation into Polish society. That is, the expectation that as education and knowledge of Polish culture spread, hopefully Jews would shed their so-to-speak medieval practices and would become, outside of the religious sphere, more or less indistinguishable from Poles. The idea of Poles and Jews sharing common interests as mutual inhabitants of one country reached its apex during the January uprising of 1863, when Jews joined Polish demonstrators opposing the Russian occupation and repressive policies. Adam Mickiewicz, in the final scene of his celebrated epic poem Pan Tadeusz, published in 1834, presented a scene of popular dancing under the sway of the Jewish fiddler Jankiel, to represent the existing true concord between Jews and non-Jews – or hopefully soon to arise.[114] Mickiewicz had Jankiel, the Jewish innkeeper, sing on a musical instrument, "long prosper our great, our dear King, Diet, Nation! Vivat each Estate! Poland has never yet perished!'"

Mickiewicz was not alone. Aleksander Świętochowski, in an 1881 article, distinguished between most Jews and those officially registered as such but who by now had adopted Polish culture and hence should be considered Poles (regardless of their religion). Relations between Poles and Jews could only be improved, he argued, by lessening the differences between the two groups, combined with energetic measures to incorporate Jews into Polish society. He proposed a series of legislative acts eliminating without exception all institutions of Jewish autonomy and obliging the Jewish population to be educated in institutions common to them and non-Jews.[115] Eliza Orzeszkowa, in On the Jews and the Jewish Question, published in 1882, stated that Poles must not consider present Jewish behavioral "faults" inevitable or immutable. Education can change all this. For, "a Jew, once having cast aside the fetters of religion and tradition, believes in, loves, and works for progress with the ardor of a convert." But, she added, the enlightenment of the poor Jews needed to be preceded by the abolition of the Jewish lower elementary religious schooling, known as *cheders* ("that fatal edifice of separatism") and Jewish children be educated in state schools.[116]

The basic assumption underlying Orzeszkowa's and Świętochowski's argumentation was that Jews needed to recognize the inherent superiority of European (and Polish) civilization over and against Jewish traditional culture, embedded in Yiddish, kosher food, and religious orthodoxy. Both of these liberal figures argued for a total assimilation into the Polish nation that, however, appalled the majority of Jews whose acceptance into the larger society appeared to them attached with conditions that spelled the wholesale revamping of their ethnic-religious existence.[117]

Assimilation attempts. Assimilation, as distinct from acculturation, is defined by Polish-Jewish historian Artur Eisenbach as "an adoption of models and values of the dominant culture in the domain of customs, attire, way of life, education of children, nourishment, interests, etc.," and is also manifested in the reform of liturgy, rites, religious practices and holidays. Jewish historian Jacob Shatzky (Szacki) defines "total assimilation," as the adaptation of the culture of another social group to such a complete extent that the assimilated person or group no longer has any particular loyalties to his former culture.[118] Such an extreme form of total assimilation could, in the Polish case, be applied only to a very small number of assimilated Jews, as the majority of assimilated, or acculturated Jews retained strong conscious ties with their Jewish origin.[119]

Initial attempts at a modest Jewish-Polish cultural symbiosis was the creation of Warsaw's Rabbinical School (*Szkola rabinów*), in 1826, with the explicit goal of producing a new generation of educated Jews to function as full-fledged members of Polish society. However, to the derision of others, in its nearly four decades of existence it produced not a single rabbi and not a single one of its graduates actually found a position at the head of a Jewish congregation. It survived until the early 1860s and is considered a failure.[120] Followers of acculturation into Polish life did not give up and published a special journal, named Izraelita. Its editor, Samuel H. Peltyn was an admirer of western culture and a firm believer in Enlightenment ideas. He held that education and mutual respect would help eliminate Polish prejudices toward Jews and bring the two segments of Polish society closer together. "What should we be?" Peltyn asked, and answered: "Let us be faithful sons of Judaism, propagators of its sublime truths, observing its humanitarian customs that are dictated by the highest love for humanity; let us raise our children in the pristine principles of faith and love, in a word, let us be Israelites." But outside of the religious and spiritual sphere, all difference should be abandoned. "Away with all separatism.…. in thought, feeling, speech or deed! Here we are no longer Jews but countrymen in the complete, most essential meaning of the word."[121] To signal the importance of Jewish attachments in the land of their sojourn, the journal even quoted the prophet Jeremiah's words to the Jews of Babylon: "Build houses and live in them, plant gardens and eat their fruit… And seek the welfare of the city to which I have exiled you and pray to the Lord in its behalf; for in its prosperity you shall prosper" (Jeremiah 29:5,7).[122]

Izraelita, too, was short-lived, and in 1906 there came into being Nowa Gazeta (New Newspaper), this time a daily paper representing an assimilation position. Nowa Gazeta espoused a total Jewish affinity with Poland and Polish culture.[123] A small group of assimilated Jews, who were strongly opposed to the speaking of Yiddish at their meetings, took part in community activities, including the building of the majestic Grand Synagogue in Warsaw, destroyed by the Germans in May 1943. These more assimilated Jews firmly rejected any suggestion that Jews constituted a separate people and nation, and they therefore opposed the Zionists (who favored the exit of Jews to Palestine) and the Bund (who espoused a secular Jewish-socialist-Yiddish ethnic existence on Polish soil) every bit as much as they condemned the antisemitism of Dmowski's National Democrats (Endeks) – to be further discussed.[124] Assimilated Jews were especially visible in finance, banking, railroad construction, and trade with Russia, all of which flourished since the 1850s. Among the most important banking houses, Jewish-sounding names were noticeable, such as: Wawelberg, Landau, Goldfeder, Natanson, Bloch, Goldstand, Peretz, and Wertheim – with many of them taking the final step toward full Polonization, by converting to the Catholic religion.[125]

However, full Polonization was far from easy. As noted by Jewish historian Jacob Shatzky, "the Roman Catholic Church played too important a role in the preservation of Polish culture to make it possible to separate Catholicism from Polonism," and this presented a serious obstacle to those among Jews who wished to become fully Polish but not at the price of a total rejection of their Judaism. Although highly critical of what they considered the backwardness of the way of life of the Jewish masses, they also appreciated the stubborn Jewish traditionalism that contained prime Jewish values, that they felt should not be lost.[126]

The only attempt in pre-partition Poland of a mass adoption of Catholicism was the pathetic event of the conversion of the eccentric Jacob Frank and his followers, in Lwów, in 1759. It ended with the disenchantment of the Catholic church of the insincere practice of the Frankists of their new religion, as they were accused of retaining certain Jewish religious rituals. Polish authorities also stepped in and soon recognized Frank as a liability, if not a complete lunatic; they arrested him, and attempted to separate him from his followers. After many adventures, the exiled Frank died in 1791 in Offenbach, Germany, to where he had moved with his small band of followers.[127]

Zionists, Bund and Others. In contrast and opposition to the assimilationists, Jews who tended to socialism created in 1897 the Bund organization (General Jewish Workers' Union), as a separate movement from the recently formed Polish Socialist Party (*Polska Partia Socjalistyczna*, PPS)[128] Radically secular, the Bund called upon the Jewish masses, especially the working lower blue collar workers, to aim for fuller integration into the Polish nation, but not at the price of abandoning the distinct Jewish ethnicity, but rather to continue to uphold and cultivate the Yiddish language. In fact, that language that derived from medieval high German had over the years become the principal language of everyday life among the Jewish masses – religious or secular. Yiddish journals and literature (such as the popular novels by the pen-named Mendele Mocher Sforim and Sholem Aleichem)[129] burgeoned in the late 19th and early 20th centuries, to the dismay and shock of many Poles, who saw in these Yiddish publications (as well as those in Hebrew) a threat to the promotion of Polish culture in the areas of the Russian empire inhabited by Poles.[130]

Another secular Jewish party, the Folkspartei (People's Party), advocated cultural autonomy, promotion of Yiddish and resistance to assimilation, whereas Agudat Israel, an orthodox religious party created in 1912, took a sharp different road from both the Bund and the Zionists, by upholding the strict religious observance of orthodox Jews and pressing for a continuous separate religious-cultural Jewish existence on Polish soil.[131] True enough, the majority of Jews in the Polish regions of the Russian Empire remained traditional in dress, worship, and world view. This strengthening of Jewish separatism (both religious and secular) heightened anti-Jewish sentiments among many nationally minded Poles.[132] The end of the 19th century, especially following a spate of pogroms in 1881, saw an increasing interest in Zionist aspirations, but Jews in greater numbers saw salvation mainly by leaving Europe and settling in far-away America.

Jewish statistics. According to Isaac Levitas, in 1847 all three annexed Polish territories accounted for 1,041,363 Jews of both sexes, and in the Russian-annexed Polish-Ukrainian provinces on the right bank of the Dnieper River, where the Ukrainians were the majority, the Jewish inhabitants outnumbered the Poles.[133] By 1881, most Jews were urban dwellers, and in the two largest cities of Russian Poland, Warsaw and Łódź, every third inhabitant was a Jew, whereas most Poles continued to live in villages.[134] The research of A. Eisenbach showed that in the 1880s, 80.4% of the Jews lived in cities and the rest in villages. Also, that as early as 1855, Jews constituted approximately 43% of the entire urban population of Polish cities, and in some places the number rose to above 50%, while in 1910, 83.6% of the much larger non-Jewish population still lived in the countryside. Warsaw's population was about one-third Jewish in the first decade of the twentieth century, as was the ratio in Łódź, and even higher percentages of Jews existed in provincial towns: Łomża—44.6%, Kielce—36.4%, Lublin—50.7%, Piotrków—37.0%, Płock—39.2%, Radom—43.1%, Siedlce—55.0%, and Swałki—54.9%. Jews were even more dominant – above 50 percent – in the smaller towns, such as Kutno, Płońsk, Mińsk Mazowiecki, Opatów, and Sejny. The Jewish population continued to grow in size, notwithstanding the large-scale emigration of Jews from different parts of Poland to distant lands, beginning in the early 1880s. The Jewish role in urban commercial venues also became more pronounced, as a wealthy Jewish merchant and financial class emerged. [135]

Violence and pogroms. Historian Bernard Weinryb, in his study of Jews in Poland up to 1800, counts at least twenty cases of physical attacks of Jews and their expulsion from certain Polish cities during the fourteenth and fifteenth centuries. Jews were expelled from Warsaw in 1482 (where in 1595, the *De non tolerandis Judaeis* rule of exclusion of Jewish residence, remained in force up to the early 1860s, although not honored in practice); from Kraków a decade later (that witnessed a riot earlier in 1407), and some years after that from Warsaw once again.[136] In 1453, following the visit from Italy of the itinerant monk preacher John Capistrano, dubbed "the scourge of the Jew, despite several months of his fulminations against Jews in Kraków, there was no anti-Jewish outbreak. It was not until 1496, when an anti-Turkish crusade led to the murder of Jews, as a consequence of which Jews moved from Kraków to nearby Kazimierz (later part of the city).[137] Despite these occasional setbacks, anti-Jewish feelings, ever present also in Poland, never reached the dimensions known in other European countries. There was never a large-scaled expulsion of Jews from all Polish lands, as took place elsewhere in Europe. In fact, the Jewish population continued to grow significantly, bolstered primarily by immigration from the west and south. [138]

Things, though, began to change in the modern period, at first slowly, such as the Warsaw pogrom of 1881, coinciding with the assassination of Tsar Alexander II, in March of that year, that prompted a large-scale wave of anti-Jewish riots throughout the Jewish-inhabited regions of the Russian Empire. The Warsaw pogrom, during Christmas 1881, began as a scuffle in a Warsaw church that turned into a general attack on the neighboring Jewish quarters, as crowds attacked homes and businesses. Property loss was much greater than actual bloodshed, though one or two Jews lost their lives and many more were injured.

More devastating than the physical damage was the moral shock, that even in the Polish capital pogroms were possible; not merely, as those in other parts of the Russian Empire. Poles had previously prided themselves on their civilized and tolerant behavior toward Jews, even as they held on to certain stereotyped negative opinions about the cultural and economic role of Jews.[139]

The Warsaw riot was followed with an anti-Jewish riot in Łódz, in 1892. Anti-Jewish violence also erupted in 1898, in the Austrian held province of Galicia. Then, there was a pogrom in 1906, in Białystok, followed soon later with another one in Siedlce. The Polish press was unanimous in denouncing these acts of violence, seeing in them the work of reactionaries and "people of a moral level lower than that of beasts." Compared with the earlier pogrom wave of 1881, these attacks were deadlier – several hundred Jews were reportedly killed in Bialystok, and around one hundred in Siedlce.[140]

There were, also, occasional calls for a total Jewish expulsion. In 1818, a pamphlet by Wincenty Krasiński, regretfully concluded that the only solution was to remove the Jews from Poland, perhaps by settling them in Tataria (the area beyond the Ural Mountains).[141] Józef Gołuchowski, similarly, in the 1850s, suggested the creation of a special Jewish province within the Russian Empire where all Jews would be concentrated, and where they would enjoy full autonomy and freedom.[142] Jan Chodźko, active in propagating Polish schooling, published in 1821, John of Swisłocz the Peddler (*Pan Jan ze Świsłoczy, kramarz wędrujący*), that fed the minds of peasant children for years, being republished in 1824 and 1825, and translated into Lithuanian in 1823, and was still in use in 1860. In a certain passage, the author exclaimed: "Oh when then, will the wise prescriptions of our Gracious Monarch, requiring the deportation of the Jews to the southern provinces of the Empire, be fulfilled? Our regions rid of this plague would flourish anew."[143]

Jan Jeleński, Roman Dmowski and the Endeks. However, larger in scope and importance was the appearance of Rola, in the 1880s, the first overtly antisemitic journal in Poland. Its editor, Jan Jeleński, was to dedicate the rest of his life to warning his countrymen of the purported

Jewish menace and encouraging non-Jews to form Christian co-ops, to isolate the Jews economically, and to encourage Jews to emigrate elsewhere. The novelty of Jelenski's Rola was that it blamed Jews for all shortcomings in Polish society. Whatever ailed Polish society, one could be sure that Jews were at fault, Rola argued. Jelenski urged Poles to "defend themselves" from economic and cultural influences of the Jews, but not through violence, but the development of Polish shops, Polish commerce, and Polish industry.[144] Assimilation was rejected, which Jeleński had in his earlier years advocated as a solution to the Jewish question. He now stated that assimilation would lead not to Jews becoming Polonized, but on the contrary – to Poles becoming "Judaized." This was a battle for the Polish soul. Jews, Jeleński charged, "don't wish to respect the sacredness of our religion but spatter it with mud in their Jewish (Yiddish) newspapers."[145] From late 1905 into 1906, the frantic tone of Jeleński's anti-Jewish, anti-socialist, and antiliberal campaign became increasingly hysterical, but short of a call to violence. In 1897, he helped found the National Democratic Party (popularly known as Endeks) – the first outspoken Polish antisemitic party. It stated that the Jews were essentially alien residents on Polish soil who must subordinate themselves to the Polish national interest. The new party would fight against Jewish economic domination and the "harmful influence of Jews" in social life, although it left room for those few Jewish individuals to be accepted as Poles who identified fully and unconditionally with the Polish cause, even when it conflicted with Jewish interests. Most Jews (even those acculturated and Polish-speaking), however, were to be excluded from the Polish nation.[146]

In the elections to the Russian first and second Duma (parliament), in 1905, the National Democrats swept the field, and Roman Dmowski who was to lead the Endeks after World War I was one of the party's elected representatives. All other Polish representatives in the following Duma elections were affiliated with the National Democratic Party in one way or another.[147] Dmowski began to play a more prominent role in the party, and the antisemitic rhetoric expanded, as shown in his brochure, The Jewish Question. In 1912, he called for an economic boycott of the Jews, and the Endek antisemitic press mounted a furious boycott campaign. Poles were admonished to avoid not just Jewish shops, but Jewish doctors, lawyers, singers, performers – in short, all intercourse between Poles and Jews was to come to an end. The anti-Jewish boycott ran from November 1912 to the outbreak of World War I, but was generally ignored by the peasantry,[148] but the anti-Jewish crusade had taken hold of large sections, even among the Polish educated society, including progressive circles.

Around 1910, several noted progressive activists, most famous among them Iza Moszczeńska and Andrzej Niemojewski, peppered their words with an increased antisemitc rhetoric. In her book Progressivism at a Crossroads, Moszczeńska called the Polish-Jewish conflict inevitable and urged her fellow Polish progressives to work against Jewish influence and "Yiddish mobilization." Assimilation was rejected other than in exceptional individual cases. Both Moszczeńska and Niemojewski, the two main "progressive antisemites," emphasized the inevitability of "struggle" and "battle" between Poles and Jews, and both prophesied the ultimate triumph of "Polishness." On the economic scene, Niemojewski and Moszczenska alike argued that Polish cities must be "dejewized" and "polonized."[149] In 1913, the erstwhile liberal Aleksander Świętochowski published articles almost indistinguishable from the Endek attack on Jews, leading the Catholic antisemitic Nasz Sztandar journal to ironically remark that "practically overnight Świętochowski has turned himself into a thundering antisemite."[150]

Pre-World War I Polish-Jewish relations. Before ending this chapter on the long history of the Jews in Poland up to World War I, let us attempt to summarize Polish-Jewish relations up to this point. The history of Polish Jews embraces eight centuries of co-existence of two communities, Polish and Jewish, side by side, so that by the early sixteenth century, Poland was becoming the home of one of the most important Jewish centers in the world. The Jews were welcomed by the monarchy as a means of facilitating trade and commercial contacts inside the country and with European countries, and in this respect were granted many liberal privileges.[151] By the late seventeenth and eighteenth centuries, Polish

Jews had become an intrinsic part of the Polish economic landscape and society – perhaps an "alienated minority," but not relegated to ghettos, as elsewhere in Europe, but living among Christians as neighbors, friends, employers, and even as masters. Especially with Polish nobles, the true rulers of the country, Jews had established a strong symbiotic relationship.[152] Polish Jews played a far more visible role in Polish lands than elsewhere in Europe. In the words of historian Theodore Weeks, "what Pole in 1900 had not drunk at a Jewish tavern, purchased food and clothing at a Jewish shop, haggled with a Jewish peddler?"[153] The general policy of tolerance brought about a delicate balance of all religious communities in the country which stemmed from the economic and social functions of the different groups that constituted sixteenth-and seventeenth-century Poland. "Jews," Stanisław Mateusz Rzewuski, in a letter to a Łuck priest, in the early 18th century, wrote, "cannot exist without the synagogue, as our towns cannot exist without them." And this was not just one magnate's opinion.[154]

One factor, however, disturbed this co-existence, this situation of *paradisus Judaeorum* – the cultural separateness of the Jewish community, despite the constant contacts between the two groups of people. As a result of this isolation, the two communities living alongside one another knew little of each other, and, as a rule, remained unfamiliar with their neighbors' customs and culture.[155] Contact between Jews and non-Jews rarely went beyond the economic sphere. The great majority of the Commonwealth's Jews lived out their lives within their own community, separated from the non-Jews by custom, law, religion, and their own institutions of self-government. The widespread use of Yiddish, the wearing of traditional Jewish garb, the consumption of different foods, and a day of rest other than Sunday, all of these factors at least made it easier to point out the Jews in Warsaw or Lublin than in Berlin or Paris, where it was more difficult to identify Jews on the main boulevards. Integration of Jews in Christian Polish life could take place only through full conversion, a rarity in Poland, but more prevalent in other countries religious affiliation in the modern period no longer played a dominant role in social relationships. Real contact of a private nature between the

Poles and the Jews existed in Poland only among a very small culturally integrated Jewish intelligentsia and to some extent among the richer urban dwellers.[156]

At no time did Polish thought attain the toleration existing in France, where in 1791 all civic rights were granted to the Jews, although, in fairness to Poland, all Jewish restrictions elsewhere outside Poland were removed very late – in Prussia only in 1848, in England in 1858, and in Italy in 1870.[157] During the Polish uprising of 1830, Jews were welcomed into the national guard – but only "enlightened" Jews who shaved their beards. As the military situation of the Polish rebellion grew more desperate, special units composed of traditional Jews were formed, and Jews also dug defensive trenches in a last-ditch effort to keep the Russians out of Warsaw.[158]

At the same time, between the 19th century and 1914, relations between Poles and Jews underwent a fundamental change. While in mid-century the ideology of assimilation, a gradual adoption by Jews of Polish cultural and linguistic norms, predominated within Polish educated society, by 1914 few Poles or Jews continued to advocate assimilation. What most critics of Jewish assimilation had in common was the belief that the Jewish question could no longer be a matter of indifference. In one way or the another, the presence of Jews as a separate, self-enclosed, very large community within Polish lands, and especially in all major cities, could no longer be tolerated.[159]

Famous novelist and publicist Bolesław Prus still upheld (late 1880s) the progressive view that insofar as the Jews are concerned, neither the Talmud, nor *cheders*, nor specifically Jewish dress was the problem, but the avoidance of agricultural work by most Jews; a serious absence, according to this author, who endorsed the romantic idea of the "noble peasant." At the same time, he doubted whether Jews could ever be fully integrated into Polish society. Even if converted, Prus cautioned, Jews remained Jews – not out of hatred of Christians or due to "race," but simply because they possessed a much older culture than Europeans. Hence, "spiritual assimilation" was impossible: "in every Jew there lives the forty-century-old Israelite."[160] In addition, throughout the nineteenth century (and beyond), the Talmud was nearly always cited by non-Jews (and at times by acculturated Jews) derogatively, and as one of the primary sources of Jewish "darkness," "immorality," and "backwardness." Complicating further the issue of assimilation, was that in the Austrian-held Galicia province a greater number of Jews who wished to distance themselves from the Jewish tradition, preferred to switch to German culture rather than Polish.[161]

At the same time, on the flip side, by the early twentieth century, Jews and Christians had moved closer to each other. Tens of thousands of Jews spoke Polish, some even as a native tongue, and while traditional Jewish garb could still be seen on the streets of Warsaw (not to mention in the numerous smaller towns), the sight of Jewish men and women dressed in European styles was no longer unusual.[162]

Enter the growing nationalistic fervor that overtook most Poles at the dawn of the modern period. This led that in the late 1800s, rather than being primarily a religious problem, Jews were viewed in terms of a national challenge for Polish society, and the feeling that the presence of such a large group of unassimilated individuals posed a threat to the Polish nation. As the 20th century dawned, the possibility of fusing Jews and Poles into a harmonious whole was overwhelmingly rejected by Polish society, unless the Jews supported the Polish cause unconditionally, even to the point of denouncing the community of their own birth. In other words, the idea that whoever was not one hundred percent "with us" was consequently not part "of us" and therefore did not belong here, and this thinking began to attract many more minds, as World War I erupted.[163]

Also, worth noting, is the role of writers and thinkers of the Polish lower middle class in shaping the rhetoric of Polish-Jewish relations. Among the lower middle classes mistrust and ill-feeling was ever-increasing, particularly between Jewish and Christian shopkeepers, peddlers or middlemen. Non-Jewish peasant newcomers, flocking into the cities in the search of a career in trade, were faced with the long-established monopolies of Jewish businessmen. The resulting economic rivalry fueled antisemitic resentment. Accusations increased that

Jewish domination of trade and commerce stymied the rise of a Polish middle class, and that, therefore, the health of the Polish nation was dependent upon the so-called Polonization of the presumed Jewish monopoly of the middle class. The growing size of the Jewish population also gave rise to alarmist opinions that the Jews may soon equal or outnumber the Christians and become the dominant power in the state.[164]

Polish writers had long claimed that antisemitism in the Polish lands was a foreign import, coming from either Germany or Russia. This was no longer so, as antisemitism was growing, and around the turn of the 20th century there were even violent incidents in the streets. There was overt animosity if not hostility.[165] Needless to say, almost all the negative ideas expressed about the Jews were by no means first heard in Poland. They were voiced all over Europe during the 18th century and were much more harshly formulated in many other countries. "Polish culture," holds Jacob Goldberg, "did not enrich the catalogue of anti-Jewish arguments: opinions which arrived from the West were simply repeated – generally in a less developed form than elsewhere in Europe."[166] One pamphlet of this time deserves mention for being both characteristic and widely quoted: Ignacy Grabowski's Ungrateful Guests, in which he warned that vigorous anti-Jewish measures were needed to save Poles, Polish culture, and Poland from ruin. Jews have lived among us, Grabowski writes, for eight centuries but have changed not at all. Poles invited them in and offered them hospitality, but the Jews remained apart and indeed took advantage of Polish weaknesses for their own profit. Grabowski's "solution" was: Warsaw and Russian Poland must become "de-judaized;" compromise and coexistence were no longer possible.[167]

Another dramatic change in the antisemitic accusations was that it was now also directed against the acculturated Jews who it was claimed threatened to infect the Polish nation with the "ethic of the Talmud," in the words of one Polish publicist. One might phrase the problem thus: not the Jew per se but the fear of "Judaized Poland" haunted Polish antisemites at the start of the 20th century. By one account, on the eve of World War I, relations between Poles and Jews were extremely strained. In a certain sense, they never recovered.[168]

CHAPTER 2
The Interwar Period (1918-1939)

Poland reborn. In 1918, at the end of World War I, suddenly and unexpectedly, Poland reemerged again as a sovereign nation, in the wake of the collapse of the Russian, German and Austro-Hungarian empires. As Poland arose under the military leadership of Józef Piłsudski – in a seemingly vengeance against the 123 years dissolution of Poland (the only major European country to undergo such torment), and in a desperate attempt to recoup its pre-dissolution size, it launched into several military adventures to aggrandize its borders at the expense of other fringe nationalities. While the rest of Europe settled down to lick the wounds of a four-year fratricidal slaughter, Poland was at war with Ukrainians, Lithuanians, communist Russians, in north and east, and ethnic Germans, in the west, that ended in 1921, and that left an expanded Poland with significant numbers of minorities within its borders, and with only two-thirds of the population ethnically Polish. In most of the eastern regions of Poland, known as the "kresy," Poles were themselves a minority. Under such circumstances, civil harmony would have demanded some sort of a pluralist approach to national issues, which was sorely lacking. In contrast to the tolerant multi-ethnic composition of the ancient Polish Commonwealth, the resurgent nationalist Poland attempted to force the Byelorussian and Ukrainian minorities to a greater identification with Polish national aspirations, leading to the closing of many non-Polish schools where these two large minority groups lived in the eastern regions of Poland.[1]

In the Polish heartland itself, the Jewish population of some 3 million, represented close to 10% of the general population. The two large communities of Poles and Jews, who had lived peacefully together for centuries, in the same cities and the same villages, but maintained for the most part separate lifestyles and religious systems, were going to be impacted in many troubling ways by the new nationalism that took hold of Poland after 123 years of enforced political dormancy. The conditions of the Jews in this new Poland, tormented with economic and political crises, during the interwar 21 years leading up to World War II, is crucial for an understanding of Polish Jewish relations during the German occupation, and even afterwards.[2]

To repeat, the two systems of thought in Polish history, the pluralist and the exclusivist, seemed to collide. The first offered a conception of Polish identity reminiscent of what it had been in the old pre-partitioned Poland, where a person might describe himself as a member of the Polish greater Commonwealth, and at the same time of the Ruthenian (Ukrainian) people, or of Jewish origin.[3] This was presently upheld for a time by the non-dogmatic Polish Socialist Party (PPS), founded in 1897 by the same Józef Piłsudski, the creator of modern Poland. The exclusivist opinion found its political focus in the National Democratic Party (*Narodowa Democracja*, ND or Endecja), founded by Roman Dmowski and his associates in the late 1890s, mentioned earlier. The Endecja (singular member "Endek") advocated a narrowly defined nationalism, based on ethnic Polish descent and the profession of Roman Catholicism; in other words, excluding primarily the Jews.[4]

Endecja argued that in the Middle Ages, at a time when a modern Polish nation had not yet emerged, Jews had been invited to develop trade in the Polish lands. But now, a modern nation cannot exist without a self-ethnic commercial class, which is now mostly in the hands of the Jews. The Jews, the Endeks concluded, consequently had to be driven out of Polish commerce and industry, even driven out of the country, and replaced by ethnic Poles.[5] The Polish left, who opposed the Endeks, commanded the allegiance of only a small part of the Polish population, most of whom still dealt in farming. The left was divided between the larger Socialist Party (PPS) and the much smaller Communist Party (KPP),[6] whereas the Endeks seemed to be gaining strength as Poland's economic woes increased during the years leading up to World War II.

During the chaotic period that followed the creation of the Polish state, and that lasted up to 1921, alarming reports were received about alleged pogroms against Jews, leading US President Woodrow Wilson to send an official commission to investigate the matter. It was led by Henry Morgenthau, Sr. (former US ambassador to Ottoman Turkey), who reported that while allegations of pogroms were exaggerated, he identified eight such incidents, and estimated the number of Jewish victims at 280. There were other isolated pogroms, particularly in Lwów (later, Lviv), during the Polish–Ukrainian war, a day after the Poles captured the city; and in Warsaw. The concerns over the fate of Poland's Jews led to a series of explicit clauses in the Versailles Treaty signed by the Western powers and Polish Prime Minister Ignacy Paderewski, that protected the rights of the Jewish minorities in the new Poland. In 1921, Poland's constitution indeed guaranteed the Jews religious tolerance, such as separate Jewish schools and respect of the Jewish Sabbath. Yet, anti-Jewish riots continued in many cities and towns of newly independent Poland, on the unfounded charge of Jewish disloyalty to the country and their favoring of a Russian style communist regime.[7] The first Polish parliament (*Sejm*) of 1922 included 35 Jewish members, who formed a separate caucus. On the political front, only the socialists (PPS), communists, and the liberal intelligentsia as a whole, were overtly pro-Jewish, with the socialists working closely with the Jewish socialist Bund movement.[8]

Józef Piłsudski, originally a military leader and favoring a certain form of socialism, by the 1920s had broken with socialism and closed ranks with the nobility, the so-called *szlachta*. Abandoning the government to parliamentary rule, in 1922, he returned in 1926 to seize power by mounting a coup d'état against the system which he himself had installed. He then ruled the country, almost singlehandedly, until his death nine years later. Parliamentary democracy thus collapsed after only eight years, and was never replaced in a consistent way. Piłsudski as a near-dictator held antisemitism in check against the more aggressive manifestations of Endek nationalism. The regime took its name as Sanacja, which may be translated as "return to (political) health," but was explained in military overtones.[9] After his death, in 1935, his successors, popularly dubbed as "Government of the Colonels," were principally led by Marshal Edward Śmigły-Rydz, with Colonel Józef Beck in charge of foreign affairs. The clique of military men who succeeded Piłsudski for the remaining four years of Polish independence abandoned his tolerant policy toward the Jews, and followed a more strident antisemitism, especially in the economic field.[10]

Economy. In relation to other European countries Poland remained industrially underdeveloped. As for Polish Jews, most were small traders and shopkeepers, artisans and tradespeople; others were wage laborers, and in the large cities, many shops were owned by Jews.[11] While some people in the retail businesses were well-to-do, and a few even wealthy, the typical Jew was far from rich. For every wealthy Jew there were thousands of Jewish artisans who worked in tiny shops, and were tailors, shoemakers, bakers, and living on the edge of survival. Many of the Jews were very poor, and by 1934 more than a quarter of them were living off supplemental welfare assistance.[12] A great many were supported by Jewish welfare agencies abroad, such as the US-based Joint Distribution Committee.[13] Many Jews also sought better living conditions by choosing the liberal professions, and they comprised 21.5 percent of the country's professional class; such as doctors, teachers, journalists and lawyers.

As the economic tribulations rose in the 1930s, the living conditions of Jews deteriorated further, also fueled by government policies aimed at facilitating the filling of better income jobs to the non-Jewish population. Jews were not welcome in state employment, and were effectively barred from a wide range of occupations, from the army and civil service, even from the schools, the state liquor monopoly, and the railways. This went even further, such as laws that restricted the sale of Kosher meat (a law not enforced), depriving Jewish shopkeepers of Sunday as a trading day (in some areas), and so forth. It is well to note that the Ukrainian and

White Russian minorities in Poland also suffered from pressures and discriminations. All in all, the essential perception of Polish Jewry at this interwar juncture was that all was not well; but neither was it unrelieved gloom; at least, not yet.[14]

Jewish population. In 1921, 69% of the total population of 25,700,000, or 17,790,00, were Poles; with the 2,800,000 Jews forming the second largest minority after the Ukrainians. 75 percent of the whole population lived in villages and did farming, with 25 percent in towns and cities.[15] By 1938, the Jewish population had risen close to 3,400,000; still slightly above 10% of the total population. The Ukrainians, 13.9%, and Byelorussians, 3.1%, were concentrated in specific regions in the east, and a smaller German minority of 2.3% was present in the west – whereas the Jews were to be found everywhere.[16] No less than 400,000 Jews emigrated from Poland for good in the two decades following World War I. Still more would have left if entry to Palestine and especially to the USA had not been restricted.[17] Still, by the time World War II began, Poland still had the largest concentration of Jews anywhere in Europe.

Jewish separateness. Probably around at least a third of the total adult Jewish population was Orthodox-traditionalist, and they were the most visible among Polish Jewry.[18] Many of them stood out clearly in their public appearance, as they dressed differently from Christian Poles.[19] The dress alone, in the case of males, signaled unmistakably that they were Jews, on top of the fact that the more orthodox men did not shave and wore beards (as well as sidelocks, *peyes*) at a time when Poles rarely did. The clothes of the more religious Jews were somber: a black caftan, known as *kapote*, worn over the trousers, and a black cap.[20] On the Sabbath and holidays, many donned the *shtraymel*, a black velvet hat with brown fur trimming.[21] Married very religious women wore their hair covered at all times with kerchiefs or wigs (*sheytl*).[22] Poland, as the center of world Hasidism and the heads of various Hasidic dynasties, the *Rebbes-Tsadikim*, continued to command the allegiance of tens of thousands of followers, inside and outside the country.[23]

At the same time, many other Jews slowly but gradually were

becoming more acculturated into Polish life, while retaining a strong Jewish identity, but progressively secular, and the Polish language, rather than Yiddish, was increasingly used by the young city-dwelling Jews.[24] Their Polish, however, retained some traces of Yiddish antecedence, manifested in intonation and grammatical structure. There was also the distinctive nonverbal language – typical gestures, facial expressions, body movements, etc., that differentiated Jews from Poles.[25]

In the first census of 1921, about 25 percent of the Jews said they were of Polish nationality. In the census of 1931, only 381,000 Jewish citizens (12%) gave Polish as their native tongue; 79% declared Yiddish as their first language, 9% being Hebrew. This number, however, may not reflect the actual state of things, since even among the Zionists, many spoke Polish as their native language, even though they considered themselves Jewish in nationality.[26] As pointed out by Władysław Bartoszewski, this points to a sharp difference with Jews living in Germany, France and England, who mostly spoke the country's language as their main tongue.[27] About 40 percent were sympathetic to Zionist views that looked forward to leaving Poland and returning to their ancient home-land, the Land of Israel, and this added to the strong feeling of national separateness of most Jews.[28] One may nevertheless speculate that had the Jews of Poland not been killed off by the Germans, the steady accultur-ation may have eventually been more widespread than it actually was, when the Germans marched in. But in the interwar period most Jews still lived outside the mainstream of Polish cultural and social lives.[29]

More significantly, in a country that was nearly three-quarters rural, Jews had increasingly become a big-city population. Although one-third continued to live in small towns, the *shtetlech*, and one-quarter remained in the countryside, nearly half of all Jews lived in cities with populations of over twenty thousand. Of greater significance, while the Jewish share in the total population was 10 percent, in the major cities it ran between 25 to 50 percent and at times even higher than that in some towns.[30] Put differently, while the Jews formed over a quarter of the urban population, they constituted only 3 percent of the rural population, while 78% of the overall Polish populace still lived in villages.[31] That did not bode well for the future relations between Jews and non-Jews, in a country at grips with a resurgent nationalism.[32]

Assimilationists. On New Year's Day 1917, in the midst of World War I, when the German and Austrian monarchs announced the birth of a not fully-independent Poland, a group of assimilated Jews reacted by creating the Association of Polish Youth of Jewish Origin–The Torch. In a special manifesto addressed to the Polish Jews, it declared that "beginning today they will prove by their behavior and actions, their sincere sentiments of gratefulness and attachment to the land which for centuries fed their forebears and where they are buried." German occupying authorities, however, became alarmed by the movement that advocated full Polish independence, and several members of the organization's national board were arrested and imprisoned.[33]

Soon after the war, on May 10-12, 1919, a general congress of 438 delegates took place in Warsaw, under the name of Association of Poles of Mosaic Faith of All the Polish Lands. The congress stated that: "Without abandoning the faith of our fathers nor renouncing its tradition and history, we take our stand unreserved in favor of Polish nationality; we give ourselves wholeheartedly to the Polish homeland and desire to serve it and co-operate in its growth and development. At the same time... we want to be Polish citizens with full rights and duties, and not second-class citizens." This association was also not active for a very long time.[34] Then, in 1924, in Lwów, another self-declared Jewish pro-Polish youth movement took form, under the name of Association of Unity Academic Youth, with headquarters in Warsaw. It downplayed the emphasis on assimilation and asserted that "Jews have been settled in Poland for more than 800 years... Thus, Poland is the only homeland of Polish Jews... So, one must abandon all thought of a concerned, obligatory, mass emigration of Jews from Poland to any destination whatsoever... The democratic impulse will build a political, cultural, and sentimental union of Jews with the State and the Polish nation."[35] Later, in 1936, an additional association – Bloc of Polish Jews of All Classes – was created in Lwów, and the following year met in Warsaw, as a national congress.[36]

These relatively small groups of the assimilationists believed that with the slow disappearance of Jewish cultural differences, the antagonism toward Jews would also disappear. They vigorously opposed the Zionists who stood for Jews leaving for Palestine, while the Yiddish tongue, spoken by most Jews, was to them the mark of low caste and low culture.[37] The more extreme Jewish assimilationists in Poland, were not content with simply adopting Polish modes of behavior, but still retain a bond with traditional Judaism (a form of mere acculturation), and went further by denying any attachment to the Jewish peoplehood, if they had not already converted to Catholicism. The total number of conversions per year was estimated by historian Aryeh Tartakower to have been between 2,000 to 2,500 in the late 1920s and early 1930s.[38] Most of these either moderate or extreme assimilationists constituted no more than one-tenth at the most of the Jewish population, which numbered over 3 million; in other words, about 270,000-300,000, but there is no way of arriving at a more exact figure.[39] The famous synagogue on Tłomackie Street, in Warsaw, which opened in 1878, and was dynamited by the Germans in May 1943, was attended by Warsaw's non-converted assimilationists on ceremonial occasions and the High Holidays, until World War II.[40]

Though few in total numbers, the assimilationists attracted some of the cultural elite among the Jews. In fact, as many as 90 percent of the leading Jewish intellectuals (many of them among the wealthy) were assimilationists, such as Jakub Natanson, professor of chemistry, and Ludwik Hirszfeld, professor of anatomy.[41] The more extreme among the assimilationists continued to sing praises to the Polish land, to the valor of Poles, and to the heights of Polish culture, art, and music. In the novels of Leśmian, Tuwim, and Słonimsky, Jews and Jewish themes hardly figure, only fleetingly if at all.[42] Some of the best-known poets, composers and renowned musicians were Jews who had assimilated into Polish cultural life, and into Polish society as well. To their great disappointment, the Polish right wing rejected this strong-willed integration, and continued to consider the assimilationists of all categories as aliens to Poles.[43] Their contribution to Polish literature, humanities, law, science, and mathematics was often interpreted as a threat to Polish culture, which was seen as being undermined (Judaized) by the presence of the assimilationists.[44]

Jews as aliens: Thus, many in Polish society saw the Jews, not as Poles but as outsiders, foreigners and strangers in their midst, in spite of the hundreds of years of Jewish presence and co-existence, and paradoxically, many Jews agreed to this estrangement, and were anxious to leave.[45] The term "Pole" was generally reserved for Christians and was seldom, if ever, applied to Jews. It was assumed that since this would never change, but last forever, even with regard to the very small group of assimilated Jews, it was better for both sides, that Jews find a home for themselves elsewhere.[46] Even with regard to the assimilated Julian Tuwim, the foremost Polish poet of the interwar period, in 1921 it was claimed that "Tuwim's writing is not Polish; he merely writes in the Polish language." The nationalist literary critic, Zygmunt Wasilewski stated that Tuwim's poetry was full of "sensual fury characteristic of the Eastern Semitic race."[47] The non-Polish names among many Jews, especially German sounding surnames; the wide use of Yiddish (a despised Germanic jargon); nonverbal language (dissimilar gestures, facial expressions, and mannerisms); typical dress, especially among very religious Jews; and food habits – all these marked Jews as different from perceptive Polish eyes.[48] Even Jewish converts to Christianity were not fully welcome. In the words of Lwów's Chur Gazette: "These individuals we ought to receive in a brotherly fashion into Christian society. But this does not mean that we have to accept them to Polish society. Conversion can make a Christian of one who was of Judaic faith but cannot make a Jew into a Pole."[49] The belief among the governing Polish elite was that Poland had reemerged as a nation state, when being a "nation" was defined as being able to absorb certain non-Polish Christian elements, such as Ukrainians, if they so desired, but not Jews.[50]

Jewish political parties. One of the basic tenets of Zionism was that antisemitism would not disappear in Europe as long as the Jews remained there, and the situation in Poland, among other countries, was used to demonstrate the truism of this claim.[51] The continued rise of antisemitism across Europe led to the growth of the Zionist movement, resulting in considerable emigration to Palestine in the mid-1930s. On the opposite spectrum, the Jewish socialist Bund movement countered that Zionism meant running away from the problem, and full Jewish social freedom would only be achieved with the advent of secular socialism. It insisted that Jewish workers involved in a revolutionary struggle for socialism had a right to continue being Jews, but not necessarily as a religious community.[52] The second largest non-Zionist party was the influential Agudat Israel orthodox party that, paradoxically, contrary to the Bund which called for a political counter activism, sought accommodation with the government.[53] In the parliamentary elections of 1922, 35 Jewish representatives were elected to the 444-member *Sejm*, but this number fell down to five in the last 1938-1939 elections.[54]

Socialists. Among many Polish socialists, the separate character of the culture of Jews was treated with some trepidation, but this was countered with the belief that with the triumph of socialism that "problem" would disappear.[55] The initial unequivocal assimilation-oriented demands gradually gave way to a more flexible stand, by which the linguistic and, to a certain extent, the cultural separateness of Jews was recognized. The Socialist Party (PPS) even included persons of Jewish origin in its leadership.[56] The party began to tilt toward the Jewish Socialist Bund party, while still retaining a critical attitude of its separate national agenda. The PPS maintained that "Jews do not constitute a separate nationality and do not possess a culture of their own," but for tactical reasons it was decided not to assert this in quite such a provocative manner.[57] At the same time, the PPS was openly opposed to antisemitism and all forms of discrimination against the Jewish population. This, of course, in the words of Jerzy Holzer, did not mean that the PPS grass roots were totally free of such sentiments.[58] Towards the end of the 1930s, with antisemitism on the steady rise, one of the top journalists of the PPS, Jan Maurycy Borski, published a brochure supporting the concept of Jewish emigration, explaining that the Jewish question in Poland was impossible to solve and that antisemitism was lasting by nature.[59] All the same, the PPS continued to maintain a Jewish section that spread propaganda among Jewish workers (often in Yiddish).[60]

As for the Bund, its main support came from Jewish workers in small, artisan workshops; whereas the PPS drew its support from large-scale industrial workers. Hence the economic interests of the two groups did not always coalesce. More important, the PPS assumed – like most non-Jewish socialists – that under conditions of political freedom Jews would assimilate, thereby shedding most cultural differences that separated them from Poles. For the Bund, in contrast, the promotion of the Yiddish language and Jewish culture remained a central concern.[61]

Political Antisemitism: In the 1930s, some political parties, other than Dmowski's Endeks, adopted increased levels of anti-Jewish rhetoric.[62] For instance, in March 1937, the centrist Christian Democratic Party, the party of the lower middle class and craftsmen, adopted a formal resolution demanding the "de-Jewification of cities, commerce, industry and the professions." The party subsequently somewhat moderated its anti-Jewish tone, underlining that we "are not proponents of solving the Jewish problem with whips, knives, and stones."[63]

On June 22, 1937, the National Radical Camp (ONR)-Falanga, a genuine Polish version of fascism, led by Boleslaw Piasecki, joined the government. The ONR platform clearly stated: "The Jew cannot be a citizen of the Polish State. Jews should be legally banned from rural commerce and trade. The de-Judaization of Polish cities and towns is an essential precondition for the healthy development of the nation."[64] Besides the Socialist PPS, which strongly condemned antisemitism, only the tiny Democratic Party and the small Communist Party stayed clear of advocating mass Jewish emigration.[65] In the atmosphere that prevailed in Poland in the last years before the German invasion, it took considerable political and personal courage to speak out on behalf of Jewish rights.[66]

The earlier-mentioned National Democratic Party under the leadership of Roman Dmowski remained the dominant right-wing opposition throughout the interwar years, largely representing many in the middle class and among the intellectuals, but also was supported among the wide strata of the population and especially among the youth and certain elements in the academic sector.[67] At the same time, generally speaking, in spite of the upsurge of antisemitic calls from various political parties, Jews in Poland continued to regulate their life as before, although increasingly concerned about their safety. Paradoxically, in December 1938, after Poland foolishly participated in Hitler's dismemberment of Czechoslovakia by acquiring a chunk of Czech territory for itself, the town of Cieszyn-Teschen, a government spokesman declared that the "Jewish question" was one of "the chief and most difficult problems facing the Polish nation" – totally oblivious of a far greater threat facing Poland; of Hitler's intentions, next-door, to soon do away completely with the Polish state.[68]

The *Żydokomuna* myth. A superstition used in a highly charged and inflated form was that Jews generally favor communism and maintain close links with the worldwide communist movement.[69] Even before the Soviet invasion of eastern Poland, in September 1939, the so-called *Żydokomuna*, or Judeo-communism conspiracy falsehood, occupied a prominent place in the nationalist diatribe, and was added to the fear that it would lead to a "Judeo-Polonia." This growing negative view had a harmful impact on relations with Jews before, during, and after World War II. This, despite that only 7 percent of Jewish voters supported the communist party (KPP) in prewar Poland. In fact, the communist party received most of its support from the Belarusian minority, whose separatism from Poland was backed by the Soviet Union.[70] However, one must also point out that the Jewish share in party membership was far higher than the proportional Jewish share in the general population. During the 1930s, Jews made up about one-quarter of the membership of the party; in large cities the proportions were even higher. Above all, Jews made up more than half of the local party leadership and most of the members of the Central Committee were of Jewish origin, and this rankled the eyes of many non-Jewish Poles.[28]

But what is overlooked is that most of the Jews in the KPP, certainly those in positions of leadership, strongly de-emphasized their Jewish origins – even used antisemitic slurs to describe other Jews.[71] It is also well to note that on the political landscape, the communists did not amount to much in prewar Poland. The total membership of the communist party in 1933 was 9,200, and the proportion of Jews in the party is estimated to have been 35 percent in 1930 and 24 percent in 1932; in other words, slightly above 2,000, out of a total Jewish population of over 3 million – very much less than a fraction of one percent.

According to the *Żydokomuna* myth, the Jews were the initiators of the Russian Communist Revolution in 1917 (witness the leading role of Leon Trotsky, creator of the Red Army) and afterwards, the primary power holders within the ruling Bolsheviks, and they as well dominated communist movements in the world. The worldwide spread of this idea in the 1920s was spurred with the publication and circulation of The Protocols of the Elders of Zion; a fraudulent document, originating in Czarist Russia, that purported to describe a secret Jewish conspiracy aimed at world domination.[72] The Judeo-Communist conspiracy myth continued to hold sway throughout the interwar period, and the years beyond that. In fact, it is still believed today by numerous people, not only in Poland, but in many other countries.[73]

Religious antisemitism: The saying that "to be Polish is to be Catholic" was held by many, if not most, Poles as a truism in a country that considered itself deeply Catholic. There were few other places in Europe where the church possessed such strength and enjoyed such wide popularity. In the minds of most Poles, patriotism and Catholicism went hand in hand; such as the poetic image of Poland as the Christ of nations.[74] Due to this strong identification with the Catholic Church, it was the only force in Poland that might have contained the spread of antisemitism, but it did just the opposite. It never let the people forget that the Jews had rejected the true faith and were implicated in the murder of the Christian divine figure.

Among the first lessons, indeed, that children learned in school from the priests was that the Jews had killed Christ. Large portions of the Polish population, moreover, still believed that Jews practiced ritual murder of defenseless Christians, especially children.[75] As told by a Jewish assimilated woman: "I personally got along well with Catholic girls. Whenever I brought them some goodies before Purim or Passover, they readily took it, even though the matzah supposedly had 'Christian blood' in it. It was no use to try to discuss this matter rationally with them... They would say, 'it is nevertheless true that you use Christian blood in the matzah. We were told this.'"[76] Historically, the first to react against the leniency of Polish kings toward Jews was the Church, in the effort to prevent social intercourse between Christians and Jews. As told in the previous chapter, the Church urged the imposition of a law requiring Jews to wear a specially shaped hat, but this was not enforced by the Polish ruling monarchs.[77]

In the modern period, right-wing elements within the Catholic community strongly denounced even those traditional Jews who sided with conservative Catholics in opposing liberalism and socialism. Father Józef Kruszyński, a professor at the University of Lublin, warned Polish Catholics not to be deceived by the apparent religiosity of Talmudic Jews. These Jews, he claimed, were full of hatred for Christians. Hence, they would always prove hostile to Poland's Catholic culture and were incapable of integrating into the mainstream Polish society.[78] As pointed out by Celia Heller, "in no other country did such a massive Catholic Jew-devouring literature exist as in Poland."[79]

Three years before the Nazi invasion of Poland, the Catholic primate, Cardinal August Hlond, drafted a pastoral letter filled with anti-Jewish venom, and which was to be read in all parishes. It stated:

> A Jewish question exists and there will be one so long as the Jews remain Jews. It is an actual fact that the Jews fight against the Catholic Church, they are freethinkers, and constitute the vanguard of atheism, bolshevism and revolution. The Jewish influence upon morals is fatal, and the publishers spread pornographic literature. It is also true that the Jews are committing frauds, practicing usury, and dealing in white slavery. It is true that in the schools, the Jewish youth is having an evil influence... upon the Catholic youth.[6]

Then, perhaps sensing he had gone a bit too far, he added: "Not all Jews are like that. I warn against the fundamental, unconditional anti-Jewish principle, imported from abroad [probably having in mind Nazi Germany]. It is contrary to Catholic Ethics... It is not permissible to hate anyone. Not even Jews." That did not stay him from calling for an economic boycott of the Jews. "One does well to prefer his own kind in commercial dealings and to avoid Jewish stores and Jewish stalls in the markets, but it is not permissible to demolish Jewish businesses, destroy their merchandise, break windows, to throw bombs at their homes... It is not permissible to assault Jews, to hit, maim or blacken them."[80] This pastoral letter well demonstrated how far the Catholic Church in Poland had traveled down the antisemitic road by the beginning of 1936.[81] "In my mind there is little doubt that prewar antisemitic attacks in Poland muted the possibility of greater Polish Catholic rescue efforts of Jews," Father John Pawlikowski of Chicago stated, having in mind later Polish attitudes during the German occupation; "even though some Catholics may have been morally troubled by the ferocity of Nazi Jewish policies," Pawlikowski added."[82]

Economic antisemitism. Worst of all for Jews struggling to make a living was the government's encouragement of an anti-Jewish economic boycott.[83] Already earlier, in 1925, when under Prime Minister Władysław Grabski, the government proceeded boldly to nationalize whole branches of commerce and industry that had been pioneered by Jews (tobacco, salt, matches, alcohol) and turn them into government monopolies, Jewish owners and laborers in this field were removed.[84] In the 1930s, credit sources were either closed to Jewish traders or operated with severe discrimination.[85] This had a disastrous economic effect on Jews.

Hand in hand with nationalization went the discriminatory hiring policy against Jews in nationalized industry as well as in the railroads, in public transportation, and government jobs.[86] To illustrate – while Jews made up about 40% of the population of Lublin, in the municipality only 2.6% of the workers were Jews. The message went out to low-level administrators to overlook Jews when hiring or to remove existing Jewish employees from their payrolls.[87] Beginning in 1936, Jews were not employed in the civil service, there were very few Jewish teachers in the public schools, practically no Jewish railroad workers, no Jews employed in state-controlled banks, and no Jewish workers in state-run monopolies (such as the tobacco industry).[88] Felicjan Sławoj-Skladkowski, as prime minister in 1936, defined his government's anti-Jewish economic policy in the following terms: "An economic struggle – by all means but without causing any harm."[89] This declaration gave a green light to students and thugs to picket Jewish stores, threatening Poles who dared to enter.[90]

The bill, for instance, to cancel the existing system of slaughtering animals according to Jewish religious prescriptions, on "humanitarian grounds," was bitterly debated by the parliament in 1936, and was seen by many as a cover for pushing Jews out of the meat processing industry. The war broke out before the bill went to the Senate.[91] The Sunday Rest Law, limiting the work week to 48 hours, made work on Saturday compulsory. Very few Jewish workers, consequently, were left in the tobacco and alcohol industries.[92]

Educational antisemitism. As early as June 1923, the Polish parliament approved a bill enforcing a numerus clausus at the universities, so as to limit Jewish attendance. The personal intervention of French premier Raymond Poincaré led the Polish government to formally retreat from this plan.[93] Reintroduced in 1937 in some universities, this numerus clausus eventually led to halving the number of Jews in Polish academic institutions. The restrictions were so widespread that, while the Jews made up 20.4% of the student body in 1928, by 1937 their share was down to only 7.5%, out of the total student population.[94] Special ghetto benches were also introduced, that forced Jewish students to sit in sections of the lecture halls reserved exclusively for them. Some Jewish students refused and instead preferred listening to the lectures while standing against the walls.[95] At all times and in all universities, Jewish students were at times heckled, humiliated, and attacked by some of their Polish fellow students – with the universities' administration abdicating to the attackers, by declining to intervene.[96]

Violent outbreaks. After a relatively respite during the Piłsudski

years (1926-1935), communal anti-Jewish violence spread again throughout the country, inspired and often led by the National Democratic
movement, the Endek party.[97] Other political groups who joined in the
fray included the National Radical Camp (ONR), Camp of Greater
Poland (OWP), and other smaller groups – who were all inspired by what
was taking place to Jews across the border, in Nazi Germany.[98] Economic
boycotts, encouraged by the government, allowed mobs to vent their
aggressive instincts and riot with impunity, occasionally smashing market stalls and small shops, with little hindrance from the authorities.[99]
Militia groups of the Jewish Bund often dispersed nationalists who were
picketing Jewish stores and preventing Polish customers from entering.
They also patrolled parks and streets where Jews were being attacked by
the nationalist hooligans.[100]

In approximately one hundred towns, violent attacks on Jews lead
to some deaths of Jews and injuries to numerous others, as a wave of
disturbances and terror swept over Poland in the years 1935 to 1937.[101]
The list is quite long and includes many cities.[102] As cases of anti-Jewish
violence came to court, the perpetrators often went free or if convicted
received short suspended sentences.[103] Attackers young of age were ex-
cused with the euphemism "emotionalism of the young."[104] As the years
moved toward the end of the 1930s, Jews began to increasingly worry
about their safety, in a country that hundreds of years before had invited
and welcomed them.

Emigration. After Piłsudski's death, in 1935, the Polish government
increased the encouragement for Jews to leave, seeing it as a desirable
solution to the Jewish question; to what they termed the Jewish "surplus population." Zionists also believed that Jewish emigration would
solve the Jewish question in Poland and other countries. The question,
however, with no practical answer – where were Jews to go?[105] The doors
of Palestine only allowed a trickle, and a stringent immigration quota
prevailed in the United States. To speed up the emigration idea, the
Polish government, came up with a fantastic idea: colonies for Poland
somewhere in underdeveloped regions, to where Jews would be directed;
and proposed this idea before the Assembly of the League of Nations

in September 1936. According to the government spokesman, General Skwarczyński, "the necessity of freeing the Polish culture from the influence of the foreign Jewish mentality" was reason enough for Poland to be allotted some territory outside of its borders.[106] Polish diplomats were instructed to actively search potential areas for concentrated Jewish settlement, either in South America, in the Middle East outside Palestine, or on the African continent.[107] In the spring of 1939, even in the atmosphere of an imminent war, Polish foreign minister Józef Beck, in a meeting in April 1939 with British prime minister Neville Chamberlain and British foreign minister Lord Halifax in London, as well as top officials of France, insisted that the problem of Jewish emigration from Poland was as urgent as the threat from Nazi Germany; that the country had room for only a half million Jews. Therefore, close to three million had to go.[108]

The Poles approached the French on the idea of a Jewish emigration to the island of Madagascar, Africa; then, a French colony.[109] It was widely publicized in the press and discussed at conferences in Paris, in October 1936, inter alia, between Polish Foreign Minister Józef Beck and the French-Jewish prime minister, Léon Blum. In the meantime, the Polish government sent a special commission of inquiry to Madagascar, but all three members of this commission agreed, each in a separate report, that the practical possibilities of settling Polish Jews or any "white immigrants" there were very limited.[110] An alternative emigration plan was discussed at the end of 1938 in talks between Jerzy Potocki, the Polish ambassador to the United States, and a group of influential American Jewish financiers, including Bernard Baruch, Edward M. Warburg, and Lewis L. Strauss. The plan called for Poland, with the help of Jewish financiers, to acquire Angola from Portugal, and use that territory to absorb Jewish mass emigrants from Poland.[14] United States President F.D. Roosevelt was in favor of this plan, and adopted it, also to divert pressures to open the gates of the United States to large-scale Jewish immigration from Eastern Europe.[111] However, Portugal's strong opposition to this plan doomed it.[112]

Pro-Zionism. During 1931-1935, an estimated 51,300 Polish Jews emigrated to Palestine, followed with 14,500 during 1936-1938 (there were then severe disturbances by the Arab population). Thousands more left during the interwar period to various other destinations.[113] In London, world Zionist leader, Dr. Chaim Weizmann, maintained direct contact with Polish foreign minister Beck and especially with the Polish ambassador in Britain, Edward Raczyński, to coordinate common efforts to apply pressure on the British government, in 1937 and 1938, to agree to a small Jewish state in Palestine so as to make possible a larger influx of Polish Jews there.[114] However, these aspirations suffered a heavy blow, with England's proclamation of the White Paper, in May 1939, effectively closing the doors of the Jewish ancient homeland to Jewish immigrants.[115]

Inside Poland, the authorities aided representatives of the Zionist secret militias, Haganah and the Irgun Zva Leumi (Etzel) by secretly selling them army equipment, by conducting army training courses in pioneer agricultural camps inside Poland, and by allowing Zionist organizations to organize the illegal flow of people to Palestine;[116] all these moves in the effort to speed up the creation of a Jewish homeland in Palestine which it was hoped would absorb most Polish Jews.[117]

Culture and Education. In spite of all these Polish government policies to frustrate hopes of a continuous Jewish existence in the country, Jewish life continued to prosper – in sharp contrast to what fellow Jews experienced across the border in Nazi Germany. Polish Jewish culture continued to dominate world Jewry in many fields, and its influence radiated throughout the world. Many religious and secular schools, numerous Jewish journals, periodicals, and books, published in both Yiddish and Hebrew; the network of Jewish libraries and cultural clubs – all these were at that time unmatched anywhere else among Jewish communities outside Poland.[118] During the school year of 1937–1938, there were 226 elementary schools and twelve high schools as well as fourteen vocational schools with either Yiddish or Hebrew as the instructional language.[119] The religious Agudat Israel movement incorporated some secular subjects into its elementary schools curriculum and founded the Beth Jacob schools for girls (numbering 250 schools in 1937 with 38,000 students).[120] In addition, there was the Yavne school system, founded by Mizrachi, the religious Zionist organization, that combined religious and secular education.[121] There were also the "grand yeshivot," for more intense Talmudic studies; many of them world famous, such as Mir, Baranowicz, Bobowa, Vilna, Grodno and Lublin (Yeshiva *Hakhme Lublin*).[122] These Polish yeshivot continued to attract thousands of foreign students, while graduates of these Talmudic academies went on to found new educational centers in Palestine, Western Europe, and the United States.

Of the Jewish secular school systems, the two largest were Tarbut – Zionist oriented, with Hebrew as the language of instruction and an emphasis on Hebrew culture, and some secular ones – anti-Zionist, and socialist in orientation, with Yiddish as the language of instruction. The YIVO Institute, founded in Vilna in 1925, became the world center for the study of the Yiddish language and Eastern European Jewish civilization as a whole.[123] The Yiddish theatre also flourished, with fifteen theaters and theatrical groups.[124] These startling statistics reveal the sharp contrast between the Jews of Poland and those in western Europe, who did not choose to remain a separate national group but wished to become more acculturated; yet, they too still suffered from antisemitic outbreaks of various degrees.

In Warsaw in the 1920s, according to incomplete statistics, there were 442 synagogues and prayer houses of various sizes for a population of about 350,000 Jews. Throughout the country, cooperatives, credit unions, orphanages, hospitals, newspapers, publishing houses, theater companies, orchestras, choirs, sports clubs, and cultural societies, many sponsored by political parties but many others independent, were the links in a far-flung network that defined the Jewish nationality of interwar Poland.[125] Judging the creativity output of the Jews in independent Poland, Nathan Davies is obviously right, that we have only to compare the flourishing of autonomous Jewish culture in that country with the situation in Germany, the Soviet Union or America, to see the startling difference. But, on the other hand, such creativity can sometimes go along with various social and economic oppressive measures.[126]

Polish freedom, and Jewish strivings, made possible the continued thriving of Jewish life, although under heightened tense conditions of a growing antisemitism.[127] On the flip side, while modern Polish nationalism too often went hand in hand with a certain antisemitism, it also inspired Polish Jewish youth to raise the banner of Jewish nationalism.[128] As underlined by Ezra Mendelsohn, Jewish history in interwar Poland was "the best of times and the worst of times." The best of times in the sense of the extraordinary creativity of Polish Jewry, the worst of times in the sense of the fulfilment of the bleakest prophecies, made mostly by Zionists, concerning the imminent bitter fate of the East European Jewish diaspora.[129]

The level of antisemitism – a summary. As Poland rebounded as an independent nation after World War I, followers of extreme Polish nationalism raged against those amidst them who were so much different than themselves in many respects; culturally, religiously and socially; even more so than against the other minorities, such as Ukrainians and Byelorussians – namely, the Jews. However, up to the end of the Piłsudski period, in 1935, it was relatively a calm time in Polish-Jewish relations,[130] as Piłsudski and his socialist associates were opposed to legislative discrimination against Jews. Some, in fact consider, with a bit of hyperbole, the period of 1926, when Piłsudski seized power, until his death, nine years later, as the "springtime" of Polish-Jewish relations.[131]

When Piłsudski died in 1935, Jews joined Poles in mourning the death of a man many called "Father" (*Ojciec*). His heirs, however, adopted antisemitic positions, calling for the massive evacuation of Jews, and publicly declaring their support of an economic boycott of the Jews.[132] The PPS socialist party rejected Piłsudski's heirs antisemitic slogans, while the Peasant Party, and other smaller parties, though not antisemitic, saw emigration for the Jews as a solution to the socioeconomic problem confronting Poland. Only the followers of Roman Dmowski's National Democrats (Endecja or Endeks), were openly hostile to Jews. Polish Jews in the late 1930s were gradually subjected to a number of ugly threats and denigrations, and to a mountainous wave of economic hardship and emotional insecurity.[133] In the eyes of the ruling circles, it was best for most Jews to emigrate to anywhere else, including Palestine, if that was possible.[134] In furtherance of that goal, these circles subscribed to measures to pressure Jews out from the country's economic life, cultural fields and professions; including boycotting Jewish factories and businesses, and introducing a prejudicial numerus clausus policy in the universities, that severely limited the admittance of Jewish students.[135] However, Poland stayed clear of enacting any Nuremberg-type racial laws against the Jews in the 1930s.

Until his death, in January 1939, Roman Dmowski argued that the presence of the Jews had prevented the emergence of a Polish middle-class.[136] As for the effort to assimilate the Jews, he felt that they were too numerous and had a too strongly marked national character for this process to be successful. In addition, the Jewish specific characteristics, developed over the centuries "are alien to our moral code."[137] Always an antisemite, he became convinced that the western democracies were dominated by Jewish influence. The rise to power of Hitler and the speed with which he was able to disenfranchise one of the wealthiest and most influential Jewish communities in Europe came as a great boost to Dmowski's political movement. It stepped up its agitation not only among students but also among workers and the lower middle class, and increased its membership from 33,000 in January 1930 to nearly a quarter million, in early 1933, when it was banned by the Piłsudski government, though it continued to exert a great political influence.[138] Dmowski's underestimation of the German danger to Poland's independence was one of the factors which created that fatal overconfidence in Poland which paved the way to the disaster of September 1939.[139]

In a study of conditions between the two world wars, Celia S. Heller described the Jews in Poland as bearing the marks of a conquered population in their social status and in the treatment accorded to them.[140] She believes, and so do other adherents of this opinion, that the years 1919-39 were a rehearsal for the Holocaust period. That the Poles pushed the Jews to the "edge of destruction," and the Nazis followed up with destroying them.[141] Joseph Lichten strongly disapproves this negative assessment, which he claims is not always based on facts, but as Heller would like to see them.[142] Joseph Marcus also challenges Heller's opinion. He states that Polish efforts to strike at the Jews' economic wellbeing through such policies as the Sunday rest law, state economic monopolies, numerus clausus, boycotts and so on, were largely ineffective. The real problem, he concludes, was Polish poverty and Jewish over-population. "The Jews in Poland were poor because they lived in a poor, underdeveloped country. Discrimination added only marginally to their poverty."[143]

However, one may question whether the difficult economic conditions in Poland rendered inevitable the state's policies and society's attitudes toward the Jewish minority. As pointed out by Ezra Mendelsohn, pre-World War I Hungary was also economically a backward country with a poor Jewish population, but its leaders, instead of urging Jews to emigrate and supporting boycotts of their stores, preached the integration of the Jewish community into Magyardom and welcomed the Jews as modernizes of the Hungarian economy. On the other hand, one may also point that Germany's wealth and the wealth of its Jewish community, did not prevent many segments of the German people from supporting radical antisemitic measures from 1933 onwards.[144]

Nathan Davies, in God's Playground, adopts a more favorable stance, and states that if things were so bad for Polish Jews then how can one explain why they were so creative and so vital a community? As he so eloquently puts it, "Anyone who has seen the remarkable records which these people left behind them, and which have been collected in YIVO's post-war headquarters in New York, cannot fail to note the essential dynamism of Polish Jewry at this juncture. All was not well: but neither was it unrelieved gloom."[145] But whether Heller's term of "conquered population" is appropriate, there is no denying of the growth and strength of antisemitism during the interwar period, and most Jewish scholars agree on this point. That by the late 1930s, both the Polish regime and Polish society were waging a bitter and increasingly successful campaign against the Jewish population, to encourage them to leave – at times, accompanied with violent outbreaks, especially during the latter 1930 years. Having said that, it cannot be denied that external events, which cannot be blamed on the Polish state or on Polish society, had a tremendous impact upon the condition of Polish Jews – the depression, for example, and the rise of Hitler in Germany.[146]

Whatever the reasons, there is no denying that by the late 1930s Jews in Poland felt excluded from first-class membership in the state, and this led to a widespread feeling among most Jews, and especially among the youth, that they had no future in Poland.[147] Possibly, one reason why Polish scholars are reluctant to admit that Poland was prop-agating antisemitic policies is, as pointed by Mendelsohn, that they are accustomed to regard Poland as a victim nation, as a result of the harsh German occupation, and victims are extremely reluctant to admit that they have victimized others. But such situations are possible.[148]

The growing antisemitism on the eve of World War Two, though less when compared to next-door Germany, was, paradoxically, a strict departure from a century earlier when opinions about Jews were also positive.[149] In Adam Mickiewicz's epic, Pan Tadeusz, published in 1834, that substantial portions of which Polish schoolchildren have memorized for generations, it included the bearded Jewish Jankiel who performs a concert of Polish patriotic music that recalls his audience to their sacred national task, under the motto, "for our freedom, and for yours."[150] But, in the post-World War I period, the persistence of Jewish separateness emerged as the main source of Polish irritation at the presence of Jews; in short, in 1930s, the gap between the two communities widened and conflicts became sharper. [151]

Impending catastrophe. In October 1940, Jewish historian Emanuel Ringelblum wrote of a joke running current, one year into the German occupation of Poland. A Jew alternately laughs and yells in his sleep. His wife wakes him up, and he is mad at her for this. "I was dreaming someone had scribbled on a wall: 'Beat the Jews! Down with ritual slaughters!'" "So, what were you so happy about," she asked? He responded: "Don't you understand? That means the good old days have come back! The Poles are running things again!"[152] However, before the war, as a leading historian of Jewish life in Poland, Ringelblum tried to counter the image of Poland as either a land distinguished by age-old traditions of liberalism and tolerance, or the contrary image of an unbridgeable Polish antagonism toward Jews and mutual alienation. Polish-Jewish relations, in his opinion, rather reflected a constant interplay of rivalry and cooperation, religious alienation and close personal ties, economic tension and mutual collaboration. Jewish historians, in Ringelblum's words, do not emphasize enough that Jews lived in Poland by right and not on sufferance. He had little patience with the idea that antisemitism was inevitable and eternal, and he attacked other scholars who exaggerated the intractable nature of antisemitism in the country.[153] As we shall later see, a traumatized Ringelblum under German occupation led him to radically change his views on the depth of antisemitism in Poland.

As the 1930s drew to a close, a growing sense of an impending disaster looming on the horizon took hold of many Jews. Something terrible was about to happen to them in Poland, but exactly how and when, in what form and by whom, one could not tell. Very few pointed to Nazi Germany as the principal author that would doom Polish Jewry. Poet Mordechai Gebirtig gave voice to these feelings in his poem, Our Town is Burning (*Es Brent*), which opened with the words: "Our town is burning, brothers, burning; our poor little town is burning. Angry winds are fanning higher; the leaping tongues of flame and fire." When it was written in 1938, it did not refer to the danger posed by Nazi Germany but rather to the sense of personal insecurity and public uncertainty that Poland's Jews were experiencing.[154]

Zionist leader, Vladimir-Zeev Jabotinsky in a public speech in Warsaw on August 7, 1938, also gave voice to this alarming feeling when he warned: "You, my sisters and my brothers, do not see the volcano that will wash over you with the fire of destruction, and I see a picture of horror and there remains only a short while in which you can be saved... If you think differently, you must drive me out of the Jewish street, but if you trust in me you must listen to my last-minute warnings. For the sake of God, each and every one of you must escape to save himself/herself while there is still time, but time is running out."[155] Up to early 1939, Poland and Germany entertained good relations, and very few people could foresee that Germany would very soon militarily subjugate

Poland, and exterminate almost all of its Jews – not even the doomsday prophet Jabotinsky.[156]

Polish-Jewish relations which many centuries ago had surged on a high note, and had in the recent interwar period suffered serious damage from an intolerant nationalism, was about to be severely tested by an infernal scenario that no one in his right mind could have imagined. As Poles across a vast spectrum of political movements continued to obsessively discuss the removal of Jews to some other distant place, they failed to take note of the more immediate existential threat to themselves by their next-door German neighbor, due to the Nazis' pronounced goals of "*lebensraum*" (living space) and "*drang nach Osten*" (expansion eastward). This would come, principally at the expense of Poland, that would have to disappear as an independent political entity, and large swaths of its territory were to be colonized by German-kindred people, coupled with the expulsion of most of its non-Jewish inhabitants to somewhere deep in Russia. For Polish Jews, the Germans had something more lethal in mind.

As 1939 dawned, Polish leaders continued to be concerned about the "surplus" Jewish population that they mistakenly considered posed a threat to the unity of the Polish nation, while blindly failing to realize the more growing ominous existential threat to their country from Nazi Germany, their next-door western neighbor, that would plunge the country into a most nightmarish six years of brutal occupation.

CHAPTER 3

World War II: Germans, Poles and Jews

a) Germans and Poles

Poland under occupation. On September 1,1939, German troops invaded Poland, from the west, followed by a Soviet invasion, on September 17, from the east, starting World War II. By the end of that month, Poland had ceased existing as an independent nation, for the second time in its history. The Polish government was reconstituted in exile under a new leadership, far away from Poland; first in France, and after that country's fall to Germany, in London.

In line with the pre-war non-aggression treaty between these two powerful countries, Germany took control of 22 million people, in western Poland, including 19 million ethnic Poles, 2.2 million Polish Jews, 550,000 Germans, and 450,000 Ukrainians. This region was subsequently divided into two; one, annexed to Nazi Germany, including Danzig-West Prussia, Pomerania (renamed Wartheland), as well as the large city Łódz (renamed Litzmannstadt), and a part of Silesia (that included Oświęcim, renamed Auschwitz); all counting 10 million people, of whom 8.9 million were Poles, plus minorities of ethnic Germans and Jews.[1] The other remaining part held by the Germans, named General Government, contained 16 million people, and included the major Polish inhabited cities of Warsaw, Kraków, and Lublin, to name a few. That

occupied part of Poland was shorn of any native administrative body, and
was harshly ruled directly by a Nazi governor from the city of Kraków.[2]

In the east, the Russians controlled about a third of the territory
of prewar Poland, with its 13 million people, including the cities of
Lwów and Bialystok, and also counting close to 1 million Jews. Until
the German attack on the Soviet Union, on June 22, 1941, 61 percent
of Polish Jews lived under the German occupation and the rest under
Soviet rule.[3]

Approximately 120,000 Jews took part in the September campaign
as soldiers in the Polish army, and an estimated 7,000 Polish Jewish soldiers fell in battle, 20,000 were wounded, and more than 60,000 taken
prisoners.[4] In Warsaw, which underwent a severe German bombing,
several thousand Jewish civilians were killed and many Jewish buildings
were destroyed.[5] The Soviets also captured some 22,500 Polish Jewish
soldiers.[6] When Germany invaded the Soviet Union, the eastern Polish
regions also came under German control, and were mostly annexed to
the occupied General Government.

In light of the Nazi design of extending Germany's borders eastward, in order to create "living space" for Germanic colonization, at the
expense of the "inferior" Slavic nations (principally, Poland, Russia and
Ukraine) – Poland was the first to feel the brutality that accompanied
this Nazi expansionist goal. In no place in German-occupied Europe was
there such a heavy concentration of German manpower as in Poland. SS
and police strength fluctuated between 50,000 and 80,000, supported
by the Wehrmacht, the German regular army, which rarely dropped
below 400,000 troops and reached heights of 2,000,000 in June 1941,
on the eve of the war with Russia. The Germans were present in all
densely populated regions, but not so in all villages.[7] As the war dragged
on and German casualties mounted, the Germans forced thousands
of Poles, considered as semi-ethnic Germans, into the German army.
Władysław Sikorski, Polish Premier in the Polish government-in-exile in
London, estimated in June 1942, that 70,000 such Poles in Pomerania
and 100,000 in Silesia were drafted into the German military, and were
mostly assigned into auxiliary formations in support of combat units.[8]

When the military tide turned against Germany, in 1944 – as the Red Army advanced toward the prewar Polish eastern border, many of these regions turned into bloody clashes between Polish and Ukrainian partisans, who vied for the inclusion of this region into future separate national states.[9] The Polish underground, the largest clandestine militia in German-occupied Europe waited until Soviet forces approached Warsaw before launching its long-awaited uprising in Warsaw, on August 1, 1944. It took the Germans two months to crush this uprising, and it ended with the loss of tens of thousands Polish lives, including an unknown fairly large number of Jews – many of whom had up to then found refuge in the city's metropolitan area, sheltered by friendly Poles. The rest of Warsaw's population, probably numbering more than 200,000, was expelled or sent to labor camps. When the Soviet army, and Polish units, trained in Russia, entered Warsaw, on January 17, 1945, they found a city in ruins and nearly uninhabited, with some 300 Jews hiding in demolished cavernous homes.[10] By end February 1945, the Russians swept the last of the German forces out of Poland.[11] Poland, although formally restored as an independent state, with a self-styled government, was actually for the next 45 years a communist client and puppet state of the Soviet Union, and whose top-level policies needed the Kremlin's prior approval, and with elements of whose army were also stationed on Polish soil under a forced military agreement, known as the Warsaw Pact. Full independence was only regained in 1990. Thus, for a half a century Poland was controlled by either Germany or Russia, an additional traumatic event in its history.

Nazi views of Poland and Poles. Ahead of the invasion of Poland, Germans troops were brainwashed into a racial hatred of the soon-to-be conquered nation; a contemptuous ill will that was largely absent in their invasion of other countries in western Europe. The Poles, as a Slavic nation, were considered racially inferior to the Germans (while Jews were downgraded as sub-humans).[12] But the Germans realized that Polish "inferiority" did not preclude a strong Polish attachment to their land, and consequently, a great resistance was to be feared to their being uprooted and exiled, to make room for German colonization. Hence, a policy of unrestricted terror was to be applied. On the eve of the war, on August 22, 1939, Hitler told his leading generals, "Our strength lies in our speed and our brutality... I have issued a command... that the aim of the war lies not in reaching particular lines but in the physical annihilation of the enemy." The enemy was to be forced to surrender by sending "man, woman and child of Polish descent and language to their deaths, pitilessly and remorselessly." Following this, "Poland will be depopulated and settled with Germans." The Poles, he told propaganda minister Joseph Goebbels, were "more animals then men, totally dull and formless... The dirt of the Poles is unimaginable."[13] After Poland surrendered, Hitler announced, on October 17, 1939, that in the captured country, a "hard ethnic struggle" will take place, "that will not permit any legal restrictions."[14] Germans secret plans for conquered Poland included the liquidation of the country's academically educated and professional classes annihilated.[15]

Nazi long-range plans for the country was for most ethnic Poles to be cleared out, exiled into deepest Russia, to make room for German or kindred settlers, who were to be served by the remaining Polish population, reduced to the status of helots to serve their new masters. In Hitler's mind, Poland was to serve the same function for Germany as Australia was for Britain, and the American West for the USA. It was to be a colony, in which most of the supposedly racially inferior indigenous inhabitants would be removed by one means or another to make room for the invading master race.[16] In the meantime, "there must be no opportunity for the Poles to reassert themselves. The standard of living in the country is to remain low; it is of use to us only as a reservoir of labor."[17]

SS head Heinrich Himmler echoing similar voices as his master, took it a step further by stating that "all Poles will disappear from the world... It is essential that the great German people should consider it as its major task to destroy all Poles."[18] This horrific extermination idea, to be carried out, not in the immediate as for Jews, but after the victory over Russia, never took place due to the changing military situation. Also, because it was only in Himmler's mind, but was never seriously considered by Hitler, who was satisfied into turning the remaining Poles, after most others had been driven into the depths of Russia, as servants of their German masters.[19] The death penalty was to be the mandated punishment for a slew of transgressions, great and small. This brutal treatment of the conquered nation must have come as a shock to most Poles, who before the war entertained amicable relations with Nazi Germany, solidified in 1934, with a 10-year non-aggression pact.

German administration of occupied Poland. Although the Poles were to be enslaved, though not exterminated, many Poles began to suspect that extermination was the Nazi ultimate goal for them.[20] The Nazi design, however, was rather to destroy Polish society so that the country would forever cease to exist as a nation.[21] According to the secret plan, termed Generalplan-Ost, whole ethnic Slav populations (Poles, Byelorussians, Russians and Ukrainians) from the Oder to the Dnieper Rivers were to be supplanted by German settlers. In line with this grand design, some twenty million Poles would be resettled in western Siberia, after the defeat of Russia, while some three to four million who were racially suitable for "re-Germanization" would be allowed to remain, while the rest were to be enslaved.[22] Hans Frank, Nazi governor of conquered Poland (the so-called General Government), triumphantly stated that once the war was won, "mincemeat can be made of the Poles."[23] The intention, Frank stated, was to make Poland as much German as possible. "There is not a shadow of doubt that the territory of the General Government must be and will be colonized by Germans."[24] In the meantime, awaiting the defeat of Russia which never took place, German oppression did not destroy the fabric of everyday life inside Poland. In addition, the Polish underground had access to large financial resources that were channeled to it from the London-based Polish government-in-exile, beyond German reach.[25]

Separate from the General Government, in the Polish territories incorporated into the German Reich, all persons were classified according to the Racial Register (*Volksliste*), and divided into four categories, in accordance with their so-called Aryan adherence. *Reichsdeutsch*, pure ethnic Germans; *Volksdeutsch*, also known as ethnic Germans, for persons who claimed German ancestry going back three generations;

Nichtdeutsch, non-Germanic – that is, all Poles with no Jewish blood connections; and at the lowest scale, *Juden,* Jews.[26] In these annexes zones, the previous local Polish administration and all existing Polish organizations were liquidated, and new administrative units were set up.[27] Polish schools, theaters, museums, libraries, bookshops, newspapers and all other Polish cultural and linguistic institutions were closed down, and the use of the Polish language was forbidden. The names of administrative districts, towns and villages were Germanized. This was accompanied with the forcible transfer of some 750,000 non-Jewish Poles to the conquered General Government, with the additional thousands of Jews forced into ghettos in the occupied zone.[28]

None of those driven out received any compensation for the loss of their homes, their farms, their properties and their assets. Altogether over a million people were arbitrarily expelled, a third of them Jewish – all becoming "beggars in one hour."[29] In place of the expelled Poles and Jews, over 400,000 ethnic Germans, from various east European regions were brought in and resettled. An undisclosed several million Poles still remained behind, as the war entered the fourth year, and their resettlement was postponed due to more pressing military exigencies.[30]

Also, much further in the east, the Zamość region (Lublin province), in the General Government, was also targeted for racial resettlement. In November 1942, the Germans began emptying 47 villages of Polish inhabitants to make room for ethnic Germans, save for those with desirable German racial traits who were allowed to stay.[31] An estimated 200,000 racially desirable Slavic children, mainly Polish, were also sent to the Reich to be fully Aryanized.[32] No similar large-scale forceful population transfers were undertaken in any of the other German occupied countries.

The direct German-occupied area of the General Government (known as *Generalgouvernement*) was divided into four districts, each named after its major city: Warsaw, Kraków, Radom, and Lublin. When Germany invaded the Soviet Union, in June 1941, a fifth district, Galicia, with its center in Lwów, was added to the General Government.[33] An additional territorial district, Białystok, with a population of 1.7 million, that was originally part of the Soviet occupied zone, was also created, and added to the General Government.[34] All of prewar Poland was, after June-July 1941, under direct German control.

In the General Government, a low-level Polish administration was permitted to function, but no autonomy whatever was granted to it. The Germans established a regime of absolute occupation in which all offices, except for those at the lowest level, were in German hands.[35] Polish secondary schools and universities were closed; education was limited to primary and vocational schools only. The Germans allowed entertainment of cheap operettas, cabarets, and pornography, and drinking was strongly encouraged to dupe the population into an atavistic and uncultured type of existence.[36] At the same time, hundreds of thousands of municipal employees, railroad workers, police, and other local officials, continued their accustomed work, although under German supervision.

Punishments. Poland also stood out as the country whose population was most severely punished by the Germans with extensive shootings for the slightest offense, as compared with other German occupied countries – months ahead of the killing of Jews. Already during the initial first months of the occupation, an estimated 16,000 people lost their lives by random execution, and serious damages were inflicted on hundreds of towns and villages for various offenses.[37] Political and resistance activists were sent to concentration camps, such as to Oświęcim, renamed Auschwitz by the Germans, where Polish political prisoners were the camp's first inmates. Later, in the summer of 1941, Soviet prisoners were also sent there. According to one estimate, approximately 270,000 Polish prisoners died in German camps.[38]

By 1943, mass killings were commonplace everywhere in Poland for people suspected of anti-German acts of the slightest nature.[39] In Józefów, Lublin region, the Germans killed many inhabitants in retaliation for the death of one German family. Even children under 16 years of age were sometimes vulnerable to the death penalty for making anti-German statements or simply demonstrating what the Germans described as a "hostile mentality." According to one source, between October 16, 1943 and February 15, 1944, there were 33 street executions which took the lives of 1,528 innocent people.[40] As a result, Poles lived in constant fear of arrest, torture, and death, and no one could be certain when they left home in the morning that they would return in the evening. This constant stress of uncertainty of one's survival made many people indifferent to the sight of suffering of others, non-Jews and Jews alike.[41]

Elimination of the Elites. To reduce the Poles to full obedience, the Germans decided that the intellectual elite of the people had to be eliminated. This included the highly educated class, mostly university professors, but also teachers, priests and army officers. In the words of Hans Frank, Nazi governor of occupied Poland: "The Fuehrer told me: 'what we have now recognized in Poland that the elite must be liquidated; we must watch out for the seeds that begin to sprout again, so as to stamp them out in good time."[42] A list of 60,000 names of Polish professionals and intellectuals had been gathered before the war, who were to be all killed or imprisoned. This was to prevent the Polish intelligentsia from building itself up to become a new leadership stratum.[43] This, fortunately, was only partly carried out, but it affected many others. Such as when on November 6, 1939, 183 (some stated 200) academics – professors and lecturers of the Jagiellonian University and the Mining Academy in Kraków were arrested, and carted off to German concentration camps, where many died.[44] This was followed with the execution of many hundreds (some claim thousands) of Polish intellectuals – professors, teachers, civil servants, and priests – after their deportation to Dachau, Buchenwald, and Sachsenhausen camps, as well as camps in the Polish homeland. In his post-war report, former Auschwitz prisoner Witold Pilecki wrote that intellectual prisoners were quickly eliminated. Over a thousand priests ended up in Dachau camp, where half did not survive their imprisonment. The Poles, thus, became the first people in Europe to experience the killings of innocents on a large scale.[45]

By 1942, the situation improved somewhat for the intellectuals because manpower shortages forced German civil servants stationed in Poland into the military, and their positions were made available to Poles.[46] In the occupied General Government, universities, schools, libraries, publishing houses, archives, museums and other centers of Polish culture remained closed. "The Poles," said Nazi governor Hans Frank, "do not need universities or secondary schools: the Polish lands are to be changed into an intellectual desert." As early as October 31, 1939, he had sarcastically declared: "For the Poles, the only educational opportunities that are to be made available are those that demonstrate to them the hopelessness of their ethnic fate."[47]

Targeting the clergy. As already mentioned in the previous chapter, in Poland, nationalism was synonymous with Catholicism, as the latter were in forefront of Polish attempts to regain their freedom during the long period of the country's partition. The Germans, consequently, singled them out for persecution, especially those in position of leadership.[48] Here, too, Poland stands out from other occupied countries, for only here, in the regions incorporated into Nazi Germany, did the Nazis arrest and imprison a great number of the clergy, whom they considered part of the remaining Polish population's intellectual elite, and hence a potential threat to full German rule over these acquired territories. Of the six bishops in the annexed Wartheland (the former Pomerania province), only one, Bishop Walenty Dymek, remained. According to one account, a staggering 80% of the region's clergy were imprisoned or deported to concentration camps. Altogether, according to one estimate, out of a total of 10,017 clergy at the start of the war, 1,811 died during the occupation, mostly those residing in the annexed territories. In the General Government, the situation was somewhat better, where 95 percent of the clergy remained in the same parish in which they had resided before the war.[49]

Execution of the mentally ill. Also slated for elimination were mental institutions that were emptied of their patients, who underwent various forms of death. Soon, after the occupation of Poland, in Kocborowo (renamed Conradstein), the patients of a mental institution were taken into a lorry and driven to a nearby killing field where many other Poles had already been killed, and were shot one by one in the back of the neck. Physically handicapped children from three other locations were also brought to Kocborowo, for execution. Altogether around 2,000 mental patients were killed, taken to that place from several other mental institutions.[50] Similar executions of mentally handicapped inmates, taken from three major psychiatric hospitals, took place in the Wartheland region. In Owińska (renamed Treskau), execution was via carbon monoxide gas, released from a canister. Altogether, some 12,000 inmates of psychiatric hospitals and homes for the mentally and physically handicapped were killed, that also included some Polish prostitutes, for good measure – mostly in the German-annexed Wartheland province, but also in other regions.[51]

Forced labor in Germany. To replenish German workers called up for army service, the government replaced them with workers from the occupied countries. Guided by these economic needs, throughout the war years, the Germans deported up to 2 million Poles to the Reich for work, in return for low wages and primitive-type accommodation.[52] It began in February 1940, when 80,000 Polish workers, a third of them women, seeking to replenish their income, volunteered for work in Germany. As this did not meet higher German expectations, more forceful methods were used, such as sudden street roundups of healthy-looking men, leaving the church or the cinema, or other public places, and shipped off without further ceremony.[53] In the summer of 1940, there were 700,000 Poles working as voluntary or forced laborers in Germany. By August 1943, the figure had risen to 1.6 million.[54]

As recorded in his wartime diary by Dr. Zymunt Klukowski, in his hometown of Szczebrzeszyn (Zamość region), on May 19, 1940:

> All young men and women born between 1915 and 1924 (from fifteen to twenty-four years of age) must register with the Arbeitsamt (Labor Office). This announcement caused a panic among parents and their youth. Fewer and fewer young people can be seen walking on the streets. Some are hiding in small villages or in the forest... [March 4, 1941] The German police, with the help of the Polish militia [probably the so-called Blue Police], are going from house to house registering

all Christians between the ages of fifteen and fifty who are suitable for labor. [August 6, 1941] The Germans began arresting people and taking them to a large, empty warehouse. Several people were beaten. Throughout the entire city people were hiding and trying to escape." [May 21, 1942] Yesterday in Zamość some 200 people were taken from offices and factories. Most were sent to Germany; only a few were set free.[55]

Sparing Aryan blood. Blind to their own racial theories, the Germans, led by SS head Himmler, were in a frantic search for so-called lost Aryan blood among the "inferior" Poles. Thus, blond-haired children, whom Himmler noticed were close to the Teutonic ideal, were kidnapped from Polish orphanages by agents of the Nazi bloodstock organization, the SS *Lebensborn* (Fountain of Life). On May 9, 1940, Himmler stated that it is an absolute necessity "to screen" the annexed Eastern territories for persons of Teutonic blood, "in order to make this lost German blood again available to our own people."[56] As he also stressed earlier, on October 5, 1939: "It is our duty to take their children with us… We either win over the good blood we can use for ourselves… or else we destroy that blood. For us, the end of this war will mean an open road to the East… It means that we shall push the borders of our German race 500 kilometers to the east."[57] A further political reason justifying the removal of the "good" Aryan blood from the Poles: "This would remove the danger that this subhuman people of the east might acquire a leader class from such people of good blood, which would be dangerous for us because they would be our equals."[58] Eighty percent of these captive deported children reportedly never returned to their families in Poland, and their whereabouts remain unknown.[59]

Other restrictions. Inside occupied Poland, the policy of the Germans toward the Polish peasantry was initially rather benevolent, since it also included the cancelling of the farmers' debts to Jewish creditors, elimination of taxes, and only a few quotas for compulsory food deliveries. This soon changed, as the German army took over a substantial number of farms to secure food supplies for its troops, and 60 percent of Polish meat production was taken off to feed the Germans back in Germany.[60] In the Zamość region, for instance, the Germans began registering pigs and other livestock kept in local farms and ordering that they could only be slaughtered for use by the German army, not for local consumption. Villages that failed to furnish the food quotas required of them faced punishment by the Germans.[61]

As for the food allotments, the Germany policy was to keep the population undernourished, so as to weaken their resolve of resistance. While the average daily food allotment for Germans was 2,613 calories, for Warsaw residents in 1941 it was 669 calories to Poles, and a starvation diet of 194 calories for Jews in the ghetto. Next to the Jews, the Poles had one of the lowest food rations of any people in German-occupied countries.[62] Not surprisingly, very few people could live on these quantities, and as a result more than 80 percent of the Polish population's daily needs were supplied by the black economy, and queues outside food stores became commonplace. To help out the food shortage, soup kitchens appeared in several cities to feed the people by local welfare agencies, at little or no cost.[63]

As the German policy aimed at the pauperization of the Polish people, a plethora of bureaucratic German agencies confiscated the property held by the Polish state and including all private property considered necessary for strategic purposes or for Germanization.[64] In the annexed territory it went even further, when on October 19, 1939 Nazi leader, Hermann Göring, announced that all major Polish and Jewish property were to be seized. A Trustees Head Office of the East (*Haupttreuhandstelle Ost*) was to administer the confiscated enterprises. By February 1941 some 205,000 businesses had been taken over without compensation to their owners, including 2,000 textile factories in Łódź (a city annexed to Germany and renamed Litzmannstadt), out of a total 2,387 textile workshops.[65] German expropriation in the General Government was somewhat milder (though, still harsh) than in the annexed lands, and after the outbreak of the German-Soviet war in June 1941, the Germans stopped the dismantling and removal of the factories there, in order to keep them functioning as close as possible to the eastern Russian front.[66]

Demoralization. The difficult economic conditions, on top of the harsh German occupation, caused mass absenteeism from work to rise to unprecedented figures. Many workers could not afford to turn up to their jobs more than two or three days a week because the black market for obtaining extra food and goods made great demands on the rest of the people's time. The Poles would have starved if they had to depend on the food rationed to them. Warsaw had become the largest illegal commercial center of any area under German occupation, as people scurried carrying and transporting by rail or horse-driven carts tons of foodstuffs in little bags sewn into their underskirts and blouses. "Never before had I seen such over-sized busts as in Poland at this time," underground activist Stefan Korboński facetiously retold.[67] This led to a severe demoralization among many people and the abandonment of the civilizing principles of human conduct. Alcoholism became a problem, which led people when drunk with blurting out information which would jeopardize the lives of others.[68]

Dr. Zygmunt Klukowski noted in his diary with despair the rapid disintegration of Polish society under the impact of such horrifying levels of violence, destruction and deprivation. Bands of robbers were roaming the countryside, breaking into people's houses, terrorizing the inhabitants, looting the contents and raping the women. Poles were denouncing each other, and collaboration was rife. Prostitution was on the rise accompanied with the spread of venereal diseases, which Dr. Klukowski was treating. Drunkenness was also growing beyond pre-war bounds.[69] As he recorded on February 19, 1940. "I never expected the morale of the Polish population to sink so low, with such a complete lack of national and personal pride."[70] A year later, it was even worse. On March 8, 1941, Klukowski noted: "Almost every day brings some events so terrifying that you cannot concentrate. Constant news about arrests, executions, death in concentration camps, and torture in prison keep the mind away from productive work."[71]

Some moderation attempts. Early in the occupation, on October

25, 1939, Walther von Brauchitsch, commander-in-chief of the German army, sharply censured some of his officers for their brutal conduct against the Polish population. Not the least perturbed by this relevation, Hitler granted a general amnesty for crimes committed by Germans against Poles. General Johannes Blaskowitz, one of the commanders of the German Army in Poland, was the most outspoken critic of the uncontrollable German killings of innocent Poles. He sent Hitler a lengthy memorandum detailing the crimes and atrocities committed by SS and police units in the area under his command. He condemned these killings as counter-productive, since it would only strengthen Polish national feeling and drive more Poles and Jews into the resistance. The result was for Blaskowitz to be relieved of his command. The administration of conquered Poland was taken away from the military and turned over to the SS and Gestapo, and the Nazi governor, Hans Frank, and the repression of Poles, including the shooting of innocents continued.[72]

However, at a much later period, following increasing German military reverses, even the brutal and merciless Hans Frank concluded that some of the German punitive actions had to be reined in. He began favoring higher Polish food rations, stopping the deportation of Poles to Germany, and the confiscation of their property, and ending public executions of women, children, and the elderly. In early 1944, in light of the approaching Russian armies, as a result of Frank's initiative, the Germans opened a Polish theater in Kraków, ended the requirement of passes for Poles using trains, and opened some religious seminaries that had been closed in 1939. Even contemplated was the opening of secondary schools and a school of medicine in Kraków staffed by Polish professors for Polish medical students.[73] In addition, to gain Polish support to the German cause, thirty-two million copies of different brochures and pamphlets were printed to convince the Poles to side with them against the Soviets.[74] This, however, proved too late to change the attitude of most Poles towards the German occupiers.

Failed political collaboration pursuits. Polish historians of the occupation justifiably pride themselves that, in contrast to other occupied countries, no political collaboration took place between the remaining leadership of the conquered country and their German masters. The severity of German administration of Poland, unquestionably the worst in Europe for an occupied country, and the Nazi attempts to begin colonizing large tracts of Poland with ethnic Germans, also unlike elsewhere in Europe, ruled out any sort of political collaboration for simply, according to German designs, there was to be no place for a Polish state.[75] But, nevertheless, some incipient attempts were made in that direction which did not go very far. Some members of the defunct Polish aristocracy and army explored possibilities of reaching some kind of political entente with Germany. In January 1940, Władysław Studnicki, a strong proponent of Polish-German cooperation, went to Berlin and presented a memorandum criticizing German occupation policies in Poland and urging the reestablishment of a Polish state. He was promptly arrested and placed in a sanitarium but because of his pro-German views, he was eventually released.[76]

That same year of 1940, the Germans twice approached Janusz Radziwiłł concerning the creation of a Polish government subservient to the Reich. Radziwiłł, however, refused to cooperate. In July 1941, the Germans made an offer to Stanisław Rostworowski, a Polish official in Hungary, proposing Polish territorial acquisitions in the East at Soviet expense in return for territory lost to the Germans in western Poland – on condition that the Poles join the Germans in the war against the Soviet Union. This alleged offer was also rejected. The Germans found a more positive responsive ear in Leon Kozłowski, a former Polish premier, to whom the German proposed to head a puppet Polish government but he imposed conditions the Germans would not accept – namely, the release of Poles from concentration camps. Then, in May 1943, a former Polish finance minister, Wincenty Jastrębski, joined by a Warsaw academician, Tarlo Mazyński, approached the German embassy in Paris with an offer to establish a Polish national Committee to collaborate with Germany, but the German Foreign Ministry ruled out this idea.[77]

Repeated German offers to the Polish underground to suspend mutual hostilities and collaborate in opposing the Soviet army's advance, and German approaches through neutral channels to the Polish government in London suggesting negotiations that would lead to collaboration, were also outrightly rejected. Even desperate German promises to create an independent Poland did not induce top Polish political or military leaders to respond favorably.[78] There were, nevertheless, some members of the right-wing National Radical Camp (ONR) who responded to Nazi appeals, and a few isolated cases where underground units cooperated with the Germans against Soviet partisans in the region of Nowogródek.[79]

Volksdeutsche. There were approximately 1,700,000 Poles of ethnic German origin in the Polish regions annexed to Germany, and some 120,000 in the occupied General Government. Many of them responded favorably to offers of collaboration in return for certain privileges, including positions in the Polish police, under overall German supervision. Known as *Volksdeutche*, many of these ethnic Germans willingly registered, and were branded traitors by the rest of Poles and the rules of resistance were applied against them. Emanuel Ringelblum, the known Jewish chronicler of events in wartime Poland, stated that much of the denunciation and informing on Jews in wartime Poland was done by these *Volksdeutsche*.[80] Dr. Zygmunt Klukowski, who chronicled events in the Zamość region in his diary, also wrote on the *Volksdeutche* where he lived. On May 23, 1943, he mentioned several people, including a former judge, and the former wife of an attorney, whose son enlisted in the *Hitlerjugend* (Hitler Youth), who now claimed were German nationals. He also noted a large group of fellow physicians who signed up on the *Volksdeutche* list (but one of whom with the approval of the Polish underground, so that person's home could serve as a safe meeting place for clandestine operations).[81] Klukowski further remarked that "it is hard to believe that practically every one of those people volunteered for this, without any pressure from the Germans." Among these "new Germans" Klukowski listed Polish army officers and Polish government employees, all with typical Polish names: Stanislaw Kiszka, Jan Flak, Ostrowski, Bielecki, and others."[82] There were undoubtedly many more similar cases of voluntary ethnic German registration, other than in Klukoswki's Zamość region, in return for additional food coupons and other privileges.

Soviet anti-Polish acts. Under the German-Russian Non-Aggression Treaty (a.k.a. Ribbentrop-Molotov Pact) that preceded the opening of the war, the Soviets occupied eastern Polish territory, with a population of 13 million. Some 200,000 Polish prisoners of war fell in the hands of the Red Army, among them 13,000 officers. During April and early May 1940, some 4,443 of these men were taken by the Soviet secret police, the NKVD, on orders from Moscow, to the Katyn Forest near Smolensk, where they were individually shot in the back of the head and buried in mass graves. The rest of the captive Polish officers were also killed. Only an estimated 450 out of the 15,000, but who were communists, or deemed capable of being converted to communism, were spared.[83] These massacres were part of much larger campaign by the Soviets to eradicate Polish national culture in Polish regions held by the Russians, during the period of the Soviet-Nazi honeymoon. In 1941, the Soviets launched a campaign of mass deportations of Poles deemed anti-Russian or anti-communists, that included aristocrats, landowners, bankers, industrialists, hoteliers and restaurateurs, and an assorted other persons who were suspected on the flimsiest suspicions of non-communist leanings.[84] Taken to the furthest recesses of the Soviet Union for the performance of hard labor, many died of frostbite and starvation.[85] When, however, Germany attacked Russia in June 1941, the Soviets granted amnesty to their Polish captives for their fictional non-committed crimes. By then, almost half of the up to one-and-a-half million Poles deported in the previous years had died due to the harsh existential conditions to which they had been exposed.[86]

Polish war casualties. At the war's end, the tally of lost Polish lives was tremendous; between 5 and 6 million (or approximately 20% of the prewar population), of which close to 3 million were Jews. The other some 2 million Polish casualties, were the result of a combination of the German invasion of September 1939, in which thousands of Polish soldiers lost their lives; followed with German killings of innocent civilians and persons dying as forced laborers. Included, are also members of the Polish underground killed in combat, and the heavy losses of lives during the Polish uprising of August-October 1944, mainly in Warsaw.

As for Jewish casualties, as further outlined, it was the result of a combination of mass shootings by the Einsatzgruppen, the gas chambers, brutal forced labor conditions, death marches, as well as from starvation and non-treated diseases, such as typhus, and including those killed by local Poles. In this context, it is well to remember that whereas all Jews were targeted for destruction, most non-Jewish Poles were forced into submission and slavery, not extermination. That distinction must always be kept in mind.[87] All the same, these combined deaths represent the highest ratio of losses of a population in any country in wartime Europe. The nation's economic assets had also been reduced by 40 percent.[88]

b) Germans and Jews

Until the German attack on the Soviet Union on June 22, 1941, the German-occupied part of Poland had a Jewish population of close to 2 million, while an estimated 250,00 had fled to the Russian-controlled zone. When that other part was added, in July 1941, the Jewish population under German control reached close to three million, while an estimated over two hundred thousand Polish Jews fled into the interior of Russia together with the retreating Soviet forces.[89] While the German treatment, rather mistreatment, of the Poles was based mostly on geopolitical grounds, mixed with an ideological disdain for the so-called inferior Slav nation, when it came to the Jews it was strictly ideological – the fight against a mythically conceived enemy of Germany and world civilization, that could not be corrected save by the physical elimination of that fictional enemy. At first, the Nazis toyed with various ideas of the removal of Jews from continental Europe to distant locations (such as to the Madagascar island), and failing that, to be exterminated, beginning with the Jews inhabiting the Soviet Union (summer of 1941), and gradually enveloping all other European Jews (spring and summer of 1942 and thereafter). In the final account, Europe was to be made "*judenrein*" – "surgically" cleaned of Jews, within the shortest possible time, and under the cover of the war.

So, although Jews and Poles shared the same enemy, the enmity of Nazi Germany toward these two groups had two different radical goals:

enslavement of the Poles and either expulsion of the Jews somewhere elsewhere than Europe, and failing that, their extermination.[90] While German terror against non-Jewish Poles was selective, aimed chiefly at the intelligentsia, the potential leadership of a reborn Poland, with the urban population much less affected, the German Final Solution of the Jews was total, encompassing all segments of the Jewish population without exception; men, women, and children of all ages.[91] True enough, both Poles and Jews suffered severely under the Nazis; however, non-Jewish Poles were able to maintain some semblance, though restricted, of a normal life; the Jews were not. As harsh as the Nazi treatment of ethnic Poles was, the Nazis brought to bear an even greater level of discrimination and terror against Polish Jews.[92] While the Jews starved to death in the ghettos and then were murdered in an assembly line manner, the situation of the Poles appeared by comparison sustainable. They preserved the right to live, a right the Jews were denied. This distinction must be kept in mind. Also, of importance, with all the German death camps on Polish soil, to where hundreds of thousand Jews from all over Europe were taken by trains to be killed, nowhere else in Europe did the murder of Jews unfold in such broad daylight and amid the visible presence of their non-Jewish co-territorial neighbors, as in Poland.[93]

The situation for Jews in Poland may be divided into two distinct periods. The first was from the early occupation period to the summer months of 1942, during which time, most Jews were first terrorized, then locked into German-supervised ghettos. Then, starting the spring and summer months of 1942, the ghettos were emptied of all, or most, Jews and dispatched to nearby extermination camps, such as Treblinka, Sobibór, Bełżec, Chelmno, and the largest of them all, Auschwitz; where most died by suffocation in the gas chambers. In Auschwitz, some were selected for hard labor, but most did not survive the brutalities inflicted on them. At the same time, already earlier, at the outbreak of the war with Russia, on June 22, 1941, the Germans launched a massive killing spree in the Polish regions heretofore held by the Russians since September 1939, encompassing hundreds of thousands of Jews who were shot in open spaces, and otherwise known as Holocaust by Bullets.

German pre-ghetto anti-Jewish acts. Violence against Jews and their institutions by the Germans began even before the enclosure of Jews into ghettos, in a display of brutality and humiliation surpassing those inflicted on non-Jews. As the German army entered Warsaw, in September 1939, the troops began looting Jewish shops and robbing Jews at gunpoint on the street. In some instances, Jews were forced to smear each other with excrement. A favorite sport was for soldiers to stop Jews and roughly cut off their beards with blunt instruments, which sometimes also tore their skin. Jewish women were forced to clean public latrines with their blouses.[94] Swastikas were branded on the scalps of some victims; others were subjected to "gymnastics," such as riding on other victims' backs, crawling on all fours, singing and dancing, or staging fights with one another.[95]

Jews, when encountered individually or in small groups by Germans, frequently aroused a degree of personal, sadistic brutality, a desire to humiliate as well as destroy, that was seldom the case when they mistreated ordinary Poles. In Będzin, on September 8, 1939, a week into the invasion of Poland, Germans burned down the local synagogue with flamethrowers, that engulfed nearby houses in the town's Jewish quarter, while Jews were indiscriminately shot when encountered on the streets. At the end of this mayhem, some 500 of the town's Jewish inhabitants were dead.[96] Jews suffered a similar fate in other places, where the military staged *auto da fe* burnings of Torah scrolls, Hebrew books, and other religious articles, and forced Jews to sing and dance around the flames and shout that the Jews were to blame for the war.[97] Within a brief initial space of the German occupation, several hundred synagogues in conquered Poland were either burned or severely damaged. Those spared were turned into stables, warehouses, bathhouses, or even public latrines. "These are no longer people," remarked Goebbels of the Jews, after visiting Łódź at the beginning of November 1939; "these are animals. So, the task is not humanitarian but surgical. Steps have to be taken here, and really radical ones too. Otherwise Europe will perish from the Jewish disease."[98] In Mława, the German military commander felt that this had gone too far. In a lone act of military justice, General Georg von Küchler ordered the arrest and disarming of a German police unit after it had shot some Jews and set their houses on fire. He court-martialed members of an SS artillery regiment that had driven fifty Jews into a synagogue near Różan, after they had finished working on buttressing a damaged bridge, and then shot them all without any reason.[99]

To further identify the Jews, the Germans ordered the registration of all Jews and the sign *Jude* was stamped on their identity cards. Toward end 1939, the Germans ordered all Jews to wear visible yellow star signs on top of their outer garments. Jewish medical doctors were forbidden to treat non-Jewish patients and Jewish lawyers were denied the right to practice.[100] All Jewish enterprises (shops, workshops, cafes, restaurants, etc., without exception) had to bear mandatory, distinct markings, with all Jewish factories and businesses confiscated or liquidated.[101] After Jews complied with registering their businesses, some 112,000 Jewish-owned businesses and shops and 115,000 workshops were arbitrarily taken over with no compensation paid to their previous owners.[102] To further humiliate the Jews, the German prohibited them from walking on the sidewalks, use public transport, and enter places of leisure, sports arenas, theaters, museums and libraries.[103]

On October 26, 1939, Nazi governor Hans Frank issued a decree according to which every Jewish male of working age was subject to forced labor, and Jews were consequently randomly seized on the streets for the performance of some work. This brought Jewish life outside the home to a virtual standstill. As a result, Jewish elders in the large cities offered to supply the Germans with a fixed quota of workers, on condition that the random roundups in the streets be discontinued.[104] By early 1941 some two hundred German-supervised Jewish labor camps were in operation, with tens of thousands of Jews forced to work there. The work consisted of flood control, road and building constructions, as well as agricultural work. At these sites, Jews were tortured and beaten, to make them work harder.

Ghettos. On September 21, 1939 Reinhard Heydrich, the SS second-in-command, ordered his officers to have all small Jewish communities in the General Government zone abolished and all Jews forced into ghettos in larger towns and cities, and near major rail junctions.[105] The ghettos were to be supervised, externally by the Germans, and internally by so-called *Ältestenräte* (Council of Elders), better known as *Judenräte* (Jewish councils), and to be headed by "influential personalities and rabbis." The councils, Heydrich added, were to be made "fully responsible... for the exact and punctual execution of all directives issued or yet to be issued" – especially with regard to forced labor requirements, based on a list of the inhabitants, divided by gender and age.[106] Each ghetto also was allowed to have its own non-armed Jewish police force to keep order.[107] Pursuant to these instructions, in 1940, the Germans enclosed most of Polish Jewry into several hundred ghettos of various sizes, and by end of 1940 the Nazis had sealed off many ghettos, including the largest one in Warsaw, from the rest of the non-Jewish population.[108]

Some of the ghettos were of short duration; others of lengthier ones. Other than the Łódż ghetto which lasted until August 1944, most inhabitants of other ghettos were liquidated by end 1942, and the ghettos closed by mid- to end-1943. The real reason behind the creation of the ghettos was first to isolate the Jews from the rest of the population (as was also the primary reason for ghettos during the Middle Ages), and separating the Jewish communities from one another, until a final decision was reached on their fate.[109] The first ghetto, in Piotrków Trybunalski, was created in October 1939, and the first large ghetto, Łódz, in May 1940, followed with the largest ghetto of Warsaw, in November 1940.[110] The Łódz ghetto was hermetically sealed (by fences and barbed wire), and was completely cut off from the outside, while the Warsaw ghetto was enclosed by a wall, but it was possible (though dangerous) to get in and out, especially in the smuggling of food and manufactured goods. In smaller places, the ghettos were open, with only a sign to indicate its boundaries; or the Jews were permitted to leave it at certain hours of the day in order to buy food. However, exiting the ghetto without a permit could cost the trespasser his/her life, for on October 15, 1941, Nazi governor Hans Frank made publicly known that all persons leaving the ghetto without permission were to be shot.[111]

The sites selected for the ghettos were usually the most squalid sections in the cities. After the Warsaw ghetto was formally closed, on November 16, 1940, an additional 140,000 Jews were dumped there from smaller cities and villages in the vicinity, raising the ghetto population to almost 450,000. Between 60,000 to 100,000 non-Jewish Poles were forcibly evicted from the area of the ghetto to make room for the several hundred thousand Jews.[112] The density was such, that in some instances over 15 people were allocated per apartment or between 6 to 7 persons to a room.[113] When the Łódź ghetto was sealed off on April 30, 1940 (ahead by several months of the Warsaw ghetto), it contained some 162,000 Jews. Thousands more were added in the succeeding months, including non-Jewish gypsy families.

A number of converted and assimilated Jews tried to obtain exemptions from the ghetto decree, such as microbiologist Professor Ludwik Hirszfeld, who after converting to Catholicism in his youth had severed all ties with Jews and Judaism. The Germans ultimately rejected his request and that of other assimilated and converted Jews.[114] Thus, the population of the Warsaw ghetto included Jewish apostates residing in a special section designated for them. They counted 1,540 Catholics, 148 Protestants, 30 Orthodox Christians, and 43 members of other non-Jewish religious denominations. Three churches that remained within the ghetto perimeter served these people on Sundays.[115] The converted Jews entertained hopes that they would be spared extermination, but this expectation, effective during previous centuries of Jewish persecutions, no longer held sway with the Germans, for whom anyone born Jewish was targeted for destruction, notwithstanding one's current religious affiliation.

Behind the ghetto walls, a world that lived under a temporarily postponed death sentence came into being. Entirely helpless, most Judenrat heads consented to a degree of cooperation with the oppressor and called for Jewish endurance; a buying of time until the hoped-for German defeat.[116] Most of the Judenrat members believed that they would be able to serve the interests of their community and protect it as best as possible under the trying circumstances by following German orders, harsh and inhuman as they may be. Some went to extremes in collaboration with the Germans, such as Chaim Rumkowki in Łódz, Moshe Merin in Zagłębie, and Jacob Gens in Vilna. The role of these ghettos heads and others that upon German demands for a certain number of victims, these leaders selected persons slated for extermination, in the hope that by sacrificing a sizable sum the rest would be spared, remains an issue of bitter debate among many survivors.[117]

Ghetto conditions. While the ghettos existed, slave labor, hunger, and recurring epidemics of typhus were the main features of daily existence behind the ghetto walls.[118] Diseases (especially typhoid) were rampant, felling thousands of Jews each month. Lack of basic hygienic conditions also added to the high mortality rate, which rose exponentially.[119] In Warsaw, the killer disease was typhus; in Łódz – tuberculosis.[120] In the Warsaw ghetto, the death rate rose from 1 per thousand in prewar 1939 to 10.7 in 1941; in Łódź it was even higher. Some 85,000 of the Warsaw ghetto residents died, mostly from starvation and infectious diseases, by the time of the full ghetto liquidation in April-May 1943 – or one out of every five original ghetto inmates.[121] Children were particularly vulnerable, with many succumbing from starvation.[122]

Food allowed for the imprisoned ghetto Jews were at starvation levels, down to 184 calories per day (the non-Jewish Poles were allotted 669 calories; the Germans – 2,613). Thus, the Jewish food ration was barely 15% of the minimum amount of food required to stay alive.[123] This led governor Hans Frank to declare to his aides that "we are starving 1,200,000 Jews to death; that is self-evident, and if the Jews do not die from hunger, anti-Jewish decrees will have to be speeded up, and let us hope that this is what will happen."[124] To avoid starvation, 80 percent of the food consumed was smuggled into the ghetto. Children smugglers were especially adept at this because they could slip more easily through holes and gaps in the ghetto wall, and sneak through.[125] Once on the other side, the children would beg for bread, potatoes, onions and other non-perishable items, and try to sneak back with these hard-to-get nourishments to their starving families.[126] Since, in the first two years of the war the United States was still not at war, the US-based Joint Distribution Committee enjoyed a certain immunity as an American organization, and its locally-appointed officials began to set up aid centers in the ghettos, beginning with soup kitchens where a bowl of soup and a piece of bread were dispensed to the hungry.[127] The special privilege afforded to the Joint ended when the US entered the war in December 1941, but food packages continued to reach some of the ghetto people through neutral venues, such as Portugal.[128] Inside the confined Warsaw ghetto, on historian Emanuel Ringelblum's initiative, an archives collection project was created, code-named Oneg Shabbes, to collect documentary material and accounts of life in the Warsaw and other ghettos.[129]

Ghetto economy. The ghettos radically changed the entire config-uration of the economic relationship between Jews and Poles. On the eve of their move into the ghettos, Jews transferred their businesses and stocks of merchandise to Polish acquaintances, in the mistaken hope of having them reinstituted only after a short while; or had their businesses and workshops registered in the name of Poles; in short, a considerable quantity of this property was transferred into Polish hands, which bene-fitted them during the difficult war years.[130] Many Poles, witnessing the German treatment of Jews, viewed them as "deceased on leave," about to die sooner or later, whether the Poles as onlookers had misgivings about this or not. When it was all over, with the Germans ousted from the country, in 1945, in an overwhelming majority of cases, perhaps 95 percent, neither goods nor personal belongings were returned, simply because the Jewish owners were no longer there. They had been killed by the Germans.[131]

It turned out that, in spite of this depletion of Jewish goods, the Warsaw ghetto, while it existed, continued to carry out lively economic transactions with the Aryan side, and economic ties created long before the war were not entirely cut off, in spite of the walls and fences separat-ing the two communities. Simply put, the ghetto continued to produce for the Polish market.[132] The Łódz ghetto, as well, included a flourish-ing textile industry which was organized by former entrepreneurs, and served German wartime interests. In Warsaw, products created included brushes, toys, aluminum industry-bowls, and spoons.[133] In some cases raw materials were smuggled into ghettos for manufacture; and the products thus manufactured were smuggled back to the so-called Aryan side of the city. There emerged an entire substructure of go-betweens between Jews and Poles as hundreds of Polish smugglers would come into the ghetto through openings in the walls or though the guard posts, and enter the forbidden ghetto with the help of bribes, and would buy old good-looking clothes from Jews in return for food items desperately needed by the starving ghetto population.[134] Smugglers sometimes sarcastically remarked to the Jews: "They'll turn you into leather anyway – sell your jacket and buy yourself something to eat."[135]

Jews in the Russian-Polish Zone. On the whole, for the close one million Jews who lived in the Soviet-controlled part of Poland, during September 1, 1939 to June 22, 1941, and adding the tens of thousands of Jewish refugees who had fled there from the advancing Germans, the Soviets provided a welcome relief from the Germans, as well for some, from harm by native antisemites.[136] A portion of the Jewish population, along with ethnic Byelorussian and Ukrainian national activists had initially welcomed the invading Soviet forces as their protectors. The general feeling among the Polish Jews was a sense of temporary relief in having escaped the Nazi occupation in the first weeks of the war. In the Soviet zone, formal civil rights were extended to everyone, and younger Jews in particular welcomed their liberation from the antisemitic hiring discrimination practiced by the previous Polish regime. Jews were consequently employed to replace the many Poles dismissed from various administrative posts by the Soviets.[137] It is well to note that in their enthusiasm for the new regime, the few among them who were professed communists discarded and castigated their Jewish identity in the process.[138] At the same time, in the eyes of Polish nationalists, not merely these handful of Jewish communists, but the entire Jewish community was made to carry the blame for working for the hated Soviet communists.

On November 29, 1940, Ringelblum noted in his diary that a man who visited the Russian side of Poland told of the great difference. There, movement was free. People can walk about as they wish, well dressed.

The cafés are full of people, and the streets not overcrowded, as in the ghettos.[139] The situation, however, was far from that rosy. All private property and private businesses were nationalized and most economic activity became subject to central planning. This was followed with the arrest and deportations of wealthy Jews and others, who refused as Polish patriots to sign up for Soviet citizenship. These steps soon dispelled the illusions of most Jews about the true nature of Soviet rule.

In addition, the Soviet annexation was accompanied by the widespread arrests of government officials, police, military personnel, border guards, teachers, priests, judges etc., followed by the massive deportation of hundreds of thousands Polish nationals to the Soviet interior and the Gulag slave labor camps where, as a result of the inhuman conditions, about half of them died before too long.[140] The Soviets closed down Polish schools and Poles were dismissed from jobs of authority and replaced with non-Polish personnel.

The Soviets also struck at the Jews, as independent Jewish organizations were abolished and Jewish activists and religious leaders were arrested. Zionism, which was castigated by the Soviets as counter-revolutionary was forbidden. As many as 100,000 Polish Jews (some estimates raise the figure even higher), including members of various Zionist factions, as well as the anti-Zionist Bund socialist party, were also deported to underdeveloped and harsh regions of the Soviet Union. Those who stayed behind would pay dearly, in retribution by native Poles and Ukrainians for the initial enthusiasm of a minority among the Jews for the Soviet invasion, when in the weeks and months of summer 1941, the Soviet army fled in haste, and the German army stormed into the previous Soviet-Polish zone.[141]

Polish prime minister of the government-in-exile, Władysław Sikorski, claimed that 30% of the Jews identified with the communists and prepared lists of Polish "class enemies," a claim contested by some historians. At the same time, at least 434 Polish Jews who had been awarded officer rank by the Polish Army were murdered by the Soviets in the Katyn massacre because of their loyalty to Poland (some place the figure between 500-600).[142] The issue of Jewish collaboration with the Soviet occupation remains controversial. Whatever initial enthusiasm for the Soviet occupation some Jews may have entertained was soon dissipated under the impact of the suppression of Jewish societal and religious modes of life by the occupiers. At the same time, the false impression left among many Poles of a supposed large-scale Jewish enthusiasm for the Soviets was to take a toll on relations between Poles and Jews throughout the years to come.[143] The old myth of *Żydokomuna* (Judeo-communism) was reinforced during the period of the Soviet occupation. It also strengthened the perception after the war that held Jews responsible for the imposition of communism on Poland.

Start of mass extermination. Nazi Germany's switch to widespread massacres of Jews was launched on June 22, 1941, with the invasion of the Soviet Union. Special organized killing units of the SS, known as Einsatzgruppen, carried out mass shootings of Jews all over the Soviet terrain, including those in the eastern Polish regions, in which totaling over a million Jews were felled. Some of the largest gruesome killing sites were in Ukraine (Babi Yar, 33,700 killed in a two-day period), and Lithuania (Ponary, 70,000 killed over a lengthier period), but also in the former Polish territory. For instance, on June 27, 1941, five days into the German invasion of the Soviet Union, men under Einsatzgruppen command drove more than 500 Jews into a synagogue in Białystok and burned them alive. At least 2,000 Jews were killed during this large-scale pogrom, and an additional 1,000 Jewish men of military age were arrested, taken out of the city and shot.[144] As for Jedwabne, the local inhabitants eagerly participated in the brutal massacre of all of the town's Jewish residents. At the same time, thousands of Jews escaped Nazi terror and local pogroms by fleeing with the retreating Russians further eastward, ahead of the advancing Germans.

Meanwhile, in the Polish ghettos, the Germans waited close to another year, until a string of extermination camps were completed, where millions of Jews were kills by suffocation of poisonous gas; those in Poland as well as from other European countries. This was preceded by a top-level Nazi gathering in Berlin (Wannsee conference), on January 20, 1942, where details were outlined on the technical and logistical plans for the extermination of all European Jewry, to take place on Polish soil, under the code-word of the Final Solution (*Endlösung*) of the Jewish Question. For this purpose, three large extermination camps were to be built: Treblinka, Sobibór and Bełżec. In the fourth killing site at Chełmno, as of December 8, 1941, people were killed by suffocation inside gas vans. These, in combination to the already existing, but enlarged Auschwitz-Treblinka camp, as well as other similar killing facilities, such as Majdanek and Stutthof (Sztutowo), were to be the slaughterhouse of most European Jews. Auschwitz, the largest killing facility on Polish soil, started its infamous career in June 1940 as an internment center of Polish political prisoners. The first killing by poison gas at Auschwitz involved 300 Poles and 700 Soviet prisoners of war. On May 4 1942, the first of the four gas chambers and crematoria consumed their first Jewish victims in the much larger nearby camp of Auschwitz annex II, but better known as Birkenau.[145]

Inside Poland, starting the summer months of 1942, Polish ghettos began to be emptied of its starving Jewish inhabitants, who were transported by cattle trains to be gassed in one of the aforementioned death camps. The so-called Great Action of the Warsaw ghetto, decimated close to 300,000 Jews during the period of July 23-September 21 1942 – with the bulk of the Jews sent to the Treblinka gas chambers. In the Łódz ghetto, the process was a bit slower, as its 210,000 residents were liquidated in stages, up to August 1944 (mostly taken to Chełmno). Many thousand others died from mistreatment in various slave labor camps that dotted the Polish landscape, such as Majdanek, Stutthof and Płaszów. In Majdanek camp, 12,400 Jews were shot on November 3, 1943, to resolve the problem of overcrowding. This was part of a killing spree, that felled thousands of other Jewish prisoners in nearby camps, and which the Germans sarcastically dubbed as Harvest Festival (*Erntefest*), and in which a total of 40,000 victims were shot – the largest single day massacre of Jews by German forces during the Holocaust. By the end of 1942, most Polish Jews, up to then imprisoned in the ghettos, were no longer alive.

Tens of thousands of Jews were also brought by train (mostly cattle wagons) from other countries (Slovakia, France, Belgium, Netherlands,

Norway, Germany, Austria, Italy, Croatia, Greece, Macedonia and Hungary), while those living in the Soviet sphere (Lithuania, Latvia, Byelorussia, Ukraine, and Russia) were done away by mass shootings, with the participation of local collaborators. Thousands of Jews also died during forced death marches of prisoners from concentration camps heading further westward, ahead of the Russian military advances inside Poland, usually over the winter months of 1944-1945. In Romania, the mass killings of Jews in the annexed regions of Bukovina and Transnistria were carried out by the Romanian army.

By the time the Germans withdrew from Poland, in February 1945, of the millions of Jews in pre-war Poland, there were hardly any left in the country, other than an estimated 50-60,000 in hiding, and some few thousands that had survived death marches and the horrors of concentration and forced labor camps, and were still alive under German control. Some two hundred thousand Polish Jews (those living in formerly eastern Poland) also survived by having fled ahead of time into the interior of the Soviet Union.

The German determination and zeal to exterminate all Jews finds expression in the words of one of its leading executors. SS officer Adolf Eichmann, who orchestrated and processed the movement of deportation trains from various European origins to the death camps in Poland, and freely and joyfully confessed to an interviewer from his place of hiding in Argentina, that "my job was to catch these enemies and transport them to their destination... Had we killed all of them, the 10.3 million, I would be happy and say, 'Alright, we managed to destroy the enemy.'"[146] An estimated six million Jews was the death toll of the German Final Solution, that lasted until the day of the German surrender, on May 8, 1945. More Jews would have died had the war lasted longer.

Polish fears of own extermination. Poles from all walks of life could not avoid witnessing the passage of trains crisscrossing the length and breadth of their country, pulling dozens of cattle wagons filled with masses of suffocating Jews on their way to the extermination camps. Many of those watching these almost daily horrible scenes, could not help wondering whether these mass killings of Jews was not a prelude to the start of the wholesale killing of the Polish population, once the last Jews were gone, to make room for resettlement of Germans and kindred so-called Aryan peoples on vacated Polish soil.[147]

On October 3, 1942, Home Army (the main Polish underground) headquarters in Warsaw received a message from the Prime Minister's office in London, of a supposedly secret order by SS head Heinrich Himmler that after the total liquidation of Jews in Eastern Europe, the Poles were to be next in line for extermination. The note maintained that the Germans were encouraged in this regard "by the silence of the world in the face of the mass murder of millions of Jews."[148] Following this unsubstantiated source, Home Army commander Stefan Rowecki wrote, on November 10, 1942: "Polish society is apprehensive that in the aftermath of the current extermination of the Jews, the Germans may proceed in the application of similar methods of extermination against the Poles... Attempts to exterminate the resistant segments of our nation by methods applied against the Jews... will encounter our resistance... The units under my command shall proceed to armed struggle in defense of the life of the nation. I order the area and district commanders to report to me without delay all confirmed instances of application against the Poles of the methods of mass extermination which the Germans currently apply against the Jews; to brace ourselves for rapid and efficient initiation of hostilities in a designated area."[149] Leaders of the Polish underground continued to discuss the precautionary measures to be applied in the event of such a terrible occurrence.[150] There were, however, no German plans for the extermination of the non-Jewish Poles, although one cannot blame Polish authorities in London, and the underground, of fearing such an eventuality, in light of the mass murder of Jews in their midst, at a scope, dimension and length of time, which to the horrified viewer (whatever one's feelings about Jews) was beyond rational explanation.

CHAPTER 4

Polish-Jewish Relations During the War Years

Poles, non-Jews and Jews alike, underwent a hellish experience under the German occupation; a brutality of horrific proportions unprecedented in the history of the two communities, that combined the political extinction of the Polish nation and the wholesome extermination of the Jewish population. While all this was being played out, one wonders, how this affected Polish-Jewish relations. Did it bring the two communities closer together and usher feelings of solidarity between the two, or did the relationship remain unchanged, or even worsen? Historians of Polish-Jewish relations during the war years are still bitterly divided on this point. We have noted in the previous chapter the prevalence of antisemitic feelings among wide strata of the population, and these feelings did not, of course, disappear overnight in spite of the horrendous sufferings of both communities by the same common enemy – the hated German Nazis. Here, an attempt will be made to draw as far as possible a fair and balanced portrait of Polish-Jewish relations during one of their common worst historic moments, while at the same time conceding that the provisional and interim conclusions reached in this study will not satisfy many readers, who have already drawn their own conclusions on the strength of antisemitism during that tragic period.

Early occupation period. "The country is full of patriotic fervor," Hebrew teacher Chaim Aron Kaplan, in Warsaw, enthusiastically wrote in his diary on September 1, 1939, when Germany invaded Poland. He continued: "All classes and all nationalities, even those that suffered persecution at the hands of the Poles in the time of peace, are ready to sacrifice their strength and wealth for the sake of the Fatherland.... It should therefore not be surprising that the Jews show their devotion to their fatherland in a demonstrative fashion."[1] For a brief period, particularly as Poles and Jews dug trenches side by side in embattled Warsaw, Polish-Jewish relations were transformed; Warsaw Jews, as Emanuel Ringelblum reported, were seized with an enthusiasm reminiscent of the solidarity experienced during the insurrections for Polish independence of the nineteenth century.[2]

On the eve of the war, an anonymous author from Kalisz noted: "In the second half of the month [August 1939] ... the Poles' attitude toward the Jewish population changed too. They came to realize that they shared a common enemy... Thus, the intense and continuous vicious anti-Jewish propaganda of the antisemitic press diminished somewhat... There was the hope that with this war, together, the bestial Jewish hatred of the Endecja [party] and the Endeks would be eliminated, and that the defeat of Hitlerism would change their attitude toward the Jews."[3] In a recent study, historian Havi Dreifuss writes that "to the Jews, it was a profound and significant change in Polish society and they hoped that it would have consequences for the future as well... The Jews of Poland believed that the Polish state that was destined to grow out of the conflict with Germany would look completely differently upon its Jewish citizens."[4] These feelings, of course, were based on the hope that Poland will somehow emerge victorious – not defeated and occupied.

These hopeful positive assessments, that prevailed during the early period of the German occupation and to a lesser degree during the start of the ghettos period, were upheld primarily by Jewish leftist organizations, such as the Bund, which proclaimed that the ghetto Jews are "bound by thousands of veins to the working classes beyond the wall."[5] The Bund downplayed the role of those belonging to different social strata who attack Jews: "The grocer, the merchant, the criminal on the Polish street... are not, in our eyes, representatives of the Polish nation.

We know a different Poland." For, "Polish antisemitism is a betrayal of Poland."[6] But these early prognoses of a better Polish-Jewish relationship took a back seat among other observers, even at this early period, and especially as the ruthless German occupation set in. As noted by the better-informed Emanuel Ringelblum: "Even before Warsaw fell, the hydra of antisemitism had already managed to raise its head."[7] Days before the Polish surrender in Warsaw, a man packing coal and noticing a Jew, shouted: "For them the good days are over, at long last. Their defenders have left already. Hitler will soon sort them out and put them in their rightful place."[8]

Indeed, after the Polish surrender, there was a perceptible increase in antisemitic manifestations.[9] At the German-controlled food distribution centers, in the early phase of the occupation, it was sometimes difficult for the Germans to distinguish between Jews and non-Jews. The antisemitic scum came to their aid and obligingly pointed out the Jews to the Germans.[10] Where water was distributed, at the demand of the antisemitic mobs, there were separate Jewish and Aryan lines. The access to water was alternately given to 50 so-called Aryans and 5 Jews. Jews carrying water packs were often knocked down, beaten, even clobbered, and their water spilled. Ringelblum, who witnessed some of these incidents, noted: "The first ties between the Nazis and the Polish antisemites were thus established."[11] As also noted by Havi Dreifuss: "The uniformity of the perceptions Jews held vis-à-vis Poland and the Poles at the beginning of the war is deceiving. In fact, the reality was far more complex."[12]

It should not be surprising to the reader that the spirit of antisemitism which affected many Poles in the 1930s, should also have had an impact on their behavior during the occupation years. While the entire Polish population was vehemently anti-German, this did not conflict in the minds of some with equally antisemitic sentiments of various degrees. While antisemitism may have taken a back seat out of hatred for the Germans in the first month of the war, it reemerged as of old soon afterwards, even blaming the Jews for the war – a typical Nazi refrain.[13] Hersh Wasser, contributor to the Oneg Shabbes Archives (created by the Jewish-Polish historian Emanuel Ringeblum in the Warsaw ghetto), stated: "Mutual relations between and Poles are very strained... Poles have started saying that the war broke out only because of the Jews."[14]

Holocaust survivors' views of Polish behavior during the war years span a wide range, depending mostly on their personal experiences. An anonymous author in the Oneg Shabbes Archives struggled with defining the wartime state of Polish-Jewish relations. Commiserating with the suffering of the Polish nation, during the early phase of the German occupation, and the pre-deportations phase of the ghetto Jews to the gas chambers, he or she wrote: "At the present time, however, the Polish people, more than any other – except the Jewish [people] – suffers the yoke of [the German] enslavement, and thus it should have shown above all compassion for companions in misery and exhibit solidarity and fraternity [with the Jewish people] at every step." Then, comes a disappointing note. "Unfortunately, this cannot be dreamed about." True enough, "the majority of enlightened intelligentsia and workers with [class] consciousness... [show] expressions of solidarity." However, "unfortunately, the [list of] sins is much longer, and filled with unforgivable signs, crying to heaven for revenge... I know, one mustn't generalize... But the [acts] of these, the mob, youth, old hags, adolescents, *lumpenproletariat* [lowest uneducated social stratum], thugs, outcasts, graduates of Endek schools," seem to proliferate. The author then takes a step backwards to point out that not all Poles are like this. There are exceptional good cases. "This does not reflect in any way the relations between the Jews and the Poles, since Polish society [also] denounces them... Every [Jewish] trader, member of the intelligentsia, or social group has some good Polish benefactor, who arranges things, helps, enables survival... Every [human] society includes these two types... Jews remember with deep emotion and gratefulness all the acts of kindness toward them and the helping hand extended to them by each of those Poles."[15]

The assimilated Ludwik Landau wrote that Jews stepping out onto the street, before the start of the ghetto period, were in constant danger of abuse and, as a result, many of them tended to avoid leaving their homes. But then, he added, "in general, the Polish Christian population is actually expressing solidary for our suffering and, in any case, there are no conspicuous expression of antisemitism."[16] Apparently, disregarding this positive comment, Landau also tells of another incident in his diary, in which he walked down the street wearing his Jewish armband, accompanied by a non-Jewish friend whose appearance could be mistaken for Jewish. He wrote that two young women who noticed his friend pointed out that it was a pity there was no German soldier in the vicinity in which they could give away this other "Jew," who they wrongly believed disregarded wearing the Jewish star.[17] In the words of historian Havi Dreifuss, Landau's comments did indeed indicate that the reaction of many Poles toward the Jews did not much change as a result of the German occupation, but remained rather negative.[18]

Poisonous Nazi propaganda also helped to reawaken native antisemitism.[19] Pedestrians walking the streets saw walls plastered with Nazi posters proclaiming "Jews, Lice, Disease."[20] As noted by Chaim A. Kaplan, in his diary entry of February 1, 1940: "The hate propaganda against Jews suited the temper and will of many groups of Poles, and perhaps – the entire Polish populace. For it was as if they [the Germans] were saying... 'All of your lives you have been struggling against the Jewish affliction and received nothing. I will show you the way.'"[21] A notable exception was the refusal of the Warsaw lawyers' Council to give in to German demands that Jews be removed from its list of attorneys; this, despite the fact that the organization's head, Leon Nowodworski, a member of the National Democratic Party (Endeks) had in the past tried to prevent Jews from entering the legal profession.[22] His reasoning was that the solution of the Jewish problem must wait till after the war;[23] quite an unusual comment by an Endek member.

Ringelblum, too, struggled with the prevalence of antisemitism among the Polish people. At first, he referred to persons who persecuted Jews as "Polish gangs," "a gang of Polish hooligans," and "thugs." At the same time, any help extended to Jews is described as the honest and authentic work of "Polish women," and "social activists."[24] In August 1941, he was hopeful, "that Polish society has undergone a profound change," for the better.[25] Ringelblum even viewed as something positive the Poles who sneaked into the Warsaw ghetto in order to trade, even though the Jews knew that some of these persons took advantage of their desperate situation to make handsome profits. Jews, nevertheless, saw this as a form of moral support, according to Ringelblum, a sign that they were not entirely isolated and forsaken.[26]

But, Ringelblum was also not oblivious of a different kind of Polish comportment – the blackmailers and extortionists. As early as February 9, 1940, he noted: "Of late, Christians have been standing around near isolated courtyard gates. They wait for a likely Jewish candidate to come along. When they catch one, they take him aside into the courtyard; the Jew emerges with empty pockets."[27] This was followed with a depressing note on Polish indifference: "From what was called good Polish society, there has been no reaction [to the attacks on Jews]. Whoever tries to react is defined immediately as 'one who serves the Jews,' and this is enough to end all involvement."[28] In this early period of the German occupation, it seems that Ringelblum could not make up his mind how to assess Polish attitude toward the Jews; at times positive; at other times negative.[29]

The Polish army. One reliable indication of Polish attitudes toward Jews, is the treatment of Jewish soldiers in the Polish army, where more than 100,000 Jewish men served during the German invasion. Here, reports are mixed, with some reporting being met with hostility by their Polish counterparts.[30] Attacks on Jewish soldiers seemed to have reached a pitch when the Polish army was defeated and thousands of soldiers were taken prisoners. During the first hours of captivity, some 61,000 Jews were separated by the Germans from their Polish brothers-in-arms. Some of the Jewish soldiers testified how Polish soldiers helped Germans identify Jews who, just a few days earlier, had fought with them side by side.[31] But, this is only one side of the story, and other accounts testify to a friendlier attitude toward Jewish soldiers; at least, not all non-Jewish soldiers displayed hostility toward their Jewish comrades-in-arm.

Pre-ghettoization violence and pogroms: During the early months of the occupation, the Germans encouraged gangs of young Polish hoodlums to attack Jews; and they sometimes also attacked non-Jewish Poles, but with less frequency. But, though some were orchestrated by the

Germans, most were spontaneous outbreaks, now that violence against Jews was not only permitted, but also encouraged by the Germans.[32] In December 1939, Ringelblum noted that such attacks are on the rise in the streets, "and have become so frequent, as if someone is forcing them to do so." Ludwik Landau, in January 1940, wrote of Jews being beaten violently in Warsaw's train station. "No-one, nowhere, dared to denounce [the attackers] – maybe not only because of fear of the Germans."[33] Mary Berg: "Today I witnessed an attack on an elderly Jewish woman by Polish hooligans who hacked her with knives. Such incidents are multiplying. Today Polish hoodlums attacked Jews in the street again."[34] To be fair, Ringelblum also noted Poles coming to the aid of Jews under attack by other Poles. "October 5, 1940: Saw this scene today. Students from Konarski's high school are beating Jews on the street. A few Christians stand up against them, and a crowd gathers. These are very frequent occurrences, where Christians take the side of the Jews against attacks by hoodlums. That wasn't so before the war."[35]

These physical attacks on Jews or exploitation of their suffering were sometimes attributed to fringe elements of Polish society or from the ethnic Germans among them, while some of them were egged on by the Germans.[36] On February 1, 1940, months before the creation of the Warsaw ghetto, Chaim Kaplan noted that the Germans "have hinted that the Jews are expendable, that the government will not adhere to the letter of the law when the victims are Jews, and such a hint is enough for hooligans. In the past few days there has been no end to attacks upon Jews in public places in broad daylight."[37] Adam Czerniaków, head of the Warsaw Judenrat, noted in his diary entry for January 27, 1940: "On Marszałkowska and Poznanska Streets Jews beaten all day and night." The next day: "At 2 o'clock in the afternoon a gang of young hoodlums who have been beating up Jews for several days now rushed past the Jewish community and smashed windows in front of them."[38] When the Germans stopped Jews with beards, and began with scissors to cut their beards, not a few passers-by shrieked with laughter.[39] It is hard to believe, as some apologists claim, that all these attackers were necessarily hoodlums and underworld people, and not a bit representative of certain strata of Polish society. Certainly, the students from Konarski high school, who Ringelblum reported were beating up Jews, were not "hoodlums" and "underworld" people.

In February 1940, a large pogrom broke out in Warsaw's Jewish quarter (again, before the start of the ghetto period) by a group of several hundred Poles. As described by Ringelblum, they "were equipped with sticks, canes, iron bars and the like; their slogans were: 'Extirpate the Jews', 'down with the Jews', 'long live sovereign Poland without Jews', and the like... They smashed the window panes of the shops marked [by order of the German authorities] with the Star of David, pulling iron bars from their shutters, breaking into the shops, robbing the Jewish passers-by, hitting them, knocking them over, beating them up to the point of unconsciousness. The plunder of the shops constituted the finale of the pogrom... All this lasted for several days with no one interfering."[40] Again, Ringelblum: "Yesterday [January 28] Polish gangs ran wild... Today... I barely escaped from them with my life."[41] "I witnessed pogroms on many streets," Emanuel Ringelblum added. The period from October 1939 to November 1940 – that is, up to the creation of the ghetto – was a period of constant anti-Jewish agitation, which steadily increased.[42] Many Jews fell victim in these pogroms, and it was a profound shock to the Jewish population, who could not understand the targeting of Jews by fellow Poles, in a country just recently brutally invaded and overrun by the Germans. No reaction against these attacks were voiced by the Polish community, at least not publicly, but only among private persons.

Anti-Jewish riots also broke out in other parts of the country. In Zakrzowek, Janów Lubelski county, a group of Poles headed by one Feliks Mazur led a pogrom on Jews, on October 9-10, 1939. The gang broke into Jewish apartments and plundered them, beating their victims mercilessly. They killed a Pole, Jan Barnaszkiewicz, who had come to assist the Jews. Similar pogroms took place in other villages and towns of the same area; such as, Wysokie, Turobin, Biłgoraj, Frampol and Krzeszów.[43] Jakub Herzig recounts the plunder of Jewish shops in Jasło, Kraków district, where groups of local Poles were acting hand-in-hand

with the Germans. In Tarnów, participation of the local Polish population in the pillage of Jewish houses occurred on November 9, 1939, the
day the Germans set the local synagogue on fire. Similar pillages were
recorded elsewhere, as well.[44] The Germans even sarcastically claimed
to protecting Jews against attacks by Poles, and made, or manufactured,
photographs of Germans saving Jews from the hands of Poles.[45] This did
not stop the Germans from encouraging a three-day long pogrom in
Siedlce, where reportedly children were also killed.[46]

The Passover pogrom of April 1940 in Warsaw, was one of the worst
such incidents, as it lasted eight days, with the participation of about
1,000 persons.[47] One Jewish witness wrote: "The pogrom was carried
out by a crowd of youths about 1,000 of them, who arrived suddenly
in the Warsaw streets... Clearly these were young ruffians specially
brought from the suburbs." German soldiers stood in the street and
happily filmed the scenes. Also, that on the corner of Nowodgrodzka
and Marszałkowska streets a Catholic priest attacked the youngsters
participating in the pogrom, beat them and disappeared. These youngsters received two złotys daily from the Germans, as reward for their
anti-Jewish acts.[48] This witness added that the attitude of the Polish
intellectuals toward the Jews was clearly a friendly one, and against the
pogrom, although during these pogroms, no one among the passers-by
intervened, and the Polish police kept silent.[49]

On June 18, 1941, when in Warsaw Jews were already locked inside
a walled-off ghetto, Chaim A. Kaplan noted sarcastically (in the notes
omitted from the published account): "the ghetto walls have spared
us from pogroms... Now the ghetto walls serve us as a shield and a
shelter; the dogs grind their teeth and bark furiously, but cannot bite
us."[50] Not willing to condemn all Poles, Ringelblum, still clinging to his
socialist ideology, added that "the significant majority of the nation, its
enlightened working-class and the working intelligentsia, undoubtedly
condemned these excesses." But, he then followed this up with some
disparaging words. "We do, however, reproach the Polish community
with not having tried to dissociate itself, either in words – sermons in the

churches, etc. – or in writing, from the antisemitic beasts that cooperated with the Germans."[51]

While claiming that most Poles had nothing to do with the anti-Jewish violence, Ringelblum was troubled by the passivity and indifference of Polish onlookers. Few seemed to care that such anti-Jewish violence played into German hands who claimed that the Polish population was more antisemitic than themselves.[52] An anonymous diarist (probably part of the Oneg Shabbes archives), of August 4, 1941, recorded a person's journey to the other, non-Jewish side of the Warsaw ghetto: "Finally, we are on 'the other' side... From all sides we are greeted by cries: 'Jews to Palestine,' 'Jews Bolsheviks.'... The policemen who escort us laugh." A few Poles "are very sympathetically disposed toward us. They ask us to tell them about the ghetto and the relations inside." But then, others throw blows and shout "boil-ridden Jews, and "Jewish son of a bitch."[53] One, however, cannot at the same time avoid speculating whether many good-hearted people would have taken a more active role in suppressing these anti-Jewish acts, had Poland not been stripped of any self-ruling Polish agencies with authority to prevent such arbitrary attacks by mobs, with German encouragement. But these attacks were nevertheless also triggered by an inbred antisemitism among many strata of the population.

Looting. As Poles watched the Germans participate in the free-for-all looting of Jewish valuables, some local persons decided to join the fray and take something for themselves, but more often than not, Germans also robbed non-Jewish Poles.[54] Some Poles who had economically benefitted from the move of the Jews into the ghettos by acquiring Jewish homes and businesses, were undoubtedly unhappy by the Polish government-in-exile's decree declaring all such actions under German occupation as illegal. "We will not return the shops and factories" were not isolated Polish responses.[55] In the general demoralization of civic values that accompanied the brutal German occupation, some behavioral patterns assumed ghoulish aspects. Such as, when in the summer of 1944 rumors spread that Jews had been buried in a certain place, but without having had their gold teeth removed, and that their clothing, supposedly full of jewelry and valuable were buried with them, large numbers of peasants and farm workers scoured the area, looking for buried treasures. When, on November 7, 1945, after the war, a member of the Polish state war crimes commission visited the site of the Treblinka extermination camp (bulldozed by the Germans and turned into cultivated fields), she found "masses of all kinds of pilferers and robbers with spades and shovels in their hands,... digging and searching and raking and straining the sand. They removed decaying limbs from the dust [and] bones and garbage that were thrown there."[56] The brutality of the German occupation had undoubtedly played a large role in the devaluation and even dehumanization of civilizing social mores among many of the conquered population. Traditional antisemitic prejudices also lent a hand in this sordid behavior.

Religious antisemitism. Anti-Jewish sentiments was also injected in a report by the Polish Catholic Church. It was conveyed to the Polish government in London by the underground, and covers the period up to July 15, 1941. It restated the pre-war Catholic position of the need to rid the country of Jews. "These highly noxious and by all standards dangerous elements live in Poland, or to be more precise, off Poland. As far as the Jewish question is concerned, it must be seen as a singular dispensation of Divine Providence that the Germans have already made a good start, quite irrespective of all the wrongs they have done and continue to do to our country. They have shown that the liberation of Polish society from the Jewish plague is possible. They have blazed the trail for us which now must be followed: with less cruelty and brutality, to be sure, but no flagging consistently. Clearly, one can see the hand of God in the contribution to the solution of this urgent question being made by the occupiers: because the Polish nation, soft-hearted and inconstant as it is, could never muster enough energy to undertake measures which in this case are indispensable."[57] This defamatory report is not surprising when compared with Cardinal Hlond's similar charges against the Jews, on the eve of the war. At the same time, as we shall further mention, quite many priests, monks and nuns were involved in the rescue of Jews, especially of children, and at great risks to themselves.

MORDECAI PALDIEL

The case of Zofia Kossak-Szczucka. The ambivalence of a deep
inbred antisemitism combined with an appeal to help Jews, including
a personal involvement in that effort, that may have existed among
many Poles, is well represented in the case of the well-known author
and publicist, Zofia Kossak-Szczucka. In fact, thanks to her efforts, the
Polish underground created a special clandestine organization for the
sole purpose of aiding Jews on the run, known as Żegota. Known for
her right-wing, conservative and strong religious beliefs during the pre-
war years, she fulminated against the Jews, considering them a threat to
the Polish people. In 1936, for instance, she wrote: "We don't like the
Jews because they are completely foreign to us, they belong to another
race... What needs to be said is this: I'm fighting the Jews for my right
to exist on my own land, either I fight or I succumb, not because I'm a
Catholic... The Jews represent a real and terrible danger for us, and it's
getting worse by the day."[58]

Then, appalled and outraged at the sight of the killing of Jews that
reached a crescendo in the summer months of 1942, she issued a manifesto to her countrymen denouncing this mass slaughter of innocents. In
her appeal to fellow Poles not to get involved in this sordid undertaking,
she added that there was nothing much they could do to derail this mass
killing spree that they were witnessing. All the same, she condemned the
silence of the world and her own people at what was happening, while
at the same restating her anti-Jewish animus. It is quite a remarkable
manifesto exemplifying the dilemmas facing many educated Poles when
confronted with the suffering of the Jews. Following are some excerpts.

> The world looks upon this murder, more horrible than
> anything that history has ever seen, and stays silent.
> The slaughter of millions of defenseless people is be-
> ing carried out amid general sinister silence... England
> and America are not saying anything. Silent is the
> ever-influential international Jewry, which was previ-
> ously oversensitive of wrongdoing to their own. Silent
> are Poles. Polish political friends of Jews limit themselves

to newspaper notes; Polish opponents of Jews show lack of interest in the problem, which is foreign to them. The perishing Jews are surrounded by Pilates who deny all guilt. This silence can no longer be tolerated. Whatever the reason for it, it is vile. In the face of murder, it is wrong to remain passive. Whoever is silent witnessing murder becomes a partner to the murder. Whoever does not condemn, consents. Therefore we – Catholics, Poles – raise our voices. Our feeling toward the Jews has not changed. We continue to deem them political, economic, and ideological enemies of Poland. Moreover, we realize that they hate us more than they hate the Germans, and that they make us responsible for their misfortune. Why, and on what basis, remains a mystery of the Jewish soul. Nevertheless, this is a decided fact. Awareness of this fact, however, does not release us from the duty of damnation of murder. We do not want to be Pilates. We have no means actively to counteract the German murders, we cannot help, nor can we rescue anybody. But we protest from the bottom of our hearts filled with pity, indignation, and horror... The forced participation of the Polish nation in the bloody spectacle taking place on Polish soil may breed indifference to unfairness, sadism, and, above all, belief that murder is not punishable. Whoever does not understand this, and whoever dares to connect the future of the proud, free Poland, with the vile enjoyment of your fellow man's calamity – is, therefore, not a Catholic and not a Pole.[59]

Kossak-Szczucka's words that her fellow Poles can do nothing at all to stay the murder of Jews; that, "we cannot help, nor can we rescue anybody," is quite a bit untrue, and she must have known it. A Warsaw resident, she must have heard of many Poles who were sheltering Jews in their homes, in diverse parts of the city's metropolis. Herself, she also sheltered for a time a Jewish person in her home. To her credit, the summer 1942 manifesto stirred her into action, and she went ahead and initiated the founding of Żegota, an organization that was active in rescuing thousands of Jews, that we will discuss in a following chapter. Herself, she also gave shelter in her home to Jews in distress. Yet, at the same time, she could not rid herself of a deeply imbedded antisemitism that did not hide a gratification that Poland after the war would be bereft of Jews. At a later period, she also stated that having saved as many Jews as possible, after the war the survivors could no longer stay in Poland, but had to look elsewhere for their destined habitations. As she stated: "I will tell the Jew: 'I saved you, sheltered you when you were persecuted. To keep you alive I risked my own life and the lives of those who were dear to me. Now nothing threatens you... Now I am depriving you of my home. Go and settle somewhere else. I wish you luck and will be glad to help you. I am not going to hurt you, but in my own home I want to live alone.'"[60]

What are we to make of this clarion call against the murder of Jews; the denouncement of fellow Poles who participate in it; side by side with a repeat of traditional anti-Jewish tropes? Is her example a reflection of the mind-set of many other Poles, but of these others not able to combine anti-Jewish sentiments with deeply held ethical values, as in the case of Zofia Kossak-Szczucka? Is she a reflection of many educated others who were prepared to help Jews on the run while simultaneously holding on to antisemitic stereotypical chlichés? On September 27, 1943, she was arrested by a German street patrol, without realizing who she really was (she went by her secret code name of Weronika). Sent to Auschwitz camp, for her underground activity, she was released in July 1944 through the efforts of the underground.[61]

Wartime antisemitism—summary. The previous discussion of antisemitism and attacks on Jews relates to the initial period of the German occupation; to approximately mid-1942, when afterwards the Germans passed to mass extermination of all Jews. In a later chapter, we will discuss Polish-Jewish relations during the post 1942 period, when after the extensive slaughter of Jews by the Germans that very year there were hardly any living Jews left inside Poland, other than those struggling to survive in the still existing ghettos, the concentration camps, and the few ones in hiding with compassionate Poles. Historians still debate the scale and spread of antisemitism among the conquered non-Jewish population. Richard Lukas, for one, who expands on Polish suffering from the Germans, argues that Jewish historians tend to make sweeping claims that label most Poles as antisemites, who did little to help the Jews against the Nazis. Polish writers also generally tend to minimize Polish antisemitism and sometimes exaggerate the amount of assistance Poles gave the Jews.[62] Lukas also makes the absurd assertion for an historian, that Polish antisemitism had much to do with the people's "outrage" at the supposed active business the Jews conducted with the Germans; that Poles accused Jews of hoarding food to keep their prices high, and many Jews preferred to have the Germans confiscate their goods rather than share them with Poles. This absurd claim, according to Lukas, is the source of Polish antisemitism during the war years.[63]

In truth, antisemitism had deeper roots, as outlined in previous chapters, and was nourished by the economic anti-Jewish policies of the successors of Piłsudski in the four-year period preceding the war. Even Lukas admits that some Poles openly approved of German policies toward the Jews, and some actively aided the Nazis in their grim mission, but he quickly adds, they were a small minority.[64] Furthermore, to be noted, that while there were antisemitic publications which delighted in the massacre of Jews, these, however, did not represent a predominant view.[65] But, one has to admit that it went quite further than this. In fact, as pointed out by Richard Evans, many Poles rather profited from the creation of the ghetto and the removal of the Jewish population from the city at large.[66] Moreover, fed by years of antisemitic propaganda and indoctrination from Polish nationalists, including senior figures in the Polish Catholic Church, many Poles, though not most, participated in some of the German acts against Jews.[67] As reported by Jürgen Stroop, the SS commander during the Warsaw ghetto uprising, certainly with some exaggeration, the Polish population "in general welcomed the measures carried out against the Jews."[68] As Evans furthermore points out, that with the widespread belief of the association of most Jews with communism, many in Poland were not sorry to see the removal of this "plague" from their midst, if it was done by the otherwise hated Germans.[69]

Nechama Tec in her groundbreaking study of Polish rescuers of Jews, and herself sheltered by a Polish family, wrote "that for most Poles it was difficult not to have internalized an anti-Semitic ideology... Even those who were saving Jews might have in some ways shared in the prevailing anti-Jewish sentiments."[70] This comes, interestingly, from a book in praise of Polish rescuers of Jews.

Jan Karski, a courier with the Polish underground, was one of the earliest war-time persons, who wrote of this prevailing antisemitic mood. In February 1940, he was asked to write his impressions on the state of Polish-Jewish relations in the homeland in the wake of the occupation. Karski expressed grave concern that in German-controlled areas, Poles were being made aware that it was permissible to rob, steal from, and even murder Jews due to the absence of any legal protections of the victims.[71] "Whoever wishes may kill a Jew, and our law will not punish him for it." Karski commented that it would have made sense for the Poles to be sympathetic with the predicament of the Jews. However, he added, "such an understanding does not exist among the broad masses of the Polish population. Their attitude toward the Jews is overwhelmingly severe, often without pity." He concluded that "this bring [the Polish population] to a certain extent, nearer to the Germans."[72] He also mentioned that while one segment of the population unequivocally condemned Nazi anti-Jewish actions, the other expressed ill-concealed joy that the Germans were solving the "Jewish question" for them. "The understanding that in the end both peoples are being unjustly persecuted by the same enemy; such an understanding does not exist among the broad masses of the Polish populace. Their attitude toward the Jews is overwhelmingly severe, often without pity."[73] The possible effect of the Karski report was so potentially damaging that Polish officials in London decided to amend the report. In the censored version, the information concerning negative attitudes toward the Jews was omitted, and the Polish population was depicted as "united in its revulsion toward German anti-Jewish actions."[74]

But not merely Karski, but a Polish underground report, of October 1940, also mentioned that "antisemitism, quite strangely, continues to be strong... I have observed few signs of compassion for the Jews even though their fate is so heavy."[75] A dispatch of the underground's Delegate Office (that represented inside Poland the Government-in-Exile in London), of December 31, 1940 gives a slightly more balanced view: "In private, many Poles express satisfaction when they see how in his city and in other cities the Jews are being removed from Polish suburbs, offices, professions, industry and commerce. But under no circumstances will they demonstrate their satisfaction in public. For they are repelled by the methods resorted;... even have some tacit compassion for the Jews, helping them whenever possible... A fraction of Poles displays favorable attitudes towards the Jews openly."[76] At the same time, Ringelblum bewailed: "The Polish people, suffering perhaps more than any other nation from the yoke of misfortune together with the Jewish people, should have, above all and at every opportunity, demonstrated sympathy, solidarity, and brotherhood with the Jews. Alas, this is but a dream."[77]

Yad Vashem historian Israel Gutman remained ambivalent on this point. He rejected the notion of all Poles having always been and continued to be endemic antisemites,[78] and pointed out that many within the circle of Polish intellectuals, and the political left, opposed the anti-Jewish measures.[79] At the same time, Gutman added, the Polish political parties during the war years retained their pre-war political programs and, with the exception of small groups of socialists and democrats, the majority continued to adhere more or less to their pre-war anti-Jewish positions.[80] One must, however, at the same time admit, that even the most extreme right-wing section of the Polish political elite referred to the Nazi extermination of Jewry as "a barbaric anti-Christian action" and one that was "alien to the Polish-Catholic ethos."[81] But many, at the same time, could not hide their inner satisfaction that the Germans in their zeal to destroy the Jews, were fulfilling a long-held Polish dream, of a new dawn in Polish history in which all Jews had miraculously disappeared – vanished forever – although the methods used by the Germans were reprehensible in the eyes of many, if not most Poles. At any rate, the Germans were making this happen and they would also bear the brunt of the blame for the methods used, so why be concerned.

To give an idea of the different responses to the hideous methods by the Germans when it applied to non-Jews as against the Jews, the following example is instructive. When word spread through the country of the pitiful plight of 30,000 children expelled from the Zamość area, a region slated for German settlement – many responded swiftly. As the trains loaded with the children moved westward across Poland, Polish women waited for hours at railroad stations in the hope of helping them. In Warsaw, residents reacted spontaneously and ransomed the emaciated and exhausted youngsters, and the same happened in several other regions of the country.[82] No such outreach occurred when Jewish children were dispatched to their death on deportation trains. However, in fairness to historical reality, the Germans would have responded more forcefully to open displays of support toward Jewish children as against non-Jewish ones. Therefore, all help to Jewish persons, adults and children alike, had to be done in strict secrecy, and at great danger to the benefactors. But the question still remains whether the compassionate zeal displayed toward non-Jewish children would also have been matched, if permitted, when it involved Jewish children? Surely, by quite some people; but, one wonders by also how many more others.

"Cognitive dissonance." Historian of Polish Jewry, Samuel Kassow (his mother and her sister were hidden by a classmate in an underground bunker in the rescuer's family barn) writes on the disparity between the "personal" and the "civic" behavior of the Polish population. While many Poles showed great kindness to individual Jews and to starving Jewish children – on the other hand, even the shared suffering at the hands of the common enemy did not soften the tendency of many to regard Jews in abstract terms, as aliens, even a hostile body, and quite beyond the sphere of Polish civic and moral responsibility. In other words, Polish kindness to Jews all too often rested on individual rather than on civic or political considerations.[83] The following story is indicative of this disparity. On July 11, 1941, Ringelblum noted of having heard a heart-warming account of a Jew who previously worked in the Alpha chocolate factory. When the Warsaw ghetto was closed, he was left with a wife and three children and no means of livelihood. He began to sell everything he had. His Polish fellow workers wrote him several times, but he didn't respond. One day, a Polish fellow worker came to his apartment at night and saw what was happening. A few days later, the workers from that man's factory sent the Jewish worker a rickshaw, together with 350 złotys to buy what he needed. Thanks to his Polish friends, the man was now able to earn a living by pedaling the rickshaw.[84]

In Warsaw, some of the Jewish beggars, especially children, on the Aryan side were, according to Ringelblum "well received, well fed, and often given food to take back to the ghetto with them. Although universally recognized as Jews from the ghetto, perhaps they were given alms for that very reason." Ringelblum added his hope that "this was an interesting symptom of a deep transformation in Polish society;" a hope that he later bewailed did not materialize.[85] Abraham Lewin, of the Oneg Shabbes Archives, was one of the few who, disregarding factual realities overstated the wishful thinking that the German terrorizing of the Polish population would forever remove the stain of Polish antisemitism. As late as June 7, 1942 (a month ahead of the mass murder of Warsaw Jewry), he exalted on the "philosemitic feelings" that the majority of Poles have been gripped. In a momentary high-spirit, he foretold: "I see Polish-Jewish relations in a bright light. I think that this war will wash this earth of ours clean of much filth and savagery… There will be no refuge here for antisemitism, at least not for public aggressive antisemitism. They will be ashamed to deal in it. I believe that the Polish people too has been purified by the terrible fire that has swept the face of the earth."[86] Chaim Aron Kaplan, who was generally critical of Polish antisemitism was at times also swept away by such hopeful wishes, noting that the Polish population "commiserate with us in our humiliation,… exclaiming, 'Better days will come!'"[87]

To explain the dissonance between a reality that contradicts what people are accustomed or wish to believe, historian Havi Dreifuss borrows the psychological concept of "cognitive dissonance." It is a perception adopted by people when the existence of certain events causes mental discomfort, and consequently leads people to produce an imaginary reality by distorting some of those new realities, since people generally aspire to create a world in which facts are compatible with certain preconceived concepts and positions that make logical sense to their life philosophies. So, one of the ways of cognitive dissonance is to excuse certain events that conflict with hard-kept preconceived notions by presenting them as exceptions to the rule and not representative of observable facts. This may explain how some Jews tried to hold on to a wishful imaginary reality by dismissing Polish antisemitism as an aberration by fringe elements.[88]

According to Dreifuss, the isolation that the Nazis imposed on the Jews, especially in the ghettos, prevented many of them from perceiving the true nature of Polish attitudes vis-à-vis the Jews, and was consequently based on the false premise that the harsh German occupation had removed the stain of antisemitism that was prevalent during the prewar years. Some of their accounts, therefore, continued to reflect a well-defined and all-encompassing positive image, and their conclusions regarding Polish attitudes toward the Jews were decidedly encouraging. This, of course, may have prevailed in the early years of the German occupation, such as up to mid-1942, the period before the massive liquidation of the great majority of the ghettos and their Jewish inhabitants.[89] One may therefore wonder whether these same people, some of whom went through a run for their lives as hunted animals among the local population after the dissolution of the ghettos, would still have held on to the same earlier views on the attitude of the larger society, beyond the ghetto walls.

CHAPTER 5

On the Aryan Side

a) Survival Among the non-Jewish Population

Fleeing the ghetto. During the period of the ghettos, to where most Polish Jews were forcibly confined under intolerable conditions, many wondered if it was not better to escape and find succor on the other side, among the non-Jewish population. It meant the difference between staying put and to a faster than usual death, or bettering their chances of survival by exiting the ghettos and passing to the so-called Aryan side, and soliciting aid from compassionate non-Jewish people, especially from those known to them. Some persons, however, withheld from such a risky adventure, fearing they lacked the physical and mental stamina for a flight into uncharted territory, while having to abandon members of their family, such as elderly parents, spouses, and children. Many were simply exhausted after long periods in the ghetto; totally weakened because of starvation; despondent, because of what they saw and what they experienced – and not willing to expend the little that was left of their strength and willpower in a risky adventure outside the ghetto perimeter among people whose liking of the Jews left much to be desired. There were also those who were reluctant to face the humiliation of having to plead before another human being, in words such as: "Save me although you are afraid. Save me, because my life is worth as much as yours."[1] Yet, there were literally thousand others who decided to make a try at this. The will to life took a hold of them over all other depressing thoughts,

and they convinced themselves that with a combination of determination and good luck they might make it. At least, it was worth a try.

Most escapes from the Warsaw ghetto took place after July 22, 1942,
during the start of the mass liquidation of the ghetto inhabitants. One
reason was that until then people still felt that the ghetto offered a better
protection, while escaping to the other side, and to a clandestine life,
seemed riskier.[2] For those seeking help within the Warsaw metropolitan
region, many felt they could find it more easily among the intelligentsia – comprising both persons of progressive views and devout Catholics
who held to strong humanitarian values. Some of these circles, indeed,
eventually joined hands to create Żegota, the special organization of the
Polish underground dedicated to helping Jews on the run. At the same
time, a substantial number of common non-organizational people took
part in the rescue work as well, usually out of pity and compassion to persons they knew from before. This happened when they were approached
and asked for whatever kind of help: nourishment, one or several nights
stay, or assistance in moving to a safe location.[3] During the peak deportations from the Warsaw and other ghettos, in the summer and fall of
1942, there were also mass escapes to villages and nearby forests.[4] Some
also made their escape from their assigned work posts outside the ghettos.[5] Venturing out of the ghetto to the other side was usually through
one of the ghetto gates after beforehand bribing the guards, who were
either Polish police or Jewish ones (who were not armed). Some tried
fleeing through tunnels constructed under a building connecting two
adjacent cellars, one on each side of the ghetto wall or fence, or through
the more accessible underground sewers connecting the two sides.[6]

Two main groups left the ghettos and crossed over to the other side;
a larger group consisting of people with means, armed with enough
currency and valuables for them to live out long stretches of time, and a
smaller group of working people, who had connections with people on
the other, so-called Aryan side, by long-standing ties of friendship and
social-business relations, as well as family connections due to the marriage with a non-Jew by someone in the family. All these escape endeav-
ors were based on advance agreement by those willing to assist. It must

be noted that the majority of former Polish friends who held back from getting involved, it was not necessarily from any animus; simply, they were too terrified of the consequences to themselves from the Germans if discovered with their Jewish friends in their flats or hideouts, and they consequently refused to get involved. In many cases, they would agree to keep a Jew on the run perhaps for only for one or several nights, but not any longer.

The number of Jews in hiding grew by leaps and bounds during the fifty-three days that the summer liquidation action lasted in the Warsaw ghetto, although many still elected to stay behind.[7] During that period, and up to the Warsaw ghetto uprising, of April 1943, that led to the final destruction of the ghetto, an estimated 10,000 people managed to leave, an average of about 50 a day. Another few thousand escaped during and even after the uprising, often by hiding in abandoned parts of the ghetto and then crossing the ghetto walls at night; or escaping from labor camps, or jumping from deportation trains.[8] One of these persons was Emanuel Ringelblum himself. Originally taken by the Germans to the Trawniki labor camp, he made a dramatic escape from there; smuggled out by two intrepid couriers, one non-Jewish and the other Jewish. Secretly returned to Warsaw, he was added to an already crowded hideout, together with his wife and son and thirty-five other Jews. In that underground hideout, in late 1943, he began to write on Polish-Jewish relations, that was published after the war. He was forced to become exactly as he had described other Jews in hiding: as a helpless child, totally dependent on his Polish protectors for everything.[9]

Those who sought help far away from the big cities often wandered from village to village, staying only briefly in each place. Others managed to organize so-called family camps in the forests; in most cases, these consisted of groups of several people, sometimes larger concentrations numbering 50-100 escapees. Still others found shelter on farms belonging to peasants who had offered to help them, sometimes without compensation. In each of those cases, the Jews were fully dependent on the goodwill of their benefactors for food and survival.[10]

German threats. When dealing with rescuers of Jews, we have always to keep in mind the circumstances where these life-saving stories took place. It was a time when helping a Jew to stay alive was a capital offense to the rescuer, with the "offender" facing the death penalty. This was especially so in Poland – where the life of a Pole was of cheap commodity – and one of the few countries where the Germans explicitly threatened the death sentence for anyone affording help to Jews on the run. Unlike in West European countries where the punishment for harboring Jews was not always as severe in all instances (but some still ended their life in concentration camps and others were executed), Poles were publicly and continuously warned of facing the death penalty for the same act.[11] The Polish population was put on notice that no tolerance and no leniency would be shown to those apprehended violating this prohibition. These warnings appeared on large billboards in the major cities, so no one could claim ignorance when caught in the act of helping a Jew avoid detection or detention.

The following few examples of such warnings will suffice. On September 22, 1942, Ludwig Fischer, the SS and police head of the Warsaw district made it known that "not only are Jews to be punished with death for illegally leaving their assigned quarter, but also those who knowingly afford them refuge. This includes not only overnight lodging, and nourishment, but also all sorts of assistance; for instance, accompanying them in a vehicle of whatever sort, the purchase of Jewish goods, etc." For those that are already hiding or helping Jews to avoid capture, if that person "reports this to the nearest police station, not later than 16:00 hours, on September 9, 1942," that person "will not be charged and prosecuted;" that is, not executed. Not so, if such a person is apprehended after that deadline, the announcement made it frighteningly clear.

Two days later, Dr. Franke, the Częstochowa military governor, warned on a billboard posted on the city's major streets that the death penalty will not only be imposed on Jews who are found outside the ghetto, but "the death penalty is a measure also to be imposed on persons, who in full conscious afford shelter to Jews, provide them with provisions or nourishment." A month earlier, on November 19, 1942, the population in Przemyśl was informed of a soon-to-be liquidation of the city's ghetto. It warned that any Pole or Ukrainian, who admits a Jew in his home, or affords him hospitality, provisions and refuge, "will be shot." Equally, for assisting a Jew "in whatever way," found outside the ghetto. To emphasize the seriousness the Germans attached to this, it added that persons to be shot will include anyone "who even attempts to commit" the previously listed "offenses." It also warned of serious measures against anyone trying to loot the valuables left behind by the expelled ghetto residents; these evidently belonged solely to the Germans.[12] If these clear German warnings were not enough to frighten off people from assisting Jews (they sure were), then the additional threats posed by persons of their own kinsfolk – professional blackmailers, persons in search of additional income whatever the methods employed, and diehard antisemites – also contributed to making people stay clear from any involvement with Jews seeking aid.

Survival on the Aryan side. To illustrate the various survival options outside the ghetto, we will concentrate on hiding possibilities in Warsaw, the city with the largest concentration of Jews. This large city seemed to offer the best possibilities of shelter in spite of the many attendant risks, due to the comings and goings in and out of the city by people from other places, and thus facilitating for Jews on the run, from Warsaw or elsewhere, to pass the city's streets undetected by others and dissimulate their presence.

In spite of this, for those prepared to make a run on the other side of the ghetto, the decision was a very agonizing one, due to the uncertain reception on the so-called Aryan side by either sympathetic or hostile Poles and the attitude of the much larger number of uninterested and passive persons.[13] The slightest mistake could be fatal. The opinion held by Jews in the ghettos was that antisemitism had of late been on the rise. Jews, it seemed to them, had been excluded from the world in which principles of brotherhood were binding, such as otherwise existed between persons involved in clandestine activities against a common tyrannical occupying country. One, nevertheless, hoped to be helped by those whom they knew from before, or lacking such people, run into good and compassionate Poles who felt a human obligation to assist anyone in need, and there were indeed quite many of such persons – but where was one to find them?[14]

As for the rescuers, they too lived under dangerous circumstances, but not only from the Germans. Not knowing whom to trust, rescuers needed to take precautionary steps even against one's own kinfolk.[15] Many Poles participated in the sport of identifying Jews circulating on the streets, or discovering Jews in hiding; then blackmailing them and their non-Jewish rescuers, and taking advantage of their vulnerability by collecting money, or worse, turning them over to the Germans for an additional reward. The Gestapo provided a standard prize to those who informed on Jews hidden on the Aryan side, consisting of cash, liquor, sugar, and cigarettes. Thus, the person who was helping Jews could himself become a victim of blackmail. Ringelblum, while hidden by a brave Pole, reports that hardly a single Jew avoided falling into the hands of extortionists at one point or another of one's travails on the Aryan side.[16]

In spite of these dangers, the Warsaw metropolitan region had the highest record of Jews hiding amidst the non-Jewish population – an estimated fifteen to twenty thousand persons. Even if these figures amount to only 5 percent of Warsaw's pre-war Jewish population, they nonetheless represent a substantial number in absolute terms when compared with any other Polish city.[17] Despite the presence of many blackmailers and denouncers, it is obvious that the concentration of such a large number of fugitives in a single area could not have been possible without the active involvement of a good number of Poles – more than the equal number of 20,000 Jews in hiding, since a single Jew at times needed the assistance of more than a lone non-Jew.[18]

With the presence of German-built extermination camps on Polish soil, all Poles knew – better indeed than persons in any other German-occupied country in Europe – the fate the Germans had in store for Jews; so that each Pole was individually aware that the life and death of a fellow human being was directly linked to his/her decision to offer or withhold assistance.[19] Aside from Żegota, the sole Polish underground organization created in late 1942 for help to Jews (and further discussed in a later chapter), Polish help to Jews was largely a private affair, conducted by individuals who assumed great responsibilities and terrible risks, in addition to undergoing excruciating mental pains, in fear of German retribution in the event of discovery of their aid to Jews.

One must also keep in mind that the ability of hiding a Jew in a very profound Christian society, where most Jews were only partially assimilated, as was the case in Poland, was a daunting task. Many Jews spoke Polish with a noticeable special accent, and used different gestures and facial expressions. In addition, Jews with specific so-called Semitic facial features (slightly curly hair and tanned skin) were particularly vulnerable. Generally, on the Aryan side, a runaway Jew had two options: to remain in the open, that is "above ground," or go underground, by constantly remain in hiding. In the first case, the Jew turns into a non-Jewish Pole (armed with appropriate false papers), and ostensibly lives legally. In the second case, the Jew (especially those with so-called Semitic appearances) hides in a place where he stays mostly indoors, and is not registered anywhere. In many cases, Jews on the run passed from one mode to another; first, passing undetected as a non-Jew, then going into hiding; or vice versa.

Living "above ground." Living in the open outside the ghetto undetected among the non-Jewish population, for those who chose this dangerous day-by-day path, was as one may imagine far from easy. Such a person had to meet several conditions: "good" (i.e., non-Jewish) looks; a certain amount of money; forged documents; a well, but not too fluent command of Polish; familiarity with Catholic rituals and modes of religious greetings; and having Polish acquaintances and contacts.[20] It also meant living in constant fear, and under constant tension of the uncovering of one's true identity.[21] A Jew circulating freely outside the ghetto could give himself away by certain bodily gestures; such as endlessly looking around in every direction to see if anyone was watching and scanning him; the nervous expression on his face; the frightened look of a hunted person; and sad-looking, melancholy, or pensive eyes. In short, all kinds of bodily behavioral modes that expressed anxiety, fear, and depression.

Such as the case of a Jewish man out on the street, whose eyes almost

betrayed him. "We were standing on the platform. I noticed a policeman pass [inside the tram]. It seems that my eyes rested on him... In
a moment, the tram stopped, and this man jumped onto the platform.
Coming straight to me he asked for my documents... He was taking me
to the police station to have my papers properly checked. I knew that
once I reached the station I would be lost... I tried to smile at him... I
said...'I cannot understand why you took me off the tram.' To this he
said, 'Maybe I'm making a mistake... You know, you don't look Polish.'
'But I am Polish,' I interrupted. 'But you have Jewish eyes,' he said. I
started to laugh. 'How is this possible?' He laughed too. I was young; it
was a nice morning, so I asked him, 'Can you give me my things back;
after all, I'm in a rush to get to my job.' He said, 'OK, take it.' Then I
asked if I could jump on the tram. 'I will stop it,' he said. And he did."[22]
This, indeed, was one lucky break, when other men stopped by a Polish
policeman did not have the same ending. Alexandra Gutter, whose appearance was Jewish, recalled, "While in hiding, I only walked into the
streets in the evenings, when people couldn't see me, because everybody
recognized me as a Jew."[23]

A Jew could also be suspected by his dark curly hair (some Jews
bleached their hair to a more brown-yellow coloring). But one had to be
careful not to overdo it. Platinum blondes gave rise to more attention
than brunettes, when one needed not to draw attention to oneself.[24] For
men, an additional factor of great concern when living "above ground,"
was the risk of being forced to remove their pants. In Poland, only Jewish
men were circumcised, and that was an incontestable proof of one's true
identity, whatever the person's looks and documents told.

Such a person must also make sure to be employed somewhere, with
fellow workers not suspecting his Jewishness. Jewish women had a certain advantage over men, since they found more easily work as servants,
housemaids, as well as in factories, hospitals, and shops.[25] If a Jew circulating freely did not actually work, he was at least required keep up the
appearance of working. He must leave his flat in the morning in order
not to give rise to suspicions, and spend long hours riding in tramways
or walk unsuspectingly in the streets. Only individuals with a so-called

"good" – that is, non-Jewish – appearance, and familiar with Polish ways and expressions as well as the Catholic religion (so as to properly greet a priest, or nun, accosted on the street), could have a chance to survive "above ground." Some people not knowing enough Polish pretended to be without voice and hearing, and wore an armband saying in German *taubstumm* (deaf-mute).[26]

Ringelblum wrote that "Mrs. I. [Batya Berman-Temkin] knows that it is not one's face but one's behavior that determines whether one can survive 'on the surface.' She always keeps calm and cheerful, is not afraid of anyone and always smiles. She wears mourning [clothes] in order to appear more dignified. If anyone glances at her in the tramway, she looks boldly back, and if anybody observes her intently, she walks up to him and asks what time it is. In the beginning she worked as a housemaid for an antisemitic employer, who tried to indoctrinate her with hatred for the Jews."[27] Some showed bravado by going to restaurants and cafes, and travelling in tramway cars reserved for Germans only.[28]

Janina Ziemian, who was passing as a self-confident non-Jewish woman in Warsaw, wrote after the war the "ten commandments" that every Jewish woman had to learn in order not to be entrapped. These included the following sound advices: When you feel being stopped by a man who says, "You're Jewish, aren't you," one has several possibilities. "If he is young and nice, ask: 'Is this the new way to start with girls? Once the approach was: 'What time do you have?'" If that doesn't help, "Start creaming: 'Help, he's insulting me! He's claiming I'm Jewish! How dare he? Shame on him!' People will gather; some will attack him; he'll start giving excuses, and in the meantime, you will be able to sneak away." To avoid being identified by pre-war acquaintances, "fully change the type of clothes you habitually wear. For instance, if you're passing as a country girl, place a shawl over your hair, walk barefooted or with sandals, and a long skirt. Avoid excessive hair dying and face powdering, for this will attract undue attention to yourself." Also, "learn well how to drink vodka – one swoop with each small glass, without this unbalancing you; for it's a well-known fact that Jews don't know how to drink." Finally, "study the church laws, even the oddest ones, so that you will be able to respond to whatever question. For instance: When does one start reciting one's confession, when you're waiting on the other side of the Confessor's booth who, in the meantime, is busy with another person? The answer: after three knocks by the priest. These are the types of questions used by persons in the business of entrapping Jews."[29]

The position of a Jew on the Aryan side could become particularly difficult if he or she was taken ill. There were cases of betrayal by non-Jewish doctors to whom Jews were referred for help. It was even worse if a Jew died while on the Aryan side.[30] For, normally, he or she had to be buried after proper certification of his/her death. This ran the risk of the disclosure of one's true identity and the place where one died – usually the home belonging to a non-Jewish person. The best solution was to somehow secretly and hurriedly dispose the body.

Documents that identified a Jew as a Christian offered some protection. Usually, when several members of a family reached the non-Jewish side of the city, they preferred to have different names. In case of an arrest, at least some could be spared, claiming not to know each other. Some identification cards were duplicates of documents that belonged to real people; some others, of people who had died.[31] In occupied Poland, everyone of age, and not Jewish, had to possess a special document, known as Kennkarte, on the basis of a birth certificate, and each person had to apply for this new identity card in person. Each Kennkarte had the owner's name, date and place of birth, present occupation, and religion. A Kennkarte holder had to register a second time with the vital records office. The requirement to appear personally in two offices stopped many Jews from getting these valid documents, and they had to rely on friends to obtain it secretly.[32] In all these instances of circulating in the open, one could not do it without the help of usually several non-Jewish persons, for help to facilitate the obtaining of new false identity cards, or finding a proper and safe apartment, alone or with others, and obtaining a proper work place. Any such helper placed himself and fellow helpers at risk, in case of one's arrest and the subsequent disclosure, while under torture by the Gestapo, of one's help confederates.

Living in hiding. Jews who hid among the non-Jewish population were usually concealed in specially prepared hideouts or inside apartments.[33] Such a life was also fraught with much danger. It was like a dynamite liable to explode at any moment due to the constant fear of exposure, such as by a neighbor, the porter, the manager of the block of flats, or suspecting blackmailers. Jews in hiding – no one, other than the person(s) caring for them were to know their presence, and visits to the host family were discouraged.[34] No wonder that Jews in hiding were often forced to switch hiding places; and this had to be done in a hurry, to avoid arrest of their benefactor hosts. People fell victim to betrayers for a host of reasons. Someone began to suspect by noticing that visitors are often received in the kitchen and not in the living room; that much more food was being bought than before; that the hosts were better dressed because perhaps of payments by Jews hidden with them, revelations that in normal circumstances would not have raised suspicious eyebrows.[35]

Women advantage. In Eastern Europe, Jewish women had certain advantages over men when passing as non-Jews. Because women were excluded from traditional religious educational pursuits, they had more freedom to engage in secular education. This was often reflected in women's greater familiarity with the Polish language. Particularly in prewar Polish towns, women had more contacts than men with local people such as storekeepers and all kinds of merchants. This in turn boosted women's acculturation and self-confidence. They could presently walk around town and pass more easily. A woman could also dye her hair, and properly dressed, she could look more like the average Polish woman.[36] It also been noted that men were usually more depressed than women, and this already began at the outset of the occupation, when they were more likely to be forced into degrading hard labor.[37] Men's special vulnerability seemed to be reflected in Nechama Tec's findings that 60 percent of the Jewish men she studied lived mainly in hiding than in the open, compared to 48 percent of women. Women also had an edge over men in the wartime economic conditions for employment. Maids, cooks, and governesses topped the list of job openings.

Transfer to Germany as a Polish laborer also looked like an attractive alternative to the constant anti-Jewish terror in Poland. Here, too, women had an advantage over men. Before being shipped off to Germany, each candidate had to submit to a thorough physical examination. For a Jewish man this meant the special danger of the discovery of his circumcision. Nevertheless, some men slipped through the medical nets, using various diversionary tactics, and ended up in Germany. Zwia Rechtman-Schwarz, who herself chose to enlist as a laborer in Germany, spoke of one exceptional case: "A neighbor of mine, a Jew, survived in Germany as a worker, and he told me that when he went to bathe with other men around him all the soap was concentrated on his genitals."[38]

The plight of Jewish children. In spring 1942, according to data that the Warsaw Municipal Administration passed to the underground, 4,000 children, half of them Jewish, were roaming the streets of Warsaw, begging for bread. These 2,000 Jewish children were risking their lives by first digging their way under the wall enclosing the ghetto, sneaking through holes to the so-called Aryan side to beg for money to buy bread, cereals or potatoes; then, sneaking back in the ghetto, without getting caught, to feed their hungry families. While out on the streets, they were usually not refused alms or food. Even plain German soldiers at times used to give them something.[39] There were, however, worse cases where persons who accosted begging Jewish children on the street turned them over to the Polish police or the Germans, who usually sent them back to the ghetto while it was still in existence, after a slight beating.[40] After the ghetto's dissolution, a worse fate awaited these children. For those in hiding, there were frequent instances when the child's protectors, having received a large sum of money for the child's upkeep, simply turned the child out into the street, due to fear or when the money ran out. Thanks to the courageous and warm-hearted help of the Catholic writer, Jan Dobraczyński, head of the Care Section of the Social Aid Department of the Warsaw Municipality, and his assistant, Jadwiga Piotrowska, a number of Jewish children smuggled out of the ghetto by Irena Sendlerowa (more on her in next chapter) and her co-workers, were sent as Polish orphans to convents and monasteries near Warsaw or locations further away.[41] By the end of 1943, there were some 600 Jewish children in various institutions in Warsaw and environs, and some more in private homes.[42]

There were also those who succeeded in passing unnoticed, not as begging children, but as non-Jewish homeless children selling various cheap and low-cost commodities to passers-by, mainly cigarettes. Such as the story of the cigarette sellers of the Three Crosses Square, in Warsaw. As told by Józef Zysman, who acted on behalf of the clandestine National Jewish Committee, after the destruction of the Warsaw ghetto. One day, in October 1943, he accosted a group of these boys, and after he had gained their confidence, they told him, "There are many more of us. We stick together and we're doing all right." Zysman was flabbergasted as they recounted their story. "Over a dozen. We sell cigarettes, we stick together and we're rough. Business is booming." As he accompanied them on one of their forays, they came upon a German soldier. "Sir, Egyptian cigarettes. How much, how much, sir? These are originals. The lot for only thirty złotys." They told Zysman that a friendly Polish woman allowed them to sleep over at her place. Some of the children also sold cigarettes near the train station, or on trams. Most of them lost their parents in the Warsaw ghetto or were deported to Treblinka camp. These boys preferred to be left alone, but Zysman persuaded his clandestine Jewish confederates to help the roving boys with some money and fake documents, and most survived.[43]

b) Threats, Betrayals, Collusion and Murder

Denunciation and informing. Further to our earlier description of German threats of the death penalty awaiting people sheltering Jews, such rescuers, to avoid detection, had to take careful measures to keep their rescue activities secret not only from neighbors, but also friends, and sometimes, even relatives. In Nechama Tec's pioneering study of Christian aid to Jews in Nazi-occupied Poland, she found two underlying impediments to aiding Jews. Besides the obvious German threat, Polish rescuers cited fear of denunciation by their neighbors as the second greatest obstacle. "The environment in which Polish rescuers lived was hostile to the Jews and unfavorable to their protection," she stated. "Not only did rescuers know that their protection of Jews would meet with Polish disapproval, but many feared that this Polish disapproval would come with actual reprisals."[44] Then, there were persons who objected to others assisting Jews, not due to fear of German reprisals, but of their personal's deep hatred of Jews. Survivor Emanuel Tanay: "I myself lived in constant fear that the Germans would kill me but I was even more afraid of Poles who were able to recognize that I was a Jew... Telling a stranger or even an acquaintance that I was a Jew living on the Aryan side with false documents would simply mean committing suicide." Tanay adds, with perhaps a bit exaggeration, that whereas an act of denunciation of underground activities was regarded as socially unacceptable, the betrayal of Jews was acceptable by many.[45]

A Polish heroine who had taken an abandoned Jewish child under her protection tells of having constantly to change her residence because she was actually driven away by her neighbors, who knew the child was not hers and was Jewish.[46] It was part of the experience of almost every Jewish fugitive on the run to come either under direct threat of an extortionist, or to run into someone he knew before the war, and was not sure if that person would denounce him. When such an unexpected encounter happened, it was best for the Jewish fugitive to make immediate arrangements for a change of address and another job, and in some cases to assume a new identity and procure a new set of forged documents as well.[47]

One of the first testimonies from a Holocaust survivor, published in November 1944 in the form of a letter to the editor of a journal in liberated Lublin, described the situation of hidden Jews during the war in the following manner: "How many more people would be saved, had it not been for the attitude of a part of society.... How many times a mean informer would frustrate the painstaking and selfless sacrifice of another Pole who risked his life for his Jewish friend or even an unknown Jew, equipping him with a forged I.D., helping him escape, relocate or find a job. Each of these actions alone carried a threat to the rescuer's life. And then, after several months of struggle, a villain came along and with one word turned to ruin the painstakingly erected structure that would be crowned with the proud inscription, 'I saved a man.'"[48] Hence, the greater admiration of those Poles who withstood such dangers to themselves and continued to afford assistance to Jews on the run, as further portrayed in the next chapter.

Blackmailers and *Szmaltsowniks.* One of the most despicable phenomena during the occupation was the prominence of people freely circulating the streets, blackmailing and denouncing to the Germans suspecting Jews and their Polish protectors. They were dubbed derisively *Szmaltsowniks* (from *shmalts* or *szmalec*, Yiddish and Polish for "grease;" in other words, extortion money). Historians debate their numbers, but their large presence in all major thoroughfares and side streets close to exit points of the ghettos, and especially mostly acting in groups, must lead to the inescapable conclusion that we are dealing with a wide phenomenon, involving more than a mere handful of such people. Many of these were from the lower classes, and some from criminal elements, but they also included persons from well-established families. These hyena-like chasers after Jews often hunted in gangs, and sometimes even Polish non-Jews with so-called Semitic features were molested by them.[49]

Aside from the various German security personnel and the German-led Polish police, the blackmailers and the *Szmaltsowniks* were an endless nightmare to Jews on the run. The moment a Jew crossed through the gates of the ghetto, or rather while still inside the ghetto gates, he was watched by swarms of blackmailers on the outside, who preyed on him the moment he was but a few feet outside the ghetto perimeter.[50] The underground journal Prawda, in March 1943, reported: "The hosts of informers and blackmailers have grown, to reach incredible, terrifying numbers. The blackmailers make life intolerable for the ever-growing number of victims of Nazi persecutions. They trail their victims relentlessly. No wonder they [Jews] feel like hunted wild animals... In no way can this conduct be justified."[51] Scattered evidence underscored this frightening reality. In a group of 308 Jews living illegally that Nechama Tec studied, an overwhelming majority (88 percent) were either blackmailed, denounced, and arrested, or came close to being arrested.[52]

Ringelblum writes that the *Szmaltsowniks* walk the streets stopping anyone who even looks Jewish in appearance. "They frequent public squares, especially the square near the central [railway] station, cafés and restaurants, and the hotels... [They] operate in organized bands. Bribing one of them does not mean that a second cohort will not appear a moment later, then a third and so on, a whole chain of *Szmaltsowniks* who pass the victim on until he has lost his last penny... They are a veritable plague of locusts, descending in large numbers upon the Jews on the Aryan side and stripping them of their money and valuables and often clothing as well."[53]

Ita Diamant, a rabbi's daughter who worked as a nurse in the Warsaw ghetto, described her journey from the ghetto gate on Zelażna Street to the main railway station on Jerozolimskie street (about one kilometer): "When we made the first three steps on the other side of the ghetto, we were assaulted by a swarm of boys, blackmailers. I didn't have the slightest idea that anything like that might happen to me on the other side. They started chasing us and... shouting that we should give them money. Of course, we were not wearing the [Yellow Star] armbands. In the beginning I thought: we will give something to this one, something to that one and they will leave us in peace. But they were like a swarm. When one departed – he sent in another one; when this one left – he sent in the third one and so on. Finally, I realized that it would not work and we would not make it... We got into a horse cab,... and suddenly – next to us – one guy on a bicycle and the second one and the third one appeared. Each reached out his hand and you had to give something to each. We could not beat it... To put it briefly: when we [got on the train] we had no money, no rings, no watches or shoes left. We had nothing."[54] These youngsters, at least, were only interested in a little handout, not like the professional *Szmaltsowniks* who would fleece the victims from whatever valuable on them; then, turn them over to the Germans, for an additional reward.

Alexandra Gutter told about a friend "who looked like a thousand Poles; he had no resemblance to a Jew." He had to move around town to make a living. Once, he was just walking the streets, and a Pole stopped him with a "come into the courtyard." He went in. The Pole threatened, made Alexandra's friend pull down his pants, and then examined his documents. In the end a handsome bribe sent the blackmailer away on his continuous hunt of Jews.[55] Before leaving, our man asked: "How did you ever recognize me?" "Well, you are the fifth one that I caught today. Some were Jews and some were not. After all, Christmas is coming and I need extra money. This is how I earn it."[56]

While the Warsaw ghetto still existed, one could observe the return of great numbers of blackmail victims, broken in spirit, stripped of belongings and money, cursing the Aryan side which had deprived them of their last haven. In embellished literary words, Ringelblum described the returning Jews as kissing the earth of the ghetto, blessing every day spent there, since at least there they could rest without continually watching out for the police and the blackmailers. They had returned to the ghetto since their shattered nerves could no longer stand the constant tension on the other side.[57]

Or, consider the story of Josef Flakowicz (today, Komem), born 1936, and his family. Originally from Kalisz, then Sandomierz ghetto, Josef and mother Cesia fled from the ghetto and moved to Brzesko, where the two, appearing under assumed names rented a room in the home of Feliksa Gardzielowa and her two children, who did know her tenants' true identity. One day, while out on the street, selling baked cookies that Cesia and Feliksa prepared at home, someone recognized Cesia from Kalisz. "Would he turn her in? Would he gossip," Josef wondered? Sure enough, it led to extortion by this man. Cesia's husband who was hiding elsewhere in Warsaw, hurried over and with the help of someone in the Polish underground, a deal was struck with the extortionist, under which he received hush money, together with the threat of retribution if he were to report the mother and son to the police.[58] Taking no chances, father and husband, also appearing under an assumed name, took his wife and son to Warsaw, where they hid in the home of Leopolda Kuropieska, 355 and her two children (her husband was in a German prisoner-of-war camp), and where Josef met his slightly elderly brother Itzhak, in hiding there. Leopolda, who knew of her wards Jewish identity told Josef "to keep quiet… I could only whisper quietly in someone's ear. I also had to walk slowly, tiptoeing in bare feet. It was forbidden to move chairs or heavy objects. I could not be near the window curtains during the day... There were also rules for flushing the toilet as silently and sparingly as possible." Two other adult sisters were also hiding in that apartment.[59]

Sure enough, here too, a neighbor betrayed them, and one day two men appeared; one, in the uniform of the Polish police; the other in civilian clothes. They knew exactly where to go – the secret hiding place behind a closet, where Josef was discovered, but not brother Itzhak. When Leopolda threatened them with retribution by the underground, the tone turned to businesslike negotiations between both sides. Again, Josef's father arranged the payment, and the two men left, assuring Leopolda and Josef's mother Cesia they would not return again for additional payments. But here, too, it was better to move on – at least for Josef, his mother and the two sisters; not so, for brother Marian, whose hiding spot was not uncovered, and he stayed on.[60] From there, Josef was moved to another temporary place; then, to the home of Stefania Łoza, son Eugeniusz, and daughter Irena Nowak, in Słotwina, not far from Brzesko. There, Josef was welcomed, but the hosts were also forced to billet two German soldiers from the nearby military caserne, who did not suspect Josef's Jewishness, with his light skin and wavy hair (and a newly-acquired Polish sounding name).[61] There, Josef stayed for over a year, until the area's liberation.

There were additional encounters with other would-be betrayers, by other members of Josef's family, who also had to be paid off, and the hiders forced to move to others locations, and similar confrontations were also the lot of other Jews hiding with friendly non-Jewish rescuers. It goes without saying that the rescuers in Josef's story were honored by Yad Vashem with the Righteous title. Then, there were some rescuers who were far from pure saints, but were eager to extort Jews sheltered by them of their valuables; then when these resources were exhausted, they evicted the Jews from their hiding places. Fear of exposure and German retribution by decent-minded people could also lead them to force out their Jewish beneficiaries.[62]

As already told, the Germans handed rewards to denouncers of

Jews. The nature of these prizes varied depending on the locality and the demands for certain goods. They might include rye flour, sugar, vodka, and cigarettes.[63] In some small places, 500 Polish złotys and a kilogram of sugar were given for every Jew captured. In other places, three liters of vodka for every Jew denounced.[64]

Some have argued that most of these professional blackmailers, on a steady day-to-day hunt for Jews, came from the very lowest orders of society and either lived on the fringes of the criminal underworld or were outright criminals themselves. They may also have included persons with no criminal past, it is argued, but whom wartime conditions freed them from all social restraints, and allowed them to indulge in their overriding desire for easy money and their innate taste for debauchery. They were also joined by rabid antisemites giving vent to their deep hatred of Jews, and there were many of that kind too.[65] Nearly every memoir mentions encounters with these persons, often several such confrontations. It is commonly held that their numbers ran into at least a thousand, in Warsaw alone, and more so when those in other cities are added. If one were to accept the claim that the bulk of the blackmailers belonged to the fringe of society, then that fringe, indeed, was quite large, encompassing many strata of the Polish population. Perhaps, hounding Jews on the run may have been the sole criminal felony of quite many of these otherwise decent citizens.[66]

As blackmailing assumed epidemic proportions,[67] on May 6, 1943, the underground (through its Delegate Office, representing the Polish government in London) issued a stern warning in its publication, Rzeczpospolita Polska: "Another type of wartime hyena has appeared. They are those who exploit the tragedy of those Jews who are in hiding from the Germans by blackmail and extortion."[68] The bulletin castigated them as depraved individuals, who do not hesitate to exploit the tragedy of Jews who are hunted by the German in order to extort large sums of money. "[They] should be treated by society with castigation and contempt. Their names should be listed and handed over to the special [underground] courts in order to enact the most severe penalties."[69] However, other than a few isolated cases, no affirmative action was taken against these gangs, as the underground routinely did in the case of other types of collaboration with the enemy.[70] From his hideout, Ringelblum noted sadly, "yet no harm befalls them. They know that where Jews are concerned, there is no law and no punishment, nobody will stand up for them. The Polish underground has as yet done nothing. Words have not been followed by deeds. This complete impunity is a clear sign for Jews that nobody is anxious to save them."[71]

Polish Blue Police. The Polish police, commonly called the Blue Police, because of the color of their uniforms (*Granatowa policja*), played a most lamentable role in the hunt after Jews.[72] Its members, with a few exceptions, became notorious as agents and accomplices of the Gestapo. It included among its ranks many Polish-born, but also several generations removed ethnic Germans known as *Volksdeutsche*.[73] The uniformed police guarded the exit gates of the ghettos; participated in deportation actions; tracked down Jews; and even shot Jews sentenced to death by the Germans.[74] Numerous sources testify to the zeal displayed by the Blue Police in anti-Jewish measures. Dr. Zygmunt Klukowski, noted in his diary of October 22, 1942 on the liquidation of Jews in the town of Szczebrzeszyn: "Today, 'our' gendarmes and the Blue Police are at work; they have been ordered to kill every Jew they catch on the spot. They are executing this order with great zeal. Since morning, they have been bringing the corpses of the Jews killed from different parts of the town, mostly from the Jewish quarter, on horse-drawn carts to the Jewish cemetery, where they dig large pits and bury them. Throughout the day, Jews have been routed out from the most varied hide-outs. They have been shot on the spot or brought to the Jewish cemetery and killed there."[75] Although at times under German orders, the actions of the police displayed a high degree of liberty and independence from their German masters, especially when it came to hurting Jews.[76]

Social anarchy. As already pointed out in Chapter 3, German punitive policies in Poland, paradoxically created a strange environment which might be called totalitarian anarchy, in which order and calm prevailed on the surface and complete chaos not far below it.[77] At the same time, paradoxically, the terror, house searches, mass arrests, and severe penalties for hiding Jews were to an extent counterproductive to what the Nazis aimed. In their attempt to terrorize the population by the threat of severe penalties – death or imprisonment in a concentration camp – for a very great variety of forbidden activities, such as black-marketing, possession of a radio, curfew violations, failing to register at the municipal offices, and so on, the effect was counter to what the Germans expected of total submissiveness. For instance, official rations were set so low that buying food on the black market became essential for survival, since no one could afford the food prices only based on income from official wages. Therefore, Polish families had to supplement their incomes illegally, and besides hiding Jews for money, although risky, so were other illegal acts such as trading in food and necessities.[78] All the same, the billboards on the main city thoroughfares threatening the death penalty for harboring Jews, while no such menacing posters appeared for other offences, made it quite clear to everyone of the seriousness the Germans attached to this issue, above and beyond any other infraction, and therefore persons knew that no leniency was to be expected to the offender found sheltering Jews, or helping them in other ways.

Scope of collaboration. According to a rough estimate by Yad Vashem historian Shmuel Krakowski, at least 200,000 men, women, and children escaped from the ghettos and camps, and maybe even more, with more wandering aimlessly through the countryside seeking help.[79] Whatever the exact number, it certainly exceeded 100,000 without counting those who sought to hide on the Aryan side in the cities, particularly in Warsaw.[80] These fugitives from German terror continued to face an uncertain future due to entrapments by many local residents, who either killed them or turned them over to the Germans. Yad Vashem files contain records of participation of local villagers in raids on the Jews in 172 localities.[81] When totaled, these estimates amount to many thousands who fell prey to raids by local vigilantes. Gutman and Krakowski estimate that the figure of over 3,000 Jews murdered by Polish civilians or turned over to the Germans are reliably authenticated.[82] Historian Dreifuss, who generally gives credence to blaming anti-Jewish excesses to "fringe" elements of Polish society, nevertheless notes that the involvement of the Poles in the murder of Jews is repeated frequently in testimonies – often with emphasis.[83]

This can be substantiated by the fact that during the Polish uprising of August 1944, most of the estimated 20,000 Jews in hiding in the greater Warsaw region elected to remain incognito. They were afraid of their neighbors, presently up in arms against the Germans, some of whom might be antisemites, blackmailers or plain scoundrels.[84] Risks from antisemitic neighbors also extended into the immediate post-war period. A confidential memorandum written in February 1946 to a US Embassy counselor in Poland recounts the plight of Jewish children who had been saved by Poles in Kraków: "Until this very day those children are kept in the garret of the house, hidden away from the neighbors for fear that the neighbors discover that the Christian family saved the Jewish children and vent their vengeance on the whole family, and this is one year after liberation."[85] This may be an exceptional case, but, sadly, there were more such similar stories.

Collective and individual participation. The widespread myth of Judeo-communism, combined with the German encouragement of open antisemitic acts, may have prompted the massacre of Jews by Poles in the northeastern Łomża province in the summer of 1941, following the German invasion of the Soviet Union. Although the Germans, through their Einsatzgruppen killing units, were primarily responsible for the massacre of Jews, some were carried out with the active participation of local inhabitants (Poles, and even more so, Ukrainians and Byelorussians). The full scope of the participation in the massacres of Jews by certain Polish villagers remains a controversial subject.[86] We will cite just a few examples.

In the village of Topola, in Pińczów county, the head of the village council, Władysław Dusza, was charged with leading the Blue police to a bunker in the field belonging to a peasant named Porada, where six people were hidden. The nighttime manhunt ended with the shooting of the victims to death in their sleep. A large number of peasants from the village arrived at the site and stripped the bodies of their clothing before throwing them into a pit.[87] As confirmed in the post-war testimony of the defendant Dusza: "Having thrown them into the pit,... we drove to the apartment of Władysław Pawlik, who invited all of us for supper and served us with vodka."[88]

Another story of organized killing by villagers, took place in Oleksin village, near Brańsk, Bielsk Podlaski county. There, Józef Adamczyk, the hamlet head led other villagers in the search of hidden Jews. That very night, they captured ten Jews. They tied them up for several days, until the Germans appeared to take them away. The ten were shot on their way to the village of Klicha. The next day, the Adamczyk group carried out another raid and captured five more Jews who were shot in Brańsk.[89] In the Białystok district in northeastern Poland, historian Joshua Zimmerman estimates that the local population participated in dozens of pogroms in local towns and villages, just two weeks after the Soviet army had withdrawn, in July 1941, in which several thousand Jewish lives were lost, with the largest in Radziwiłł on July 7 (400 deaths) and Jedwabne on July 10, in which at least 300 (and perhaps more) Jews were tortured and beaten to death by the local population. The Polish Institute for National Remembrance identified twenty-two other towns that had pogroms similar to Jedwabne.[90]

The underground Home Army reported that covering the period of July 1-15, 1941, "in a number of cities (Brześć, Łomża, Białystok, Grodno) pogroms took place – unfortunately, in collusion with German soldiers." This is the only known document produced by the underground that explicitly mentions civilians participating in the pogrom wave of June-July 1941.[91] The rise of these incidents went so far that on October 15, 1942, the underground publication, *Biuletyn Informacyjny*, felt compelled to condemn Poles for taking part in looting and anti-Jewish violence.[92] Such as the report of the underground's Delegate Office expressing shock at the behavior of the local Poles during the deportations of the Piotrków Trybunalski ghetto, on October 27 1942: "Our people behaved scandalously; they plundered, stole, and broke into empty houses, taking away whatever they could carry."[93]

In the post-war trial of Zygmunt Wiśniewski, he stated: "I confess to taking part in murdering Jews between the villages of Wysokie Małe and Wysokie Średnie, village district Jurkow, county of Sandomierz. The murder was carried out as follows. It was summer time, 1943, I was at home at the time and heard a shot, so I went out... I noticed five or six Jews shot to death, and one Jewess and one Jew still alive. In my presence, the Jewess and the Jew were told to take five steps, after which Kazimierz Domagała shot the Jewess twice, she was hit in the stomach and fell to the ground. [Three more names of participants in the killings are cited]... Three people were still not shot... Kazimierz Domagała told me that there was no more ammunition to shoot those three Jews. So Domagała told me and Sosnowski to go bring some rope in order to hang those three Jews, and both of us went to get the rope from a farm in the village of Wysokie Małe... After we brought the rope... we took those three Jews. ... We brought them to a ditch," where the three victims were brutally murdered. "From Domagała I received a short coat of the Jewess who was shot, and in the collar, at home, I found 110 dollars, and also got 10 dollars from Domagała, which belonged to the murdered [Jews]."[94]

The Jedwabne massacre (Łomża district) of the town's entire Jewish population, soon after the Russians retreated in July 1941, has been widely reported. In their rage against the previous Russian occupants, the local inhabitants took it out on all of the town's Jews; men and women, young and old. It was an act of genocide of an entire community that had in common one thing: they were all Jews.[95] In a post-war arrest of a few of the perpetrators, in 1949, the fifteen men arrested included small farmers, seasonal workers, two shoemakers, a mason, a carpenter, two locksmiths, a letter carrier, and a former town-hall receptionist. Some were family men (one a father of six children, another of four); others still single. The youngest was twenty-seven years old, the oldest sixty-four.[96] Hardly imaginable to classify all these participants as belonging to "criminal" and "underworld" elements, as claimed by some apologists of these criminal acts.[97] And the list of more such betrayals goes on.[98]

What is especially galling about these stories is the participation of so many in each of these ghastly undertakings. Arguably, many of the perpetrators may have been prompted by social pressure to act in unison, when so many others joined the fray. In some cases, the entire village took part, either as passive witnesses or active participants, and it became a secret to be kept after the war, since it implicated the village as a whole.[99] The events in question are still taboo. In the words of one villager: "Better not to talk about it, because we'll be turned into [another] Jedwabne."[100]

Sheltered then killed. Mind-boggling as some of these stories may be, one is even more appalled by stories of the murder of Jews by persons who originally sheltered them; in some cases when the hiders could no longer pay their host; in other cases, when the host was either overcome with fear or when the greed compulsion took possession of the rescuer. Such as the seven Jews, gruesomely murdered by the Środa family who had earlier sheltered them in their barn, in the village of Klemencice, Wodzisław village district. According to the testimony of the accused, Jan Środa, in his post-war trial, the Jews had paid him 4,000 złotys for sheltering them and 3,000 złotys for food. The Środa family decided to murder them in April 1944. Their motivation was to despoil the hidden Jews of the "riches" that they allegedly had with them.[101] Some rescuers eliminated their Jewish hosts due to fear of their own lives. Yehuda Ehrlich testified in Israel, in the 1960s, that he was hiding in the home of Jan and Maria Wiglusz in Sietesz, a nearby village of Markowa. In the spring of 1944 a Jewish family was discovered hiding with Polish peasants. The Polish family – eight souls, including a pregnant wife – was killed together with the hidden Jews. As a result, there was enormous panic among the Polish peasants who were hiding other Jews. The next morning 24 corpses of Jews were discovered in the fields. They had been murdered by the peasants themselves, farmers who had kept them hidden during the previous twenty months, probably in return for payment – in fear of being discovered, and their own death.[102]

c) Conclusion

The previous discussion of the severe conditions of Jews in German-occupied Poland, who sought outside help is quite disheartening.

Unquestionably, the most sensitive barometer of Polish-Jewish relations during the Second World War must surely be the extent of Polish help to Jews on the run. Some survivors are sharp in their condemnation of Polish attitudes during that horrific period. Such as the following passage in Rabbi Joseph Guzik's diary, extensively mentioned in Dreifuss's study, which covers a wide spectrum of Polish-Jewish relations during the German occupation – the good and the bad. "July 26, 1943: We've stopped believing in the Polish people; because of them so many of our brethren have met an untimely and bizarre death... Most of them agree with the dastardly Germans and assist them, and only a few oppose them and have been helping us in our tragedy... Observe the extent to which the toxin of their hatred of us has penetrated them."[103] Having read this person's unfavorable opinion about the Poles, one must also mention the other, positive, side of the story – that the rabbi and his brother were hidden by a Polish farmer, and thus they both survived.

Others, such as historian and eyewitness Emanuel Ringelblum, were not prepared to draw a final line in one direction, and mixed their words with both praise and condemnation. Such as in the following: "I myself am concrete proof that the contention of some Jewish circles that the whole Polish population is supposedly delighted over the fate of the Jews, that there do not exist on the Aryan side people with aheart, who are pained by the tragedy of the Jewish people in Poland, is far from the truth."[104] But, while paying tribute to the "thousands of noble souls" who risked their lives to help Jews, Ringelblum also bewailed what he believed were the too few numbers of person readying themselves to help Jews on the run. He ascribed this omission to various factors: "German terror, mass arrests and house searches, severe penalties for hiding Jews, and a widespread antisemitism. These factors created non-favorable conditions for the mass concealment of Jews."[105] Most Poles, he felt, were indifferent, while "hundreds, perhaps thousands" in Warsaw alone occupied themselves with blackmailing Jews or betraying them to the authorities for profit.[106] Some actively helped Jews, others actively worked against them, and the great majority stayed aloof from either these two options.[107] As also stated by the Jewish underground courier Feigele Peltel (a.k.a.

Vladka): "There is no doubt that more Jews would have been saved if there had been more Poles who were men of heart and conscience."[108]

All the same, what is sometimes overlooked, when discussing aid to Jews, is that there was no compelling pressure from the society at large, or the country's secret political leadership in the form of the Delegate's Office, or the church leadership, to urge people to do their best to save Jews; to persons to whom they were not necessarily obligated due to close familial relationships. At the same time, the repeated German warnings of the death penalty awaiting those Poles caught sheltering Jews, added to the fears of the German rule by terror prevailing in the country, and this undoubtedly inhibited many from getting involved.

However, as also pointed out by Jan T. Gross and Michael Steinlauf, the low societal approval of rescuing Jews cannot be explained solely on the basis of fear of German reprisal: that such reasoning is a bit misleading.[109] As Steinlauf points out, "what limited Polish aid to the Jews was not just fear of the death penalty. In occupied Poland, death was mandated for a host of transgressions great and small, and was sometimes merely a result of being on the street at the wrong time. Nor did the fear of death keep hundreds of thousands of Poles from joining the underground."[110] On the other hand, one must not forget that hiding Jews was more dangerous than, for instance, distributing underground literature. Also, in light of the popular attitudes about Jews, someone hiding a Jew could be less certain of his or her neighbor's reaction than learning of someone distributing an underground paper.[111] Having a Jew in one's home, with the danger of disclosure day in and day out, was psychologically far more frightening and distressing than, for example, illegally selling bread rolls on the street.[112] It may, therefore, have been wiser for rank and file Poles to stay clear of any additional potential harm to their person, and avoid helping Jews – the chief targets of the Germans. But, that does not excuse the many others who either took part in denouncing Jews to the authorities, and participated in the hunt and killing of Jews. At the same time, thousands of others, each one separately, decided to lend a helping hand to Jews, in spite of the risks to themselves, and acted thus for the simple belief that every living being, whether liked or not, had a fundamental right to life, and they wished to be agents in making that possible, when called upon to act.[113]

In 1988, in an international conference attended by Polish historians, Israel Gutman, himself a survivor of the Warsaw ghetto uprising, stated: "There is no moral imperative which demands that a normal mortal should risk his life and that of his family to save his neighbor. Are we capable of imagining the agony of fear of an individual, a family, which selflessly and voluntarily, only due to an inner human impulse, brings into their home someone threatened with death? Are we capable of understanding the pressure of those fears?" Therefore, "such willingness to sacrifice could have been only a marginal phenomenon."[114] A divergent view was stated by Maria Kann, recognized as a Righteous by Yad Vashem, in her November 1943 brochure, "Before the Eyes of the World," where she asked: "Cannot Poland do more than what it is currently doing?"[115]

To summarize, one must be careful before running to conclusions on the behavior of all or most Poles toward Jews during the German occupation. Antisemitism there sure was plenty; also, much blackmail and betrayals; and plenty of personal participation in the murder of Jews, especially in outlying villages. But, there were also many stories of self-sacrificing help to Jews; stories of personal courage by Poles that surpass anything in comparison with rescue stories that have come to light in other German-occupied countries. As shocking and incomprehensible as are the murder of innocent Jews by local non-Jews, even without German prompting, one cannot but be moved and spiritually uplifted by the stories of other persons who stood fast on the high moral ground, in their determination to save Jewish lives, in spite of the inestimable risks to themselves. To this inspiring epic, we turn in the next chapter.

CHAPTER 6

Rescuers of Jews

In this chapter, we turn to the various forms of help to Jews by Polish rescuers – persons who Ringelblum terms "idealists," for they "help Jews very devotedly at the risk of their lives."[1] These "idealists," in Ringelblum's words, "will forever remain engraved in our memories, the names of heroes who saved thousands of human beings from destruction in the fight against the greatest enemy of the human race."[2] Ringelblum then points out that there "there are thousands of idealists like these in Warsaw and in the whole country, whether among the educated or working class [but rarely, in his mistaken opinion, among the middle class], who help Jews most devotedly at the risk of their lives."[3]

In this regard, one must keep in mind that, not only in Poland but throughout German-occupied Europe, the initiative for going into hiding came mostly from the Jewish side; that help was rarely offered unless it was asked for.[4] Such as in the case of Chaya-Helena Elbojm-Dorembus, who smuggled herself and her family out of the Warsaw ghetto and lived for a time disguised as a Pole. She first approached a person she had known in the past. She wrote: "When I walked into the small shack... Stach crossed himself as if he were seeing a ghost. His wife dropped a spoon she had been drying. "Jesus-Mary, you look terrible, Madam Helena!" Chaya: "Can I spend the night with you?" Stach: "What do you mean, spend the night? And what'll you do tomorrow, Madam Helena? And where's your husband, your mother, Hilda? The whole family?" Chaya: "Listen to me, Pan [Mister] Stach. I'm carrying around a death sentence with me, but I've no right to impose it on others. Tomorrow I'll leave for one of the villages, maybe I'll find work there. My husband's still in the ghetto. My mother, my husband's mother, my daughter – they're no longer alive." Stach buried his face in his hands and cried. "You're staying with us," he said after regaining his self-composure. "And I'll take your husband in with us too. We are as dust at your feet, and if death strikes at you, let the devil take us too. Yes, I put my trust in the good Lord to protect us."[5]

But there were also stories where help was first offered by the rescuer. Such as the good luck that befell Sonia Orbach, as she related. "As we were sitting in the woods contemplating what to do next, a peasant appeared... He approached us and said: 'I know your family and would like to help you. If you find a place for yourself in the deep woods I will be happy to bring you food.'... He came back without the police, and a great friendship started between us. What can I tell you?... As they used to say [in Poland], if that man was still alive I would wash his feet and drink the dirty water."[6]

Generally speaking, people who knew Jews from before the war were more likely to help them than if the Jew on the run was a total stranger. According to one account, perhaps over 75% of rescue stories are of persons who were saved by someone whom they personally knew from either before the war or during the initial phase of the occupation, or by members of their respective families who knew each other."[7]

What's also important to underline—most rescue acts were not group initiated (with the major exception of Żegota, discussed in the next chapter), but individually launched with perhaps the collusion of very few others, sworn to secrecy. Rescuers, even those associated with the underground, mostly kept their aid to Jews to themselves and withheld this additional activity from their underground confederates unless absolutely necessary.[8]

Then, there are also stories of help in return for pay; small or large sums.[9] Such as Feliks Ząnkiewicz, a poor farmer near the village of Wisnicz Nowy, Bochnia region, who sheltered a young Jewish girl for two years, and some other Jews for shorter periods. The parents of the girl paid him for this. In the village of Mogiła near Kraków, Adam Kowalski for two years sheltered as many as ten members of the Lieberman family in return for pay. All ten survived. Perhaps some of these payments were for the additional upkeep of the hidden persons, and not necessarily profitable rewards to the rescuers for their magnanimity.[10]

Contrasting these active rescuers, one must also mention the passive ones, who themselves did not save but provided information and advice that aided Jews to better their escape plans. Such as some of the Polish railroad workers, who were the first to warn Jews about the destination of the trains they serviced, going to Treblinka, and what really awaited them there.[11] Also to keep in mind – it was more difficult to hide Jewish people in the countryside than in towns and cities, because in villages people usually know one another, and any unusual thing – such as large purchase of food by a villager – could raise suspicions and give the rescuer away by an informer to the Polish police or directly to the Germans.[12] Yet, many rescue stories that came to light also occurred in villages; usually in houses that were a bit isolated and at the far ends of the village.

At times, rescuers moved hiders from one place to another for their own safety, and this involved much careful planning to avoid detection. Such as in the story of Leon Eitel, who beginning January 1943, arranged for Halina Wolman, who had fled from the Warsaw ghetto, a series of haphazard comings and goings from one place to another, after staying the first two nights with Leon's parents. Eitel's second wife was related to Halina's husband, who in the meantime remained behind in the ghetto. Halina then contacted Antonina Gacz, who moved her and her mother to Antonina's mother, until Antonina's brother came to live there, and Halina and her mother had to move elsewhere, under false identities. Watching the ghetto flames shoot up, in April 1943, the apartment landlady exclaimed: "Finally we are rid of the Jews." Then, suddenly two police agents raided that home, stole all the belongings of the two Jewish women, and warned them to quit the apartment.

Halina and her mother then headed to Leon Eitel's hat shop. He took Halina's mother to Natalia Młynarczyk for temporary shelter, while Halina moved in with Juliana Nowak, a cleaning lady in Mrs. Eitel's home, as well as a worker in Eitel's store. In the meantime, Halina's husband made good his escape from the ghetto, with his brother, and they passed two nights at the home of Natalia Młynarczyk. Then, Eitel took both men to his parents' home, and from there to Juliana Nowak's place, whose home was in the back of Eitel's store. Back at Antonina Gacz's home, in May 1943, she readmitted Halina, her husband and brother-in-law. As for Halina's mother, Leon Eitel found for her a place with Maria Głębicka.[13]

In this story, it is at times hard to follow all the twists and turns that started with the lone rescue of Halina Wolman whose husband was related to the rescuer's wife, and this then evolved into a multiplicity of other rescue acts – to four more Jews aided in bits of time by altogether eight non-Jewish rescuers who knew of their wards' true identity. Not all stories are of alike nature, of constant comings and goings, but most Jews hiding in the sprawling city of Warsaw were forced to move from one place to another several times, as circumstances dictated, and also to be a step ahead of those who wished them harm.

The rescuers in the preceding story were honored by the Yad Vashem Holocaust Memorial, in Jerusalem, as Righteous Among the Nations – a traditional Jewish title originally mentioned in the Talmud. Here, it is applied to non-Jews who risked their life in their effort to save Jews during the Holocaust. All further stories mentioned in this chapter were certified by Yad Vashem, and the rescuers honored under the Righteous program.

(a) Knew Each Other From Before

As earlier alluded, most rescue stories that have come to light are of persons who knew each other from before the war years, or during the early ghetto period. Presently, as some Jews made attempts to flee the ghettos, they either, in most cases, secretly approached their former acquaintances and asked for assistance, or these non-Jewish acquaintances volunteered to assist those they already knew, and took the initial steps in that direction. In many cases, when the rescuer agreed to admit a pre-war Jewish acquaintance, others not known to the rescuer, who hitched along with the known person, were also admitted. The common form of assistance was finding a hiding place for the fugitive person or persons. In large cities, it may have been an uninhabited back room, or a room hidden from view with a fake partition, or inside a cupboard, or again, in the attic or far corner of the basement. In outlying areas and villages, the most common hiding places were in newly dugout pits under the dwellings of the rescuers, or existing ones that served as storage, and were now a bit enlarged. Also, in pits or haylofts of barns and pigsties. Only very late at night could the hiders be allowed to exit these stifling conditions, sometimes referred as "tombs" and step out, unseen, for a whiff of fresh air. Fear of betrayal, capture and immediate death was a daily nightmare to be faced and overcome, and rescuers had to keep a watchful eye from fellow kinsfolk as well. The following case stories will illustrate these points further.

After the breakout from the Sobibór death camp, on October 14, 1943, Esther Terner made her way to Stefan Marcyniuk's farm, in Janów, near Chełm, whom her family knew from before the war. As she first sneaked into the Marcyniuk farm, she discovered her brother, long thought dead, already in hiding. The next morning, Stefan Marcyniuk told her: "If God has sent you here I will not send you away and whatever happens will happen." The Marcyniuk children were sworn into secrecy.[14] In Czernelica, a small town near Horodenka, (today, in Ukraine), Ignacy Ustjanowsky and the Shikler family entertained friendly relations before the war years. "He used to drop in almost every day," Mordechai Shikler recalls. "He was like part of the household." Escaping from the Janowska camp in Lwów, Shikler was taken in by Ustjanowski and wife Bronisława (and three children) who hid him and two other fugitive Jews in the pigsty. After the war, Ukrainian partisans exacted revenge on this Pole who dared rescue so many Jews. They looted his home, then put it to the torch. The Ustjanowskis luckily escaped and relocated to a different region of Poland.[15]

In the Łomża region, in northeast Poland, Stanisław Gosk first

sheltered his pre-war acquaintance, Yitzhak Shumowitz, and four companions, in an abandoned windmill, near the town of Modzele. Then,
Yitzhak's group was moved to an underground shaft in Gosk's pigsty. In
August 1944, as the front approached and the Germans occupied Gosk's
home, Shumowitz's group fled into the fields, only to be accosted by a
group of local residents who threatened them. "What? There are still Jews
left," one of them exclaimed? But suddenly, Russian soldiers appeared in
sight, and the would-be aggressors fled.[16]

Jan Mikulski, a forester in the Biłgoraj region of southeastern Poland,
invited Benzion Rosenbaum, a prewar timber business acquaintance, for
occasional meals and overnight lodgings, including Ronsebaum's fellow
fleeing forest Jews, not known to Mikulski. During the 1942-1943 winter, some were sheltered in a pit of the pigsty. In the story of Józef Fink, he
was a former customer of Pinhas Rafaelowitz's textile store in Sokołów-
Podlaski, near Węgrów. When Pinhas and his family of six persons asked
for help, Mikulski decided to hide them in a hole under the haystack of
a small barn owned by him. There, the six Jewish fugitives stayed for 22
months, cared by the Fink family (wife and two children). In Frampol,
Stanisław Stańczyk invited Samuel Brik and his daughter Hanna (born
1929), known to him from before the war, to hide in his barn. Food was
usually brought by Stanisław's daughter, Klementyna. "She would come,
singing on the way, so as to make us a bit happy. She addressed the horse,
but it was meant for us, since she was afraid she would be observed by
suspicious eavesdropping neighbors." After four months, the fugitive
hiders had to leave as suspicions mounted by neighbors that Stańczyk
was hiding Jews. Fleeing into the forest, Samuel Brik was killed by local
vigilantes. Daughter Hanna survived in the forest.[17]

Returning a favor. Some rescuers saw their sheltering of Jews as
returning a favor from previous days. Before the war, Josef Kleinman
worked in a brick factory, in Nadwórna (today, Nadvirna, Ukraine),
owned by Wawrzyniec Bruniany, and both had become friends. When,
under the Russian occupation during 1939-1941, Bruniany was threatened as a "bourgeois capitalist" with deportation to distant Siberia,
Josef interceded on his behalf and caused the deportation order to be

anulled. In October 1942, under German rule, Bruniany admitted Josef and his cousin for hiding, in a non-functioning brick factory, for 17 months. In another story of repaying a charitable act from before the war, Jan Puchalski guarded the summer cottages in Łosośna forest of the Zandman family, who lived in the city of Grodno. In March 1943, Jan's wife, Anna, admitted the fleeing youthful Alex Zandman, as an act of recompense. As she explained to him, many years ago Alex's mother arranged for Anna to deliver her baby in a hospital, and under a doctor's case, instead of inside her home. "I prayed that one day I could repay that, and here you are, God sent you!" Five more people benefitted from Anna's magnanimity, and were hidden in a hole under the floor of Puchalskis' bedrooms. Two left, and four remained there, sequestered for 17 months.[18]

Saving many people. We continue with stories where unbelievably more than 10 persons were sheltered by a single family, counting children. Wacław and Jadwiga Gołowacz (with 3 children) hid 13 people in the cellar of their home, in the Praga section of Warsaw, with the help of their housemaid, Stanisława Strzelec, who was sworn into secrecy. Chawa Cymerman, one of the hiders, was a prewar acquaintance. Some stayed there from July 1942 to August 1944, when the Russians came in. In Staszów, southeast of Kielce, Maria Szczecinska, a widow with children, knew well the Roman Segal family from before the war. In October 1942, she agreed to shelter the whole Segal family and their friends, totaling 14 persons, in an underground bunker beneath the master bedroom. The hidden persons remained in almost total darkness for an unbelievable long duration of 21 months.[19]

We continue with Franciszek and Tekla Zalwowski and their four sons, who were farmers in a village near Zbaraż, north of Tarnopol. Franciszek admitted his youthful friend Michael Zemora, and his family for hiding, first in the granary loft, where they were surprised to meet another Jewish family, while some others were hidden elsewhere on his property. In all, the Zalwowskis cared for 12 persons in their home and 8 out in the fields.[20]

We follow with stories, primarily where the rescuers took the initiative in inviting their Jewish acquaintances into their homes. In the summer of 1942, Stanisław Krzemienski, a farmer in Jackowka, near Tłumacz, in southeastern Poland, invited his pre-war friend Shlomo Blond to stay in his home. Shlomo's family members moved into an underground hiding place, while Shlomo left for Buczacz. Then after losing two sons to the Germans, Shlomo showed up before Krzemienski, in summer of 1943, and found seven persons in hiding, in three bunkers – one in the garden, another beneath the unfinished part of the house, and the third in the barn hayloft. They all stayed there until liberated in August 1944.[21] In Stryj, south of Lwów, before the war, Yitzhak Nussenblat taught the sons of Rozalia Paszkiewicz in the local high school. In June 1943, Rozalia (her husband was overseas in the Polish army) invited Yitzhak and brother Pinhas to hide with her. When five persons showed up, startled at first, she welcomed them all in, then left for the ghetto to bring along, two small girls. A total of seven persons were now in Rozalia's charge, hidden behind a large wardrobe. One of the hidden women gave birth, and the father had to suffocate the new-born baby to avoid its weeping to disclose the persons in hiding. Altogether the seven hidden people were sheltered for 14 months.[22]

In Sokal, Franciszka Halamajowa (her husband having left for Canada) and her grownup daughter, Helena, sheltered 13 persons in the pigsty loft next to her home, prompted on a prewar acquaintance with Moshe Maltz, one of the hiders. One of the hidden women died from typhus after a painful three-month illness, and her body was secretly buried beside a tree. On July 19, 1944, when Sokal was liberated, the 12 hidden Jews were surprised to learn that, unbeknownst to them, Halamajowa had hidden three more Jews in her home cellar. A further surprise was to find a German soldier who had deserted, hidden in the attic. In all, the two Halamajowa women had saved 16 Jewish persons (one of whom died in hiding) and one deserting German soldier.[23]

Stanisław Jacków's story is even more amazing. He and Max Saginur were friends going back to high school years, in Stanisławów (today, renamed Ivano Frankivsk, in Ukraine). On January 31, 1943, Stanisław began sheltering Max and his family, and eventually extending his hosting so that 31 persons were hiding in a specially constructed bunker under the kitchen. Jacków kidded of running "the biggest underground hotel in Stanisławów." After liberation he told Saginur; "if they caught me saving only you, they would kill me. I might as well be killed for thirty-two as for one."[24] In Dębica, medical doctor Aleksander Mikołajków and wife Leokadia, and their two sons, sheltered the 13 Chaskiel Reich family members, his former patients, in his home for two long years, with one woman dying while in hiding. When the Russians arrived in August 1944, Dr. Mikołajków was hit by a stray shell shrapnel shell and died.[25] Finally, in one more of many unbelievable stories, Dr. Jan Żabiński, a famous zoologist, and in charge of the Warsaw zoo, together with wife Antonina, sheltered Jews fleeing from the ghetto for shorter or longer stays, in cages previously emptied of their animals during the German bombing of September 1939. Hundreds passed through Żabiński's zoo. "The largest group that ever stayed simultaneously included 50 persons," Żabiński noted, other than those few who stayed there permanently, for lack of other options.[26]

Opposition by some of the rescuer family. Not always, did all members of the rescuer family, or close friends who were privy to the story, agree with the decision of one family member to shelter fugitive Jews; mostly, for fear that in case of detection, all others involved in the hiding action would suffer retribution by the Germans. Or, some, who agreed at the start, changed their mind during the hiding period. Or, again, some in the family were complicit in acts against Jews on the run.

In late 1942, Władysław Kołodziejek, a pre-war business acquaintance of the Zissman family, admitted for hiding the two sisters Sima and Nechama (ages 29 and 25), who had fled the Żelechów ghetto, near Warsaw, in late 1942, and remained hidden in Kołodziejek's home for 22 months. Danger threatened when Kołodziejek's son-in-law brought home a blood-stained jacket from a recently murdered Jew and asked Sima and Nechama (not suspecting their Jewish origin) to mend the bullet marked jacket. These increasing dangers even made Władysław's wife insist that the women be sent off in the interest of their own family's safety, but Władysław remained adamant that the two women stay on.

In another story, when in September 1942, six members of the Abraham Yom-Tov family escaped from the Węgrów ghetto (east of Warsaw), and arrived at the home of Jan Joniuk, a farmer in the village of Grochów, per his invitation, his wife suggested to inject poison in their food, so as to be rid of them. Jan's daughter, Leokadia, from his previous marriage, reacted that in that case she would denounce her step-mother as the person who had initiated the rescue operation. The six hidden persons remained there for a full two years.[27]

In Łuck (today in Ukraine), starting August 8, 1942, lung disease specialist, Dr. Wiktoria Struszinska sheltered her Jewish pediatrician friend, Dr. Tatiana Goldstein, in a bunker underneath the woodfire storeroom; then inside the potato storeroom under their home. More were later added for a total five persons. When in September 1943, Struszinska's husband, Zygmunt, was arrested and shot for his underground participation, Boris, her late husband's colleague in the Polish underground, a man who had previously himself helped Jews in distress, now urged Wiktoria to poison the food prepared for the five persons in the interest of her and her two children's self-preservation. "I was shocked to hear this from a man who himself was active on behalf of Jews. I did not listen to him and did not poison the persons who were given to my care and mercy. I continued in efforts to help all." To ease the burden on Struszinka, two persons left, and with her help, were hidden by her relatives in another city. The remaining three persons stayed on until liberated, on February 2, 1944.[28]

Rescuers also faced threats from local antisemitic elements. Adam and Stanisława Suchodolski and children Jadwiga and Stanisław, in the village of Krzynowłoga Wielka, north of Warsaw, in April 1943, sheltered Michal Schaft, whom they knew from before, for two years. On January 15, 1945, a group of still-active partisans stormed into the Suchodolski home and asked to hand Michal over. Young Stanisław held them off, long enough to allow Michal to jump out from the back door. The attackers gave chase but failed to catch up with him. In revenge, they ransacked the Suchodolski home. Late, at night, Michal came back. Soon thereafter, Michael and Jadwiga married and left, and eventually settled in Israel.[29]

(b) Met During the War Years

In the previous section, we spoke of rescuers who saved people, some of whom were known to the rescuers from pre-war times. Presently, we tell stories of rescuers who saved Jews that they had met only recently, during the times of the German occupation.

In March 1943, Tadeusz Soroka, who worked for the railways, and occasionally traded food for clothes, while meeting with Aron Dereczynski, on his work site outside of the Grodno ghetto, volunteered to help him flee to Vilna-Vilnius, on the eve of the final liquidation of the Grodno ghetto. Together with Lisa Nussbaum, and her brother Robert Raczki, the three left the ghetto and Soroka led them to the railway station, and the four jumped aboard a German ammunition train and laid down unseen on the roof, for a 180-kilometer ride to Vilna. After jumping off at a certain spot, Soroka placed them astride a group of Jews returning to the ghetto from a work shift. Soroka made four such journeys, saving a total of 9 lives.[30]

Like many other Poles, Andrzej Kostrz was evicted from the Baltic sea shore town of Gdynia by the Germans, when that town was annexed to Germany. Resettled in Kraków, in touch with some ghetto Jews, Kostrz sheltered them in his Kraków home for short stays. He then accompanied individual Jews to the Slovakian border to the south, from where they continued on their own into Hungary, where conditions for Jews were relatively safe until March 1944. He eventually joined one of these groups, and arrived with them in Budapest. It is estimated that, all told, Kostrz, with some help by others, aided some 100 Jews.[31]

Romance between rescuer and rescued also served as backdrop in the following story. In mid-1940, Jerzy Bielecki was imprisoned in Auschwitz as a political prisoner. In August 1943, he worked repairing agricultural equipment in the subcamp of Babice, where he met Cyla Stawiska Cebulska, a Jewish woman that with other workers were repairing flour bags, and the two fell in love. This led Bielecki to the decision to attempt escaping with her. With the help of a fellow prisoner, Bielecki was able to get an SS uniform, a gun holster and an SS staff sergeant insignia of *Rotterführer*. Jerzy and Cyla escaped on July 21, 1944, as they made their way past the guard at the tower post, with Bielecki in his SS uniform explaining he was taking her to the Gestapo office in the main camp for interrogation. They eventually made their way to Jerzy's uncle, in the village of Muniakowice, and from there to other locations.[32] All these aforementioned rescuers, as well as those that follow, were honored by Yad Vashem as Righteous Among the Nations.

(c) Strangers to Each Other

There were also rescuers that hid people not known beforehand, as the two sides met accidentally when the rescuers were approached by a fleeing Jew seeking help. In September 1943, Szymon Calka, a farmer in a village outside of Parysów, answered a knock on the door, and there stood before him Josef Czarny, one of the few lucky persons to successfully make their escape from the Treblinka extermination camp, during the revolt there. After being fed by Helena, the man's wife, Calka disclosed to Czarny that he was helping a group of Jews in the vicinity, whom Czany later met. The fugitive Jews stayed on Calka's farm for many months; then, they fled to a nearby forest to await liberation from there.[33]

In Wielopole village, near Rybnik, as Stefania Zimon mounted the ladder into the family barn, she encountered three Jewish fugitives hidden in the hay. A day earlier, on January 18, 1945, Michael Goldman, Hanan Ansbacher and Eli Herman, had slipped away unnoticed from the Auschwitz death march, as they passed Wielopole, and quickly mounted the attic of a barn and buried themselves in the hay. Presently, to their surprise, the youngish Stefania placed an urn and a loaf of bread, and left. She returned that afternoon, and continued feeding the three for a whole week – twice a day. The three men were then invited into the Zimon home, where they continued to be sheltered by Stefania's parents, Konrad and Regina Zimon, until the arrival of the Russians, toward the end of January.[34]

On May 1, 1943, Benjamin and wife Zlata Markowitz jumped a train taking them from the Łuków ghetto to the Treblinka death camp.

During the jump, Zlata was injured from shots fired by Ukrainian guards on the train, with a bullet in her thigh, while Benjamin landed safely at the foot of the railway embankment. After local inhabitants had robbed them, Stanisław Nowosielski, from the village of Sołdy, between Łuków and Siedlce, approached the two fugitives, and in Benjamin's words, "carried my wife on his back to an isolated spot. He gave us a bottle with milk and an Easter cake. For the following three weeks, he visited us every night, bringing along potatoes, cooked in milk, and a loaf of bread." After three weeks, this total stranger took the two in the evening to his farm, where he hid them for 15 months in the hay on top of the stable, until liberated by the Russians in July 1944.[35] In July 1944, Abraham Szajner and Arieh Lustgarten fled from the Hermann Goering arms factory in Starachowice, and wandered aimlessly in the nearby forest. Władysław Jeziorski, in a stroll in a nearby forest, saw from a distance the two Jews lying on the ground. He shouted at them: "Jews! Friends! Take care! The Germans are only half a kilometer from the forest. When it gets dark, come to us in the first house in this direction [and he pointed out the way] and you can sleep in the granary." That evening, Szajner and Lustgarten dragged themselves over to the Jeziorski home, in the village of Wierzbnik, where the man's parents, Władysław and Anna Jeziorski hid them in the granary until liberation time.[36]

We continue with other stories of help by total strangers. On a snowy day in late 1942, Stefania Job, while walking on a side road leading from Dębica to Tarnów, noticed a girl struggling in the deep snow, with a man walking ahead of her. Walking up to the girl and seeing her condition, and her swollen legs, Stefania said: "Don't be afraid. I know you are Jewish, but I won't harm you... Let's walk together." Then, walking up to the man ahead of the girl, she learned that he was her father, Berl Szturm. Stefania rushed home to alert her father, Józef Job. 12-year-old Helen Szturm related: "He picked me up and carried me to his home, in the village of Lipiny." His wife, Wiktoria, her two brothers and her sister, removed Helen's ice-filled boots. Bringing her father along, the Job family then decided that the two would remain with them for an indefinite period, and were sheltered in the attic of a next-door half-finished new home until the area's liberation, staying there, even after Józef Job left, when he was called up for labor in Germany.[37]

Fleeing from the Sosnowiec ghetto, in August 1943, 19-year old Hanna Piller, alighted from the train in Katowice. Calling at the first address given her by friends back in Sosnowiec, it turned out they were not home. Calling upon the second address, she was invited to join them for lunch, then was shown the door and told to leave immediately or else she would be turned over to the authorities. Hannah had one final address to turn to. She stopped a woman on the street, pushing a stroller with a baby, and asked her for instructions to reach that particular street. After Hannah admitted she was Jewish, the woman urged Hannah to try her luck with someone else, the Jadwiga Kieloch family, living in a country house outside the city. Arriving there, she was greeted by one of the family girls. "I told her I am on the run and need a place to hide, and that my only sin is being Jewish." After the girl's mother, Jadwiga Kieloch, arrived, the whole family decided to shelter Hannah for an indefinite period, and keep this a secret from everyone, even their close relatives. She stayed there until the area's liberation in January 1945.[38]

Finally, in beleaguered Warsaw, after the suppression of the Polish rising, on October 3, 1944, and the ghost city under tight German control, Władysław Kowalski hid a group of 49 Jews in the underground caverns of one of the destroyed buildings, for three months, with hardly any food left to feed such a large group, but they miraculously survived. After the war, Kowalski discounted his role in this rescue operation. He stated: "I did nothing special and I don't consider myself a hero. I only fulfilled my human obligation towards the persecuted and suffering ones... I sought no compensation for what I did... In summary, I should like to re-emphasize that all I did was to help 49 Jews survive the Holocaust. That's all."[39]

Help by some, harm by others. In those days, it goes without saying that not everyone could be trusted. Some helped; others saw a golden opportunity to either fleece the Jews of whatever they had on them, or report them to the authorities in return for a paltry reward, while others decided to shut their eyes and turn the other way. Jan Mirek from

Jordanów, south of Kraków, helped the Isaac and Hanna Windenstreich family that he met in the forest, on September 26, 1942, with food and other provisions, after they had fled from a German killing raid of Jews in Naprawa village. A while later, a group of Poles fell upon the Windenstreich family, stripping them of all their valuables in return for the promise of not betraying them to the authorities. Another farmer, known to the Windenstreichs promised to help, but then alerted the Germans. The Windenstreichs escaped under a hail of bullets by the Germans, losing some friends who had come along with them. The survivors then sought out again Mirek, and he hid them in the attic. However, a few days later, under the pressure of his wife (terror stricken for herself and the children), he took them to an age-old abandoned shack deep in the forest, unknown to the villagers. There he cared for them throughout the winter of 1942-43. He then moved them to another location, and provided them with nourishment. In the words of one of the survivors: "He would crawl over to us at night carrying food, and picking his steps carefully through difficult terrain; he did all this out of compassion."[40]

In autumn 1942, Jan Charuk, of the village Lechówka in the Chełm region, stepped out to fetch hay for his animals, when he discovered a group of six fleeing Jews hiding in the hay – the family of Esther Pechter. They related that while in the forest with other Jews, they had been accosted by local inhabitants, armed with axes, about to strip the corpses of the Jews slain by the Germans, but had not harmed this family. Charuk hid them on his farm's silo; then in the pigsty. One day, a group of antisemitic partisans raided his home, after he had sent his Jewish wards in the forest for a temporary stay. Charuk: "They beat me with great cruelty... As they swung the butt of their rifles on me, they shouted, 'turn us over the Jews.'" Charuk stood his ground and they finally left. The six Jews returned to Charuk's pigsty, where they stayed until the area's liberation.[41]

The final story in this section takes us to 26-year-old Leonard Gliński, a technical draughtsman in the firm of Stanisław Pacha's road construction company, who in September 1943, dropped over at Pacha's home, in Warsaw, to secretly listen to the BBC news on Pacha's wireless set. While there, he could not avoid overhearing Mrs. Pacha tell her husband that they ought to take the Jewish Alina Potok, who had been referred to them, out somewhere, supposedly to meet her cousin, then dump her on the street and immediately notify the Germans of her whereabouts. Finding the frightened 13-year-old girl hidden in a side room, Gliński told her, as related by her, "if the Pachas told me that they would take me to my cousin, I should refuse to go." He then told the Pachas to keep the girl for several more days until he found a way to help her. As a member in the Polish underground, Gliński obtained a false identity card for Alina, a baptismal certificate (stating she was a Roman Catholic), and a General Education Secondary School Certificate. That solved Alina's immediate problem, but Gliński felt it best to have Alina registered on the Labor List for domestic work in Germany. Again, utilizing his underground contacts, Gliński saw the girl off at the train station, then received letters from her, from Vienna where she was doing domestic work with a family who treated her well, not aware, of course, of her true identity, and she survived.[42]

(d) Clergy Assistance

In spite of Cardinal August Hlond's 1936 pastoral anti-Jewish tirade,[43] a number of war-time memoirists report that when they disclosed during church confessions their help to Jews – in most but not in all cases – the response they received was that they were doing a good and noble thing.[44] We shall, presently, recite a few stories of aid to Jews by lower-level clergy; men and women, honored as Righteous by Yad Vashem.

Inside the Warsaw ghetto, Father Marceli Godlewski, known for his prewar antisemitic diatribes, headed the All Saints Church for converted Catholic Jews, who lived in a special section of the ghetto, and numbering up to 1,500 persons. Godlewski, consequently, arranged hiding places for the mostly converted Jews with former parishioners on the Aryan side.[45] He also reportedly provided false baptismal certificates to Jews wishing to flee to the non-Jewish side of the city and he aided Irena Sendlerowa (later in this chapter) in smuggling children out of the ghetto. However, when the deportations commenced, the SS took no notice of the cross which protected the street blocks where the converts lived, and all inhabitants of the parish blocks were deported to Treblinka extermination camp. When Godlewski died in December 1945, it is not known whether his witnessing of the Holocaust caused a reversal of his pre-war strong theological anti-Jewish views.[46]

In the case of Father Stanisław Falkowski, a vicar in the village of Piekuty Nowe, southwest of Białystok – one evening in September 1942, a teenage Jewish fugitive boy approached him for help. Joseph Kutrzeba had escaped from a deportation train heading from Wołomin and Zambrów to Treblinka, and had been roaming the countryside from place to place until he stumbled onto Father Perkowski who, upon discovering the lad's true origin, referred him to Father Falkowski. That priest gave him a thorough washing and delousing and treated his bodily boils. He then removed him to a friendly Polish farmer (who was not told of Joseph's Jewish identity). After about a year, Father Falkowski arranged for Joseph a set of false identity papers with which he was able to register for labor in Germany under his assumed non-Jewish identity.[47]

Father Michała Kubacki, in Warsaw, helped young Halina Engelhard, who before she jumped from a deportation train from the Warsaw ghetto, was told by her mother (who stayed on the train): "Go to Father Kubacki, at the Basilica church. Take tramway number 5 and ride to the last stop. He will surely help you. Go and believe in your luck." Reaching the church, Kubacki listened to Halina's story, and provided her with a false birth and baptismal certificate, and concocted a story that she was a childhood acquaintance of his, and presently a refugee from Płock. She was treated warmly by the house governess (a nun, sworn into secrecy), and Kubacki began teaching her some basic Catholic prayers and customs, and she was given various assignments. Halina was then referred to a certain Sister Bernarda, at the Saint Magdalena convent, where she saw a long line of persons waiting to be received, many of them with Jewish-looking faces. Sister Bernarda then sent Halina to a certain convent, where she shared a room with two other women. A few days later, Sister Bernarda came to visit. "How are you, my daughter, do you feel well here? … Remember, my girl, that you are Jewish. Be proud of it. The Jews gave the world great persons; our Lord Jesus, he too was Jewish. When the war is over, go to Palestine, live and work there. Only there will you be really happy." Halina then learned that Bernarda was sought by the Gestapo for her help to Jews, and had to live underground.[48]

We follow with the unusually remarkable story of Sister Dolorosa (Genowefa Czubak) of the Order of St. Ignacy de Loyola, in Prużana, northeastern Poland (today, Pruzhany in Belarus). When she took ill, a nun was sent to the ghetto to fetch the highly reputed Dr. Olga Goldfein, with German permission. Dr. Goldfein treated Sister Dolarosa's illness, then returned to the ghetto. On January 28, 1943, during a German killing raid on the ghetto's diminishing Jews, Dr. Goldfein fled and was admitted by Sister Dolorosa, given a nun's habit, and a new identity card in the name of another Sister (Helena), and both she and Sister Dolorosa walked out of the convent on a life of wandering nuns, and supporting themselves with alms from kindhearted people. Reaching Sister Dolorosa's hometown of Olszyny, Goldfein remained sheltered by Sister Dolorosa's family for a full 15 months.[49]

Finally, Matylda Getter was the Mother Superior of the Order of the Franciscan Sisters of the Mary Family, that operated homes for the crippled, the epileptic, handicapped children, and unwed mothers. During the Nazi occupation, she allowed an untold number of Jewish children smuggled out of the ghetto to be sheltered in the Order's institutions. Margareta Frydman and her sister were moved to the Order's home in Płudy, 12 kilometers east of Warsaw. Frydman stayed in that convent until May 1945, when her father came from Budapest and her mother from Germany to fetch her. Sister Louisa remembers: "The Jewish children were in my charge. There were about 20 – a group of older girls, between 10 and 15… There were about 50 Jews in hiding at the Płudy orphanage; adults and children."[50]

(e) Saving the Children

We need constantly to remind ourselves that the Germans during the Nazi period, heirs to a civilizing culture, targeted Jewish children for extermination, for no other reason than simply for being born, and the Nazis were determined to eradicate every living Jewish soul. Parents wishing to save their children from death had only a few choices from which to choose. Other than turn them over to Catholic religious homes (convents and orphanages), that offered a better chance for the child's survival, but also facing the risk of the children's conversion to another religion, the best other option was to hand them over into private non-Jewish hands, under various arrangements, and hope to reconnect with them, if the parents survived. If not, at least, have the children survive by being cared by the non-Jewish host families. We begin with nursemaids who saved the little ones they had once helped raise before the Nazi avalanche that burst upon the Jews in Poland.

Nursemaids. Gertruda Babilińska, a nursemaid in the Stolowicki household, fled from Warsaw to Vilna (today, Vilnius) in late 1939 together with her matron, Lidia Stolowicka and her 4-year-old son Michael. Lidia's husband was away in France, and communications with him proved impossible. In April 1941, gravely ill, Lidia made Babilińska swear that she would eventually take Michael to safety in Jewish Palestine. After the death of her mistress, in July 1941, Gertruda passed the child off as her son. To support herself, she helped local people draft petitions to the occupation authorities in the German language which she, as a native of the mostly German-speaking Danzig (today, Gdańsk), was proficient. In exchange, she received eggs, milk products and fowl as payment. After the war, keeping her vow, she bid farewell to her family and set out with the child for then Palestine.[51]

In Piotrków Trybunalski, in 1942, Aniela Krzysztonek fetched the 12-year-old Hanna Fiszgrund from the ghetto where her parents were forced to stay, and both left for Kraków, where they huddled in a basement dwelling. When neighbors began to gossip about the strange looking child, Aniela took Hanna on a train ride to Warsaw, to look up some persons for their help. Alighting from the train, they were arrested and taken to a Polish police station. Hanna: "We underwent a difficult interrogation, as they forced us to admit that we were Jewish. After difficult tortures which I could not support, I admitted I was Jewish, but that Aniela was Polish. The interrogator left the room, and a Polish police officer entered and said to me: 'I have a daughter your age, and a pity for your life, for you face a certain death.'" He allowed them to escape; a rarity for a policeman in those days. Eventually, Hanna was admitted in the Nasz Dom (Our Home) orphanage, headed by Maryna Falska, who kept Hanna's Jewishness a secret from others. There, she stayed until the war's end.[52]

Some more children stories. In autumn 1942, Apolonia and Aleksander Oldak, in the village of Dzierzkowice, not far from Kraśnik-Lubelskie (southeast of Lublin), took in a baby girl found abandoned by the villagers after they returned from a hunt of Jews in the nearby woods. The villagers refused to provide Apolonia with milk for the 8-month-old baby. Once, a group of men invaded the Oldak home and demanded to turn the child over to be killed. Husband Aleksander pulled out a gun and ordered them to leave. Years after the war, after Aleksander died, Apolonia decided to take the child with her to Israel to be reunited with her relatives, with whom Leokadia had been corresponding for some time.[53]

In the Częstochowa ghetto, in the summer of 1942, one-year-old Lilian Brenner was smuggled out of the ghetto in a bag, and turned over to a tailor named Nowokowski, who then invited his married daughter, Irena Ogniewska-Jorasz, living in Stalowa Wola, some 250 kilometers east of Częstochowa, to take the little girl. Returning to her hometown with the little girl, Irena and her husband Bogdan concocted a story that Lilian was the product of an illicit affair between Bogdan and another woman. This ruse worked only for a while. As suspicions mounted, the couple moved to a different town, eventually settling in Częstochowa, near Irena's father.[54]

In September 1941, after moving into the Vilna ghetto, Rachela Kryski was able to turn over Sarah, her 21-month-old daughter to

Wiktoria Rodziewicz. Returning to her village, Wiktoria introduced Sarah as Irena, and explained her sudden presence as the product of a prewar out-of-wedlock affair by Wiktoria. To support herself, Wiktoria sewed aprons, prepared hamburgers and sold them on market days. In 1945, mother (after surviving several concentration camps) and daughter were reunited after a 3-year lapse.[55] As for Genowefa Pająk, married and mother of three children, in Będzin, she agreed to shelter Tamar Cygler, a young girl from the ghetto. Tamar, now known as Bogumila, or affectionally Bogusia, shared the life and travails of her benefactress. As in the previous story, here too Genowefa fabricated an out-of-wedlock story, with a man who lived in a village with her old aunt and, according to the story, her husband had not known of it. Now her aunt having died, she was forced to take the child with her and her husband finally agreed to adopt the child. Thus, the child survived.[56]

In another story, also originating in Będzin, in August 1943, when Dora Rembiszewski learned that two stranger women were prepared to save her 5-year-old daughter, Mira, the young child was thrown over a fence. Maria Dyrda, one of the two women, took the child with her, bleached her hair and eyebrows to look like the other children, taught her the Catholic prayers and gave her a cross to wear and on Sundays they took her to church. The Dyrda children two children, aged 12 and 14, were told to treat her as their own sister. Maria's husband Pawel was himself hiding from the Gestapo, after someone informed that he was listening to a foreign radio broadcast. To her neighbors, Maria explained that Mira, now Marysia, was her sister's child. Both Mira's parents survived, and were reunited with their daughter after the war.[57]

Not always did all family members agree to admit Jewish children in their home, mainly due to fear of detection. In early 1943, in the Warsaw ghetto, Hanna, the aunt of the three Gutgold brothers, David, Shalom and Jacob, tried to figure out a way to save the young boys. Their father had left for Russia and their mother died before the war. The aunt decided to look up the family's pre-war private chauffer, living outside the ghetto. At the chauffeur's home, she learned that the man had been arrested on a smuggling charge and shot. Noticing Hannah's dejected look, a neighbor asked if he could help. When told of Hanna's predicament, this stranger offered to shelter Hanna's three nephews. His name – Aleksander Roslan. The Roslans had two children of their own. The boys' aunt returned to the ghetto, and was eventually deported, and did not survive. The ongoing tension of keeping the boys hidden in their apartment caused Amelia, Aleksander wife's, to bang the door behind her in a fit, saying she was going straight to the Gestapo. Aleksander ran out after her. He found her sitting in a field, alone and weeping. He calmed her nerves and she returned home.[58]

In another dramatic family-contentious story, one day, in 1943, Maria Maciarz stepped out of her home, and ran into Helena, her daughter-in-law, who lived in the same building, and holding in her hand little Jack Twersky. The daughter-in-law stated that she was on the way to turn over the boy to the Gestapo. The widowed mother-in-law, in an on the spot decision, grabbed the boy out of Helena's hand, saying that he will stay with her. Maria Maciarz supported herself by selling old clothing on the market. Luckily, Jack's parents survived the concentration camps, and met the rescuer of their son. Before leaving Poland, Natalia Twersky, little Jack's mother, turned her parents' home over to Maria Maciarz, who signed the deed with the sign of the cross. "Illiterate, but with the heart and feelings of a saint," Natalia wrote.[59]

As for Józef Zwonarz, in Lesko, southeastern Poland, he hid the 5 members of the Dr. Nathan Wallach family in an underground shelter of his workshop shack, unbeknownst to his wife and three children. At times he asked that his meals be brought to him at the workshop shack, where he could turn it over secretly to the hidden persons there. His wife berated him, suspecting him of dallying with another woman – "you ought to be ashamed, carrying on like this at sucha late age." Only much later, as the Russians were closing in, did he bring her into the secret to whom the missing food was intended.[60]

A giant of a hero. We finish this section with the unbelievable story of a legendary savior of countless Jewish children. Born 1910 as Irena Krzyżanowska, in 1931 she married Mieczysław Sendler. Captured as a soldier by the Germans in September 1939, he remained in a German prisoner of war camp until the end of the war. In the meantime, Irena Sendlerowa (name ending, in Polish, when referring to a woman), obtained a permit by the municipality to her and her closest collaborator, Irena Schultz, to enter the ghetto without hindrance, to report on health conditions, especially for signs of typhus, a disease the Germans feared most to be themselves infected. With the cooperation of several ghetto tenement building administrators, Sendler began to smuggle Jewish children out of the ghetto, provide them with false identity documents and sheltering places. When the parents asked what guarantees there were of success, in Irena's words, "we had to honestly answer that we could offer no guarantees. I spoke frankly; I said I couldn't even be certain I would safely leave the ghetto with a child that very day." Some Jewish mothers would spend months preparing their children for the Aryan side. They would say to their terrified little ones: "You're not Itzek, but Jacek. You're not Rachela, but Roma. And I'm not your mother, I was just the housemaid. You'll go with this lady and perhaps over there your mummy will be waiting for you."

Children were smuggled out in various ways; through underground cellars connecting houses in the ghetto with those outside the ghetto, or driven out tucked into various cars and trucks. Babies were put to sleep and hidden in crates with holes, so they could breathe. Once outside the ghetto, a young child had to be taught Polish, how to pray, sing Polish songs, and recite Polish poems. They were washed, dressed in new clothes, and fed. Considerable trouble was taken to calm them down, to ease the pain of being separated from their loved ones.

In late 1942, Irena Sendlerowa joined the newly founded Council for Aiding Jews, better known by the codename Żegota, created by the Polish underground for helping Jews on the run (more on Żegota in the next chapter). Under the codename Jolanta, and with the help of her coworkers, by September 1943, she took over the leadership of Żegota's Department for the Care of Jewish children. In that capacity, she supervised a team of workers that was responsible, according to some estimates, for the up to 2,000 children in Żegota's care. About 25% of the Jewish children were placed by Sendlerowa's network with Polish families, while 75% in various religious orphanages.

On October 20, 1943, Sendlerowa was betrayed and arrested by the Germans and taken to the notorious Pawiak prison, and brutally interrogated. One day, taken out to be executed, she was instead released. She later learned that her Żegota confederates had bribed the Gestapo with a huge sum to have her freed. She later stated: "Every child saved with my help is the justification of my existence on this earth, and not a title to glory." She added, "As long as I live and as long as I have the strength I shall always say that the most important thing in the world and in life is Goodness."[61]

(f) In a Class by Themselves

We also have stories of rescuers who helped Jews survive, not necessarily by sheltering them in their homes, but in other unusual and awesome ways. We begin with the story of Wacław Nowiński.

It was late afternoon on April 9, 1943, when Aleksander Bronowski, out on a Warsaw street, was arrested by two German secret police agents, who in spite of his impeccable credentials, they suspected he was Jewish. As it was already late in the day, they decided to drop him off at a local Polish police station, promising to return early the next morning to take him to Gestapo headquarters for a grueling interrogation. It was 11 in the evening when Bronowski asked the cell guard to be allowed to sit in the hallway, across from the desk sergeant, named Wacław Nowiński, so as to warm himself a bit before returning to his cold cell. Sitting across Nowiński, Bronowski admitted to his being Jewish and then asked the policeman to do him a favor; to take him out to the outhouse, then shoot him in the back, and claim it was done in response to Bronowski's faked attempt to escape. Bronowski said he preferred such a death instead of being shot by the Gestapo, after a painful and grueling interrogation. Nowiński declined, stating he would not shoot an innocent person. At two o'clock in the morning, Sergeant Nowiński suddenly stated, "I must save you;" got up and left, locking the prison door from the outside. Four hours later, he reappeared and told Bronowski that through his underground contacts he was able to buy off the Gestapo in return for 5,000 złotys, that Bronowski was to hand them when they came to fetch him. An hour later, the two German secret police agents arrived, made a note in the police register that Bronowski had been erroneously arrested. They then took Bronowski outside. He gave them the 5,000 złotys as instructed and walked off. Bronowski repaid Nowiński that amount, so that, in Bronowski's words, he may use it in another attempt to free an innocent person by bribing the Gestapo.[62]

As for Władysław Misiuna, he was part of a team of Polish prisoners in a labor camp near Radom that also held some Jewish women. At times, Misiuna stole food meant for the rabbits that the Germans also kept there, for the women prisoners. When one of the women, Rachela Mitzenmacher, fell ill, with her whole body covered with suppurating wounds, Misiuna decided to save her by infecting himself with Rachela's sickness. He then visited the camp doctor and asked for a proper medicine, which was granted to him. This medicine helped him as well as Rachela, and they both were restored to good health.[63] We then have the story of Feliks Kanabus, a plastic surgeon, in Warsaw, who perfected a method to remove the circumcision sign from Jewish persons living in the open, during the occupation. This was done to help them pass inspection, when in spite of their "good looks," and authentic credentials, they could still be "defrocked" as Jews simply by submitting to the request of removing their pants to check whether they were circumcised, in a country where only Jews bore this very ancient traditional sign on their bodies. Dr. Kanabus performed these circumcision removal operations with the help of his wife, Irena, and several trusted medical doctors. The medical term for this type of operation is known as Elongatio Preputii. Kanabus stated that he performed about seventy anti-circumcision operations. "Satisfactory results were obtained in more than half of these cases... I performed these operations either in my office or in the homes of my patients. It was impossible to perform these operations in a hospital." Dr. Kanabus thus helped many people survive by removing this traditional Jewish sign on their bodies.[64]

Our final story takes us to a totally different scenario. Jan Kozielewski was a courier in the Polish underground, passing messages to the government-in-exile in London. On the eve of another such trip, in the summer of 1942, under his new underground name of Jan Karski, he was asked to meet two Jewish leaders of the Warsaw ghetto, in order to relay a message from them to the Polish government-in-exile. Fearing that his report on the fate of the Jews would be received with skepticism, Karski asked to be smuggled inside the Warsaw ghetto to personally witness the mass roundup of Jews on their way to the Treblinka gas chambers, and this was arranged for him. Still not satisfied, Karski asked to be smuggled into one of the deportation camps, to witness the happenings inside, and dressed as one of the Latvian militiamen who served the Germans as guards in some of the concentration camps.

Five weeks later, he was in London. As expected, his words were met with incredulity and disbelief. Resolved to carry the message of Polish Jewry to the United States, Karski arrived there in 1943, and personally reported to President Roosevelt (arranged by the Polish ambassador in the USA) and other high American officials. Roosevelt listened attentively to events inside Poland. But when it came to the Jewish part, Karski felt he had fallen on deaf ears. With his name and underground role revealed, he could not return to Poland, and he remained in the USA, making his wartime undercover name of Jan Karski, official. Years later, he stated, "all those great individuals, presidents, ambassadors, cardinals, ... they lied. They knew or didn't want to know. This shocked me.'"[65]

(g) Rescuers punished for aiding Jews

German punishment. As earlier mentioned, the German threats of the death penalty for would-be helpers of Jews inhibited many from getting involved in rescue activities. Indeed, a yet not fully known number of Poles who were apprehended for aiding Jews on the run paid with their lives. To cite some examples, of those honored by Yad Vashem – on October 22, 1942, Jan Kurdziel and Stanislaw Kurdziel, both from Zarki, were arrested in Częstochowa, for helping two Jewish women escape from the ghetto, and on December 10, 1942, Stanislaw Kurdziel was sentenced to death and executed.[66] In Markowa village – in 1943 or

1944, the Józef and Wiktoria Ulma family took into their home eight members of the Golda and Layka Goldman and Schall families from nearby Łańcut. On March 24, 1944, the German gendarmerie from Łańcut, accompanied by several Polish policemen, descended on the Ulma house and executed both the hidden Jews and the Poles who had granted them shelter.[67]

As for Jadwiga Deneko, active in the Polish Socialist Party, she served as a courier for the children's section of Żegota (the underground organization created to assist Jews). Arrested in November 1943, while sheltering 13 Jewish children in Warsaw, she was executed by a firing squad in Warsaw on January 8, 1944 in Pawiak prison.[68] Adam Sztark, a Jesuit priest and rector of a church in Słonim, was active in the rescue of Jewish children by issuing predated Catholic birth certificates. In June 1942, as the Słonim ghetto was being liquidated, Sztark was seen creeping, alongside the ghetto fringes hoping to pick up Jewish children, which he took to safe places. Sztark publicly called upon his parishioners to extend help to Jews. Arrested in December 1942, he was shot together with other Jewish victims.[69]

Not all rescue stories ending in German punishment are as detailed as the following one, based on interrogation records. On November 11, 1942, Franciszek Antczak, in Boguszyn village (northwest of Warsaw) admitted Moshe Kuperman and Józef Lewin for hiding. According to Lewin's interrogation by the Germans after his and Kuperman's arrest on March 2, 1944, when Kuperman and Lewin first arrived, Antczak agreed to shelter them, but his wife objected. He nevertheless hid the two without his wife's knowledge for 5 days; then during a German police patrol search of the village, Antczak told the two they could no longer stay with him, and he moved them to his sister Zofia Sztok, living in nearby Nowy Nacpolsk village, and they were taken there by his 12-year-old son. When they arrived, they said they would only stay for a few days, but this actually lasted much longer. Zofia's 27-year-old son, Kazimierz befriended them, and decided to build a bunker in the barn. Zofia's daughter, Genowefa, brought them food, three times per day. Evenings, they stepped out for fresh air. As a result of their arrest, in March 1944,

Franciszek Antczak was sent to a concentration camp where he died. His sister, Zofia Szkop was sentenced to three years imprisonment, and saw liberation in 1944; her 27-year-old son Kazimierz was sentenced to death and executed, for helping build the underground hiding place. As for the two Jewish fugitives, Kuperman was shot trying to escape, but Lewin successfully escaped and survived.[70]

Similarly, in the Sophie and Jakob Gargasz case. Here, the German judges went to considerable length to explain the justification of the death penalty. The Gargasz couple was tried by a German court in Sanok, on April 19, 1944, for having sheltered in their home the 65-year-old Heni Katz. At first, Mrs. Gargasz kept her hidden for a full year in the hayloft without informing her husband. When, according to his statement, he accidentally discovered her, he insisted that she leave, but acceded to his wife's pleading to keep her for a while until Mrs. Katz had recovered from an illness. In the meantime, someone informed on them and they were arrested. At the trial, the judges rejected Mrs. Gargasz's claim that as a practicing Adventist, her religion forbade her to expel a sick host, and she was consequently sentenced to death. As for her husband, since he later agreed for the Jewish woman to stay until she was back in good health, he was an accomplice in the sheltering scheme, and the judges also imposed on him the death penalty. Upon appeal by their Polish lawyers, the death sentences were commuted by Nazi governor, Hans Frank, to imprisonment in concentration camp. It is reported that they miraculously survived.[71] Perhaps the 1944 date of this trial, with a German defeat on the horizon, led Hans Frank to try mending his tarnished record, and moderate the death sentence, upon appeal.

We continue with the story of Anna Bogdanowicz, whose husband served as temporary mayor in Kielce. In November 1942, Anna was arrested and sent to Auschwitz camp, where she died, for organizing the escape of the Jewish Sara Diller from Jasło, and arranging her clandestine stay in the Kielce region. Bogdanowicz's rescue conspirator, Julian Ney, in Jasło, was shot. Turning to another story – in Radomsko, Natalia Abramowicz and her housemaid Weronika Kalek were arrested in May 1943 for sheltering Jews in her home, including Michael Steinlauf, his

family and relatives. Sentenced to death, it was commuted to imprison-
ment, due to Abramowicz's *Volksdeutsche* (ethnic German) status. Not
so her maid, Weronika Kalek, who was shot with other members of the
Steinlauf family, with the exception of Michael who managed to escape.
Imprisoned in several camps, Abramowicz saw liberation in a camp near
Lübeck, Germany, in April 1945.[72] We already told of Irena Sendlerowa
who was sentenced to death for aiding Jewish children escape from the
Warsaw ghetto, but her life was spared due to a hefty bribe paid to the
Gestapo by her fellow underground affiliates.

There are of course, many more such accounts; how many, one is not
sure, for at times it is difficult to separate punishment for regular underground activity (the Polish underground was the largest in Europe) with
those for aiding Jews. What one must keep in mind is that while rescuers
of Jews in other German-occupied countries also faced risks to their
lives, and some indeed paid it, nowhere else was it so strictly enforced as
in Poland, and nowhere else was the local population repeatedly warned
of the dire consequences to them for affording aid to Jews on the run.[73]

Antisemitic retribution. When talking of the risks facing rescuers,
one cannot, at the same time, overlook the danger not only from the
Germans, but from other Poles who were not beyond betraying and even
punishing fellow Poles for sheltering Jews. This doubled-edged punishing sword hanging over the heads of the rescuers amplifies even more
their courage, who on top of German retribution, also faced retaliation
from certain fellow die-hard antisemites, as in the following examples
of Polish rescuers honored by Yad Vashem.

In March 1942, in Połaniec, southeast of Kielce, Czesław Kubik
invited his pre-war friend Marek Verstandig to stay with him, then
arranged for Marek and his wife a hiding place with a certain Korzak
who also sheltered other Jews. Marek Verstanding then related what
happened. "On the night of May 31, 1944, a unit of the AK (Home
Army) raided the farm house of Korczak requesting the farmer to deliver
the Jews he was hiding on his farm… The unit consisted of 11 armed
men… I suddenly pushed one of the rear guards into the ditch, ran a few
meters away and jumped into the same ditch. I heard a shot over me, but

I was already under the water." Marek then heard another shot; it was his wife who was hit by a dum-dum bullet that entered her shoulder and slid to the middle of the back, exploding and detaching a piece of flesh. Four more shots exploded, "and I knew my two cousins Leah Ostro and Mindla Lehman and a certain Mrs. Kleinan and her 12-year-old son David were killed by Poles, members of the AK." With the help of a compassionate Pole, Marcin Walas, the Verstanding couple found other hiding places. After the war, Walas supplied Marek Verstanding with the full list of names of the AK unit which raided Mark's hiding place. In 1946, Antoni Makson, one of the men who shot Marek's wife, fled the police who came to arrest him, and was shot dead.[74]

In Szydłowiec, north of Kielce, Antoni and Helena Duda and Franciszka Ognowska sheltered ten Jewish persons in two places. As told by Yitzhak Mintz, a unit of the Polish underground, members of the intensely antisemitic NSZ partisan faction, raided Ognowska's home, in May 1943, and demanded to be shown the hidden Jews. Not complying with these wishes, the NSZ partisans shot dead Franciszka's son, 30-year old Władysław and severely wounded in both legs his 32-year-old brother Stefan. After this tragic incident, some of the hiders left the place and spread out. Two family relations of the hidden persons were caught by NSZ partisans and murdered. Some returned to the Duda family and were readmitted.[75]

In the village of Pieczonogi, near northeast of Kraków, Konstanty Celuch with wife Justyna (and four children) hid on the roof of his farm (in a section of the chimney) Herman Figowicz and his girlfriend, Rachel Brzeska. One night, in Rachela's words, "members of the AK [Home Army] invaded the house, and demanded of Konstanty to disclose to them the hiding place of the Jews. Konstanty denied the claim … and the Poles gave him a terrible beating until he lost consciousness." After the beatings, he stayed in bed for a long time. Herman and Rachela continued to stay in Celuch's home until liberation time.[76]

In another story of great courage by a Polish rescuer, in Komodzianka village (Zamość region) – on November 2, 1942, Jan and Stefania Sosnowy hid Eli Ashenberg (whom they knew from before) in a hole underneath the house floor. In March 1943, a group of armed men, described by Ashenberg as AK partisans, invested the Sosnowy home. "They broke down the door and began physically to beat Jan saying they knew he was hiding a Jew. He denied this and they indicated they were taking him out to be killed and commanded him to say goodbye to his wife. Stefania indicated that she also wanted to go along with her husband, to share his fate." After 15 minutes, Jan and Stefania returned. The partisans did not carry out their death threat on the Sosnowys. Perhaps, they believed them. Eli Ashenberg stayed on there, at his rescuers' insistence, until the area's liberation in July 1944.[77]

Some rescuers of Jews suffered retribution, not during but after the liberation, as happened to Włodzimierz and Anna Daniluk. In May 1945, the Daniluks, in the village of Solniczki (Zabludów county, Białystok district), invited over four persons they had earlier hidden and some of their relatives to celebrate the victory over Nazi Germany. In the middle of the party, armed men broke into the home, opened fire and shot dead seven people, while others were severely wounded. Włodzimierz Daniluk, and two of those he rescued were among the victims. It is reported that the murderers belonged to a certain faction of AK, the Home Army. The story is as reported by the rescuer daughter Raisa Daniluk.[78]

More such sad stories are on the record, as they came to light in the accounts of survivors, and also based on post-war Polish records, and they represent a stain in the history of Poland during the occupation – especially, in light of the deep sufferings of the Polish people at the hands of the Germans. At the same time, these betrayals by some Poles (whose numbers are debated by historians), paradoxically, throws a greater light on the other Poles, who sheltered Jews. As Emanuel Ringelblum asked himself, while hidden with 30 other Jews with the help of Mieczysław Wolski: "Is there enough money in the world to make up for the constant fear of exposure, fear of the neighbors, the porter and the manager of the block of flats, etc.?" Himself hidden with wife and son, and 30 Jews, in a large underground shelter under Wolski's vegetable garden, in Warsaw, it was one of the biggest secret structures of its kind, with financial responsibility shared by Jewish and non-Jewish clandestine organizations. Unfortunately, on March 7, 1944 the hideout was disclosed due to betrayal by an unknown person (a version has it that it was his former female sweetheart companion, in revenge after he left her), and all those in hiding paid with their lives, including Ringelblum, his wife and son, and their rescuer, Mieczysław Wolski.[79]

(h) Possible motivations

The debate by students of human behavior on the motivation of rescuers of Jews did not so far lead to any definite conclusions. We mention here three opinions by two sociologists and one psychologist, where they agree on some points and not on others. Socialogist, Nechama Tec, who made a study of Polish rescuers, found that most of them were armed with a powerful inbred system of beliefs that ran counter to those held by their surrounding society. What characterized many of the rescuers, according to Tec, was a trait she terms "marginality," or more positively, "individuality," and their view of Jews in universal instead of ethnic terms. Not as the Others, towards whom one's moral obligations did not apply, but as equal members of a worldwide human family. In other words, they were persons who did not follow the trend, but made their own decision on what is right and wrong behavior. This rare quality permitted such people to face not only Nazi terror but also the indifference and hostility of much of their society.

Samuel and Pearl Oliner, Tec's sociological dissenters, drew different conclusions from their research of rescuers – that they were quite well acclimated within their societies, and were not at all "marginal," but had absorbed to the full the ethical teachings of their societies (that others only paid lip service), and the values inculcated by their parents to help others in need, even the strangers in their midst.[80] Psychologist Eva Fogelman posited a different portrait. She described the rescuer as a person nurtured by certain values during childhood, and these then fully blossomed during the Holocaust when such a person lent a helping hand to a victimized Jew. This, then, led to a transformation of the rescuer's personality; a different self was formed, that became an integral part of the rescuer's identity in the postwar years.[81]

Interestingly, the French-Jewish philosopher, Emmanuel Levinas, came up with a different idea to explain one's sudden arousal to help out. He wrote that such a positive response was predicated by proximity and an eye-to-eye confrontation between two sides; the helper and the stranger. This is especially so when facing society's Other; the person considered outside one's own close social circle, such as the Jews, that society disowned from responsibility and moral obligation. However, in situations of proximity and eye-to-eye contact, a person may suddenly be inundated by some outside force, that then becomes part of oneself, and this helps that person to turn aside, even momentarily, one's socially constructed system of prejudices, and triggers that person into a rescuer. In the words of Levinas: "Since the other looks at me, I am responsible for him." It then becomes a responsibility without conditions. "The face of the other ordains me." This existential responsibility has nothing to do with any contractual obligation; it is a non-symmetrical relationship. Whatever one may think of Levinas' explanation, true enough, many rescue acts during the Holocaust had their origin in this face-to-face encounter between the two sides.[82]

Here, it is also worth mentioning Kristen Monroe, who specializes in political psychology and ethics. After an in-depth study of 28 rescuers, she characterizes them as people who make no distinction between themselves and others; they are "at one with all humanity."[83] She terms the Holocaust rescuers as John Donne's People, after the 16th century British poet, who stated: "Any man's death diminishes me, because I am involved in Mankind. And therefore, never send to know for whom the bell tolls; it tolls for thee." She also notes the sudden and instinctive nature of the rescuer's response to the request for help, such as in the words of one rescuer: "I don't make a choice. It comes, and it's there.... It happened so quickly." Little time to think of alternatives. Another rescuer stated that "when they're standing at the door and their life is threatened, what should you do in this situation? You could never do that [turn them away]." Still another rescuer explained what made him decide to help: "I never made a moral decision to rescue Jews. I just got mad. I felt I had to do it."[84]

Monroe holds that none of the sociocultural predictors traditionally offered by analysts (age, gender, education, or socioeconomic background) accounts for altruism. Also, that "the altruist's early childhood and relations with parents reflect those of the rest of humanity: they are complex and varied," and cannot therefore be utilized to explain the motivation of the Holocaust rescuers. The only strong factor shared by all rescuers, she points out is seeing themselves as "individuals strongly linked to others through a shared humanity;" and such a positive feeling, sadly, was missing by many people during the Nazi years.[85]

In summary, while sociological and psychological students of human behavior are still debating the nature of altruism under different conditions, when speaking of rescuers during the Holocaust, especially those in Poland – what they all shared, in spite of different backgrounds and personal prejudices, is the belief that every human being, whether liked or not, had a right to life. So, when challenged by the proximity of Jews threatened with death for simply being born, these brave persons rose to the occasion, and momentarily putting aside their fears, and also their prejudices, and with the limited resources at their command, helped to save as many of the fugitive Jews as they possibly could. They thus demonstrated a type of altruistic behavior of an unprecedented elevated moral dimension. It goes beyond saying that they merit that all others listening to their stories should be eternally grateful to them, as well as learn from their example, to also perform good deeds within the realm of their possibilities.

CHAPTER 7

Organizational and Diplomatic Assistance

(a) Żegota—Council for Aiding Jews

In Poland, a non-Jewish organization was established for one purpose only – to aid Jews on the run for their lives. It was the sole such non-Jewish organization ever created in any German-occupied country, and is testimony to the wish to help Jews to stay alive that prevailed in certain parts of Polish society. Żegota, the code name for the Council for Aiding Jews (*Rada Pomocy Żydom*) was established in autumn of 1942, under the auspices of the Delegatura, the political underground in the occupied homeland representing the government-in-exile, in far-away London. Formed during the late summer months of 1942, Żegota began operating in December 1942.[1] The organizational structure was without parallel elsewhere in occupied Europe and it had the effect of exerting a moderating influence on the hostility of other Poles toward Jews. Zofia Kossak-Szczucka, not a great friend of Jews, laid the groundwork for the undertaking, when in August 1942, she urged in a proclamation that "anyone remaining silent in the face of this murder becomes an accomplice to the murder."[2] The newly-found organization included representatives of some of the underground political parties, but not of all, especially not the National Democrats, the Endeks, who made no secret of their outspoken antisemitism.[3]

As told, the initiative for Żegota's creation was Kossak-Szcuczka's manifesto "Protest," written and distributed in Warsaw in August 1942, while trains were dispatching Jews to the Treblinka gas chambers. A provisional council named Konrad Żegota, was founded on September 27, 1942, led jointly by Kossak-Szczucka (representing the Front for Polish Rebirth) and Wanda Krahelska-Filipowiczowa (Democratic Party). By the end of November, it had representatives in fourteen cities outside of Warsaw, although its principal center of activity remained Warsaw and environs.[4] The most important branch of Żegota elsewhere was in Kraków.[5] In that city, the Jewish Miriam Hochberg, who passed as the non-Jewish Maria Mariańska, was a principal Żegota activist, who worked closely with others belonging mainly to the Socialist Party.[6]

Konrad Żegota disbanded in early December 1942, and was reconstituted on December 4, 1942, and simply code-named Żegota.[7] It is well to note the three-year long lapse since the start of the German occupation for the Polish underground to create such a help organization. Julian Grobelny (code-named "Trojan"), representing the Socialist Party (PPS), headed Żegota.[8] He was arrested in 1944 but luckily survived. His deputies were Tadeusz Rek ("Rósycki") of the Peasants Party, and Ferdynand Arczynski ("Marek"), of the Democratic Party, who served as treasurer. During the period of the provisional council or committee, the Young Catholics were represented by Władysław Bienkowski ("Jan"), and Władysław Bartoszewski ("Ludwik").[9] Żegota also counted two Jewish members on its board of directors – Leon Feiner ("Mikolaj"), of the Jewish Socialist Bund party, and Dr. Adolf Berman ("Adam," "Ludwik"), representing the Jewish National Council, who served as secretary.[10] Berman contends that the reason the Catholics withdrew from Żegota was their opposition to having Jews present in the Council's deliberations or to having them included in the organization's leadership.[11]

At its founding, Żegota set itself the following tasks: (1) establish contact with existing Jewish societies, and Jews in hiding, and offer them financial assistance; (2) provide Jews escaping from the ghettos with apartments and temporary sleeping quarters, and locate more permanent housing for them; (3) clothing, food and work for runaway Jews;

(4) forged identity papers to fleeing Jews so they could pass as Poles; (5) medical care for Jews in hiding; and (6) a special section dealing with sheltering Jewish children, spirited out of the Warsaw ghetto.[12]

Ringelblum puts the number of Jews in Warsaw who benefited from Żegota's assistance at 300 families. According to its own sources, aid eventually extended to over 1,000 individuals.[13] In a postwar study by Teresa Prekerowa (herself a wartime Żegota operative), she comes up with a greater number of persons helped – that by the middle of 1944, about 3,000-4,000 person benefitted from Żegota's financial relief (of which 600 in Kraków, and at least 120 in Lwów). Prekerowa adds, that when the additional persons aided separately by the two Jewish organizations, Bund and the Jewish National Council are added, the total number of aid recipients included about 12,000 people.[14] In Warsaw, Żegota had several apartments at its disposal, where it could put up Jewish fugitives for a few nights, and a number of "mail drops" at which messages and funds were delivered and picked up.[15] Żegota agents were constantly confronted by the dilemma of having to decide whether or not to reveal to a landlord, with a room or an apartment to rent, that a prospective tenant was Jewish. With the mixture of either passivity, fear of the Germans and local informers, or outspoken antisemitic feelings among many, it remained uncertain how many Poles were prepared to offer shelter to Jews, especially to persons whom they knew not from before.[16]

Manufacturing and supplying false documents were some of the principal activities of Żegota for Jews on the run, who were either passing as non-Jewish Poles or were hidden in their homes. During the occupation, every resident of Poland was required to possess a variety of personal documents besides one's identity paper, such as work papers, if only as a guarantee against seizure for forced labor in Germany. As a general rule, a birth or baptismal certificate was the principal document that determined eligibility for any of the others, including identity papers, known as *Kennkarten*, and residence permits. Polish and German police carried out frequent identity checks. To obtain these documents, a regular black market in forged documents had developed throughout Poland.[17]

Adolf Berman, in a post-war article, writes: "The Council [Żegota] organized within its own domain a 'factory' for the manufacture of thousands of birth certificates, baptismal certificates, marriage certificates, prewar identity papers, identification certificates (*Kennkarten*)... These documents were of the highest quality. According to need, documents would arrive blank, and were then filled in, down to the last detail and with a precision that could hardly be matched, mostly to the specifications ordered by the secretariat of the Council... This 'factory' for documents was run by a former mayor of one of the cities in Poland... He fell into the hands of the Gestapo and was shot... The Council gave all of these documents away to Jews at no charge."[18] Since workshops producing documents for Żegota were also forging them for other sections of the underground, it makes it almost impossible to arrive at any but a general estimate of the total figure for Jews, other than that Żegota's work in the field of documents legalization was quite extensive.[19]

Żegota's Medical Department employed a number of trustworthy physicians, who visited Jewish patients in hiding, organized by Dr. Ludwik Rostkowski, the representative of a clandestine medical association. Some of these doctors included the earlier mentioned Feliks Kanabus, and Andrzej Trojanowski; both of whom performed plastic operations in order to remove signs of circumcision.[20] In autumn 1943, secret post boxes were set up where addresses of the sick persons and the descriptions of their ailments were deposited by the heads of the medical section. Żegota's liaison workers made rounds of these post boxes a few times a week to collect calls and to pass them on to Dr. Rostkowski. He then decided what specialized help was necessary in each case and which medical doctors should be asked to see particular patients.[21]

Żegota placed a special emphasis on saving Jewish children, and a separate such section was established in September 1943, headed by Irena Sendlerowa ("Jolanta"), who in an earlier period singlehandedly managed to spirit many children out of the Warsaw ghetto. Up to 2,000 children (some sources mention a higher figure) were placed, previous and after that date, in children's homes and religious institutions, such as convents and orphanages in the Warsaw area, with others in private homes.[22] About 50 percent of the children were placed with so-called foster families, with the other half enrolled in orphanages or children homes. Foster families generally took those children whose features were not typically Semitic, so they could pass as members of the family. The children who had the most Semitic features tended to be taken in by convent orphanages, since it was less probable that the presence of Jewish, that is non-Catholic, children would be present there there by Germans conducting a search. Such children were protected behind the convent walls, beyond the reach of blackmailers and informers. They could also play freely with other children of their age – a vital need by young children.[23]

Żegota emissaries also provided camp prisoners with money, medicine, and letters from their political parties and from their families and friends. Couriers maintained contacts with a number of forced labor camps, such as in Budzyń (a branch of Majdanek concentration camp), Trawniki, Zamość, Częstochowa, Piotrków, Radom, Pionki, Skarzysko-Kamienna, and Plaszów, as well as with the ghettos in Łódź, Białystok and Vilna. There were also frequent contacts with people in Lwów, particularly with the labor camp on Janowska Street, from where several prisoners were extricated – Holocaust narrator Maksymilian Boruchewicz (after the war, Michel Borwicz) being one among them. One of the most outstanding achievements was spiriting Emanuel Ringelblum out of the camp at Trawniki and organizing his flight to Warsaw, in autumn 1943, with the assistance of the railway worker Teodor Pajewski.[24]

Żegota published four broadsheets of its activities – three to the Polish public, in twenty-five thousand copies all told, and one in German in five thousand copies, and they were distributed to homes, posted on the walls of houses in Warsaw and cities in the provinces, and sent to various offices.[25] Financial resources for Żegota's activities included contributions by Jewish organizations abroad, that couriers of the Polish underground helped smuggle into the occupied country.[26] All in all, according to Prekerowa's research, a total of 34,000,000 złotys were made available for all these diverse activities. Individuals being cared for usually received monthly allowances of 500 złotys, that was considered as sufficient for a modest living in those times. When money from overseas did not arrive in time, smaller payments were made, such as 350-400 złotys, or even as little as 250-300 złotys per month.[27] According to Prekerowa, higher amounts than those of Żegota were paid separately by the two Jewish organizations, the Bund and the Jewish National Council, but during a shorter period of time than that of Żegota.[28]

The struggle against blackmailers. One item constantly appearing on Żegota's agenda was the ongoing victimization of Jews by informers, blackmailers and betrayers, whose activities cast a pall of terror over the surviving Jews in hiding. From the moment of its inception, Żegota demanded severe and immediate punishment of extortionists and denunciators whose criminal acts brought about the death of many people in hiding and, frequently, their protectors as well.[29] Żegota appealed to underground authorities to do all they could to combat this plague and created a separate branch of its organization to propagandize against it. It requested the Delegate Office to declare in the underground press the condemning of murders and stigmatizing displays of antisemitism.[30] On March 4, 1943, Żegota received a reply, signed by the Delegate's representative in Żegota and the man in charge of the Jewish section in the secret civil underground, who stated that "because of the impossibility of excepting the Jewish sector from the annihilation campaign which involves all of the citizens of the Polish Republic, there will be no special call made to the public on the matter of assistance to Jews." As for a public appeal against extortions, this too was inadvisable since "until now technical reasons have been the cause of postponing the publication."[31]

Żegota appealed again on March 25, 1943, asking for the posting of public announcements of death sentences carried out against extortionists.[32] In a sharply worded letter to the Delegate Office, it stated: "The number of Polish blackmailers is increasing daily and is a plague visited on us by criminal elements of the society." It urged the Delegate Office to treat blackmailing "as a crime subject to the death penalty."[33] The answer from the underground, veiled in legal verbiage, was that nothing could be done because it was a judicial procedure – a trial was required; and given the circumstances of the occupation, it was not possible to carry out proper investigations.[34] Żegota responded that it would take independent action by issuing proclamations that warned of dire consequences for blackmailing Jews,[35] and it went ahead and distributed a circular in May 1943, that read: "Every Pole who cooperates in the ruthless extermination either by blackmailing or denouncing Jews... commits a grave crime in light of the laws of the Polish Republic and will be punished without delay. If that person manages to escape punishment, let him be assured that the time is near when he will be prosecuted before the court of justice of Reborn Poland."[36]

On July 12, 1943 Żegota's directorate asked, in a letter to the Delegate's representative in Żegota, for a list of cases which were prosecuted to date, and information about the number of sentences passed and the number that had actually been carried out. The official reply came on August 9, 1943, in an evasive letter, from the Jewish section of the Delegate's Office, that the issue of prosecutions is a "top secret" matter and cannot be revealed. Testifying after the war, Witold Bieńkowski, claimed to have "personally signed 117 death sentences against extortionists throughout the country, 89 of which were carried out... A total of 220 death verdicts were adjudicated for crimes coercion."[37] However, Żegota furnished no evidence to this claim, and Bieńkowski's figures, in the opinion of historians Gutman and Krakowski, seem excessively high when considered in light of the evidence contained in the documents on hand at Yad Vashem.[38]

No more than 8 cases of blackmail and victimization of Jews had, in truth, been brought before the special underground courts, and only two of these had been prosecuted in full, with the sentences actually being carried out. The first death sentence was carried out in Kraków in 17 July 1943 and was announced in the *Biuletyn Informacyjny* (the main underground information bulletin) on 2 September. Jan Grabiec, a tailor, was sentenced to death for blackmailing both Poles and Jews. Two weeks later the same source communicated that Jan Pilnik was shot for blackmailing and for denouncing Jews to the Germans; only Jewish victims are mentioned on this sole occasion.[39]

It is worth mentioning, that the Polish underground conducted an energetic fight against Polish traitors who collaborated with the Germans or worked for them in activities not relating to Jews. From January 1943 to June 1944, more than 2,000 death sentences were carried out against informers and German agents among the local Polish population.[40] On April 6, 1943, for a lack of other measures, Żegota even suggested some imaginary sentences to be publicized against *Szmaltsowniks* to intimidate others, but the proposal was rejected by the Delegatura, which feared this would lead to creating doubts of the credibility of its other statements, even if that fictitious announcement could have led to a temporary relief of the blackmailing plague. To note that 150 Gestapo informers of Polish nationality were put to death by the end of April 1943, but blackmailing of Jews was not anywhere mentioned as the reason of these executions.[41] Clearly, failure to punish extortionists of Jews facilitated their acting with impunity and expanded the scope of their criminal behavior.[42]

Statistics. In all, Żegota was active over a period of 21 or 22 months,[43] as with the outbreak of the Polish uprising in Warsaw in August 1944, Żegota's organizational structure collapsed.[44] One cannot say with certainty how many people totally were saved by Żegota.[45] The number certainly runs into several thousand, as claimed by former Żegota workers,[46] although most of the Jews who survived the German occupation of Poland were saved by Poles who were not necessarily connected with Żegota. Adolf Berman estimates that 4,000 Jews benefited from monthly allowances by Żegota. Gutman and Krakowski claimed that this estimate is far too high; that it was in the range of 1,000 to 1,500.[47] Coinciding with Żegota's operation, the Jewish National Council, headed by Adolf Berman, that operated separately on the Aryan side of Warsaw, after the suppression of the Warsaw ghetto uprising, extended aid to 5,000 to 6,000 Jews, and Leon Feiner's Bund organization to 1,500 to 2,000 Jews. So, the total number of Jews in Warsaw and the environs who received help from the two underground movements, non-Jewish and Jewish, may have totaled up to 12,000 and perhaps slightly higher than that.[48]

Whatever the real figures, words of thanks and appreciation are due to Żegota for its exclusive and lone role, within the much larger underground network, to save as many Jews as possible within the limited means at its disposal, and having to face the apathy and indifference of certain circles in the underground's Delegate Office, toward whom it was subordinate and answerable. To reiterate, in no other country of Europe under the Nazi occupation was a similar network created to attempt to rescue the Jewish population; a secretive organization that represented a wide spectrum of socio-political platforms, and was linked to the main underground.[49]

(b) General Rescue Statistics

As to the estimate of how many Jews benefitted from the aid of non-Jewish Poles, and how many rescuers were involved in that endeavor, here too opinions are divided. Some claim that to hide one Jew, the cooperation of many more was required, although that may not be so in all cases, since absolute secrecy was needed for the success of the rescue operation, thus keeping the knowledge of one's involvement to a bare minimum. At the same time, admittedly, most rescue operations involved a husband and wife team, with some of their children, and possibly a handful of relatives sworn to secrecy.[50] Another way of looking at the rescue figures is the number of Jews liberated on Polish soil who mostly survived thanks to the aid of non-Jewish Poles. Some historians give mostly exaggerated figures in this regard and argue that Poles saved some 100,000 Jews, while others give a more modest number, of 40,000-50,000. True enough, Emanuel Ringelblum, an eyewitness to events in Warsaw, and himself a recipient of aid by Poles, who in his writings from a hiding place often caustically criticized the Poles for not doing enough to help his kinsmen, praises the "thousands" of "idealists," in Warsaw and the whole country, who saved "thousands of human beings from certain death."[51] At the same, he was careful not to venture a more accurate figure, since he realized that from his secret hideout he was not able to back up with evidence any more precise figures.

According to a very detailed study by Lucjan Dobroszycki, and according to the findings of Shmuel Krakowski, the number of Jewish survivors on Polish territory who benefited from non-Jewish aid did not

exceed 30,000, with almost half of them in the eastern territories of
prewar Poland. This, of course, is a conservative figure and the actual
number may be higher and closer to 50,000, and perhaps slightly more
than this, if one were to take into contact those who benefited from help
by non-Jews, but then fell victim to blackmailers and murderers. Simply
put, further research is needed on Jews in hiding or on the run, who were
either helped and survived, plus those aided but did not survive due to
natural death, and those caught and murdered, either by the Germans
or by local individuals, and vigilante groups.[52] As for Warsaw and its
environs, most credible historians agree to the figure of 15,000 to 20,000
Jews who sought sanctuary in that metropolis.[53] One would then also
have to take into account those sheltered in other Polish locations; cities,
villages and forests.

As for rescuers, Jewish historians tend to point out the lower figures,
while Polish historians favor the higher ones, with some suggesting that
as many as 1,000,000 Poles were involved in sheltering Jews, including
the claim that 1,000 Poles from Lwów were killed in the Bełżec concentration camp for aiding Jews. However, the Germans executed many
Poles for a whole host of reasons, and it is difficult if at all impossible
to arrive at a close estimate of those killed or otherwise punished solely
for aid to Jews.[54]

Teresa Prekerowa, a former Żegota activist, sought to determine as
scientifically accurate as possible the proportion of Poles actively engaged
in helping Jews. She calculated that between 160,000 to 360,000 Poles
aided Jews, out of an adult Polish population of 15 million; in other
words, between 1.0 and 2.5 percent of the Polish population provided
safe haven to Jews fleeing Nazi persecution.[55] According to Gutman and
Krakowski, these are inflated figures and have no correspondence whatsoever with historical realities.[56] To attempt at a fair estimate, although
not accurate, if we take the fifteen to twenty thousand Jews in hiding
in the capital, and combine it with a similar figure of fifteen to twenty
thousand Polish people in Warsaw helping to hide Jews – reckoning a
husband and wife team for each rescuer (some cases involved only one
person, whereas others involved more adult members of one's family),

then doubling the 15 to 20,000 figure, we come up with 30,000 to 40,000 persons who were directly and actively involved in the rescue of Jews, in Warsaw alone.[57] If, the accepted total number of Jews saved everywhere is 50,000, then based on the same calculation we can safely assume that at least 100,000 Poles, and perhaps slightly more, were actively, or in some other forms, involved in the various rescue operations of at least 50,000 surviving Jews.

Swedish-Canadian historian, Gunnar Paulsson, claims that an estimated 17,000 Jews were hiding in the Warsaw region alone; he then adds an unknown figure of several thousands who escaped from the Warsaw ghetto but headed elsewhere, plus the approximately 3,500 who gave themselves up in the summer of 1943 in the notorious Hotel Polski affair; and adds to this the thousands (about 6,500) who were caught, or died of from accelerated natural causes.[58] After a lengthy and convoluted discussion on hiding places, followed with mathematical equations hard to follow, Paulsson further inflates the figure of Polish rescuers, to as possibly as high as 90,000, in Warsaw alone.[59] If, in Paulsson's estimate, Warsaw represents only a fourth of helpers from throughout the country, he easily multiplies the 90,000 figure by four, and comes up with the fantastic number of 360,000 possible rescuers – all them including direct and indirect helpers. But, he is willing to settle for half of that number, 160,000, as also suggested by Perekerowa, to be on the safe side. It seems that Paulsson's figures need a further close and meticulous recalculation.[60]

The final and even approximate estimate of Polish helpers to Jews is still left undecided, and equally the number of Jews who benefitted from their help; those that were aided and survived, and those apprehended and died. But, calculating the estimated 50,000 Jews who were aided and survived, one may safely assume that there were at least 100,000 non-Jewish Poles (on the principle of a husband and wife team) who made this survival possible. And, one may safely assume that there were slightly more such brave rescuers, but not overwhelmingly more.

Also, well to remember, that the vast majority of Polish Jews who survived World War II, it was not due to help on the local scene, but to their escape and eventual stays in the hinterland regions of Russia, beyond the reaches of the deepest advance of the German army – an estimated 200,000 to 250,000 such persons.

c) The Ładoś Group[61]

Background. One of the most inspiring rescue stories to come to light recently is that of a group of Polish diplomats who acted in concert with Jewish rescue activists, to help at first hundreds and eventually thousands of Jews to avoid deportation. It concerns the involvement of the Polish diplomatic legation in Bern, Switzerland, headed by Aleksander Ładoś, in an operation unparalleled by diplomats of other countries, who also tried to help. Together with his two principal subordinates, Stefan Ryniewicz and Konstanty Rokicki, the three Polish diplomats acted in tandem with several Jewish activists in Switzerland in a wide-ranging scheme to help Polish Jewish nationals, residing in various parts of German-dominated Europe, to avoid deportation, by supplying them with illegal Latin American passports, especially that of Paraguay – in stark violation of diplomatic procedures and Swiss laws. The passport holders were able to either postpone or completely avoid deportation to the death camps. Jewish rescue activists had nothing but words of praise for these courageous diplomats. What follows is based on documentation obtained by this author from Polish and other sources, including personal testimonies by those involved in this rescue conspiracy.

Passports. Following the German occupation of Poland, the Polish government-in-exile, in London, continued to conduct diplomatic activity through its offices in some European countries not at war with Germany, such as Switzerland. Since 1940, Aleksander Ładoś, headed the Polish Legation in Bern, together with Stefan Ryniewicz and Konstanty Rokicki. The Jewish Julius Kühl, an equally important legation staffer, was hired by Ładoś to deal with Jewish refugees in Switzerland, in addition to general matters affecting Polish-Jewish citizens.

Before the war, the policy of the Polish government had been to revoke the passports held by Polish citizens who lived in other countries and did not take the trouble to renew their passports, and many of these were Jews who had left Poland for other European destinations, mostly for economic reasons. After the German conquest, the Polish London-based government-in-exile ruled that in all such cases, the persons affected will have their citizenships reinstated even though their passports had lapsed. There were thousands of such cases in Switzerland, of Jews who had fled there seeking security and were at risk of being expelled. The Polish legation in Bern, led by Aleksander Ładoś, kept busy reinstating their Polish citizenship as well providing them with assistance in the various refugee camps that the government in Switzerland had placed them. For example, on December 10, 1943, Ładoś announced to his government in London that approximately 5,000 additional Jewish refugees who arrived from France were being cared by the Polish legation in Bern, with a major part of the budget being assigned to this purpose. Myself, my parents and my 5 siblings, were among those refugees, have crossed illegally into Switzerland from France, in September 1943, fleeing the Germans who had occupied the Italian zone.

According to Julius Kühl, the Jewish staff-member in the legation – after the forcible takeover of East Poland by the Russians in September 1939, a scheme was devised for getting many Jews out of there. Dozens of documents were obtained from Rudolf Hügli, the Paraguayan honorary consul in Bern, in return for payment, in which ostensibly Polish-Jewish citizens were converted into citizens of Paraguay, and this allowed the Soviet authorities for these people to depart to Japan where, free from Soviet inspection, they received new Polish passports by the Polish envoy there, with which they continued to other safe destinations. Furthermore, passports were also obtained by the Polish legation staff in Bern from the consuls of Peru, Honduras, Costa Rica and Haiti, that together with the Paraguay passports protected the documents recipients during the war years, in countries held by the Germans, from immediate deportation to the camps. Instead, they were sent to detention camps in Germany and France, with the intention of freeing them in exchange for the thousands of German nationals living in countries that the Nazi regime desperately wanted their return to Germany, in order to replenish the ranks of men in the German army. This work in the Polish legation was done in close cooperation with three Jewish organs in Switzerland; foremost, Avraham Silberschein, who headed the Relico section of the World Jewish Congress; Rabbi Chaim Israel Eiss, of the Agudat Israel organization, and the Yitzhak and Recha Sternbuch couple, who represented in Switzerland the Vaad Hatzalah organization that was created by the orthodox Agudat Israel movement in the USA.

As told by Avraham Silberschein during his interrogation by the Swiss police, on September 1, 1943, after the passports scheme came to light to them – in mid-1943 he met with the two Polish legation staff members, Stefan Ryniewicz and Konstanty Rokicki, upon their request. They told him of the existing black market of buying and selling false passports by private groups, and asked Silberschein take this operation under his responsibility, in full cooperation with the Polish legation. Silberschein, whose main activity had been finding as many escape routes for Jews as possible, agreed to this proposal, and he began to obtain passports from Latin American consuls, but mainly from Hügli, the consul representing Paraguay, in return for a certain payment to him. These, he turned over to the Polish legation, and there, especially Rokicki but also Ryniewicz and Kühl, entered the names of Polish-Jewish citizens who lived mainly in occupied-Poland, but some also in other German-held countries. The passports included dates of birth and names of family members, some based on data that Silberschein provided them, and others on information available in the Polish legation. The passports were returned to the consul of Paraguay, for his signature and appending the consulate seal, which made them official. The purpose was to make it possible for the passport recipients to get out from German-dominated countries, and move elsewhere, but not at all to the countries of these fake passports. In his testimony, Silberschein underlined, "I did this with the full cooperation of the Polish legation people;" and it goes without saying with the full knowledge of Aleksander Ładoś, the legation head. Thus, thousands of ostensibly legitimate, but in truth illegal, passports were manufactured for the sole purpose of saving Jewish lives.

In addition to the passports, Paraguayan citizen certificates were obtained for Polish Jews for whom no full personal information with photos were on hand, and no passports could therefore be prepared for them. It was, consequently, decided to momentarily provide them with citizenship confirmations in the form of official letters, known as *Promesas*, in the hope that these would eventually be converted into legal passports, with the receipt of the additional required data. These mostly illegal Paraguayan documents were done, with the complicity of that country's honorary consul, Rudolf Hügli, but without the knowledge of the government that he represented. Upon disclosure of Hügli's involvement by his superiors, he was immediately dismissed.

When Ładoś learned that the Germans were placing doubts on the validity of these passports held by Jews in the Vittel detention camp, in occupied France, he hurriedly dispatched many letters to various parties, under his signature, so as to uphold the credibility of these passports, and avoid the deportation of the passport recipients to the death camps in Poland.

One must also mention in this context the fully legal Polish passports that the Polish legation printed herself, without the mediation of others, to persons who, at times, were not at all Polish citizens, but needed such documents in order to secure escape from persecution. Such as Dr. Joseph Burg, later a minister in the Israel government, who was then a senior official in the Palestinian Jewish Agency. He had come to Switzerland to attend the August 1939 Zionist congress in Geneva, when the war that broke out a month later prevented his return to Palestine via France, as he was a German national, where he was born and educated. The danger for him was of arrest by the French authorities (this was before the fall of France to Germany in June 1940). He consequently, obtained a Polish passport, although never a Polish citizen, and this allowed him to return to Palestine via France. Likewise, for the Jewish Pierre Mendès-France, later a French Prime Minister, who had been arrested and imprisoned by the Vichy regime as a leading member of the Socialist party. He had escaped and fled to Switzerland, where he lived in hiding. To help him avoid arrest by the Swiss authorities, the Polish legation issued him a Polish passport, under the name of Jan Lemberg, and with this false document, he secretly made his way to Portugal, via France and Spain, and proceed to England, where he joined the forces of Free France, under General Charles De Gaulle.

The Secret Transmitter. An additional scheme of help to Jews by the Polish legation in Bern, headed by Ładoś, was by way of communicating secret messages to the free Western countries, and especially the USA, on the condition of the Jews in countries under German occupation, via a secret transmitter in the Polish legation, thus circumventing the strict Swiss censorship against transferring whatever information that included negative portrayals of Nazi Germany. Ładoś was warned several times by the Swiss police against the use of a secret transmitter, but he disregarded it and continued to transmit messages. Journalist David Kelley, in his letter of November 19, 1941 to a British Foreign Ministry staffer, writes: "the Pole told me… that 1.5 million Jews who were living in Eastern (recently Russian) Poland have simply disappeared altogether; nobody knows how and where." Historian Walter Laqueur added to this: "The report is of considerable interest: it is one of the first, if not the very first, indication that the activities of the Einsatzgruppen have reached the West and also the fact that hundreds of thousands of Jews had been killed. The source was Alexander Lados, the Polish diplomatic representative in Bern."[62] Isaac Lewin, of Agudat Israel, living in New York, who received such messages via the Polish consulate in New York, writes in his books and articles that starting December 1941, when the USA entered the war, the US censor forbade any mention originating in Germany or countries under its control. In his words, "the principle was followed that it was better to stop ten innocent news items rather than to pass one that could be useful to the enemy." Then, suddenly, in mid-1942 a breach opened. This was the transmitter in the Polish Bern legation, Lewin added. These messages went both ways, back and forth, on the ever-expanding Holocaust affecting European Jewry.[63]

Such, as the frightening news sent by Yitzhak and Recha Sternbuch, via the Polish transmitter, on 3 September 1942, to Yaakov Rosenheim, president of the World Agudat Israel, in the following words: "According to recently received authentic information, the German authorities have evacuated the last Ghetto in Warsaw, bestially murdering about one hundred thousand Jews. Mass murders continue.... Do whatever you can to cause an American reaction to halt these persecutions. Do whatever you can to produce such a reaction, stirring up statesmen, the press, and the community. Inform [Stephen] Wise, [Eliezer] Silver, Lubawiczer [Rebbe], [Albert] Einstein, [Jacob] Klatskin, [Nahum] Goldman, Thomas Mann, and others about this." As a result of this and additional similar dispatches, Dr. Stephen Wise called an emergency meeting of Jewish leaders, although Wise still placed doubts in the exactitude of these frightening allegations. It was decided to ask for a meeting with President Roosevelt, and the delegation was received by the Assistant Secretary of State Sumner Welles, who promised to undertake a study of the facts.

Similar to the news by the Sternbuch couple – on March 12, 1943, Avraham Silberschein transmitted the following message via the Polish legation in Bern: "Based on absolutely reliable information, only 10% of Jewish population in the General Gouvernement [occupied Poland] is still alive. Therefore, I considered it my first duty to organise rescue for the survivors, including in particular outstanding figures and young Halus [sic; Hebrew for pioneer] Jews. As part of the action we are obtaining South American passports, mainly Paraguayan and Honduran ones, from respective consuls friendly to our interests. The document stays with us, while the photograph is sent to occupied Poland [the passports were reproduced, and copies were mailed out]. This saves people from death, because as 'foreigners' they are placed in fairly good conditions in designated camps, where they are supposed to stay until the end of the war and where we can contact them by letters. We made a written declaration to the consuls that the passports will serve no other purpose than saving these lives." Silberschein also sadly added that the US legation in Bern disagreed with the passports scheme, due to fear that it will facilitate the travel of German spies. But these concerns, Silberschein adds, have no foundation, since the original passports remain in Switzerland. He added: "The action has the full support of the Polish Legation in Bern, which has been doing its utmost to help us.

Please, pass on the above to the Jewish World Congress, for the attention of [Stephen] Wise, [Nachum] Goldman and [Arieh] Tartakower, with the following annotation: 'Help us expand our reach. The lives of the *Sh'erit ha-Pletah* [catastrophe remnants] depends on that." To which, the Polish envoy, Ładoś, significantly added: "This request has my full and complete support."[64]

Dangers and fears. On October 13, 1943, Swiss Foreign Minister Marcel Pilet-Golaz summoned Ładoś on the matter of the Latin American false passports. There ensued a shouting confrontation between the two. Pilet-Golaz charged: "We found that members of the embassy and consular staff had conducted activity that was beyond the scope of their competence and duties. From the moment we learned about this, we had to set things in order... The passports were invalid, and did not meet the conditions under which they are normally issued." To this, Ładoś responded angrily, that his government will not be able to accept the Swiss decision. That "his Government will never understand that we now treat with absolute severity actions... inspired by very noble reasons – the desire to save the lives of a certain number of good people." The Swiss Foreign minister remarked that the fact that the Germans did not yet raise the issue is no guarantee that they will not react at all, "unless they are forced to do so by a scandal for which I can find no justification." In the end, Ładoś asked the Foreign Minister to reconsider his stand on the passports, which the Foreign minister declined. Thus, ended the somewhat stormy confrontation between the two diplomats, as recorded by Pilet-Golaz.

Unbeknownst to both the Swiss Foreign minister and the Polish envoy, on August 23, 1943, the notorious Jew baiting SS officer, Alois Brunner, in a letter from Paris to Adolf Eichmann, in Berlin, asked to take measures in order to curb the passports scheme of Latin American countries, whose recipients had no knowledge of "their assumed homeland." He charged that under the passports scheme, "the worst Jewish criminals from Warsaw succeeded in leaving Warsaw." Brunner asked that the IIB4 department within the RSHA (*Reichssicherheithauptamt*), the highest SS and Gestapo central office, investigate this matter, and added a pointed threat toward Switzerland. "It is imperative to show Switzerland that criminally fake Jewish citizens cannot be brought out of the Reich."

Already, three months before the Ładoś—Pilet-Golaz confrontation, the Swiss authorities were considering punitive measures against those involved in the false passports scheme, including Rudolf Hügli, Avraham Silberschein, and the two Polish diplomatic staffers, Stefan Ryniewicz and Konstanty Rokicki. In this context, the Swiss police report emphasized that Ryniewicz, Rokicki and the Jewish Julius Kühl, all took part in writing the names into the fake passports, and also brought them to consul Hügli of Paraguay for his signature and the affixing of the official seal. The police also noted Hügli's testimony of the pressure by Ryniewicz for him to cooperate, as the representative of a country allied to Poland. The Swiss authorities decided that Ryniewicz, Konstanty and Kühl were to be summoned (which was done) and warned of the severe consequences against them if they persisted in the fake Latin American passports scheme.

Numbers and conclusion. There is as yet no fully precise statistics how many Jews benefitted from the Latin American passports scheme, and foremost of Paraguay, but according to estimates, their numbers reach into many thousands. Based on a careful study by Jakub Kumoch, the former Polish ambassador in Switzerland, in coordination with the Pilecki Foundation, and made public, Kumoch identified 3,262 names, of whom at least 796 survived thanks to the passport scheme. However, when adding the family members that are also included in many of the passports, the total number of passports beneficiaries is probably higher, up to 8,000, of which up to 2,000 may have survived.[65]

In light of acts that violated the Swiss policy of strict neutrality, Aleksander Ładoś was well aware the he stood before the risk of (a) being declared a "persona non grata," and be asked to leave Switzerland, followed with (b) the closure of the Swiss legation in Bern, as Germany strongly demanded these many years. For reasons, why the authorities eventually withheld from such sharp steps, this may have to do with the changing military situation in October 1943, after the terrible German debacle in the Stalingrad battle, the German withdrawal from North Africa, and the fall of Fascist rule in Italy. This may have led Switzerland to conclude, as many other neutral observers, that the tide of war was turning against Germany, and, consequently, the possibility of a German invasion into Switzerland was no longer perceived as an immediate realistic threat. The time, therefore, had come to switch to a neutrality stance that was subtly tipped toward the presumptive victorious Allies. One, therefore, had to avoid severe punitive steps against the Polish diplomats, close allies of countries at war with a presumed doomed Germany. At the same time, the diplomats in the Bern Polish legation, who lived under constant fear of punitive measures, lacked any foresight of such a possible policy shift by the Swiss government that would ultimately benefit them, when they earlier undertook a series of illegal acts, in contravention of acceptable diplomatic conduct.

The Jewish rescue partners in this vast operation, Abraham Silberschein, Chaim Israel Eiss and Yitzhak and Recha Sternbuch had nothing but words of praise for ambassador Aleksander Ładoś, his fellow diplomats, Stefan Ryniewicz and Konstanty Rokicki, as well as Julius Kühl, the lone Jewish staff member. Chaim Israel Eiss, before he suddenly died in November 1943, wrote to his Agudat Israel colleagues in London, "Beg Polish government in London to thank the Polish ambassador and consul in Bern for helping me to save Jews." In a January 21, 1944 letter by H.A. Goodman, head of the Agudat Israel office in London, to K. Kraczkiewitz, of the Polish Foreign Office, Goodman wrote of "the most helpful attitude adopted by our Minister in Berne, Dr. Lados... He has been helpful in every possible direction and without his assistance many of the activities which we have undertaken could not have been fulfilled." Julius Kühl, too, had words of praise for Ładoś. In his post-war memoirs, Kühl, an orthodox observant Jew, terms Ładoś a true Righteous Among the Nations. He writes that Ładoś "made sure to approve all the Polish passports that I made out at the request of the Sternbuchs and other Jews... Ambassador Ładoś also approved the use of the secret Polish diplomatic code, which enabled the Sternbuchs to send or receive messages with no interference from the Allied or the Swiss censors."[66]

What is currently reffered to as the Ładoś Group is one of the most amazing story of a close collaboration between Polish diplomats and Jewish rescue activists in a joint effort to try to save as many Jews as possible even if it meant flouting international diplomatic standarts of legitimate behavior. Both these two groups realized that the reality of the Holocaust called for such unorthodox responses in fulfillment of the biblical command: "Do not stand idly by while your neighbor's blood is shed."[67]

CHAPTER 8

The Polish Government-in-Exile and the Underground

a) Polish Government-in-Exile

After the fall of Poland, in late 1939, a Government-in-Exile was constituted. It met first in Angers, France; then after France's fall in June 1940 it moved to London, where it stayed throughout the war years, and was recognized as the legitimate government of Poland by the countries at war with Germany. While Władysław Raczkiewicz served as the symbolic head of state, real power was in the hands of prime minister Władysław Sikorski, who presided over a political and military structure that included a National Council (*Rada Narodowa*) – a kind of parliament. It was composed primarily of four political parties: Christian Democratic Labor Party (*Stronnictwo Pracy*), National Democratic Party (*Stronnictwo Narodowe*), better known as the Endeks, Polish Socialist Party (*Polska Partia Socjalistyczna*), and the Polish Peasant Party (*Stronnictwo Ludowe*).[1] Two Polish Jews represented separate political movements in the National Council: Dr. Szmuel Zygielbojm – Bund, and Dr. Yitzhak-Ignacy Schwarzbart – Zionists.[2] On July 4, 1943, Sikorski died in a plane crash and was succeeded as prime minister by Stanisław Mikołajczyk. The fact that this government operated far from Poland caused it not to be fully obeyed by the various underground structures that existed inside occupied Poland.[3] Especially with regard to the Jewish question, Polish leaders in London were conscious of the unambiguous opposition to antisemitism among Poland's Western Allies on whose support they relied.[4] To this was added an imaginary exaggerated Polish belief of the Jewish influence on American and British ruling elites, finance, and media, and that this supposed leverage could either aid or harm the Polish cause. Whether fact or fiction, the belief of an exaggerated international Jewish influence played a role in wartime Polish-Jewish relations.[5]

The Delegate Office (Delegatura). The London-based government-in-exile was represented in occupied Poland by the Delegatura, or Delegate Office or Bureau, that remained the underground's supreme political authority, and was headed by a Delegate head whose responsibility was to coordinate government policies with the activities of the main underground diverse organs, including the underground Home Army (*Armia Krajowa*).[6] Practically every prewar political party that went underground was represented in the Delegate's Bureau, except the communists.[7] It oversaw up to twenty departments along the lines of prewar ministries. The Delegatura also had its own press, and once every three months it reported detailed conditions inside Poland to the London government, including local attitudes toward the Jews.[8] At the same time, each individual party produced its own publications, took part in separate underground social and cultural work, as well as at times in separate military actions. Until the fall of 1942, there were no Jewish representatives in the Delegatura. Afterwards, it was limited to Żegota, a Delegatura offshoot, but not a political body as the other Delegatura participants. The two Jewish main rescue organizations, based in Warsaw after the destruction of the Warsaw ghetto, the Jewish National Committee, and the Bund, were welded with Żegota, although, not directly integrated as a section of the Delegate's administration.[9]

Polish relations with Russia. As a result of the Soviet-German treaty of August 1939, that cleared the road for Germany's invasion of Poland, and the division of the country between these two major powers, most Poles held a deep hatred of the Soviet regime, with which it had been at war two decades earlier. This changed, however, after

Germany's attack on the Soviet Union, on June 22, 1941. Sikorski began to look toward establishing some sort of rapprochement, and he signed a treaty with the Soviets in July 1941, which also provided for a Polish army, organized by General Władysław Anders, composed of Poles imprisoned up to then by the Russians. The treaty restored diplomatic relations between the two countries, annulled by the Soviet invasion of 1939, and promised amnesty to Poles detained in the Soviet Union.[10] Sikorski also hoped that with British and American support, the Soviets would recognize the 1939 Polish-Soviet border that existed under the Riga treaty of 1921. Britain and the US, however, held back. Toward the end of the war, the Soviet Union upheld the so-called Curzon line that placed most of eastern Poland beyond the Bug River within Russian territory, with Poland to be compensated by annexing land which formed part of eastern Germany before the war.[11] When the Katyn massacre of thousands of Polish military officers by the Soviets came to light, in April 1943, with the Polish government demanding a full-scale investigation by the International Red Cross, the Soviet Union, denying responsibility for this massacre (admitted 50 years later when Poland regained full independence) responded by breaking diplomatic relations with the London-based Polish government.

Government-in-exile and the Jewish issue. The outbreak of war in 1939 initially led to high expectations of a favorable change in Polish policy toward the Jews. It was, after all, a war in which Poland, an ally of liberal Western democracies, stood against Nazi Germany – the very symbol of intense antisemitism.[12] The government, now in exile in London, issued several pro-equal rights proclamations, such as the November 3, 1940 resolution that "Jews, as Polish citizens, shall be equal with the Polish community in duties and in rights in liberated Poland. They will be able to develop their culture, religion, and folkways without hindrance."[13] Jan Stańczyk, the minister of labor and social welfare, in a speech on April 20, 1941, reaffirmed the Polish commitment to full Jewish legal equality, and denounced German-style racial antisemitism, which was "foreign to the psyche of the Polish nation." He acknowledged and expressed shame for the political groups in prewar Poland that had advocated anti-Jewish discriminatory programs.[14] On March 9, 1942, Prime Minister Sikorski referred to the courage of Polish Jews; "the spirit with which the Jews in Poland bear their sufferings must fill us all with admiration." But this remark was omitted in the report which appeared in the Polish press on that occasion, and also was not cited in air broadcasts to Poland.[15] On October 29, 1942, in a London public speech, Sikorski condemned in sharp language the German mass murders of Jews, and promised full equality for Jews in postwar Poland.[16] These words were also excised when his other words were broadcast in Polish.[17]

In spite of the earlier few pro-Jewish pronouncements, the political parties that made up the Polish wartime government, with the exception of the Socialist party, still held on to the idea of the emigration of Jews after the war as the best solution of the Jewish question, and this was also the government's position although, paradoxically at the same time, upholding equal rights to Jews.[18] Sikorski was at times ambivalent on this matter. In August 1942, he stated that while Jews had every right to emigrate from Poland to their National Home (i.e., Palestine), it was not something essentially required of them, neither should they be pressured to do so. As late as 1944, after most Polish Jews had been exterminated, Ignacy Schwarzbart, the Jewish member in the National Council, stated, "the fear of the allegedly 'too many Jews in Poland' continued to hold Polish thought captive during the war," although the Final Solution had made it a moot point.[19]

In London, the exiled Polish leaders were receiving messages from their own underground network that included critical reactions to the government's favorable declarations in Jewish matters. A letter from the homeland in late November or early December 1940 warned that while the Polish population categorically disapproved of the German treatment of Jews, "it would nonetheless be a grave error to suppose that antisemitism among the Poles is a thing of the past. Antisemitism still exists among all segments of society... These facts should be taken into account in London."[20] The Delegate man in charge inside Poland cautioned the government against its "exaggerated" love of the Jews. "The government goes too far in its philo-Semitism, especially as the Jews are not liked in the country."²¹ Repeated hints continued to reach London that the government need not go out of its way to defend the Jews.²²

Even outside Poland, some government officials did not hide their anti-Jewish sentiments. Such as Polish ambassador to Russia, Stanisław Kot, who stated on November 25, 1941: "Polish society is terrified of excessive Jewish influence. It is afraid that the need to import foreign capital into a decimated Poland would give the international financial Israelite magnates excessive power in the country, and that this might, in turn, enchain the country to 'an economic Jewish slavery.'" He added that "not only has the Jewish question not lost its sharpness, but it has, to the contrary, become significantly inflamed."²³ One must also not forget that one of the leading parties in the London government, the National Democrats (the Endeks), one of the strongest parties in pre-war Poland, was shamelessly antisemitic.²⁴

The imaginary claim that the Jewish rebels in the Warsaw ghetto uprising, during April 1943, were Russians and Soviet agents was to some degree accepted even by some of the leaders of the Polish government-in-exile. Reviving the prewar fear of a Jewish-Communist conspiracy, the Polish defense minister, in London, General Marian Kukieł, in a cable to the head of the military underground, queried: "Was the resistance of the Jews of Warsaw during the liquidation of the ghetto really led and organized by Soviet officers and noncommissioned officers parachuted into the ghetto, and were arms, ammunition, and anti-tank guns supplied in the same fashion?"²⁵

News of the Holocaust and Allied responses. Radio contact between occupied Poland and Polish outlets in some other countries was established as early as spring of 1940. The Poles produced many transmitters and receivers of their own; 6 to 8 transmitters monthly by 1943. According to one observer, "Polish clandestine wireless was judged at the time to be 'outstandingly good,' in advance of any comparable service in the world, and at time as many as 100 sets were working at once out of Poland to bases in England and Italy." The Polish underground also developed an efficient courier system to the West.²⁶ Aware of what was happening to the Jews inside Poland, as early as 1941 and into 1942, the

Polish government published several reports, including the first edition of a Black Book in January 1942, which included the plight of the Jews with that of the Poles during the early years of the German occupation.[27]

The first known information about mass killing of Jews that made its way to London was the Delegate's report of August 30, 1941. It was a short description of the execution of 6,000 Jews in Czyzew near Łomża on August 27, 1941, when the Germans occupied what was previously the Soviet zone of Poland. Two days later Dziennik Polski (the daily London newspaper in Polish for Polish immigrants) printed the news in bold type on the front page. In November 1941, Polish underground head, General Stefan Rowecki, reported that 3,000 Jews were shot in Vilna, but this item did not appear in the London press.[28] In mid-January 1942, Minister Stanisław Mikołajczyk provided Ignacy Schwarzbart with the Delegate's report of late September 1941 that stated that mass executions of the Jews, indiscriminate of sex and age, had taken place in the Białystok district since September 1941. Furthermore, that in Lithuania almost all Jews have been already murdered, with details of the remaining Jews in several locations. The report also described the mass executions in Ponary, near Wilno-Vilna and emphasized the Lithuanians' participation in the crimes. In the section of Volyn province, the report told of the massacres of 8,000 Jews in Pinsk, 6,000 in Brześć, all the Jews of Homsk, Motol, and Kobryń, and more than 10,000 in Wlodzimierz, where "the grave of the victims of the murder is about one kilometer long." Most of this information, however, was withheld and not made public by the Polish Ministry of Information.[29]

It must also be pointed out that the first news of the genocide was discounted by non-Jewish and Jewish sources alike as exaggerated and were disbelieved. Dziennik Polski mentioned that "in Boryslaw, Molodeczno, and Mohylów there is not a single Jew left;" that they "disappeared," not killed, despite reports from Poland that explicitly mentioned killings.[30] The Bund report, of May 11, 1942, dispatched from Warsaw on May 21, and reaching London less than two weeks later via the Polish underground, was the first lengthiest report on the extermination of Jews in Poland. It provided a detailed description of the Nazi actions against the Jews in Poland, which for the first time was defined as part of a plan for total extermination, and estimated the number of murdered Jews at 700,000.[31] It gave a grim litany of the number of Jews who had perished in various places in eastern Poland: 3,000, Lwów; 15,000, Stanisławów; 5,000, Tarnopol; 50,000, Wilno-Vilna; and so forth. The Bund asked the Polish government to urge the western allies "to apply the policy of retaliation against the Germans" (a request Sikorski had already made two months earlier to Roosevelt) and against Germans living in the Allied countries ("the fifth column"), a demand rejected by the Western democracies.[32]

The Polish government (and other Allied government officials, as well as some in the Jewish leadership) doubted the reliability of these reports. Polish leaders in London could not believe the key Bund information of a plan of total extermination, with 700,000 Jews already murdered. As stated by Adam Pragier, a socialist member of the National Council, "I did not believe in this number [700,000]... How can one believe in the killing of 700,000 people? The Bund should have written, that [the Germans] killed 7,000 people. Then we could provide the news to the British, with a slight chance they would believe it."[33] As Zygmunt Kaczyński, a top official of the Ministry of Information, told the Jewish representative in the National Council, Ignacy Schwarzbart: "Hitler murdered many Jews but you [Jews] exaggerate the numbers." [34] Even Szmul Zygielbojm, the second Jewish representative, initially doubted the accuracy of the report of his own Bund party. He changed his mind after having read other Polish reports and became the most outspoken alarmist and doom-monger of the terrible truth.[35]

In spite of these doubts, this time, the Polish government not only publicized the Bund report, but on June 6, 1942, the cabinet issued a memorandum to the Allied governments protesting German crimes against the civilian population, including the Jews: "Extermination of the Jewish population is reaching an unbelievable scale. In towns such as Wilno, Lwów, Kolomyja, Stanislawów, Lublin, Rzeszów, Miechów [the Germans are] slaughtering tens of thousands of Jews.... The Jews in Poland are suffering the most horrible persecution of all their history."[36]

Three days later, Sikorski warned that the Jews of Poland were "doomed to destruction in accordance with the Nazi pronouncements on destroying all the Jews regardless of the outcome of the war."[37] It is therefore remarkable that it took the Americans and the British so long (until November 1942) to confirm the truth of these horrifying messages, including the one by Gerhart Riegner, the World Jewish Congress representative in Switzerland, in August 1942, of the planned extermination of all of Europe's Jews, that Riegner received from a confirmed source.[38]

When the Germans launched their so-called Great Action against the Warsaw ghetto Jews, on July 22, 1942, deporting the vast majority to the gas chambers in Treblinka – Tadeusz Bór-Komorowski, the deputy to the Home Army commander Stefan Rowecki, wondered why nothing of this was heard on BBC radio, in spite of the reports sent to London.[39] On August 11, 1942, Stefan Korboński, of the Delegate Office, wrote to London: "From the [Warsaw] ghetto, 7,000 are taken daily for slaughter. President of the Jewish council, Czerniaków committed suicide." It took a month before the BBC broadcast this news. Korboński learned later that the information in his messages was disbelieved: "Neither our government nor the British would believe them," one Polish emissary told him.[40]

On August 19, 1942, Home Army commander, Rowecki, dispatched a message (received in London on August 25), which read: "Since July 22, liquidation of the Warsaw ghetto (400,000 inhabitants) has continued with great cruelty by the German police and Latvian auxiliary police. Till now 5-6 and at present 15 thousand [people] daily have been deported. Apparently, the majority [of victims] is murdered in Bełżec and Treblinka, a part seems to be assigned to [forced] labor behind the front line. Mass killings and robbery [take place] along with deportation. Several tens of thousands of skilled craftsmen and their families are to remain in the ghetto. To this point more than 150,000 have been deported."[41] When the underground courier Jan Karski arrived in London, in November 1942, he gave an extensive personal chilling account on the scale of the Jewish genocide, witnessed by him inside the Warsaw ghetto and a concentration camp.[42] Sadly, first in London, then in Washington,

Karski's message was either disbelieved or shrugged off with the excuse that nothing could in the meantime be done, but only after the defeat of Nazi Germany.[43]

According to Richard Lukas, the Polish government-in-exile was the first official body to propose Allied bombing of railroad lines leading to and including the German death camps.[44] One needs to mention in this context the Polish fears that the extermination of the Jews would be followed with the start of the extermination of non-Jewish Poles. Already, when the Germans began the mass removal of Poles in the Zamość region late in 1942, to replace them with ethnic Germans, it appeared to the Poles that the Germans intended to exterminate the Polish people even before they had finished off the Jews. In general, the Polish government shared the belief of many Poles that Jews and Poles both faced elimination, one way or another.[45] On November 27, 1942, at an extraordinary session of the National Council in London, Deputy Prime Minister Mikołajczyk added a generally-held Polish fear that "the enemy is determined to exterminate both nations; only the Jews, being fewer in number, are being exterminated faster."[46]

On September 17, 1942, the Polish government approved a public protest against the extermination of the Jews, but held back on calling Poles to give shelter to the Jews, nor for Jews to seek refuge with Poles.[47] On December 9, 1942, Polish Foreign Minister, Edward Raczyński, wrote to British Foreign Secretary, Anthony Eden, reiterating the German goal of the total extermination of the Jewish population of Poland, and giving details of the actual liquidation process; Warsaw, tens of thousands; Wilno-Vilna, 50,000; Lwów, 40,000; Równe, 14,000; Kowel, 10,000; as well as victims in Lublin, Stanisławów, Tarnopol, Stryj and Drohobycz. Also, of the murder of thousands of Jews in the Bełżec, Treblinka, Sobibór and Chelmno death camps. The number of victims, the note stated, "exceeds one-third of the 3,130,000 Jews" who, according to this estimate, lived in Poland before the war.[48]

Finally, on December 17, 1942, the Allies publicly confirmed the German extermination of all Jews that was actually taking place. The declaration spoke of "several hundred thousand" victims, which was less the numbers in Raczynski's note, less than reports from Poland, and much less than the actual figures. But the silence in which the West passed over the massacre of Poland's Jews was finally broken. By that time, sadly most of the Jews in Poland had already perished, but many tens of thousands still remained.[49] The Allied governments promised retribution against those responsible for the mass murder of Europe's Jews, to be done after winning the war as quickly as possible, but nothing was stated what was to be done to mitigate the ongoing mass murder of Jews while the war was still on.[50]

At the same time, it must also be noted that on December 18, 1942, the President of the government-in-exile, Władysław Raczkiewicz, wrote a dramatic letter to Pope Pius XII, begging him for a public condemnation of both murdered Poles and Jews – an appeal that remained without a proper response.[51]

However, regrettably, the Polish government's official press and radio broadcasts into Poland avoided direct calls to the population there to show solidarity and unity with the Jews, but confined itself to merely verbally protesting against the extermination of Jewish citizens in Poland.[52] Only on May 5, 1943, after most Polish Jews had already been killed, Prime Minister Sikorski, in London, appealed to the population of Poland: "The greatest crime in human history is being perpetrated... I ask you to extend all possible aid and, at the same time, to soften the sting of this terrible brutality." There were no further similar direct appeals.[53] Gutman and Krakowski report that a certain Lieutenant Jur, a Polish courier who arrived in London on June 12, 1944 suggested in a lecture to publicly announce that persons hiding Jews will be considered members of the Polish underground, even when they did not belong to it. "After all," he added," those who hide the Jews imperil their lives no less so than those who fight in the ranks." His suggestion was not accepted.[54]

Jan Karski, Polish underground emissary to the West, in November 1942, in a face-to-face meeting with Prime Minister Sikorski, on the problem of the *Szmaltsowniks*, told him what the dying representatives of Polish Jews in Warsaw asked him to relay the following message: "We know there are Poles who blackmail, who denounced us to the

Gestapo. We are Polish citizens – there is an Underground... So, take action against them!... Kill them and then publish the names of those whom you killed in the underground press, including the nature of their crimes."[55] Similarly, Moshe Sneh (Kleinbaum), of the Jewish Agency in Palestine, asked Stanisław Kot, Polish envoy in the Middle East, on November 27, 1942, that the government enact a decree making any-one taking part in the murder or persecutions of Jews liable to criminal responsibility.[56] Also, that the Polish government call the Polish clergy to speak out and protest, in the same way as some of the clergy in the western democracies did. Kot's reply was evasive. In subsequent meetings between the two, on December 5 and 13, 1942, and on January 25, 1943, Sneh asked to prevail upon the Polish population to supply relief to Jewish survivors. The discussions between the two were at times tense, and did not lead to any positive outcome.[57]

Certain politicians within the Polish government continued to up-hold the pre-war stance that the majority of Polish Jews who would sur-vive would have to leave after Poland had regained its independence. As early as 1940 Stanisław Kot, then minister of information, and Edward Raczyński, the Polish government's ambassador in London, advanced such a proposal in separate conversations with representatives of British Jewry. In his memoirs, Selig Brodetsky, one of the Jewish interlocutors, wrote: "Professor Kot gave a long history of the Jews in Poland, which, he said, had treated Jews well for centuries. But Jews were a foreign body in Poland... He said that there were too many Jews in Poland, Hungary and Romania. About a third of them could remain, the rest would have to go elsewhere."[58] In the spring of 1942, the Polish National Council (which acted as a sort of parliament-in-exile) passed a resolution endorsing the project of the massive emigration of Polish Jews from the country in the future.[59] Prime Minister Sikorski's view on emigration of Jews as a national necessity also did not change during the war. In January 1942, he told British Foreign Secretary Anthony Eden that "it is quite impossible... for Poland to continue to maintain 3.5 million Jews after the war. Room must be found for them elsewhere."[60] At the time of Sikorski's remark, there were much less Jews alive in Poland, though still in great numbers.[61]

The Jewish response by the Bund organization to these demands, was: "It should be stated clearly and frankly that the notion of a 'surplus' of Jews is preposterous and unspeakable. We are not 'unneeded' citizens in Poland... Jews have been in Poland since the time the Polish state was formed and are not foreign *arrivistes* [newcomers] who should be forced to emigrate... It is true that Jews will begin to emigrate immediately after the war.[62] However, it will be a voluntary emigration, just as non-Jews will emigrate voluntarily."[63]

Jews in the Polish Army of General Anders. After Germany attacked the Soviet Union, in June 1941, Stalin allowed the many Poles forcibly removed to Russia during the Soviet control of eastern Poland, to be freed if they joined a newly created Polish army to help in the war against the common enemy. This new Polish army eventually totaled 72,000 men, and was commanded by General Władysław Anders. After training on Soviet soil, the army was evacuated to other battlefields outside Russia. According to Jewish sources, thousands of Jews flocked to join this army, numbering initially 10,000 men, including the future prime minister of Israel, Menachem Begin.[64] Some Polish military units consisted as many as 30 to 40 percent Jews. Polish antisemites in the army wanted but failed to get General Anders to limit the number of Jews, while Zionists asked for separate fully-Jewish detachments which, they hoped, would eventually find their way to Palestine.

In some of the training camps, in Russia, Jewish soldiers were separated from their non-Jewish colleagues into special units, to avoid confrontations.[65] This led General Anders, on November 14, 1941, to write to his senior officers: "I order all my subordinate commanding officers to fight relentlessly against any manifestation of racial antisemitism." The Jew was to benefit from the same laws that apply to all Poles. However, some two weeks later, a second order was issued, the wording of it and its general tenor virtually cancelling out all that was positive in the first order of the day.[66] The second order reads: "I well understand the reasons underlying antisemitic manifestations in the ranks of the armed forces."

However, Anders explained, the current policy of the Polish government, tied as it was to the policy of Great Britain, made it imperative to treat the Jews favorably, since the Jews wield considerable influence in the Anglo-Saxon world. Therefore, for the time being, any overt expression of the struggle against the Jews was totally forbidden and whoever was found guilty of such would be severely punished. "However, after the battle is over and we are again our own masters, we will settle the Jewish matter in a fashion that the exalted status and sovereignty of the home-land and simple human justice require."[67] Anders, however, categorically denied he had written such words. "That order is a falsification from A to Z."[68] The debate on this has not been settled.

Meanwhile, back in Russia, in May 1943, Stalin allowed, or en-couraged, the creation of a second Polish army, the Popular Polish Army (*Ludowe Wojsko Polskie*), to be formed, under the command of Zygmunt Berling. It originally numbered 45,000 soldiers, and it rose to an esti-mated 100,000 men by August 1944, and upward that figure later. Jews made up a significant component of Berling's army, estimated at 20 percent in February 1944. This force fought alongside the Red Army as it advanced into occupied Poland.[69] In the eyes of the Polish underground, Jews were again conflated with the Soviet and communist threat, and General Berling was repeatedly referred to as a Jew even though he was baptized at birth in a parish church in Limanowa.[70]

b) The Polish Underground

During the German occupation of Poland, a so-called "underground state" arose that had a highly developed network of political, mili-tary, and social institutions. They were divided into two major political groups: the larger non-communist camp, known as The Home Army (*Armia Krajowa*-AK), composed of the majority of prewar political parties, and accepted by most of the Polish population; and the much smaller communist camp, People's Army (*Armia Ludowa*, AL), rep-resented by one main party, the Polish Workers' Party (*Polska Partia Robotnicza*, PPR), and backed by the Soviet Union.[71] AK became a large military organization that incorporated numerous military groups with different political views and affiliations.[72] Except for the the fiercely antisemitic *Narodowe Sily Zbrojne* (National Armed Forces, NSZ), up until March 1944, on the right, and the communist *Armia Ludowa* (AL), on the left, all political shades of opinion were represented in the *Armia Krajowa*.[73] Many military and political groups held their own counsel and pursued their own goals, often at variance with the official policy of the AK central command.[74] Thus, the Home Army was more of an umbrella organization of armed groups originally organized under the authority of individual political parties.[75]

As the Soviet army drew nearer to the prewar Polish frontier, in March 1944, a rapprochement took place between the Home Army and the NSZ – the only underground organization that openly declared war on surviving Jews, and was active in hunting them down, while other underground units may have intermittently acted likewise, but not as a matter of official policy.[76] At this point, with the Russians very close, the struggle between the larger AK and the much smaller AL became more intense, and led to armed confrontations between both groups.

As early as September 1940, the Home Army had 40,000 fighters and a relatively large supply of weapons, secretly stockpiled from the dismembered Polish Army (including hundreds of heavy machine guns and submachine guns, and thousands of rifles and pistols), in spite of the country's intensive German military occupation.[77] The size of the Home Army continued to grow, to 236,000 in September 1943, and peaked at 350,000 in June 1944. By then, it was the largest underground resistance force in German-occupied Europe.[78] Poland was fairly rich in forested areas and small villages, which provided good cover for guerrilla warfare.[79]

The Home Army targeted the SS and Gestapo among the Germans, as well as members of the Polish, so-called Blue, police, who participated with the Germans in hunts after underground members and against Jews on the run. Also, among AK primary targets were German labor offices and the railroad system. According to Richard Lukas, by 1944, in Warsaw alone the underground was killing 10 Germans every day.[80] Prior to the outbreak of the general Warsaw uprising in August 1944, according to Lukas, the AK lost to the Germans an estimated 62,133 men.[81] If these numbers are correct, the Home Army was indeed a very active underground and, hence, also capable of affording aid to Jews inside and outside the ghettos, if it so wished.

Though it conducted extensive sabotage, diversion, reprisal, and intelligence operations, the Home Army's primary goal was preparations for an eventual general uprising which would be launched when, as the Russians neared Polish territory and with the Germans in full flight, the Poles would reassert their military and political authority over their own country, ahead of the Soviet army.[82]

Train derailments. The argument that nothing could be done to stop or at least slow down the deportation of Jews to the death camps by substantial damage to the trains or railways tracks leading the victims to their miserable end, does not bear out when one takes into consideration that the Germans employed an estimated 30,000 Polish railroad workers, who many under underground orders played a major role in delaying and damaging German rail transports throughout Poland during the occupation years. One of the sabotage methods employed was adding a chemical to the grease in the box of the railroad engine which disabled it.[83] Explosives and track derailments were some of the other methods used.

By 1942, AK extended its diversionary operations to Warsaw itself where on October 8, six rail lines leading out of Warsaw were cut. In retribution for these losses, the Germans executed thirty-nine men and women.[84] As pointed out by Richard Lukas, Polish railroad workers played a critical role in sabotaging trains and related installations. Already in February 1941, as a result of the activities of the underground unit, called Union for Revenge, 43 percent of the locomotives in the General Government were inoperative.[85]

Dr. Zygmunt Klukowski reports in his diary some of the actual rail sabotage by the underground in his Zamość region, during the first months of 1943:

> January 1, 1943: Approximately sixty armed men surrounded the [Szczebrzeszyn] station; they threw six

hand grenades. The passengers were ordered to lie flat on the floor. They were assured that nothing would happen to them... The water tower was set on fire... Everything went smoothly. Also, on New Year's Eve, two bridges blown up, a small one in Minkowice, another in Ruskie Piaski. There the passengers had to walk on narrow planks to get to the other train waiting on the opposite side of the bridge.[86] January 5, 1943: More and more attacks on the railroad are taking place in different locations. The trains between Dlugi Kat and Krasnobrod are under constant machine gun fire. Trains were blown up near Krasnik and Trawniki.[87] March 29, 1943: A train derailed between Zwierzyniec and Krasnobrod. March 30, 1943: Tracks were damaged and two engines, with six cars, were thrown from the tracks. In retaliation several forest rangers were killed. April 23, 1943: In Susiec, an attack on a train took place. A tanker loaded with gasoline was set on fire. Train traffic was interrupted for several hours. May 15, 1943: Last night, near Susiec a German armored train was blown up, and today near Tereszpol a train was derailed. On the Tanwa River in Biłgoraj County a bridge was destroyed. Last night a train derailed between Susiec and Mazila (this one by a Soviet partisan group).[88]

Klukowski points out that Polish units target mostly German transport trains, or trains bringing ethnic German to replace Polish settlers, but Polish passenger trains are not targeted.[89] Thus, in response to a German reprisal raid that took the lives of 280 Poles, AK in June 1943 burned a German-colonized village in which 69 ethnic German settlers perished. Retaliatory operations continued, included attacks on railroad, military, and government targets.[90] German authorities in Poland grew progressively more nervous about the frequent attacks on German communication lines and supplies, especially in the important districts of

Kraków, Warsaw, Lublin, and Radom. By 1943, the Polish underground had escalated their attacks so much that trains on many lines moved only at certain times and under guard, or not at all. A report for the period January 1, 1941 to June 30, 1944 listed 6,930 locomotives damaged; 803 locomotives delayed in overhaul; 732 transports derailed; 979 railroad cars destroyed; 19,058 railroad cars damaged; 443 transports set on fire; and 38 railroad bridges blown up.[91]

These brave efforts by the Home Army, begun slowly in 1942, and picking up speed in 1943, contrasts with the lack of any efforts to sabotage trains taking their human cargo to the death camps, operations which it could have attempted to carry out – at least on some of them. At the same time, the same charge can be placed at the door of Jewish partisans who targeted German troop and supply trains, but not those transporting fellow Jews to the death camps. In fact, the only such derailment by a clandestine Jewish group, took place in distant Belgium; the 20th convoy, on April 19, 1943. None in Poland. Some defenders of this lack of activity point out that the Home Army attacks on German trains indirectly and temporarily benefitted the Jews by creating logjams in the transportation system.[92]

Whatever the excuses, the Polish underground (the largest of its kind in German controlled countries) could have attempted to sabotage the railroad tracks leading to Treblinka, or other extermination camps, or even attack the extermination camp itself (German military personnel in some of these camps, other than Auschwitz, was relatively small; most of the guards were Ukrainian, Lithuanian or Latvian militiamen), but did not undertake any such action for various reasons; also for fear it would result in inordinately heavy losses to the attackers.[93]

Jews in the Underground. The Polish underground, for all its exemplary democratic structure and its exalted national mission, was essentially meant for non-Jewish Poles only. Its powerful bond with the country's inhabitants was based primarily on culture and blood, not citizenship, and in this intimacy it mirrored popular attitudes that, sadly, saw the Jews as outsiders; not part of the Polish social community.[94] At the same time, several hundred Jews were admitted in various Home

Army units as individual members, especially in those subordinated to units of Socialist leanings, with the new recruits mostly masking their Jewish identity, to play it safe.[95] In general, a Jew wishing to join an underground movement had to take extra precaution not to encounter an extreme right-wing unit which could prove fatal for the Jew, such as a radically antisemitic NSZ unit.[96]

The accidental discovery of a Jew in an underground unit did not necessarily, or always, lead to fatal results. For instance, Jozeph Halperin joined a Home Army unit in Warsaw under an assumed name, on April 20, 1944, not telling the recruiting officer that he was Jewish. Eventually, one day after Halperin was chosen to head a nine-man team, and his platoon stopped at a lake for a few hours, "like all the others, I undressed and jumped into the water. "Oh, you're circumcised,'" some noted; but they did not mind, and he remained a squad commander. Halperin added that in his Home Army platoon, he did not notice any hostility toward the Jews.[97] In another story, such a discovery had a different, though not fatal, finale. The Jewish Chil (Hillel) Cejlon served in the underground in Warsaw. In 1943 a school acquaintance of his hometown Sandomierz who had come to Warsaw recognized him and started to blackmail him. When Cejlon revealed to his commander that he was Jewish and asked for help in getting rid of the blackmailer, he was told instead to leave both the organization and Warsaw.[98] Some claim that an estimated 1,000 Jews, who mostly managed to successfully hide their Jewish identity, were members in units of the Home Army.[99]

Since Jews, identified as such, continued largely to be excluded from the Home Army, they usually formed separate fighting units.[100] They had to fend for themselves, since they could hope for little support from the Home Army, in acquiring arms, guidance, intelligence or liaison assistance with the outside world.[101] This general refusal to admit Jews into underground ranks went hand in hand with repeated references to Jews as either outright communists or strongly leaning towards it. Such references can be found in reports of the Delegate's Office and the Home Army, such as the following: "The partisan units are commanded by Bolshevik officers. The vice-commander is often a

Jew;" "Jews are completely alien to us and are hostile to Poles in various areas. They are threatening the local population with Bolshevism."[102] One underground report stated: "The Warsaw ghetto is still the seat of the communist base in Poland... Politically, Jewish communists... aim for a Sovietized Poland in the future."[103] A situation report of the Home Army for September 1943 on the remaining Jews in Sokołów stated: "They are mainly young Jewish men of whom 90% are communist."[104] As the realization set in that Poland would be liberated from the east by the Soviet army, there was a corresponding rise in fear of a supposed Jewish communist takeover. This often led to gross exaggerations of the real proportion of Jews as communists.

The Underground and antisemitism. Henryk Woliński, in charge of the Jewish information section in the Delegate's Office, related to author Lukas that, "never, not in the slightest way, did I come across signs of anti-Semitism, either from the side of the High Command of the Home Army or from the BIP [Bureau of Information and Propaganda];" that is, in the very upper ranks of the underground. Although that statement refers to some senior officers in the Underground, anti-Jewish feelings could ran high among some of the rank and file of lower-ranking fighters.[105] The same Henryk Woliński also reported that "the Polish lower middle-classes, freed from economic competition with the Jews by the Germans [tacitly support] the extermination policies of the occupier towards the Jewish people."[106] Some antisemitic opinions proliferated even among personnel of the Delegate's Office.[107] Such as in its issue of No. 5, of August 31, 1943, that stated: "While appalled by the dreadfulness of the methods, and while revolted by the disgrace of murdering women and children, ... [the Jews] were entirely and forever alien to our culture, our traditions, and our statehood... There probably is no other human collectivity that would be so repulsive, that would abound with individual characteristics as distinct and as offensive as those which the Jews share."[108] Similar anti-Jewish motifs could also be found in some provincial papers of the Home Army.[109]

Some underground publications went further in anti-Jewish tirades. *Słowa Prawdy* (Words of Truth), October 30, 1943: "The Jews have beset

us, like a plague. Poland was their breeding ground, a place for incuba-
tion... getting fattened off our Polish misery."[110] *Praca I Walka* (Work
and Struggle), Issue No. 6, March 27, 1944: "The accursed Jewish incu-
bus has left so much poison in the blood of civilized nations, produced
so much evil and so many calamities, that the time has finally come to
mete out a well-deserved punishment."[111] Reporting on the elimination
of the Warsaw ghetto, the National Democrats' (Endeks) *Młoda Polska*
gloated: "Victory has been achieved."[112]

On September 25, 1941, General Stefan Rowecki, Home Army commander, responding to Prime Minister Sikorski's statement in London
that after the war Jews will enjoy equal rights as non-Jews in liberated
Poland, wrote to London: "I report that all the steps and pronouncements
of the government and members of the National Council regarding the
Jews in Poland arouse the worst possible impression and greatly enables
propaganda that is unfavorable or even hostile to the government...
Please accept it as a completely genuine fact that the overwhelming majority of the country is of an antisemitic orientation"[113] He added, that
"hardly anybody advocates imitating the Germans. However, even those
underground organizations under the influence of the prewar executive
groups of the Democratic Club or the PPS [Socialist Party] accept the
emigration project for Polish Jews as a solution to the Jewish problem."[114]
In fact, nine out of thirteen of the major political groups attached to the
Delegate's Office, in 1943, favored the emigration of Jews after the war,
and only a few were willing to grant them equal rights.[115] In the summer
of 1944, in one of his reports, Jan Stanisław Jankowski, the government's
last head of the Delegate Office, criticized in harsh terms the London-
based government's presumed "love toward Jews." Although, Jankowski
conceded, that this is to some extent necessary as far as Polish foreign
relations are concerned, nevertheless such attitudes should be restrained.
The government should bear in mind "that inside the country Jews are
disliked."[116]

The Socialist Party, PPS, was the only major political group in
the Polish underground which advocated full equal rights for Jews in
the post-war period,[117] and it was the only group within the Delegate's

Office that maintained any contact with at least one Jewish resistance group: the Bund.[118] The disenchantment by the Delegate's office with the London-based government-in-exile's sometimes pro-Jewish statements was no better illustrated than in the memorandum by Roman Knoll, in August 1943. A onetime foreign minister in the prewar Polish government, he now headed the Delegate Foreign Affairs Commission. Under the heading of "The Jewish Question," he wrote that the whole middle-class continues to pay homage to antisemitic ideology and was pleased that the Nazis had solved the Jewish problem in Poland. "Thanks to Hitler, the members of the Polish middle class have at one stroke got rid of their unwanted creditors – the Jewish banks and merchants – and thanks to the mass slaughter of Jews, the scheme of 'numerus nullus' [not any number] has been achieved in its entirely in industry, labor, commerce and economic life as a whole."[119] Knoll warned that "in the Homeland as a whole… the return of the Jews to their jobs and workshops is completely out of the question, even if the number of Jews were greatly reduced. The non-Jewish population has filled the places of the Jews in the towns and cities; in a large part of Poland this is a fundamental change, final in character." Restoring Jewish property and jobs now held by Poles, Knoll warned, would meet with strong, perhaps even violent, public opposition in Poland. He added that the government was correct in assuring world opinion that antisemitism will no longer exist in Poland, "but it will no longer exist only if the surviving Jews do not endeavor to return to Poland's cities and towns en masse." As a solution to the Jewish question, he suggested creating a Jewish center somewhere else in Europe, rather than in Palestine, due to Arab hostility; and he added incredulously, "our attitude in this matter should be philo-Jewish rather than anti-Jewish."[120]

On June 30, 1944, Żegota protested strongly against the publication by the agricultural department of the Delegate's office, entitled *Nowy Wspolny Doni* (New Common Home), where Jews were portrayed as only concerned with business, and do not love Poland, but the war was gladly bringing "some positive developments" by the "disappearance and future reduction of alien forces."[121] Żegota charged that this publication "offends the honor of the Polish nation by portraying the most horrible crime of Hitler as the historical fate of the Jewish people and by evaluating it as a positive development for Poland." It added that such words "paralyzes to a significant degree its [Żegota's] activities, which are undertaken with huge effort and risk."[122]

The Home Army and the Warsaw ghetto uprising. Another controversy dividing historians is the role of the Polish underground in help to Jewish insurgents during the Warsaw ghetto uprising, that started on April 19, 1943, by the some 50,000 remaining Jews.[123] Tadeusz Bór-Komorowski, the deputy Home Army commander at the time, in his post-war memoirs, The Secret Army, wrote of the offers of help by the Home Army during the previous deportation of Warsaw's Jews in the summer of 1942, that were supposedly rejected by the Jews, but which Jewish sources assert is a figment of the general's imagination.[124] He wrote: "The Jewish leaders, however, rejected the offer, arguing that if they behaved quietly the Germans might deport and murder 20,000 or 30,000 and perhaps even 60,000 of them, but it was inconceivable that they should destroy the lot; while if they resisted, the German would certainly do so."[125] According to historian Israel Gutman, himself a Warsaw ghetto resister, not a single one of the details in Bór-Komorowski's description is based upon fact.[126] Quite the opposite is true. In the text of a message sent by General Stefan Rowecki to London, on January 2, 1943, he stated: "Jews from all kinds of groups, including communists, have turned to us lately asking for arms, as if we had depots full of them. As an experiment, I took out a few revolvers. I have no assurance they will use these weapons at all. I shall not give out any more weapons, for you know that we ourselves have none."[127] In fact, the Home Army had much more than "none." According to an authorized representative of the Polish government stationed in the United States, in the spring of 1943 the AK (Home Army) had in its possession 25,000 rifles, 6,000 revolvers, 30,000 grenades, and other types of even heavier weapons.[128]

In fact, the newly-created Jewish underground in the ghetto had taken the initiative and appointed a delegation, headed by Aryeh Wilner ("Jurek"), to contact Polish resistance forces on the Aryan side of

Warsaw.[129] This took place in August 1942, and according to Woliński, Wilner met with an unfavorable response.[130] Thus, it was the Jews rather than the Poles who made the first liaison attempt, which was rejected by the Polish side.[131] It took two more months, when in October 1942, Woliński put two representatives of the Jewish Fighting Organization (ŻOB) in touch with Zbigniew Lewandowski of the underground, for instructions on manufacturing explosive devices.[132]

Earlier, following Jan Karski's secret meeting with two Jewish leaders, in Warsaw, in September 1942, he reported their request for weapons to Rowecki, but got no positive response.[133] An additional ten pistols were, however, delivered with instructions in diversionary actions, and how to make Molotov cocktails, and starting December 1942, members of the Jewish resistance regularly visited a secret Home Army location on Marszałkowska Street, where they received military training.[134] Only after January 18, 1943, when Jews for the first time shot back at the Germans during another deportation roundup, did Rowecki and his comrades change their views on the effectiveness of Jewish resistance.[135] He then ordered the delivery of more weapons.[136]

Altogether, up until the ghetto uprising of April 19, 1943, the AK secretly handed over a total of 90 pistols, magazines and ammunition, 500 defensive hand grenades, 100 offensive grenades, 15 kilograms of explosives with fuses and detonators, 1 light machine gun, 1 submachine gun, material to make Molotov cocktails, and sabotage material such as time bombs and safety fuses, and this was later followed with a second shipment of light weapons.[137] In comparison with the existing supply of arms kept by the Home Army, this delivery of arms and ammunition did not diminish its capacity for underground activity.[138]

Important to note that the overwhelming majority of the remaining ghetto Jews were not combatants during the uprising; most of them hid in bunkers and remained passive until the fighting was over,[139] while the fighting by the ŻOB was limited to about five hundred men. Shortage of arms was the principal factor. Only one pistol was available for every seven men, one rifle for every fifty men, and one machine gun for more than every one hundred and fifty men.[140] The ghetto uprising that began on April 19, 1943, pitted a small group of poorly armed Jewish fighters against an overwhelming enemy force armed with heavy weapons at its disposal, including tanks, armored vehicles, and aircraft. This struggle, in Ringelblum's words, was "between a fly and an elephant."[141] As Wilner previously told Woliński, "We do not wish to save our lives. None of us will come out alive. We wish to save our human dignity."[142]

During the Warsaw ghetto uprising, Captain Józef Pszenny, of the Home Army, made an unsuccessful attempt to blow up part of the ghetto wall in order to allow for mass escape. After a brief confrontation, and losing some of his men from German fire, Pszenny ordered his troops to retreat with the dead and wounded.[143] A second attempt, led by Captains Jerzy Lewinski and Zbigniew Lewandowski, was made in a different section of the wall, on April 23. Outgunned and outmanned, the Home Army unit withdrew after killing several SS soldiers; the wall-breaching mission failed, and the ghetto remained sealed.[144]

When ŻOB leader Yitzhak Zuckerman asked that automobiles and people be prepared in time to get the survivors out; that houses be readied to conceal the fighters, the response of the Polish underground spokesman was: "We don't believe you. We believe that the ghetto is no more than a base for Soviet Russia... The Russians were the ones who prepared the revolt in the Warsaw ghetto, and you have far more weapons that you let on; and I am sure that on May 1, 1943, they will land in the Warsaw ghetto."[145] When a year later, on August 1, 1944, the Polish underground launched its large-scale Warsaw uprising, it did not at all mind help from the Soviet communists. In fact, the underground pleaded for such help to ward off defeat, which sadly for the insurgents was only halfheartedly forthcoming, but Soviet army units did participate in that uprising. Historians, critical of Jewish partisan aid from some Soviet partisan units, are surprisingly silent when it comes to the complaints of the Polish underground of not receiving sufficient military aid from the Soviets during the bloody fighting in Warsaw and its suburbs, in August and September 1944.[146]

After the Warsaw ghetto uprising was suppressed and most of its last inhabitants were either dead or deported, the Polish underground press showered praise on the Jewish fighters. *Myśl Państwowa* (Government Thinking), on April 30, 1943: "The Jews have risen to the level of a fighting people… The Polish public look upon this phenomenon with unrestrained admiration, affords it moral support, and hopes that the resistance will continue for as long as possible." The Home Army': "Dying with weapons in hand might introduce new values into the life of the Jewish people and bestow upon the death of Polish Jews …the halo of a struggle for the right to life."

Nevertheless, a considerable part of the Polish clandestine press still kept up its vicious anti-Jewish campaign even during the weeks of the fighting in the ghetto. *Walka*, on May 5, 1943: "Even the Jew fighting for his life understands that he can move the world with the name of Poland, but not by his own fate, merited a hundredfold." *Wielka Polska*, on the same day: "There is no heroism in it at all, or even any risk. Nor has it anything in common with the Polish cause."[147] *Prawda Młody* (The Truth of the Young), the organ of the Catholic youth in the underground, added an antisemitic sting to its words of praise: "Who knows whether the Jews will not emerge from the fire purified; if the wandering, parasitical, dangerous Jews will not return to being a normal people that will embark upon an independent, creative life wherever they may be. The Warsaw ghetto may not be an end but a beginning; whoever dies as a human being has not perished in vain."[148]

The Underground and the killing of Jews. The most frightening aspect that has stained the Home Army's record, in spite of its valiant struggle against the German invader, were the increasing forays against Jews by various underground formations. This began slowly toward the end of 1942 and picked up steam in the months thereafter, as Poles were witnessing the German armies in their headlong retreat before the Russians who edged ever closer to the prewar Polish border with the Soviet Union. But instead of celebrating such an event, most Poles saw the specter of one hateful occupier being replaced by another – the equally hated Russians, who in August 1939 signed a treaty with Nazi Germany, sacrificing Polish independence, and were presently in the process of liberating Poland from the Germans, only to probably impose a communist regime in its stead, directed from Moscow – a most terrible scenario for Poles. This again brought to the foreground the *Żydokomuna* charge; of Jews being the avant-guard of a communist-dominated Poland. This accusation, spiced with a still prevalent traditional antisemitism led certain disgruntled elements in the Home Army to the determination to clean the country of as many Jews as possible before the Russians moved in.[149] Thus, when Jewish fugitives continued to fear the Germans who spared no effort to find and murder them, they also had to contend with surprise attacks by certain armed elements of the Polish underground – mainly units of the right-wing and fiercely antisemitic NSZ, but also other units of the Home Army proper.[150]

Although it joined the mainstream AK in March 1944, the NSZ continued to act as a dissident militia organization. Numbering in the thousands (their claim of 72,439 fighting members is perhaps an exaggerated figure), it targeted communists, and any Jews they came across. No mercy was shown to those apprehended, be they men, women and children, even Jews who were officer members in the Home Army. In the last stages of the war, members of the NSZ Holy Cross Brigade were even assisted by the Germans to flee westward, to avoid capture by the advancing Soviets.[151] In truth, there were also isolated incidents of Jews killed by members of communist *Gwardia Ludowa* (later, *Armia Ludowa*),[152] but a whole lot more such cases were carried out by the aggressively antisemitic NSZ.

There were also bandit groups, in search of loot and plunder, who falsely claimed membership in the Home Army, and terrorized Jewish fugitives they came across, and also peaceful Polish village residents. As also reported by Klukowski, during the spring and summer months of 1943, throughout all the small villages, so-called partisans were taking food from the people. "It is nearly impossible to find out who they are; Polish, Russian, even German deserters or plain bandits."[153] Many brigands were local people who had become criminals after the Germans forced them from their homes. Others were already before members of the criminal world. Jews, occasionally joined these groups or formed groups of their own, and they included some criminal elements among them, as told by Reuben Ainsztein of such a "wild group" in the northeast regions of Poland.[154]

Jewish partisan units operating in forest lairs were especially vulnerable to attacks by either certain elements of the Polish underground, who branded Jewish survivors (men and women of all ages, and their children) as "bandits," who were in collusion with true bandits, and thus legitimizing their killing. Such as the Home Army order, by commander Tadeusz Bór-Komorowski, in August 1943: "Banditry... Men and women, especially Jewish women. ... I placed emphasis on the necessity of liquidating the leadership of these bands... [and] to ensure the participation of the local population."[155] No mention that the plundering women be treated with consideration, since they were probably out for food to feed their starving families hiding in the forests.[156] A further order, on September 15, 1943 called upon local Home Army commanders to "liquidate" the leaders of bands that were robbing local Poles; again, "in particular Jewish women." [157] As noted by Antony Polonsky, "nothing in the document indicates any sympathy for fugitives from the Nazi genocide: no appeal is made to villages to provide them with the food and shelter, which, in the absence of such assistance, they could only seize by force, and no understanding is shown of their predicament."[158] Bór-Komorowski's order was later withdrawn, according to one source.[159] Notwithstanding this, assaults by Home Army detachments upon Jewish partisans increased in frequency.

Home Army reports from the Nowogródek region in September 1943 mentioned that in order to survive (food and provisions), Jews were at times forced to pillage local farms.[160] This led the rural population to retaliate and mercilessly and systematically hunt down Jews, or hand them over to the Germans, but not necessarily because of their search for food.[161] As testified by Adolf Wolfgang, who fought in the Home Army while concealing his Jewish origin. After making sure he was not identified as Jewish, they explained to him that lately there were many Jews hiding in the forests whom they had shot dead [because] they desire a Poland without Jews.[162]

Following are a few more examples. In Lublin province, Eliahu

Liberman testified of an attack on a Jewish detachment commanded by Jechiel Grynszpan: "Some Home Army units in the village of Makoszka in the Parczew forest region – whenever they came upon a lone Jew, they would kill him... Many from our ranks perished by their hands."[163] In the vicinity of the village Majdan Tyszowski, Tomaszow Lubelski county, a Jewish partisan unit, commanded by Cadok established contact with local units of the Home Army. There ensued a number of joint operations against the Germans. Two weeks after a joint and successful operation, the Home Army unit invited the Jewish combatants for a feast. Caught unawares, the Jews were first served poisoned vodka, and then fired upon. No one survived.[164]

Moving further south, in the Kielce region, on February 9, 1943, near Ostrowiec Swiertokrzyski, fifteen Jews who escaped from the Ostrowiec labor camp, were murdered by a unit of *Związek Odwetu* (Revenge Union), an organization which acted under Home Army orders.[165] This happened during a swearing in ceremony under the white-red banners of Poland, when they were all assembled together. Of the seventeen, only two succeeded to escape the entrapment.[166] In a post-war, 1949 trial, unit commander Józef Mularski freely admitted: "I, the commander of a ZWZ [Union of Armed Struggle, Home Army] sabotage unit, ordered my unit deputy... to execute, together with the subordinate members of the unit... a death sentence by shooting all the people of Jewish nationality staying in the dugout in Bukowie near Kunów. A similar killing of a group of Jews in the Kielce district, who had escaped into the forest, and wished to join the Home Army, were lured to a certain spot, and then all nine Jews were shot and killed, including one woman."[167]

In Opatów county, 40 miles east of Kielce, a large partisan detachment, known as *Barwy Biale* (White Colors), participated in several killings of unarmed Jews in hiding. The last incident, in Siekierzyn, in 1944, involved the murder of a large group of Jews, numbering as many as fifty-eight. Edward Sternik, one of the insurgents who took part in the murder testified that at the head of 60 Home Army members, in Siekierzyn, Kielce district, they came upon a shelter containing about 30 people of Jewish nationality, some women among them. "I ordered...

to carry out the death sentence on these persons of Jewish nationality...
I saw the Jews killed, lying in the field." In February 1950, the Kielce
Appellate Court sentenced squad commander Edward Sternik to death,
and five of his soldiers were given sentences ranging from the death
penalty to five years in prison. All the sentences were subsequently commuted to lighter sentences.[168] And there are many more such accounts.[169]
Some of these attacking units may also have been involved in raids on
fellow non-Jewish Poles for either loot, or political reasons, as evidences
by the war-time diary of Dr. Klukowski, but with a stark difference.
Only when Jews were targeted, no one was spared; not even defenseless
women and children.

In May 1944, Żegota in a communication to the Delegate Office
condemned the "murders committed by a certain segment of Polish society against Jews in hiding... The shameful murder of thirteen Jewish
fighters who were on stand-by in villages in the area of Koniecpol...
Those involved were NSZ or AK units under the command of someone
known as Orzel... In the region of Częstochowa, Radom and Kielce
such units had murdered about 200 Jews in hiding."[170]

The only area of prewar Poland in which a close cooperation between
Home Army units and Jewish partisans was the rule took place in a
certain place in the Wolyn region – for a special reason. The dominant
rival force there were the Ukrainian nationalists who frequently assailed
the Polish minority, ravaging entire villages in the most atrocious manner. The Poles, consequently, looked on the Jewish partisans as most
desirable fellow defenders. Sergeant Kazimierz Wojtowicz ("Brier"), was
stationed with his men in the village of Hanaczów, 12 kilometers north
of Przemyślany. There, his men and the Polish populace supplied the
Jewish partisans with foodstuffs free of charge, and the villagers permitted the Jews to set up quarters in the village itself.[171] The number of Jews
hiding there is estimated at 250.[172] In the words of one of the Wojtowicz
brothers: "The fact that around 250 Jews could be hidden in one village
of whom close to 180 survived... is perhaps without parallel in wartime
Poland." Indeed, without parallel; and the Wojtowicz brothers (Alojzy,
Kazimierz and Antoni) were honored as Righteous by Yad Vashem.[173]

The pro-communist People's Army (*Armia Ludowa*) and its prede-
cessor, the People's Guard (*Gwardia Ludowa*), were generally friendlier
toward Jewish partisans, and this attracted Jews to these units who
wished to fight the Germans, since they could rely not to be harmed by
them.[174] However, here too, the conduct of the People's Guard varied,
and one could never be sure how they would react to the presence of
Jews in their midst.[175]

Village attacks. While one may debate the "banditry" justification for attacks on armed Jewish partisans, what justification was there
in targeting individual unarmed Jews on the run from the Germans?
Beginning with December 1942, some Polish underground formations
undertook searches for Jews hiding in villages and small towns. When
they were discovered, they were shot on the spot. Beginning with the
summer of 1943, crimes of this type reached a high frequency.[176] In
Gutman's and Krakowski's study, cases of murder of Jewish fugitives by
Polish underground groups (NSZ and some of the Home Army) were
found in 120 different localities or forest ranges.[177]

One of these gruesome murders was committed by the Marian
Soltysiak ("Barabasz") partisans that caused the death of six Jews –
women and children included – and including the Polish man who
was sheltering them, Stefan Sawa, in the village of Zagórze outside of
Daleszyce, 17 kilometers southeast of Kielce. Sawa had been sheltering in
his rented house six members of the Zelinger family, whom he had earlier
helped escape from the Kielce ghetto. When the Barabasz group learned
of the presence of Jews at Sawa's residence, an order was given to "liquidate" Sawa, and the Jews he was hiding, after Sawa was warned to expel
the Jews, but he declined. Sawa's punishment was acted upon on the
night of February 24, 1944, when an execution squad led by Władysław
Szumielewicz raided Sawa's home. After the war, Szumielewicz gave the
following account: "All four of us then took aim at Stefan Sawa, who was
in the kitchen, and shot him on the spot. Next, we turned our guns on
two Jews whom we shot and killed... We found three women and one
child of Jewish nationality whom we shot dead... We helped ourselves
with men's and women's clothing, men's and women's shoes, as well as

jewelry, including a gold necklace, rings, as well as one gold and two ordinary watches... We set the house on fire to destroy all traces."[178] The post-war sentences of the perpetrators were surprisingly light. Most were sentenced to a few years' imprisonment, but were released after only a short prison stay. By 1957, all remaining prisoners had been freed. As for Marian Soltysiak ("Barabasz"), the group leader, he was released in 1953, due to "poor health." To add, insult to shame, in June 1992, the Kielce District Court overturned the 1951 conviction, pronouncing Soltysiak innocent of all charges.[179] As for the martyred Stefan Sawa, he is honored as a Righteous by Yad Vashem, on the Polish slate. [180]

Polish 1944 uprising and Jews. In July 1944, the Soviet army crossed the Bug River, and on July 22, liberated Lublin, the first major Polish city.[181] When in late July 1944, Soviet forces approached Warsaw, the Home Army decided that the time had come to take matters into their own hands; especially, to preempt the Red Army, who were still on the other side of the Vistula River, from taking over. The order was given to challenge the Germans, who were thought to be on the point of withdrawing, by a general uprising, and take control of the country's capital.[182] So, on August 1, 1944, the Home Army launched the long-awaited revolt, that lasted sixty-three days of intense savagery.[183] In the first four days, the insurgents occupied the city's central suburbs, but thereafter they were mostly on the defensive as the Germans brought in heavy reinforcements, and used three battalions of starved Soviet prisoners, known as the Russian National Liberation Army (RONA in Russian initials) in the suppression of the Polish uprising.[184]

Still hoping for a political and military victory, the Poles – incredibly – put their faith in the Soviet Union (overlooking their previous accusations of Jewish collusion with the hated Soviet communists). Across the Vistula River, the Russians attacked the German position in the Praga suburb, to relieve the pressure on the insurgents inside Warsaw proper, with the help of the pro-Soviet First Polish army, led by General Zygmunt Berling, but held back from a full-blown attack on Warsaw itself.[185] By September 28, Home Army commander Bór-Komorowski, still hoping for deliverance with Russian aid, continued to haltingly parley with the Germans surrender terms.[186] On October 2, 1944, with the Russians still on the other side of the Vistula River, the final surrender terms were agreed upon with the Germans, under which Home Army soldiers were to be treated as prisoners-of-war, while the whole civilian population was to be evacuated from the heavily ruined city, mostly to Pruszków, some 10 miles southwest of Warsaw, and tens of thousand others to various labor and detention camps in Poland (some, even went sent to Auschwitz), or further in Germany.[187] Polish military losses included some 20,000 killed and wounded, and a much larger number of civilians – the estimates vary into as many as 100,000.[188] The Germans systematically dynamited most of the remaining homes, with 93 percent of the dwellings destroyed or damaged beyond repair, and Warsaw was turned into a ghost town.[189] On January 17, 1945, the Soviet army resumed its offensive, and entered Warsaw, and two days later, General Leopold Okulicki, the last commander of the Home Army (AK), formally dissolved it.[190]

While the fighting inside Warsaw was still raging, another trial faced Jews, as the regions in the city where thousands of Jews were believed hiding were all caught up in the fighting. Many of them emerged from their hiding places and shared in the momentary euphoric sense that gripped all the city's residents at the start, as they watched the insurgents unfurl the red and white symbols of the Polish flag over the buildings that they secured.[191] It has been estimated that between 400 and 500 Jews took part in the fighting, with many of them dying, and perhaps 100 murdered by hostile Poles.[192]

On August 5, 1944, the Polish Zośka battalion liberated the Gęsiówka labor camp in the area of the former ghetto, which was holding some 340 Jewish inmates (mostly men) for cleaning up the remnant valuables left by the former ghetto inhabitants. Thirteen of the men were subsequently enlisted in the Home Army under the command of Lieutenant Wacław Micuta.[193] Here too, amidst the joy of a temporary freedom, antisemitism raised its ugly head. As one witness recalled, "alongside the beautiful and moving scene of soldiers sincerely welcoming the liberated Jews, there were also very unfortunate antisemitic pronouncements and anti-Jewish blows by some soldiers. And sometimes without any reaction from the commanders."[194]

The Home Army's relations with Jews continued to be a troubled one during the two-month long Warsaw uprising.[195] A Home Army unit commanded by Captain Wacław Stykowski reportedly killed at least twenty-two Jews and three non-Jews during the uprising.[196] Jewish activist Feigele Peltel (code name, Vladka) recounted one such Home Army attack: "On the fifth day of the rebellion several Jews... with distinctive Jewish faces, were detained by an insurgent guard of the Armia Krajowa. The men proceeded to beat them, declaring cynically that there would be no place for Jews in liberated Poland. Two of them – Lutek Friedman and Adek – managed to jump out of the window under a hail of bullets... The third one—Yeshieh Solomon—was murdered on the spot."[197] Eyewitness Chaim Goldstein: "I see Jewish fighters murdered by their own comrades-in-arms – killed purely and simply because they are Jews."[198] Marian Igrán tells that someone in his unit had discovered he was a Jew and intended to kill him the following day, and fortunately for him, his officer came to the rescue.[199]

Samuel Wittenberg related that when asked for his real name during the first days of the uprising, believing that the Polish rebellion signaled a new era for the surviving Jews, he confidentially replied "Samuel Wittenberg." "When I noticed the curious stares of the company, I added, 'I'm a Jew, and I was at Treblinka.' No one said a word." Soon, afterwards, some members of the radical NSZ were threatening to kill him. "That very day, as I was in my position shooting at the Germans, a shot came from behind me and whizzed past my ear. Turning around, I caught a glimpse of a rifle barrel disappearing into an opening of a building. I was stunned at the thought that my comrades at arms – after all we had gone through together, after all the battles we had fought as partners – were out to kill me because I was Jewish." Wittenberg left his post and found a friendly fighting force – a small Polish socialist militia.[200] When the uprising began to falter, Jacob Celemenski remembered hearing anti-Jewish invectives all around him. "The Jew again became a scapegoat for the [uprising] failure: 'Jews brought on the war,' 'Jews started the uprising', 'Jews prevented the Bolsheviks [The Russian army, which camped across the Vistula River] from coming', and similar antisemitic sentiments. We had to listen to this in the streets and yards and cellars, while Nazi bombs were dropping from overheard."[201]

The negative, the positive, and the indifferent. In the years leading up to World War II most Poles wished to see the Jews gone from their country, but never in the form it took during the war years – of mass murder. In trying to assess the true nature of Polish-Jewish relations during the war years, one is confounded with a mixture of the bad, the good, and the indifferent, as in the following story.

Halina Zawadzka, while still in the Konskie ghetto, met Olga Słowik, from Starachwice, who had come to trade, and had given Halina's family her address, to seek shelter with them, if it ever came to that. Fleeing the ghetto, eighteen-year-old Halina arrived at the Słowik home, and was warmly welcomed.[202] However, Olga's mother, Karolina, fearing discovery by the Germans of the sheltered Jewish woman, wanted Halina to leave and pleaded with her daughter to agree with her. But Olga declined. According to Halina, "they were too gentle, too warmhearted, to physically throw me out." While there, Halina met a certain Stanisław, who was active in the *Gwardia Ludowa*, the Polish communist underground. By January 1943, Stanisław had acquired for Halina new set of false identities, and she was now named, Józefa Czajkowska.[203] The other neighbors in that building, in Halina's words, were openly antisemitic and described Jews as "swindlers, the cause of the prewar poverty, masters of international intrigues, carriers of diseases, personifications of the devil and so on. They talked about mass murders of the Jews with such indifference – as if the Jews were animals, not humans. I never heard a word of sympathy concerning the Jews' present fate." Halina also encountered similar views from others. A male friend who took a liking to Halina, not knowing her true identity, during a walk with her, stated how he admired the Germans for one thing – getting rid of the Jews. He added that the Poles should build a monument to Hitler for solving the country's Jewish problem.

In the spring or summer of 1943, Halina learned that her hosts were members of the Polish underground. Their home was the town's liaison point of the local organization, and it included a box that the Słowiks kept in their attic in which messages were received and passed on to members of the local Home Army.[204] Sometime later, for her security, Halina was told to go into a certain forest and link up with a partisan group. Arriving at the partisan location, she saw young men sitting on the grass beneath a white-red Polish flag fluttering in the air. "I was moved. I had come across free Poland." That evening, they all shared a meal. It was during the conversation over dinner that Halina learned that the unit had recently come across a Jew hiding in the forest. The unit commander explained that he ordered his men to kill him. "When I bravely asked 'why?', I was told that this was a safer way for everyone." Halina, under her new name, joined the unit and was handed a loaded pistol. Some time later, Halina returned to Starachowice and to Karola's home.[205]

In the fall of 1944, the NSZ began to operate in the Starachowice region. At a meeting with two NSZ members, talking about Jews, they were so overt about their antisemitism that Halina's face turned red and the two men immediately suspected she was Jewish. One of them told Halina that the NSZ killed Jews regularly without any moral qualms because Poland had to be Jew-free after the war. She was being spared only in consideration of Olga, a dedicated member of the Polish underground.[206] Halina Zawadzka survived thanks mainly to Olga Słowik, a woman she had accidentally met in a ghetto, to be able to tell her story.

In a 1986 monograph, Yad Vashem historians Israel Gutman and Shmuel Krakowski, both Polish Holocaust survivors, concluded that the over-all balance between the acts of crime and acts of help, is disproportionately negative. They accounted this negative balance to a large extent by the hostility towards the Jews on the part of large segments of the Polish underground, and, even more importantly, by the involvement of some armed units of that underground in the murder of Jews.[207] Some find this conclusion too harsh; others, a fair description of reality.

Poland, the most victimized of all German-occupied country, where so many suffered martyrdom – at times for no reason at all; at others times for resisting their oppressors – was also a country that counted over 3 million Jews before the coming of the Germans, with only some 50,000 left on Polish soil when the Germans were evicted (thousand others survived the concentration camps, and tens of thousands by having fled into the Soviet Union). The question whether Poles could have done a bit more to prevent or reduce the scope of the mass murder of a people that had lived in their midst for nine centuries, will continue to haunt students of that period for years to come. At the same time, while dismayed by those who participated in anti-Jewish excesses, one draws inspiration from the thousands of Poles who saved Jews from death, while at the same time risking their own lives, and some paying for it.

CHAPTER 9

Postwar Situation

World War II was an unprecedent tragedy in Polish history; a period of great suffering of all Poles, and many times more so of all Jews. The ties that had bound the two communities for hundreds of years, and had started to fracture in the years leading up to the war, finally broke asunder during the bitter five and half years of the harrowing German occupation. When the dark clouds lifted, and the dust had settled, most Poles were still there; none, but a small fraction of prewar Jews were to be found. As for Poland itself, it underwent a new painful phase, a situation only imaginable in the worst nightmares – a country transformed into a communist state, and ruled from afar, from Moscow; from the same rulers that in 1939 made possible the start of the war and the end of Polish independence. To most Poles, this new situation was as bad, if not worse, than the country under German occupation. In their frustration and rage, Jews were again much blamed for this; the old *Żydokomuna* myth resurfaced with added animus.

Outwardly, with most Polish Jews gone, it would seem that Polish dreams of Poland without too many Jews had in some miraculous way come about – a favor unintentionally bestowed upon the country by the Nazi Germans who, paradoxically had intended to also do away with the Polish nation politically, though without exterminating its people. Instead of feeling content at such an unforeseen favorable outcome, the opposite happened. Antisemitism again raised its ugly head, leading to two years of anti-Jewish violence, for two principal reasons. In the eyes of some, there were still too many Jews left in the country, especially when one adds the tens of thousands who returned from exile in the Soviet Union. But, of greater frustration, after the martyrdom of so many Poles, mainly to the Germans, Poles had to submit to a communist regime, a satellite of the Soviet Union, and to concede the redrawing of the county's borders to the advantage of the Soviet Union. Seeking explanations for this sad outcome, the fact that some self-denying Jews occupied prominent positions in the new political configuration, inspired many disillusioned elements within the population with new acts of violence against the country's mostly non-communist remaining Jews. As violence gradually abated, it erupted again in the years 1967-1968, as a campaign by the communist-led regime to expel the last remaining Jews from the country – accused this time, not of being too pro-communist as in years past, but of being only communist in appearance, but wishing to undermine communism, in collusion with foreign governments. Jewish life in Poland had come full circle, as the curtain came down on the few remaining Jews in Poland.[1]

Poland as a communist state. In the first meeting of the three main anti-Axis Allies (the Soviet Union, the U.S.A. and Britain) in the Tehran Conference, during November 28-December 1, 1943 – without even first consulting the Polish government-in-exile, in London, it was agreed that after the war, Poland's eastern border with the Soviet Union would be shifted westward to the so-called Curzon Line (proposed in 1919 by the British Lord Curzon). In other words, the territories taken by the Soviet Union under the Nazi-Soviet August 1939 treaty would remain in Soviet hands. At the Yalta conference, of February 4-11, 1945, it was decided that Poland was to be compensated for its territorial loss in the east by the annexation of German lands in the west: the provinces of East Prussia, Pomerania and Lower Silesia.[2] In summary, Poland was to be moved bodily 241 kilometers westward.[3] However, while the territory lost (178,220 square kilometers) greatly exceeded the territory gained (101,200 square kilometers), the resources of the western territories more than compensated for the republic's diminished area. The territory lost to the Soviets included mostly primitive undeveloped rural districts, while the territory gained from Germany included rich coal and iron deposits, complex industrial installations, a modern network of roads and railways, and a large number of cities and seaports.[4]

The population of Poland in 1945 had fallen by almost one-third from the 1939 figure, to a mere 23.9 million, but the pre-war national minorities that made up a large part of the population had also disappeared. Over 90% of the Jews were dead, the Germans in the acquired territories expelled, and the Byelorussians and Ukrainians in the east incorporated in the USSR. The new Poland was homogenously solid, inhabited only by Poles, who were all attached to the Roman Catholic church, but also subservient to a communist regime, headed by a revamped communist party, the Polish Workers' Party (*Polska Partia Robotnicza*, PPR), which took orders from Moscow, and this was to last for 45 years.[5]

With the dismantling of the anti-communist Home Army, and the presence of Soviet troops on Polish soil, a new era began for the country, renamed People's Republic of Poland; in reality, a Soviet satellite state.[6] In the eyes of most Poles, one occupier had simply replaced another, and Poland had been betrayed and abandoned by the West.[7] As elsewhere in the Soviet bloc, links with the West were discouraged, newspapers and books were strongly censored; and artists and writers were required to adhere to the so-called banal norms of Socialist realism. Priests were arrested; yet the Church was far from crushed and it also managed to retain legalized religious instructions for the young and allowed to retain its own press.[8]

Post-war Jewish population and cultural life. The small number of Jews that resurfaced in Poland on the morrow of the German defeat were an infinitesimal fraction from the pre-war Jews there, and also of a different composition. Hasidic Jews were hard to find, likewise Bund Jews, whose leadership was eliminated by Stalin. Yiddish/ Hebrew circles were almost non-existent. It was a different and culturally poverty-stricken Jewry compared that what it had been only six years before – the mainstay of a universally significant cultural-religious center. In June 1945, some 55,000 Jews had registered with various committees throughout liberated Poland, although some more who were passing as non-Jews preferred to remain incognito, not sure of their reception as Jews by the public at large. In January 1946, the number had risen to 86,000, most of whom, assumingly had either hidden on the so-called Aryan side or survived the concentration camps, with smaller numbers also surviving as combatants in partisan units and in the Polish army. This was followed with a significance surge of some 250,000 Polish Jews who made their way back from the Soviet Union, to where they had earlier fled, and returned under a repatriation program.[9] If one were to add the Jews who did not bother to register with Jewish organizations, as well as the still hidden children, the gross total figure could well be over 300,000 Jews; in other words a sizable number but a mere 10 percent of the prewar Jewish population.[10] This number of Jews, substantially larger than the original 55,000, was viewed alarmingly by antisemitic Poles, who feared a "re-inundation of Poland by Jews."[11] Of greater import, one of the main reasons for the new spate of antisemitism and anti-Jewish violence was the fear among Poles that Jewish survivors would demand the return of their homes and properties, and the possessions and assets they had left in the safekeeping of Polish acquaintances.[12] The old bogey of Jews as communists, now in a country under a hated communist regime, intensified this negative feeling about Jews.

Despite the lack of freedom under the communist regime, six state Jewish elementary schools and three Jewish high schools (all in Polish language) continued to function until 1967, and a Yiddish Theater remained active in Warsaw.[13] A handful of surviving Jewish historians founded the Central Jewish Historical Commission that, in 1947, as the Jewish Historical Institute (*Żydowski Instytut Historyczny*, ŻIH), in Warsaw, became the repository of archives relating to Jewish life before and during the Holocaust. Above all, in 1946 and 1950, some of the Ringelblum Archives of Oneg Shabbes were found and dug out of the rubble of the destroyed Warsaw ghetto. ŻIH's activity paralleled that of Polish historians working in the High Commission to Investigate Nazi Crimes in Poland (*Główna Komisja Badania Zbrodni Hitlerowskich w Polsce*), established by the Polish government in 1945.[14]

During the occupation, thousands of Jewish children were hidden either with private families or children homes of various sorts, including Christian religious ones. Some of these children were returned into Jewish hands, sometimes after difficult negotiations and payments of money for the children's wartime upkeep. The official Jewish committees maintained 11 boarding schools with a total of 1,135 orphans, and day schools and nurseries which cared for about 20,000 children, but with education oriented toward Polish assimilation. A separate organization, the Jewish Religious Council, sent people to redeem children from Polish homes, particularly at the request of religious relatives. These children were delivered to their relatives abroad, or sent to be adopted by Jewish families in the United States, United Kingdom, and other countries. A third organization was established by the Zionist movement, and given the abbreviated name of *Koordynacia* (Coordination). Its emissaries wandered through Poland to rescue children, very often risking their lives in doing so. The *Koordynacja* established four children's homes, which housed hundreds of children aged between two and twelve, in advance to their movement to Palestine/Israel. Funds were supplied mainly by the American Jewish Joint Distribution Committee (JDC). This situation lasted into 1949, when the Polish communist government ordered Jewish children organizations to cease operations and leave the country.[15]

Jewish life under the oppressive communist regime proved difficult, and in the years 1948–49, all remaining Jewish schools were nationalized and Yiddish was replaced with Polish as a language of teaching. *Folks-Shtime* (People's Voice) remained the sole Yiddish weekly newspaper.[16] On April 19, 1948, a Warsaw Ghetto Memorial was unveiled. Constructed out of bronze and granite and designed by Natan Rappaport, the memorial is located where the Warsaw Ghetto once stood, at the site of a command bunker of the Jewish Combat Organization (ŻOB).

Jews viewed as communists. Some Polish political writers and historians attribute the renewed antisemitism to two factors: (1) the alleged widespread collaboration of the Jews with the Soviet administration in eastern Poland between 1939 to 1941, and (2) the relatively large presence of Jewish survivors in the Polish communist administration after the war.[17] Many Poles continued to retain the belief that communism was a Jewish conspiracy imported from the Soviet Union, and that both the Soviet invasion of eastern Poland in September 1939 and the installation of a communist government after the Second World War were the work of Jewish communists, whose presence in the post-1945 government, and especially the security police, did not pass unnoticed.[18] People claimed that they were presently living under a regime that was essentially not Polish, but Jewish; the creation of the Jews working under Soviet tutelage. The Jews were held responsible, in a word, for the renewed enslavement of Poland.[19]

Overlooked was that communists never constituted a majority among Jews in general. Also, conveniently sidestepped was that most communist Jews were hardly Jewish, and not a few were embarrassed by their Jewish origins and made efforts to hide it.[20] Except for a handful of Yiddish-speaking communists, most of the Jews who served in the Polish government had assimilated linguistically and culturally to Polish norms or were attempting to do so. For most of these officials, their connection to anything Jewish amounted to an accident of birth.[21] In total, no more than a few thousand Jews, many of them fully secular and also non-communist, were employed in the government bureaucracy and other key national sectors, so that in terms of numbers Jews made up an insignificant percentage.[22] But this presence of Jews in government agencies, in sharp contrast to the total absence of Jews in pre-war governmental positions, and against the background of a Moscow-imposed communist regime, rekindled the antisemitic fires of prewar years.

Widespread anti-Jewish violence. There were several factors that led to the outbreak of anti-Jewish violence in the immediate post-war years. One of these was undoubtedly the traditional religious Jew-hatred. The traditional view of the Jews as aliens and unpatriotic was an additional factor. Whatever the real causes, Jews began to feel physically unsafe. Many Jewish testimonies collected immediately after the war contain the recurrent line: "We had to move to a bigger town because they were killing Jews, because they threatened to kill us." And these were no hollow threats. Hundreds of such accounts are preserved in

Warsaw's Jewish Historical Institute's archives and in published memoirs, marking a new sad phase in the history of Jewish life in Poland.[23] All over Poland, there were secret murders of Jews who had been saved, Jews who had come back from the camps and from the partisan units. This included women and children as well.[24]

It was the period of the worst anti-Jewish violence in the history of Polish-Jewish relations. Beginning in 1945 the assaults upon Jews swiftly assumed mass proportions.[25] From 1944 to 1947 between fifteen hundred and two thousand Jews were murdered, most of them specifically because they were Jews.[26] In March 1945 alone, while the war still raged elsewhere, but there were no more Germans on Polish soil, 108 Jews were killed and 9 wounded, according to the official information of the Ministry of Public Security (MBP). The situation worsened in June and August 1945, when serious riots broke out in Dzialoszyce, Przemyśl, and Rzeszów. During the Rzeszów event, the same pattern appeared that would be repeated later in Kraków and Kielce: the rumor of the ritual murder of a Christian child igniting the pogrom flames.[27] Assaults took place in Chełm, Opatów, Sanok, Lublin, Grojec, Gniewoszów, Rabka, Raciąż near Płońsk, and other towns.[28] The attacks spread throughout the country, and in 1945 alone 353 Jews were reported murdered. The wave of anti-Jewish excesses continued well into 1946 and subsided in 1947, which coincided with the panicky flight of most Jews from the country.[29]

The two largest pogroms were in Kraków, on August 11, 1945, which led to widespread robberies, the demolishing of apartments, and the beating of Jews on the street, and the even greater Kielce pogrom on July 4, 1946, when 42 Jews killed and more that 100 wounded – both based on a false ritual murder charge.[30] Before the war, Kielce had about 20,000 Jews, now only some 250 were present. The Kielce pogrom had a traumatic effect on the Jewish community. It was also a turning point in the attempt to rebuild a Jewish community in Poland. Kielce convinced most survivors that Poland held no future for them.[31]

Jewish responses. Anti-Jewish riots and killings in postwar Poland led an uncertain number of Jews to retain their wartime hidden non-Jewish identity. It was simply safer not to disclose one's Jewish origins. As a result, many Jews remained unknown – some for a long while; others, forever. They were often intermarried and sometimes did not tell their spouses about their true identity. In the meantime, these hidden Jews begat children who had no knowledge of their Jewish ancestry.[32] To these one should add the several thousand Jewish children who had been adopted by Polish families or found refuge in monasteries, convents and boarding schools, and who either remained undiscovered or were not returned.[33] Child survivor Pinchas Gruszniewski recalled: "It was already November of 1946. In my village people talked about one woman who had saved a Jew and was robbed by the bandits as revenge. ... [Going to see her], I told her, 'I am a Jew. I can't take it here any longer. I know you hid a Jew, help me too, please.' She took me to Łomża, my hometown. I was terrified that somebody might recognize me and kill me, because there was not a single Jew there. She took me to Białystok, to the Jew she had saved. For the first time in four years, I found myself among other Jews. I was thrilled, could hardly speak, all shaking of joy that there are still Jews."[34]

Yonas Turkow, a distinguished Jewish actor and Holocaust survivor, organized a special radio broadcast in newly liberated Lublin. Known in Yiddish as *Zuchvinkel fun Kroyvim* (Search for Relatives), this program publicized the names and addresses of survivors provided by the Jewish committees as well as by individuals. However, after receiving hand-written threats, Turkow decided to omit from his broadcasts the addresses and the Christian names still used by Jews who had recently emerged from hiding. Turkow was concerned that exposing these survivors' Jewish identities could prove more dangerous than thwarting their relatives' attempts to trace them.[35] Even some members of the Zionist parties behaved this way. Yitzhak Zuckerman, one of the leaders of the Warsaw Ghetto uprising, used his Polish name of Stanisław Bagniewski and similarly on documents while traveling in the country on Zionist missions.[36]

Catholic response to anti-Jewish violence. After the Kielce pogrom, demands began to mount for the Catholic Church to respond to the outrages against Jews, but for the most part church leaders avoided taking a stand. Only Bishop Teodor Kubina of Częstochowa spoke up openly in his diocese in defense of the Jews and strongly condemned the Kielce pogrom. As for Cardinal August Hlond, on July 11, 1946, a week after the pogrom, he was finally moved to issue an official statement on the subject. Similar to his pre-war letter, he began with an anti-Jewish tirade: "Blame for the breakdown in these good relations [between non-Jews and Jews] is borne to a great extent by the Jews. In Poland they occupy positions in the first line of the nation's political existence, and their attempt to impose forms of government completely rejected by the great majority of the people is a pernicious game, for it is the cause of dangerous tensions." Not a word of condolence to the stricken Jewish community that was mourning its dead and was troubled by an uncertain future.[37]

It took many years for the Catholic church to revise its age-long teaching of contempt toward the Jews. In October 1978, Karol Wojtyla, the archbishop of Kraków, became Pope John Paul II. In June 1979, he visited Auschwitz. Noting the plaques at the foot of a memorial in Birkenau, John Paul II asked his listeners "to pause ... for a moment at the plaque with an inscription in the Hebrew language. This inscription evokes the memory of the nation whose sons and daughters were intended for complete extermination. This nation originates with Abraham, who is the 'father of our faith'[38] (Romans 4:12), as Paul of Tarsus expressed it. This nation, which received from God the commandment 'Thou shalt not kill,' itself experienced killing in special measure. It is not permissible for anyone to pass this plaque with indifference." His later declaration of the Jews as "elder brothers" to Christianity, would inspire a new and more positive dialogue of the shared values between Christians and Jews.[39] On January 21, 1991, Catholic Polish bishops, in an effort to improve relations, issued an unprecedented statement taking a clear stand against all manifestations of antisemitism. Read in churches, it presented Vatican II teachings on the relations between the two faiths and dealt with a number of controversial issues such as Polish responsibility for the

Holocaust, alleged Jewish responsibility for communism, and antisemitism past and present.[40]

The communist regime and the Jews. The new Polish communist government claimed to represent a complete break with everything "reactionary" in the Polish past; in particular, with the heritage of antisemitism – that it claimed was a product of class oppression.[41] But, in 1949 and 1950, when all non-communist political parties were banned, this also including Jewish ones. All Jewish institutions – from schools to theaters – were nationalized.[42]

In the meantime, the vast majority of Jewish survivors began leaving Poland in the years following the end of the war. Some, because they did not want to live under a communist regime. Others, because of the antisemitic violence they faced in postwar Poland, and because they did not want to live where their family members had been murdered. Especially, the July 1946 Kielce pogrom and other acts of violence against Jews led to a stampede of Jews out of the country. By the spring of 1947, all that was left were about 80,000 to 90,000 Jews. There were several more waves of Jewish emigration from Poland afterwards. Altogether, between 1945 and 1948, some 100,000 to 120,000 Jews had departed. During 1956 to 1960, an additional forty thousand Jews left Poland for Israel. By 1961, the official Jewish population of Poland was down to 45,000,[43] and by the mid-1960s, it numbered no more than thirty thousand. It was an aging, fear-ridden group, with no qualified rabbi, and only a handful of functioning synagogues.[44]

During the forty-five years of communist rule, the story of the Holocaust was distorted in a way to fit with the official communist line, of explaining this tragedy as part of the last stage of monopoly capitalism. In the second half of the 1960s, this orthodox communist narrative began to unravel. It was replaced by a so-called anti-Zionist (in truth, anti-Jewish) campaign, led by a faction of the communist party headed by Interior Minister, General Mieczysław Moczar.[45] They proclaimed a struggle against a worldwide anti-Polish conspiracy whose agents, they claimed, were Germans and Jews.[46] The Moczar period also witnessed a state-sponsored campaign of antisemitic agitation of hysterical intensity directed not only at the alleged non-existent Zionist activists at the time but principally against Jews in general, both real and imaginary. It resulted, during the years 1968-1970, in the ruin of thousands of careers, the emigration of some twenty thousand Jews, and in what was perceived as the definitive end of the millennial Jewish presence in Poland.[47] The Jewish ethnic origin of those expelled was invariably either hinted at or emphasized.[48]

There was scarcely any protest in Poland against the anti-Jewish campaign.[49] A smaller group of assimilated Jews remained. They retained Polish names, were married to non-Jewish Poles, and were in the process of abandoning ties with the Jewish community. It seemed that the thousand years history of the Jews in Poland had come to an ultimate end – on a bad note.[50]

Lanzmann's Shoah. In 1985, French-Jewish Claude Lanzmann's film Shoah premiered in Paris. Nine and a half hours long, eleven years in the making, the film contained no documentary images, but nearly entirely Holocaust witnesses – Jews, Germans, and Poles – interviewed by Lanzmann. Jews were shown retelling their sufferings and miraculous survival. Germans spoke in euphemisms, and Polish bystanders appeared indifferent to the fate of the Jews. The bystanders that Lanzmann presented were nearly all peasants and residents of small towns who lived near death camps and deportation trains. No rescuers of Jews were shown, except for Jan Karski, who tried to warn the world of what was happening. Most of the Poles in the film sometimes expressed sympathy for the Jews, but also repeated common antisemitic tropes.[51] The situation was exacerbated by Lanzmann himself, whose public statements, unlike his film, were filled with accusations against Poles.[52] Shoah provoked impassioned and unprecedented discussions in Poland. The great majority of responses denounced the film as anti-Polish, as an unjust accusation against Poles that required a defense of Polish national honor and morality.[53]

Jan Błoński on Polish guilt. Lanzmann's Shoah film had barely begun to recede from public awareness when another similar event exploded. It was occasioned in January 1987, when Jan Błoński, a professor of literature at the Jagiellonian University, in Kraków, followed up on two poetic writings by Czesław Miłosz, written in 1943, as he watched the Warsaw ghetto went up in flames. The first Miłosz poem was titled A Poor Christian Looks at the Ghetto. It tells, metaphorically, of the poet confronting an underground peculiar apparition: a "guardian mole ... with a small red lamp fastened to his forehead," who counts burned bodies, and "distinguishes human ashes."[54] In the second poem, Campo dei Fiore, Miłosz describes the "happy throngs [that] laughed on a beautiful Warsaw Sunday," as they played on a merry-go-round outside the ghetto walls, oblivious to "those dying alone, forgotten by the world," as the Germans were at the same time liquidating the remnants of the Warsaw ghetto inhabitants.

Presently, Błoński explained the paradigm of the mole in Miłosz's first poem. "This mole burrows underground but also underneath our consciousness. This is the feeling of guilt which we do not want to admit. Buried under the rubble, among the bodies of the Jews, the 'uncircumcised' fears that he may be counted among the murderers... When we read such a poem, we understand ourselves better, since that which had been evading us until now is made palpable."[55]

What Błoński was pointing to was the uncontrollable guilt born from not necessarily having committed any crime, but from witnessing the Holocaust, and indifferently watching it unfold. Błoński portrayed the Jew as someone who "shared our home, lived on our soil, [whose] blood has remained in the walls, seeped into the soil, [and] has also entered into ourselves, into our memory." But this Jew is simultaneously someone who, insofar as he "shared our home," was, metaphorically, made to "live in the cellar." And as a result, "eventually, when we lost our home, and when, within that home, the invaders set to murdering Jews, did we show solidarity towards them? How many of us decided that it was none of our business? There were also those (and I leave out of account common criminals) who were secretly pleased that Hitler had solved for us 'the Jewish problem.' We could not even welcome and honor the survivors, even if they were embittered, disoriented and perhaps sometimes tiresome."[56] Błoński argued that the destruction of European

Jewry, although not conceived of or implemented by the Polish nation, had tainted Polish soil forever. As witnesses to that event, Poles "shared responsibility" by failing to do more to prevent the Nazi barbarism from achieving its aims.

Błoński boldly declared: "We must stop haggling, trying to defend and justify ourselves... But to say first of all – Yes, we are guilty... Our responsibility is for holding back, for insufficient effort to resist. Who of us could claim that there was sufficient resistance in Poland?" And here, Błoński added fuel to the fire by maintaining that prewar Polish antipathy to Jews had shaped wartime Polish responses: "More significant is the fact that if only in the past we had behaved more humanely, had been wiser, more magnanimous, genocide would perhaps have been 'less imaginable,' would probably have been considerably more difficult to carry out, and almost certainly would have met with much greater resistance than it did. To put it differently, it would not have met with the indifference and moral turpitude of the society in whose full view it took place."[57] But Poles have blocked the memory of this part of their history because "when we consider the past, we want to derive moral advantages from it... We want to be completely clean. We want to be also – and only – victims."

How to get rid of this mole "who burrows in our subconscious, Błoński asked?" It may not be possible to do so. But to the extent that it was possible, he suggested that the only remedy was to "acknowledge our own guilt, and ask for forgiveness." But forgiveness for what? Certainly not for participation in the Holocaust, Błoński was careful not to overcharge Polish sensibilities, but for what the author terms "shared responsibility," and above all, for the Polish attitude toward Jews before the Holocaust.[58]

Never before had a Polish intellectual of respectable standing challenged the common held apologetic explanation that nothing more than actually done could have been added to save Polish Jews. Not surprisingly, Błoński's article ignited a ferocious controversy. In the words of Jerzy Turowicz, the editor of a journal which printed the article: "The reaction was greater than anything known in the course of the 42 years during which I have edited that paper. I cannot remember any article which provoked such a strong reaction on the part of the readers."[59] As with the Shoah film, most of the reaction was negative. What was rejected above all was the notion that Poles had wronged Jews; many denied altogether the existence of antisemitism in Poland.[60]

The Jedwabne disclosure. The revelation of the mass murder of Jedwabne Jews in the summer of 1941 again revived the question of the collusion of some in the murder of Jews during the Second World War.[61] The study of that massacre by Jan Tomasz Gross, in his book Neighbors?, was based on court trials, archival documents, and Jewish and Polish testimonies. [62] Neighbors? chronicled, in painstaking detail, the horrific events that took place in Jedwabne when, in July 1941, two weeks following the Soviet withdrawal from the city, local Poles, encouraged but not necessarily forced by Nazi officials, went on a murderous rampage that left many hundreds of Jews dead. Gross attacked the conventional wisdom that only 'socially marginal' individuals in Polish society – the so-called *Szmaltsowniks*, or the blackmailers "scum," were involved in causing harm to the Jews. This "scum" theory could no longer be held in light of the fact that, in Gross's words, one half of a town's population murders its Jewish half.[63]

Appearing first in Polish in 2000, Neighbors? sparked the most wide-ranging debate on the Polish response to the murder of Jews by the Germans, and led many to question the myth of total innocence, widely held among many Poles.[49] Halina Bortnowska, a former editorial board member of the Polish journal *Znak* drew the following conclusion: "The book by Jan Gross, Neighbors?, calls into question a view I had so far held, and which could be put in a nutshell as follows: in Poland, antisemitism has existed and was commonly accepted; however, it has nothing to do with the extermination of Jews under Nazi occupation... Now, this paradigm of innocence has crumbled."[64] Father Stanisław Musial, a longtime activist in Catholic-Jewish dialogue, wrote that "Poles have believed in the myth that they have been solely victims ... and that they themselves never wronged anyone... The work of Professor Gross has shattered this myth."[65] Myth, or no myth, most historians agree that there were more than a mere few persons among the local population that colluded in one way or another with the Germans to facilitate their roundup and liquidation of the Jews.

The 1990s revival of Jewish life. With the fall of communism in Poland, in 1990, a renewed and organized Jewish community also came to light, but very reduced and hardly noticeable. According to official statistics, in 1993 the Jews numbered a paltry 4,415; those involved in Jewish affairs most often cite the figure of 5 to 10,000. The problem stems from the difficult question as to who is to be counted as "Jewish" – is it to include non-religious Jews with only a Jewish father and a Catholic mother – that orthodox Jews consider non-Jewish, in view of the importance of the mother's lineage? Some believe that in today's Poland there are more marginal Jews, who "have not come out of the closet" than there are official members of the Jewish organizations; that the standard estimate of between 5,000 and 10,000 is misleading.[66] Whatever the true number, this is a very far cry from the once large and vibrant Jewish community.[67]

At the same time, Jewish cultural, social, and religious life has been undergoing a revival, some with the help of the US-based Ronald Lauder Foundation and the Taube Foundation for Jewish Life and Culture. There are several Jewish schools and associated summer camps as well as several periodicals and book series sponsored by the above foundations. Jewish studies programs are offered at major universities.[68] Very recently, a Polish Jewish museum (named Polin Museum) opened in Warsaw that narrates the 1,000 years history of Polish Jews. There are also ongoing efforts to restore and maintain Jewish cemeteries and monuments.[69] There is simultaneously also a general growing interest in Jews, Judaism, and Jewish culture. Festivals of Jewish culture are increasingly popular, as are Jewish restaurants, cafes, shops, and assorted souvenirs.[70]

A process of de-assimilation has also begun. This is a novelty in the history of Jews in Poland. While in the nineteenth century and the first half of the twentieth century more and more Jews assimilated into the majority culture, aspired to rootedness in it, and loosened their Jewish commitments, many other Jews in today's Poland have been regaining their Jewish identity and knowledge of their Jewish roots that their parents withheld from them. As stated by one re-converted Jew: "Unlike our ancestors, we do not need to aspire to being Polish, because we have been raised Polish. We can be as Polish and Jewish as English Jews are English and Jewish."[71] This de-assimilation in most cases does not mean de-Polonization; most "reborn" Jews in Poland remain involved in Polish life. But in no Polish Jewish family is Yiddish any longer the language of communication.

With regard to former children, a very interesting and unique organization has been formed – the Association of Hidden Children of the Holocaust, consisting of individuals who were either hidden Jewish children during the war, or the product of mixed marriages after the war, and were raised and have lived as Catholics since then. Having begun with a few individuals, they now number hundreds of members. Some of them are university professors; others, women who married in the village in which they were hiding.[72]

Opinions about Jews. One of the questions haunting students researching Polish attitudes toward the Jews is how much of the earlier stereotyped views of the Jews have undergone major changes? Put more directly – the experience of being either the prime witnesses of the Holocaust, for the older generation, or the knowledge that their country had been chosen by the Germans as the slaughterhouse of European Jews, for the younger generation – in what ways did it transform conventional opinions about Jews? For those still recalling the horrific events of the German occupation, the memory of the Jews is especially haunting. It is Poles, after all, who watched the ghettos burn, saw their neighbors herded into sealed trains, watched the "transports" arrive at their destination, smelled the smoke of the crematoriums, and witnessed the hunting of escapees.[73] As put by Jerzy Andrzejewski, "for all honest Poles the fate of the Jews going to their death was bound to be exceedingly painful, since the dying. . . were people whom our people could not look straight in the face with a clear conscience."[74]

Admittedly, the continued image of the Jew in Polish folk culture attest to the existence of many antisemitic motifs in speech and art which have survived the absence of Jews because they have sunk deep into the Polish mentality, even for persons who have never seen a Jew.[75] Then, there is the religious antisemitism that found its most brutal expression in accusations of Jewish ritual murder; the belief, dating back to the Middle Ages, that Jews once used the blood of Christian children for their religious rituals.[76] In the 1990s, a Polish man pointing to a painting, in a church in Sandomierz, that depicted Jews killing a Christian child for his blood, asked the priest why such a painting was still displayed. At first puzzled by the question and then angered by the young Pole's persistent questioning of a depiction he assumed was fictional, he asked the questioner to leave the church.[77]

One possible explanation is that even outside of Poland, in the liberal and multi-cultural societies, the fact remains that most people prefer others who are like themselves to those who are not. The "in-group" is preferred to the "out-group;" "we" to "they." In Poland, Jews were the perfect out-group – the Other. As already described in the first two chapters, in pre-war Poland most Jews differed from Poles in every external marker conceivable: they looked different, dressed differently, spoke a different language, ate different foods, and were forbidden from eating typically Polish food such as ham – and very importantly in the Polish Catholic context, Jews believed and prayed in a totally different religion. Even when more and more Jews began to lose their external markers and dress, and speak, and eat like Poles, they were often resented for trying to "pass" and insinuate themselves into Polish society.[78] Too many Poles, to put it most mildly, did not like Jews. This did not as a rule mean that Poles wished to see the Jews murdered, but simply leave to somewhere else, even preferably Palestine.[79] Jan Błoński described Zofia Kossak-Szczucka, founder of Żegota, as such an example. "She was prepared to give her life for Jews; if nevertheless – through some miracle – they vanished without any particular harm being done to them, she would have been relieved, since she saw neither the need nor the possibility for co-existence."[80]

A pastoral letter by Polish bishops, read in all parishes in January 1991, reaffirmed, on the twenty-fifth anniversary, of Vatican II's historic

Nostra Aetate's revocation of the charge of deicide against Jews, that included the following on Polish-Jewish relations during the Holocaust: "In spite of so many heroic examples of help on the part of Polish Christians, there were also people who remained indifferent to this incomprehensible tragedy. We are especially disheartened by those among Catholics who in some way were the cause of the death of Jews. If only one Christian could have helped and did not stretch out a helping hand to a Jew during the time of danger or caused his death, we must ask for forgiveness of our Jewish brothers and sisters... We express our sincere regret for all the incidents of antisemitism which were committed at any time or by anyone on Polish soil."[81]

The Righteous Among the Nations. Since 1962, the Yad Vashem Holocaust Memorial in Jerusalem has honored non-Jewish rescuers with the title of Righteous Among the Nations, and rescuers from Poland top the list. This does not necessarily mean that there were more rescuers in Poland than elsewhere, since the work under this program is primarily based on the availability of eyewitness accounts by those who benefitted from the help of the rescuers. At the same time, the record of the Polish stories does however point out to a situation that existed primarily in Poland. That this most harshly occupied country was also where the Germans made it absolutely clear that the death penalty would be imposed on anyone affording any aid to a Jew. These warnings were affixed on billboards in the major cities for all to know and fear, if they wished to stay alive. Considering this Damocles sword hanging over the heads of rescuers in Poland, it is quite amazing, to use an understatement, that there were nevertheless thousands of Poles (whatever their real numbers) who braved the risks to themselves and their families, and decided that if life had any meaning for themselves, it also obligated them to help Jews (the ones they knew or came across) to survive, in spite of the grave risks to themselves. In making such a decision, many of these rescuers were able to put to rest (even if only momentarily) whatever previous notions they had about the Jews. The principle of the sanctity of human life overrode all other considerations.

In closing, it is worth repeating Kristen Monroe's portrayal (mentioned in an earlier chapter) of these rescuers, as John Donne's People; of the 17th century English poet who wrote that when hearing the death bell toll, it also "tolls for thee." For, "no man is an island entire of itself… Any man's death diminishes me, because I am involved in mankind." So, when discussing Polish responses during the Holocaust, the story of these Yad Vashem honored Righteous Among the Nations needs also to be told. These Polish rescuers have written a most glorious chapter in history's annals of moral conduct and humanitarian behavior. It is, therefore, incumbent to learn and teach of their deeds as role models and educational tools for persons everywhere else.

CONCLUSION

It is a painful task for anyone to fairly, and without prejudice, summarize Jewish history in Poland, but an effort must nevertheless be made. I find myself still puzzled by the mystery of the ups and downs of this centuries-long dual relationship; of an auspicious beginning, and such tragic endings. It began with Jews being invited to settle in the country, which ever expanded its borders, and were granted freedoms for several centuries unparalleled elsewhere. Life for Jews in the centuries-long pluralistic environment of Poland before the modern era was close to the best by comparison with other European countries. This freed the Jews to expand population wise and to experiment with various religious and secular innovations that spilled over and affected Jewish communities beyond Polish borders. This paradisical situation may have gone on undisturbed if Poland had not gone through the trauma of being wiped off the map of Europe as an independent entity, that lasted 123 years, and was not the result of any grandiose military defeat but due to contrived political machinations.

Reborn in 1918, not as a result of a successful rebellion, but due to the collapse at the end of World War I of the three powers that had divided Poland among themselves, and having missed the social, religious and economic advances of other countries when Poland did not exist, the new-born country tried to catch up with the rest of Europe by adopting a stringent nationalism, allied to a medieval Catholic mindset, that left anyone not able to cohere to this new type of social inclusiveness outside the Polish frame of reference – principally the Jews. The centuries long period of tolerance had allowed the Jews to develop a strong

257

self-conscious Jewish identity that was too deeply ingrained to allow the type of acculturation and assimilation experienced by fellow Jews in other more liberal countries, and able to mold into the framework of a resurgent Polish nationalism.

The abandonment of the traditional tolerance and ethnic plurality that characterized the early Polish kingdom, and its replacement by a nationalism with a vengeance, that left no room for anything else than a full identification with Polish social and religious aspirations, was something that Jews, 10% of the general population, could not adhere. This was especially so when the new Polishness also went hand in hand with a Catholicism that, in contrast than the Catholic churches in western Europe, still saw the Jews through Middle Ages lenses as a reprimand people that ought to be subject to the teaching of contempt. This view of the Jews, always socially, culturally and religiously different than the ethnic Poles, were under the new nationalism spirit stigmatized as the ultimate aliens; hence, dangerous, and the pressure was extended to make them leave by the institution of various restrictive laws. This placed the Jews in Poland, the largest concentration in any other European countries, in a vulnerable position.

Józef Piłsudski, Poland's liberator, tried to stem the rising anti-Jewish tide, but it rose again after his death, with various discriminatory laws, to pressure the Jews to leave and find rest and repose elsewhere. Had World War II not intervened, the situation of the Jews would inevitably have continued its downward slope, with additional restrictive laws to make their stay in Poland unbearable, while encouraging them to get out as fast as possible. In summary, Jewish life in Poland, under the conditions prevailing in the 1930s could no longer be sustainable in the long run, even without the onset of Holocaust. At the same time, one must caution that what Poles wanted most was for Jews to leave, and find repose and a self-sustained social life elsewhere – not a solution through mass extermination as was carried out by the Germans. Such a frightening option never entered the mind of Poles, of all political pesuasions.

At the same time, this anti-Jewish virus propagated by Polish political leaders in the interwar period spilled over into the many criminal acts against Jews during the German occupation, and immediately afterwards, when the country came under Russian sway. The German extermination of 90% of the country's Jews was followed with a failed attempt to restore a modicum of Jewish life, and ended with hardly any Jews, exception for a small hardly visible Jewish community, still not sure of their reception by the larger society, a few empty synagogues, and many tombstones.

Whatever the future holds for recent attempts to revive Jewish life in Poland, it is quite clear that Poland can no longer attain the status it had for Jews, as the center of cultural and religious creativity of world Jewry, especially now that that the attention of most Jews is riveted toward the Jewish state of Israel and its continued prosperity.

In 2018, Poland's Senate, angered by critiques of Polish participation (or indifferent passivity) in the German extermination of Jews on Polish soil, passed a controversial law titled, Amendment to the Act on the Institute of National Remembrance, that criminalized any mention of Poles as "being responsible or complicit in the Nazi crimes committed by the Third German Reich." Only scientific research into the war and artistic work are exempted – a passage that raises more questions than offers clear definitions. The proposed legislation raised concerns among critics about how the Polish state will decide what it considers to be facts. "We have to send a clear signal to the world that we won't allow for Poland to continue being insulted," Patryk Jaki, a deputy justice minister, told reporters in parliament. This turning of the clock backward sparked outrage in many academic circles outside Poland, calling it an attempt to silence historical-based criticism of events in Poland that could tarnish the Polish image during World War II.

The absence of a vibrant Jewish community is still on the mind of many Poles, although they had hoped for such an outcome right before the onset of World War II, but not actually in the way it was carried out. In 2003, Polish sociologist, Barbara Engelking-Boni wrote: "I think that Poles still fear Jews. They fear their silent absence, which is a reproach. Absent Jews also demand something of us. They demand our respect for their suffering. They demand our memory. They still give us Poles a chance. So far, we have failed to do it… And today we Poles need Jews. We need them to better understand our own past, our own Christian tradition and identity, our own experience. We need them to finally accept the Holocaust not only as a fact of Jewish history but as an extremely important experience belonging also to the history of Poland."[1]

Not to be overlooked and forgotten in this reassessment of Polish-Jewish relations are the stories of the many Poles who helped the Jews to survive, at great risks to the lives of the rescuers, and were honored by Yad Vashem as Righteous Among the Nations. The importance is not in their numbers, although they may counted in the thousands or beyond that, but in acts of rescue themselves that called forth great courage, determination, stamina and persistence, not usually associated with altruistic acts under normal conditions. Since the dangers facing them stemmed not only from the Germans but also from fellow Poles, then, indeed, they sublimely stand out as the morally best to ever have appeared on the human stage. Their motto may be summed up in the immortal words of that unforgettable rescuer of many Jewish children, Irena Sendlerowa (mentioned earlier): "As long as I live and as long as I have the strength I shall always say that the most important thing in the world and in life is Goodness."

NOTES

Introduction

1   Jacob Goldberg, "On the Study of Polish-Jewish History." In, Adam Teller,
     ed., *Studies in the History of the Jews in Old Poland*. Jerusalem: Magnes
     Press, 1998; 9-13; 9. Goldberg adds, that this is especially true since almost
     all Polish historian also mention in their works the issue of Polish Jews at
     all stages of Poland's development.

2   Golda Meir, later Prime Minister of Israel, was born in nearby Kjiv,
     Ukraine, and there is a plaque on the outer wall of the house where she
     first saw the light of day. Her family had to flee to the United States due to
     unending pogroms against Jews, spurred by the Tsarist regime.

3   This is also true of certain Talmudic centers in Lithuania transposed else-
     where. For instance, the famous Talmudic yeshiva in Panevėžys-Ponevezh
     is today a leading Talmudic academy in Israel, and still calls itself Ponevezh
     Yeshiva. Similarly, Telšiai, presently the Telz or Thelse Yeshiva, in Wickliffe,
     Ohio. Also, the Mir yeshiva, in Jerusalem, originally in Mir, Poland. All
     three still go by their original city names, although no Jews are left there.
     These city titles recall the great importance of these religious schools as
     international centers of Talmudic studies, and inspire students to continue
     in the tradition of these famed religious schools.

4   Michael C. Steinlauf, *Bondage to the Dead: Poland and the Memory of the
     Holocaust*. Syracuse, N.Y.: Syracuse University, 1997, *ix*.

Chapter 1

1   Celia S. Heller, *On the Edge of Destruction: Jews of Poland Between the Two
     World Wars*. New York: Columbia University, 1977, 1.

2   Heller, *Edge*, 3, 13.

3   Jerzy Wyrozumski, "Jews in Medieval Poland." In, A. Polonsky, J. Basista and A. Link-Lenczowski, eds., *The Jews in Old Poland 1000-1795*. London, New York: I.B. Tauris & Co, 1993, 13-22; 14. Aleksander Gieysztor, "The Beginnings of Jewish Settlement in the Polish Lands." In, Chimen Abramsky, Maciej Jachimczyk and Antony Polonsky, eds. *The Jews in Poland*. Oxford, UK: Basil Blackwell, 1987, 16-21; 16-7. The conversion of the Khazar king, renamed Joseph, was lauded by the Spanish Jewish theologian Judah Halevi, in the 12th century, in his book *The Kuzari*. The more recent well-known author and journalist Arthur Koestler also speculated on the origins of eastern European Jews to the Khazars. See his book, *The Thirteenth Tribe*. New York: Random House, 1976.

4   Heller, *Edge*, 14.

5   Steinlauf, *Bondage*, 1.

6   Israel Gutman, "Poland;" in, *Encyclopedia Judaica*. Vol. 13. Jerusalem: Keter, 1971, 709-89; 711-2.

7   Steinlauf, *Bondage*, 3.

8   Heinrich Graetz, *History of the Jews*. Vol IV. Philadelphia: JPS, 1949; Vol V. Philadelphia: JPS, 1956; 4: 111. The number of Jews stated to have been killed in Poland in pre-modern times bears no relation to the enormous multitudes who fell victims in German lands. Graetz, 4: 1356.

9   Graetz, 4: 419-20.

10   Graetz, 4: 265, 632, 642.

11   Magda Teter, *Jews and Heretics in Catholic Poland: a Beleaguered Church in the Post-Reformation Era*. Cambridge, UK: Cambridge University, 2006, 30. Antony Polonsky, "Introduction." In, Polonsky, *The Jews in Old Poland 1000-1795*, 1-9; 1.

12   Jacek Staszewski, "*Votum Separatum* to Research on the history of the Jews in Pre-Partition Poland." In, Adam Teller, ed., *Studies in the History of the Jews in Old Poland*. Jerusalem: Magnes Press, 1998, 224-32; 227. Polonsky, "Introduction;" in, Polonsky, *The Jews*, 2.

13   Teter, *Jews*, 4, 23-24.

14   Polonsky, "Introduction;" in, Polonsky, *The Jews* 1-2.

15   Theodore R. Weeks, *Assimilation to Antisemitism: The 'Jewish Question' in Poland. 1850-1914*. DeKalb, Illinois: Northern Illinois University Press, 2006, 14-5.

16   Israel Gutman, "The Jews in Poland;" in, *Encyclopedia of the Holocaust*, Vol. 3, New York: Macmillan, 1990, 1151-76. Haim Hillel Ben Sasson, "Poland;" in, *Encyclopedia Judaica*, Vol. 13. Jerusalem: Keter, 1971, 709-89; 712. Weeks, *Assimilation*, 13.

17   Polonsky, "Introduction;" in, Polonsky, *The Jews*, 3. Shmul Ettinger, "The Council of the Four Lands;" in Polonsky, *The Jews in Old Poland 1000-1795*, 93-109; 95. Jacob Goldberg, "The Privileges Granted to Jewish Communities of the Polish Commonwealth as a Stabilizing Factor in Jewish Support." In, Abramsky, *The Jews in Poland*, 32-54. See 36 and 40, on additional Jewish privileges granted by Polish kings. Graetz, *History*, 4: 264. There were unconfirmed rumors that Kazimierz had a romantic relation with a beautiful Jewish mistress named Esther (Esterka), who bore him two sons (Niemerz and Pelka) and two daughters. The latter are said to have remained Jewesses. Graetz, *History*, 4:112.

18   A burgher was a rank or title of a privileged citizen in medieval times, who formed part of the pool from which city officials were drawn, and their immediate families formed the social class of the medieval bourgeoisie, or nascent middle class.

19   Stanisław Grodziski, "The Kraków *Voivode*'s Jurisdiction over Jews: A Study of the Historical Records of the Kraków *Voivode*'s Administration of Justice to Jews;" in, Polonsky, *The Jews in Old Poland, 1000-1795*, 199-218; 203. Goldberg, "Privileges;" in, Abramsky, *The Jews*, 41-3.

20   Goldberg, "Privileges;" in, Abramsky, *The Jews*, 53-4.

21   Graetz, *History*, 4: 631.

22   Heller, *Edge*, 24.

23   Steinlauf, *Bondage*, 4. Polonsky, "Introduction;" in Polonsky, *The Jews*, 6.

24   Heller, *Edge*, 23. Graetz, *History*, 4: 420.

25   Ettinger, "Council;" in, Polonsky, *The Jews*, 100. Jacob Goldberg, "The Jewish Sejm: Its Origins and Functions." In, Polonsky, *The Jews in Old Poland 1000-1795*, 147-165; 148. In the sources, this body is referred to as "General Congress," "General Jewish Congress," "Jewish Congress," *Congressus Judaicus*," "General Jewish Meeting." "Meeting (*Zjazd*)," "Leadership (*Generalność*) of the Crown Synagogue," and "Leadership." This body is also referred to in the sources as a *Sejm*-parliament. Anatol Leszczyński, "The Terminology of the Bodies of Jewish Self-Government;" in, Polonsky, *The Jews*, 132-46; 143. Heller, *Edge*, 23-4.

26   Lesczynski, "Terminology;" in Polonsky, *The Jews*, 141.

27   Ettinger, "Council;" in, Polonsky, *The Jews*, 98.

28   Polonsky, "Introduction;" in Polonsky, *The Jews*, 6. Gutman, "Poland;", in, *Encyclopedia Judaica*, 726. Wikipedia, "Council of Four Lands; 2018." Gutman, "Jews;" in, Gutman, *Encyclopedia of the Holocaust*, New York: Macmillan, 1990; 1152.

29   Graetz, *History*, 5: 3.

30   Ettinger, "Council;" in, Polonsky, *The Jews*, 97,105.

31   Israel Bartal, "The *Pinkas* of the Council of the Four Lands;" in, Polonsky, *The Jews*, 110-8; 111. Ettinger, "Council;" in Polonsky, *The Jews*, 104.

32   Goldberg, "Jewish Sejm," in, Polonsky, *The Jews*, 147.

33   One of the last important congresses was held in Jarosław in the fall of 1753. Among other matters debated was the famous dispute between the rabbis Jacob Emden and Jonathan Eybeschutz over the Sabbathean movement, resulting in Eybeschutz's acquittal on the charge of heresy. Wikipedia, "Council."

34   Ettinger, "Council;" in, Polonsky, *The Jews*, 94, 101.

35   Goldberg, "Jewish;" in, Polonsky, *The Jewish*, 164. Polonsky, "Introduction;" in Polonsky, *The Jews*, 8.

36   Graetz, *History*, 4: 641-2, 644. 5: 3-4, 387.

37   Graetz, *History* 4: 420, 634.

38   Graetz, *History* 5: 4. Norman Davies, *God's Playground: A History of Poland*. Volume 2. Oxford: Clarendon Press, 1982, 245.

39   Heller, *Edge*, 24-6.

40   Polonsky, "Introduction;" in, Polonsky, *The Jews*, 5. Wikipedia, "History of the Jews in Poland; 2019." Gutman, "Poland;"in, *Encyclopedia Judaica*, 711, 729. Graetz, *History* 4: 639.

41   Gutman, "Poland;" in, *Encyclopedia Judaica*, 730.

42   Ettinger, "Council;" in Polonsky, *The Jews*, 106. Gershon Hundert, "The Implications of Jewish Economic Activities for Christian-Jewish Relations in the Polish Commonwealth;" in, Abramsky, *The Jews*, 55-63; 56.

43   Goldberg, "Privileges;" in, Abramsky, *The Jews*, 54.

44   Joseph Lichten. "Notes on the Assimilation and Acculturation of Jews in Poland, 1863-1943;" in, Abramsky, *The Jews*, 106-129; 109. Based on: E. Kupfer, *Ber Meisels*. Warsaw, Żydowski Instytut Historyczny, 1953, 105.

45   Davies, *God's*, 253.

46   Wyrozumski, "Jews;" in, Polonsky, *The Jews*, 18.

47   Ettinger, "Council;"in Polonsky, *The Jews*, 102-3.

48   Teter, *Jews*, 24-25. Antoni Podraza, "Jews and the Village in the Polish Commonwealth;" in, Polonsky, *The Jews*, 299-321; 316. This, according to some, led to Poland to lag behind in the creation of a strong city-centered middle class, in contrast to other European countries, where the monarchs established centralized bureaucracies loyal to them. Daniel Tollet, "Merchants and Businessmen in Poznań and Cracow, 1588-1688;" in, Abramsky, *The Jews*, 22-30; 22.

49   Teter, *Jews*, 29-30. Maria Bogucka, "The Jews in the Polish Cities in the 16th-18th Centuries;" in, Teller, *Studies in the History of the Jews in Old*

Poland, 51-66; 52. Tollet, "Merchants;" in, Abramsky, *The Jews*, 25; Weeks, *Assimilation*, 12.

50   Teter, *Jews*, 5, 32. Some Jews felt secure enough to confiscate the goods of Christians or to arrest them, even nobles, for dereliction of payments. On October 8, 1615 in Słonim, for instance, a nobleman Pawel Masiukiewicz filed a complaint charging that his imprisonment by a Jew, Mayer Shimonivich, for an unpaid debt was illegal. Teter, *Jews*, 34.

51   Adam Teller, "Radziwiłł, Rabinowicz, and the Rabbi of Świerz: the Magnates' Attitude to Jewish Regional Autonomy in the 18th Century;" in, Teller, *Studies in the History of the Jews in Old Poland*, 246-69; 247-8. Goldberg, "The Privileges;" in, Abramsky, *The Jews*, 35. Teter, *Jews*, 25.

52   Polonsky, "Introduction;" in, Polonsky, *The Jews*, 8. Tollet, "Merchants," in Abramsky, *The Jews*, 28; Teter, *Jews*, 28; Hundert, "Implications," in Abramsky, *The Jews*, 62; Podraza, "Jews," in Polonsky, *The Jews*, 320.

53   Polonsky, "Introduction;" in Polonsky, *The Jews*, 5. One publicist, named Piotr Hadziewicz, was indignant that this "once devout Christian kingdom has in fact been transformed into a Jewish state by the greed of the voracious barons." Jerzy Michalski, "The Jewish Question in Polish Public Opinion During the First Two Decades of Stanisław August Poniatowski's Reign;" in, Teller, *Studies in the History of the Jews in Old Poland*, 123-46; 127.

54   Gershon Hundert, "On the Problem of Agency in 18th Century Jewish Society;" in, Teller, *Studies in the History of the Jews in Old Poland*, 82-9; 86-7.

55   Jan M. Małecki, "Jewish Trade at the End of the Sixteenth Century and in the First half of the Seventeenth Century." In, Polonsky, *The Jews in Old Poland 1000-1795*, 267-81; 274. Weeks, *Assimilation*, 72; Gieysztor, "Beginnings," in Abramsky, *The Jews*, 18.

56   Artur Eisenbach, "The Four Years' Sejm and the Jews;" in, Polonsky, *The Jews*, 73-89; 74. Malecki, "Jewish;" in, Polonsky, *The Jews*," 273-4.

57   Ettinger, "Council;" in, Polonsky, *The Jews*, 108. Hundert, "Implications;" in, Abramsky, *The Jews*, 57. Weeks, *Assimilation*, 56-7. Judith Kalik, "Patterns of Contacts Between the Catholic Church and the Jews in the Polish-Lithuanian Commonwealth: the Jewish Debts;" in, Teller, *Studies in the History of the Jews in Old Poland*, 102-22; 105.

58   Ettinger, "Council;" in, Polonsky, *The Jews*, 106.

59   Goldberg, "Privileges;" in Abramsky, *The Jews*, 39. Daniel Tollet, "La législation commerciale régissant les Juifs des grandes villes royales de Pologne sous les règnes de Wasa;" in, Teller, *Studies in the History of the Jews in Old Poland*, 277-302; 282.

265

60   Maurycy Horn, "The Chronology and Distribution of Jewish Craft Guilds in Old Poland, 1613-1795;" in, Polonsky, *The Jews*, 249-66; 253, 256, 258.

61   Horn, "Chronology;" in Polonsky, *The Jews*, 265; Tollet, "Législation;" in, Teller, *Studies*, 302.

62   Tollet, "Législation;" in, Teller, *Studies*, 285-286, 291-292, 301; Goldberg, "Privileges;" in, Abramsky, *the Jews*, 44; Horn, "Chronology;" in, Polonsky, *The Jews*, 255, 289.

63   Staszewski, "Votum *Separatum* to Research on the history of the Jews in Pre-Partition Poland;" in, Teller, *Studies*, 224-5. Grodziski, "Kraków;" in, Polonsky, *The Jews*, 199-200.

64   Weeks, *Assimilation*, 4.

65   Polonsky, "Introduction;" in, Polonsky, *The Jews*, 4, based on the study of Bernard Weynrib, *The Jews of Poland* (1976), 308-320. Ettinger, "Council;" in, Polonsky, *The Jews*, 95.

66   Bogucka, "Jews;" in, Teller, *Studies*, 56. Polonsky, "Introduction;" in, Polonsky, *The Jews*, 4. Zenon Guldon and Karol Krzystanek, "The Jewish Population in the Towns on the West Bank of the Vistula in Sandomierz Province from the Sixteenth to the Eighteenth Centuries;" in, Polonsky, *The Jews in Old Poland 1000-1795*, 322-39; 338.

67   Guldon, "The Jewish;" in, Polonsky, *The Jews*, 327-328. Polonsky, "Introduction;" in, Polonsky, *The Jews*, 5.

68   Steinlauf, *Bondage*, 2.

69   Polonsky, "Introduction;" in, Polonsky, *The Jews*, 2; Ettinger, "Council;" in, Polonsky, *The Jews*, 107. Guldon, "The Jewish;" in, Polonsky, *The Jews*, 331.

70   Heller, *Edge*, 26. Gutman, "The Jews," in Gutman, Encyclopedia of the Holocaust, 1152; Wikipedia, "History."

71   Guldon, "Jewish Population;" in, Polonsky, *The Jews*, 67-81, 69.

72   Graetz, 5:8-11, 14. Historians are still divided on the actual number of Jewish casualties.

73   Polonsky, "Introduction;" in, Polonsky, *The Jews*, 2, 7-8; Teter, *Jews*, 53.

74   Steinlauf, *Bondage*, 5; Gutman, "Poland;" in, *Encyclopedia Judaica*, 731; Gutman, "The Jews;" in, Gutman, *Encyclopedia of the Holocaust*, 1152.

75   Eisenbach, "Four Years;" in, Polonsky, *The Jews*, 74. Podraza, "Jews;" in, Polonsky, *The Jews*, 299, 303, 306. Graetz, *History* 4: 632. Davies, *God's*, 240.

76   Teter, *Jews*, 28, 32.

77   Janusz Tazbir. "Anti-Jewish Trials in Old Poland;" in, Teller, *Studies in the History of the Jews in Old Poland*, 233-45; 233.

78   Teter, *Jews*, 88.

79   Teter, *Jews*, 90.

80   Teter, *Jews*, 82, 97.
81   Teter, *Jews*, 88-9.
82   Tazbir, "Anti-Jewish;" in, Teller, *Studies*, 235-6; Teter, *Jews*, 116-7.
83   Tazbir, "Anti-Jewish;" in, Teller, *Studies*, 235-6.
84   Tazbir, "Anti-Jewish;" in, Teller, *Studies*, 239-40.
85   Tazbir, "Anti-Jewish;" in, Teller, *Studies*, 239. The element of cruelty was emphasized in the titles chosen for the anti-Jewish pamphlets. Father Przecław Mojewski wrote "Jewish Cruelties, Murders and Superstitions" (1589). Similar was the title of Aleksander Hubicki's booklet "Jewish Cruelties to the Most Holy Sacrament and Christian Children" (1598). Mateusz Bembus wrote: "Whenever they can, they cruelly murder Christian children." Tazbir, "Anti-Jewish;" in, Teller, *Studies*, 237.
86   Tazbir, "Anti-Jewish;" in, Teller, *Studies*, 20.
87   Gutman, "Poland;" in, *Encyclopedia Judaica*, 714-5.
88   Teter, *Jews*, 17. Wyrozumski, "Jews;" in, Polonsky, *The Jews*, 19-20. Daniel Tollet, "The Private Life of Polish Jews in the Vasa Period;" in, Polonsky, *The Jews in Old Poland 1000-1795*, 45-62; 49.
89   Gutman, "Poland;" in, *Encyclopedia Judaica*, 715.
90   Michalski, "Jewish;" in, Teller, *Studies*, 133.
91   Podraza, "Jews;" in, Polonsky, *The Jews*, 317-20.
92   Eisenbach, "Four Years;" in, Polonsky, *The Jews*, 75. Teter, *Jews*, 61.
93   Teter, *Jews*, 61.
94   Weeks, *Assimilation*, 78.
95   Teter, *Jews*, 81, 85, 87. Kalik, "Patterns;" in, Teller, *Studies,*107.
96   Kalik, "Patterns;" in Teller, *Studies*, 103, 111. Moshe Rosman, "The Indebtedness of the Lublin Kahal in the 18th Century;" in, Teller, *Studies in the History of the Jews in Old Poland*, 161-88; 168-9.
97   Kalik, "Patterns;" in, Teller, *Studies*, 108; Rosman, "Indebtedness;" in, Teller, *Studies*, 179-81.
98   Rosman, "Indebtedness;" in, Teller, Studies, 172, 178.
99   Teter, *Jews*, 85.
100   Kalik, "Patterns;" in, Teller, *Studies*, 111.
101   Steinlauf, *Bondage*, 6. Wikipedia, "History."
102   Steinlauf, *Bondage*, 9.
103   Steinlauf, *Bondage*, 10.
104   Steinlauf, *Bondage*, 9. Weeks, *Assimilation*, 41. Czeslaw Madajczyk. "Poland: General Survey;" in, Israel Gutman, *Encyclopedia of the Holocaust*, 1143-51; 1143. Gutman, "Poland;" in, *Encyclopedia Judaica*, 737. Wikipedia, "History."
105   Davies, *God's*, 247-8; Weeks, *Assimilation*, 41.

106 Ryszard Bender, "Jews in the Lublin Region Prior to the January Uprising, 1861-1862;" in, Abramsky, *The Jews in Poland*, 91-6; 92. Stefan Kieniewicz, "Polish Society and the Jewish Problem in the Nineteenth Century." In, Abramsky, *The Jews in Poland*, 70-7; 73-4. Weeks, *Assimilation*, 49.
107 Einsenbach, "Four Years;" in, Polonsky, *The Jews*. 81, 84-5.
108 Weeks, *Assimilation*, 19-21.
109 Eisenbach, "Four Years;" in, Polonsky, *The Jews*, 87, 89.
110 Steinlauf, *Bondage*, 8.
111 Gutman, "Jews;" in, Gutman, *Encyclopedia of the Holocaust*, 1153. Wikipedia, "History." Davies, *God's*, 245-6.
112 Davies, *God's*, 246, 248, 250, 253-4. Graetz, *History*, 4: 21.
113 The archaic English term *pale* is derived from the Latin word *palus*, a stake, extended to mean the area enclosed by a fence or boundary. Wikipedia, "History." Davies, *God's*, 241.
114 Weeks, *Assimilation*, 4. Daniel Beauvois, "Polish-Jewish Relations in the Territories Annexed by the Russian Empire in the First Half of the Nineteenth Century;" in, Abramsky, *The Jews in Poland*, 78-90; 80.
115 Weeks, *Assimilation*, 76-7.
116 Weeks, *Assimilation*, 83-5.
117 Weeks, *Assimilation*, 85.
118 Lichten, "Notes;" in, Abramsky, *The Jews*, 107-8.
119 Lichten, "Notes;" in, Abramsky, *The Jews*, 108.
120 Weeks, *Assimilation*, 27-9.
121 Weeks, *Assimilation*, 64, 66.
122 Lichten, "Notes;" in, Abramsky, *The Jews*, 110-1. Weeks, *Assimilation*, 65.
123 Lichten, "Notes;" in, Abramsky, *The Jews*, 114-5.
124 Lichten, "Notes;" in, Abramsky, *The Jews*, 114. Weeks, *Assimilation*, 144.
125 Weeks, *Assimilation*, 55-6.
126 Lichten, "Notes;" in, Abramsky, *The Jews*, 112, 128. Weeks, *Assimilation*, 38. Kieniewicz, "Polish;" in, Abramsky, *The Jews*, 74.
127 Staszewski, "Votum," in Teller, *Studies*, 229. Weeks, *Assimilation*, 17-18.
128 Weeks, *Assimilation*, 117.
129 Their true names were Sholem Abramowicz and Solomon Rabinowich, respectively.
130 Weeks, *Assimilation*, 149-150.
131 Gutman, "Poland;" in, *Encyclopedia Judaica*, 737. Wikipedia, "History."
132 Weeks, *Assimilation*, 86, 136, 177.
133 According to the Russian Governor-General's annual report for 1840, the numbers of the three ethnic groups there were as follows. In the provinces of Volhnyia, Kjiv and Podolia: Jews, 457,547; Poles, 410,212; and

Ukrainians, 4,282,390. Beauvois, "Polish-Jewish;" in, Abramsky, *the Jews*, 78-9.

134 Weeks, *Assimilation*, 73.

135 Weeks, *Assimilation*, 151. Gutman, "Jews;" in, Gutman, *Encyclopedia of the Holocaust*, 1153. Gutman, "Poland;" in, *Encyclopedia Judaica*, 735-37.

136 Weeks, *Assimilation*, 14-15. Guldon, "Jewish;" in, Polonsky, *The Jews*, 329.

137 Wyrozumski, "Jews;" in, Polonsky, *The Jews*, 18.

138 Wyrozumski, "Jews;" in, Polonsky, *The Jews*, 18. Tollet, "Merchants;" in, Abramsky, *The Jews*, 27.

139 Kieniewicz, "Polish;" in, Abramsky, *The Jews*, 76. Weeks, *Assimilation*, 72, 80. *Gazeta Polska*, a daily journal not well known for Judeophile sympathies, in explaining away the recent outbreaks of anti-Jewish violence in 1881, printed a long article claiming that antisemitism was of German import and quite alien to Poland. Specific anti-Jewish agitation was blamed on "outsiders" and was deemed ipso facto un-Polish. Weeks, *Assimilation*, 78.

140 Weeks, *Assimilation*, 107, 120, 137.

141 Weeks, *Assimilation*, 24-5.

142 Weeks, *Assimilation*, 31.

143 Beauvois, "Polish-Jewish;" in, Abramsky, *The Jews*, 87.

144 Weeks, *Assimilation*, 89-92.

145 Weeks, *Assimilation*, 69-70, 93, 143.

146 Weeks, *Assimilation*, 114-5, 142.

147 Weeks, *Assimilation*, 148,150.

148 Weeks, *Assimilation*, 164-6.

149 Weeks, *Assimilation*, 156.

150 Weeks, *Assimilation*, 166.

151 Jacob Goldberg, "On the Study;" in, Teller, *Studies*, 10. Polonsky, "Introduction, in, Polonsky, *The Jews*, 2-3.

152 Teter, *Jews*, 31-32, 107.

153 Weeks, *Assimilation*, 172.

154 Andrzej Link-Lenczowski, "The Jewish Population;" in, Polonsky, *The Jews in Old Poland*, 44. Tollet, "Merchants; in, Abramsky, *The Jews*, 27.

155 Goldberg, "Study; in, Teller, *Study*, 13.

156 Weeks, *Assimilation*, 16-18, 176. Władysław Bartoszewski, "Polish-Jewish Relations in Occupied Poland, 1939-1945; in, Abramsky, *The Jews in Poland*, 147-160; 154.

157 Beauvois, "Polish-Jewish;" in Abramsky, *The Jews*, 81.

158 Weeks, *Assimilation*, 26-7.

159 Weeks, *Assimilation*, 3, 27.

160 Weeks, *Assimilation*, 101-2.

161   Weeks, *Assimilation*, 28, 121.
162   Weeks, *Assimilation*, 170.
163   Weeks, *Assimilation*, 4, 24, 152.
164   Kieniewicz, "Polish;" in, Abramsky, *The Jews*, 75; Michalski, "Jewish;" in Teller, *Studies*, 128; Weeks, *Assimilation*, 5, 8, 176.
165   Ezra Mendelsohn, "Interwar Poland: Good for the Jews or Bad for the Jews?" In, Abramsky, *The Jews in Poland*, 130-146; 133. Lichten, "Notes;" Abramsky, *The Jews*, 111.
166   Michalski, "Jewish Teller, *Studies*, 125.
167   Weeks, *Assimilation*, 162-3.
168   Weeks, *Assimilation*, 6, 177.

Chapter 2

1   Davies, *God's*, 259, 409.
2   Richard C. Lukas. *The Forgotten Holocaust: The Poles under German Occupation, 1939-1944*. Lexington: University Press of Kentucky, 1986, 123. Steinlauf, *Bondage*, 15.
3   Steinlauf, *Bondage*, 12.
4   Steinlauf, *Bondage*, 13.
5   Steinlauf, *Bondage*, 13-4.
6   Heller, *Edge*, 130, 253.
7   Israel Gutman, "The Jews in Poland;" in, Gutman, *Encyclopedia of the Holocaust*, 1153. *Wikipedia*, "History of the Jews in Poland." Gutman, "Poland;" in, *Encyclopedia Judaica*, 738.
8   Davies, *God's*, 255, 262, 408.
9   Davies, *God's*, 421-2.
10   Davies, *God's*, 419. Steinlauf, *Bondage*, 16. Yisrael Gutman and Shmuel Krakowski, *Unequal Victims: Poles and Jews During World War Two*. New York: Holocaust Library, 1986, 3.
11   Davies, *God's*, 416. Richard J. Evans, *The Third Reich at War*. New York: Penguin, 2014, 49. Lukas accuses the Jews of discriminating against Poles as they supposedly had done for centuries; that Jews did business with each other and distrusted Jews who developed relationships with Polish Gentiles. Such a statement places great doubts on the credibility of this author when discussing Jewish Polish relations; Lukas, *Forgotten*, 124.
12   Evans, *Third Reich*, 49.
13   Gutman, "The Jews;" in, Gutman, *Encyclopedia of the Holocaust*, 1154; "Poland;" in, *Encyclopedia Judaica*, 736; Steinlauf, *Bondage*, 17;

Gutman-Krakowski, *Unequal,* 13-4; Heller, *Edge,* 74. The economic categories breakdown are as follows: Extremely poor, 12.4%; Poor, 27.6%; Minimum wage earners, 0.8%; Sufficient income, 18.4%; Moderately well-to-do, 9.2%; Wealthy, 1.6%. Gutman-Krakowski, *Unequal,* 26, note 10.

14   Davies, *God's,* 260, 409; Lukas, *Forgotten,* 125.

15   Davies remarks with reference to these figures that a society in which two-thirds of the population was engaged in subsistence agriculture and where one-third consisted of national minorities, could hardly afford the gradualist, liberal climate of prosperous and well-established western countries. Davies, *God's,* 410.

16   Heller, *Edge,* 71-2. Most Ukrainians lived where Poles were not the majority, such as Tarnopol, Stanisławów, and the regions of Wolyn and Polesie; Gutman, "Poland;" in *Encyclopedia Judaica,* 738. Davies, *God's,* 404-5, 426.

17   Davies, *God's,* 261.

18   Heller, *Edge,* 144. Havi Dreifuss (Ben-Sasson). *Relations Between Jews and Poles During the Holocaust: the Jewish Perspective.* Jerusalem: Yad Vashem, 2017, 33.

19   Evans, *Third Reich,* 49.

20   Under the caftan appeared the *arba kanfot:* an undergarment which was a truncated white prayer shawl (with a hole in the middle so it could be slipped over the head), with silk tassels (*tsitsit*) at the four corners that often showed.

21   Heller, *Edge,* 145-6.

22   Heller, *Edge,* 146.

23   Heller, *Edge,* 152.

24   Dreifuss, *Relations,* 33.

25   Heller, *Edge,* 64, 69.

26   Dreifuss, *Relations,* 33; Lichten, "Notes;" in, Abramsky, *The Jews,* 121-2; *Wikipedia,* "History."

27   Bartoszewski, "Polish-Jewish;" in, Abramsky, *The Jews,* 148.

28   Lukas, *Forgotten,* 123.

29   Heller, *Edge,* 66.

30   Steinlauf, *Bondage,* 16.

31   Gutman-Krakowski, *Unequal,* 8

32   Gutman-Krakowski, *Unequal,* 8. Heller, *Edge,* 72. *Wikipedia,* "History." Gutman, "Poland;" in, *Encyclopedia Judaica,* 740; "The Jews;" in Gutman, *Encyclopedia of the Holocaust,* 1153, 1155. Davies, *God's,* 410. Jews constituted between one third and one fourth of the total population of each of

the five major cities of the country: Warsaw, Łódź, Wilno-Vilna, Kraków and Lwów. Prior to World War II, the 233,000 Jews in Łódź constituted one-third of the city's population. Lwów had 110,000 Jews in 1939 (42%). Jews in Wilno (now Vilnius, in Lithuania) counted nearly 100,000 souls, about 45% of the city's total. In 1938, Kraków's Jewish population numbered over 60,000, or about 25% of the city's total population. In 1939, there were 375,000 Jews in Warsaw or one third of the city's population. Similarly, in Lublin where Jews comprised around 40%, and almost likewise in Białystok. In some very small towns the population was almost entirely Jewish, serving the peasantry in the surrounding areas.

33   Lichten, "Notes;" in, Abramsky, *The Jews,* 117.

34   Lichten, "Notes;" in, Abramsky, *The Jews,* 121.

35   Lichten, "Notes;" in, Abramsky, *The Jews,* 118.

36   Lichten, "Notes;" in, Abramsky, *The Jews,* 124.

37   As expressed by child educator Janusz Korczak: "Polish phrases like Polish field flowers arrange themselves into happy fields or rise clearly and burst into rays like the sun." But Yiddish is generally "the screaming and ordinary jargon of quarreling and name calling." Heller, *Edge,* 193.

38   Heller, *Edge,* 196.

39   Heller, *Edge,* 186, 188.

40   Heller, *Edge,* 35. In Lwów, a Progressive Synagogue, opened in 1898, in which an organ and mixed choir were introduced.

41   Heller, *Edge,* 36, 188.

42   Heller, *Edge,* 194. One example of this strong pro-Polish feeling among the assimilated Jews is the story told of the famous Jewish-born poet Julian Tuwim, in a conversation with an Israeli journalist in 1969. When asked how he felt about the creation of Israel, Tuwim replied, "I am happy and proud of the establishment of the Hebrew state. Could it be otherwise? For it is a state established by Jews from Poland, and I am also one of them." For Tuwim, Israel was a veritable overseas Polish Jewish project. In 2013, the Polish parliament declared a year-long "Year of Julian Tuwim" in honor of his legacy. His statue stands on the main street of Lodz, his hometown. Meyer Siemiatycki, *The Jerusalem Post,* December 24, 2019.

43   Gutman-Krakowski, *Unequal,* 15-6.

44   Heller, *Edge,* 195. A very brief summary of names include Bruno Schulz, Julian Tuwim, Marian Hemar, Emanuel Schlechter and Bolesław Leśmian, as well as Konrad Tom and Jerzy Jurandot, who made important contributions to Polish literature. Some Polish artists had Jewish roots, such as singer Jan Kiepura, born of a Jewish mother and Polish father. Some Polish Jews who gained international recognition include Ludwik Zamenhof (the

creator of Esperanto), physicist Georges Charpak, and classical pianist Artur Rubinstein, just to name a few from a long list. Raphael Lemkin (1900–1959), a legal scholar, coined the term "genocide," adopted by the UN after World War II, while Leonid Hurwicz was awarded the 2007 Nobel Prize in Economics. *Wikipedia*, "History."

45   Heller, *Edge*, 58.

46   Heller, *Edge*, 61-2, 64.

47   Heller, *Edge*, 127. Joshua D. Zimmerman, ed., *Contested Memories: Poles and Jews during the Holocaust and its Aftermath*. New Brunswick, New Jersey & London: Rutgers University, 2003, 5.

48   Heller, *Edge*, 63, 70.

49   Heller, *Edge*, 200

50   Mendelsohn, "Interwar;" in, Abramsky, *The Jews*, 137.

51   Heller, *Edge*, 260, 265. Dreifuss, 34.

52   Heller, *Edge*, 41; Gutman, "Poland;" in, *Encyclopedia Judaica*, 750-1. Dreifuss, *Relations*, 34.

53   Heller, *Edge*, 250. Sadly, the Bund's two leading leaders, Wiktor Alter and Henryk Ehrlich were later executed on orders of Stalin, when they fell in Soviet captivity. Heller, *Edge*, 264.

54   Heller, *Edge*, 273. *Wikipedia*, "History." Gutman, "Poland;" in, *Encyclopedia Judaica*, 749-51.

55   Jerzy Holzer "Relations Between Polish and Jewish Left-Wing Groups in Interwar Poland." In, Chimen Abramsky, Maciej Jachimczyk and Antony Polonsky, eds. *The Jews in Poland*. Oxford, UK: Basil Blackwell, 1987, 140-6, 140.

56   Holzer, "Relations;" in, Abramsky, *The Jews*, 144.

57   Holzer, "Relations;" in, Abramsky, *The Jews*, 141.

58   Holzer, "Relations;" in, Abramsky, *The Jews*, 144.

59   Holzer, "Relations;" in, Abramsky, *The Jews*, 144.

60   Weeks, *Assimilation;* 117.

61   Weeks, *Assimilation;* 117-8.

62   Joshua D. Zimmerman. *The Polish Underground and the Jews, 1939-1945*. New York: Cambridge University, 2015, 27.

63   Zimmerman, *Polish*, 28-30.

64   Zimmerman, *Polish*, 17-9.

65   Zimmerman, *Polish*, 31.

66   Steinlauf, *Bondage*, 22.

67   Gutman-Krakowski, *Unequal*, 17.

68   Steinlauf, *Bondage*, 22; Gutman-Krakowski, *Unequal*, 8.

69   Gutman-Krakowski, *Unequal*, 11; Heller, *Edge*, 51.

70 Steinlauf, *Bondage*, 35; Zimmerman, *Polish*, 240; *Wikipedia*, "*Żydokomuna*," June 2019.

71 Steinlauf, *Bondage*, 35.

72 Wikipedia, "Jewish Bolshevism," May 2019. During the 1920s, Hitler fulminated that the mission of the Nazi movement was to destroy "Jewish Bolshevism." Ian Kershaw, *Hitler: 1889-1936*. New York: W.W. Norton, 1998, 303, 253.

73 Heller, *Edge*, 255. In Great Britain, On February 8, 1920, future wartime Prime Minister Winston Churchill penned an editorial entitled "Zionism versus Bolshevism," which was published in the *Illustrated Sunday Herald*. In the article, Churchill asserted that Zionism and Bolshevism were engaged in a "struggle for the soul of the Jewish people." He called on Jews to repudiate "the Bolshevik conspiracy" and made clear that "the Bolshevik movement is not a Jewish movement," but then added that: "[Bolshevism] among the Jews is nothing new. From the days of Spartacus-Weishaupt (sic) to those of Karl Marx, and down to Trotsky (Russia), Bela Kun (Hungary), Rosa Luxemburg (Germany), and Emma Goldman (United States), this world-wide conspiracy for the overthrow of civilization and for the reconstitution of society on the basis of arrested development, of envious malevolence, and impossible equality, has been steadily growing." Winston Churchill, "Zionism versus Bolshevism;" in, *Illustrated Sunday Herald, February 8, 1920;* Steinlauf, *Bondage*, 19-20.

74 Heller, *Edge*, 109.

75 Heller, *Edge*, 112.

76 Heller, *Edge*, 112.

77 Heller, *Edge*, 16.

78 John T. Pawlikowski, "Polish Catholics and the Jews during the Holocaust: Heroism, Timidity, and Collaboration;" in, Zimmerman, *Contested Memories*, 107-119; 115.

79 Heller, *Edge*, 111. Józef Kruszyński's *The Talmud, What it Contains and What it Teaches*, was a compendium of lies and distortions which supposedly instructed Jews in wickedness. The eminent Polish orientalist Tadeusz Zaderecki (who knew Hebrew) refuted these fabrications in *The Talmud in the Fire*.

80 Heller, *Edge*, 113; Gutman-Krakowski, *Unequal*, 19. Zvi Gitelman, "Collective Memory and Contemporary Polish-Jewish Relations;" in, Zimmerman, *Contested Memories*, 271-290; 273.

81 Heller, *Edge*, 114.

82 Pawlikowski, "Polish;" in, Zimmerman, *Contested*, 114.

274

83 Gutman, "Jews;" in Gutman, *Encyclopedia of the Holocaust*, 1154; "Poland;" in, *Encyclopedia Judaica*, 739.

84 Heller, *Edge*, 100.

85 Gutman-Krakowski, *Unequal*, 13.

86 Heller, *Edge*, 100.

87 Gutman-Krakowski, *Unequal*, 13.

88 Zimmerman, *Polish*, 17; Heller, *Edge*, 106. The authorities in the small towns and provincial districts started to change the days fixed for the open market fairs to Saturdays and Jewish holidays, to make it hard for the Jews and prevent their part in the fairs from which they made their living. Emanuel Ringelblum, *Polish-Jewish Relations During the Second World War*. Jerusalem: Yad Vashem, 1974. Footnotes by Joseph Kermish and Shmuel Krakowski, 14, note 4.

89 Melzer, *Contested*, 20.

90 Heller, *Edge*, 116.

91 Heller, *Edge*, 107. Gutman-Krakowski, *Unequal*, 21-22. Ringelblum, *Polish-Jewish*, 20, note 12.

92 Heller, *Edge*, 101.

93 Gutman-Krakowski, *Unequal*, 12.

94 *Wikipedia*, "History."

95 Gutman-Krakowski, *Unequal*, 21. Heller, *Edge*, 123.

96 Heller, *Edge*, 121. Some future Israeli leaders studied at the University of Warsaw, including Menachem Begin and Yitzhak Shamir.

97 Heller, *Edge*, 53.

98 Heller, *Edge*, 115.

99 Ringelblum, *Polish-Jewish*, 15.

100 Heller, *Edge*, 290.

101 Zimmerman, *Polish*, 16.

102 See the list in Ringelblum, *Polish-Jewish*, 11-2, note 2, of the 36 towns and cities that underwent violent outbreaks against Jews during the years 1935 to and including 1937 -- especially the notorious pogrom in Przytyk, March 1936, where 3 Jews lost their life and 22 were wounded.

103 Heller, *Edge*, 118, 287.

104 Heller, *Edge*, 108-9.

105 Emanuel Melzer, "Emigration versus Emigrationism: Zionism in Poland and the Territorialist Projects of the Polish Authorities, 1936-1939." In, Zimmerman, *Contested Memories*, 19-31; 21. Heller, *Edge*, 136.

106 Heller, *Edge*, 136-7.

107 Melzer, "Emigration;" in, Zimmerman, *Contested*, 22.

108　Zimmerman, *Polish*, 19. Melzer, "Emigration;" in, Zimmerman, *Contested*, 23. In October 1938, when Nazi Germany expelled some seventeen thousand Jewish Polish citizens, who had been living in Germany, the Polish authorities responded by establishing the Jewish Colonization Committee in Poland under the chairmanship of Rabbi Professor Moshe Shorr, a historian and former Senate member. Among the committee members were the former Sejm deputies, the Zionists Yehoshua Gottlieb and Henryk Rosmarin, as well as Rabbi Yitshak Meir Lewin of Agudat Yisrael and some assimilationists. Its task was, among others, to maintain contacts with foreign Jewish organizations so as to explore Jewish emigration possibilities from Poland and launch a fund-raising campaign. In the short period of its existence, the Jewish Colonization Committee did not achieve any positive results. Melzer, "Emigration;" in, Zimmerman, *Contested*, 27.

109　Gutman-Krakowski, *Unequal*, 23. Zimmerman, *Polish*, 20.

110　Melzer, "Emigration;" in, Zimmerman, *Contested*, 22. As late, as July 1940, Hans Frank, the Nazi governor of conquered Poland upheld in a speech the Madagascar idea, "which [defeated] France would have to give up as soon as possible," as a solution to the Jewish population of continental Europe. Zimmerman, *Polish*, 115.

111　Melzer, "Emigration;" in, Zimmerman, *Contested*, 22-3.

112　Chaim Weizmann, president of the World Zionist Organization, proposed that French premier, Léon Blum consider a plan to settle a significant number of Polish Jews on the Syrian coast and in Lebanon, which were at that time under mandatory rule of France. Such a plan, according to Weizmann, might be especially attractive to the Maronites in Lebanon, on the one hand, and to the Jewish prospective emigrants from Poland, on the other hand, because of the closeness of this territory to Palestine. Blum's immediate reaction to Weizmann's proposal is not known. Among the various Jewish emigration plans that the Polish authorities initiated and considered in the late 1930s, is the rather interesting one to settle Polish Jews in the Sinai Peninsula. This plan, if it had been realized, could have been very attractive to the Zionists because of the close proximity of this territory to Palestine. It was officially submitted in January 1938 by Alfons Kula, the Polish chargé d'affaires in Cairo, on the basis of personal contacts with the local Anglo-Egyptian administration and with influential Jewish elements in Egypt. In the same year, the Polish consul in Tel Aviv, Tadeusz Piszczkowski, delivered to his government a written survey of the possibilities of Jewish emigration in Transjordan. Syria, and Iraq. Emanuel Melzer, "Emigration;" in, Zimmerman, *Contested Memories*, 19-31; 23-4.

113　Gutman-Krakowski, *Unequal*, 16, 23.

114   Melzer, "Emigration;" in, Zimmerman, *Contested,* 24.

115   Heller, *Edge,* 7.

116   Melzer, "Emigration," 21-2; Gutman-Krakowski, *Unequal,* 23.

117   The New Zionist Organization (NZO) by the Revisionist movement was even more eager to cooperate with Polish official circles on the Palestine issue than its rival World Zionist Organization. NZO leader, Vladimir (Ze'ev) Jabotinsky, kept very close relations with the Polish authorities. In one of his frequent visits to Poland, in September 1936, he published his "Ten-Year Evacuation Plan" in the Polish conservative daily, *Czas.* According to Jabotinsky's plan, of the 1.5 million Jews whose emigration he sought from Europe to Palestine, 750,000 were to come from Poland. Melzer, "Emigration;" in, Zimmerman, *Contested,* 25.

118   Heller, *Edge,* 219.

119   *Wikipedia,* "History."

120   Heller, *Edge,* 156, 158.

121   Heller, *Edge,* 222.

122   Heller, *Edge,* 159.

123   Steinlauf, *Bondage,* 18-9; Gutman-Krakowski, *Unequal,* 16.

124   *Wikipedia,* "History."

125   Steinlauf, *Bondage,* 18.

126   Mendelsohn, "Interwar;" in, Abramsky, *The Jews,* 136.

127   f Mendelsohn, "Interwar;" in, Abramsky, *The Jews,* 138.

128   Mendelsohn, "Interwar;" in, Abramsky, *The Jews,* 139.

129   Mendelsohn, "Interwar;" in, Abramsky, *The Jews,* 139.

130   Gutman-Krakowski, *Unequal,* 5-6.

131   Gutman-Krakowski, *Unequal,* 17.

132   Gutman-Krakowski, *Unequal,* 5.

133   Davies, *God's,* 263; Lukas, *Forgotten,* 126.

134   Melzer, "Emigration;" in, Zimmerman, *Contested,* 19-31.

135   Gutman-Krakowsk, *Unequal,* 4.

136   Antony Polonsky, "Roman Dmowski and Italian Fascism. In, R.J. Bullen, H.Pogge von Strandman, A.B. Polonsky, *Ideas into Politics: Aspects of Human History 1880-1950.* London & Sydney: Croom Helm; 130-146; 133.

137   Antony Polonsky, "Roman;" in, Bullen, *Ideas,* 133-4.

138   Polonsky, "Roman;" in, Bullen, *Ideas,* 135, 143.

139   Polonsky, "Roman;" in, Bullen, *Ideas,* 144. Władysław Bartoszewski, writing after World War II, states that the image of the Jew in the mind of the Polish peasant was that as a stranger, more or less as he similarly saw German descendants living in Poland, the Polish burgher, or even the

peasant from another village. He maintains that it is completely wrong to believe that the Polish peasant was an antisemite, a modern term which he says is connected with the rise of modern nationalism and foreign to the peasant mentality. True, Bartoszewski adds, the peasants did think of the Jews as Christ killers and as users of Christian blood for baking their matzos, but these beliefs, did not influence the behavior of the peasants. Mendelsohn, "Interwar;" in, Abramsky, *The Jews,* 132. Others, such as Mendelsohn, disagree with this mitigating assessment by Bartoszewski; Mendelsohn, "Interwar;" in, Abramsky, *the Jews,* 136.

140   Heller, *Edge,* 3, 13; Lichten, "Notes;" in, Abramsky, *The Jews,* 107.

141   Mendelsohn, "Interwar;" in, Abramsky, *The Jews,* 131.

142   Lichten, "Notes;" in, Abramsky, *The Jews,* 107.

143   Mendelsohn, "Interwar;" in, Abramsky, *The Jews,* 131.

144   Mendelsohn, "Interwar;" in, Abramsky, *The Jews,* 135.

145   Mendelsohn, "Interwar;" in, Abramsky, *The Jews,* 133.

146   Mendelsohn, "Interwar;" in, Abramsky, *The Jews,* 135.

147   Mendelsohn, "Interwar;" in, Abramsky, *The Jews,* 130.

148   Mendelsohn, "Interwar;" in, Abramsky, *The Jews,* 138.

149   Gitelman. "Collective;" in Zimmerman, *Contested,* 272.

150   Steinlauf, *Bondage,* 10

151   Israel Gutman, "Some Issues in Jewish-Polish Relations During the Second World War;" in, Zimmerman, ed., Contested *Memories,* 47-53; 47.

152   Emanuel Ringelblum. *Notes from the Warsaw Ghetto: The Journal of Emanuel Ringelblum.* New York: Schocken Books, 1974, 79.

153   Samuel Kassow, "Polish-Jewish Relations in the Writings of Emanuel Ringelblum." In, Zimmerman, *Contested Memories,* 142-157; 142. Israel Gutman, ed., *Emanuel Ringelblum: The Man and the Historian.* Jerusalem: Yad Vashem, 2010, 189-205; 189-190, 193. One of the ideas that strongly influenced and molded Ringelblum was the Polish socialist ideology, that he felt was also consistent with the belief in reason and progress of society and civilization. Before the war, Ringelblum belonged to the strongly Marxist Zionist Poalei Zion Left wing. It is now recognized that Ringelblum erred in his war-time assessment that ordinary workers had a better record than other Poles in saving Jews. This is not borne out by the more recent research. Samuel Kassow, "Polish-Jewish Relations in Emanuel Ringelblum's Writings." In, Gutman, *Emanuel Ringelblum,* 197; Barbara Engelking, "Moral Issues in Emanuel Ringelblum's Writings from World War II." In, Gutman, *Emanuel Ringelblum,* 207-27; 208.

154   Dreifuss, *Relations,* 37-8.

155   Dreifuss, *Relations,* 38-9.

156   Dreifuss, *Relations*, 37; Gutman, "Poland;" in, *Encyclopedia Judaica*, 751;
       Madajczyk, "Poland: General Survey;" in, Gutman, *Encyclopedia of the
       Holocaust*, 1144.

Chapter 3

1   Lukas, *Forgotten*, 6. Evans, *Third Reich*, 12. Łódz had been an important
     industrial center, boasting a textile manufacturing center in 1939 that
     employed 700,000 people. Upper Silesia, was a major center of industrial
     war production, especially synthetic oil and rubber and chemical plants.
     Lukas, *Forgotten*, 7.
2   Zimmerman, *Polish*, 39. Evans, *Third Reich*, 13.
3   Bartoszewski, "Polish-Jewish;" in, Abramsky, *The Jews in Poland*, 149.
4   Zimmerman, *Polish*, 41. Another source gives 32,216 killed and 61,000
     taken prisoners by the Germans. Dreifuss gives the figure of 100,000
     Jewish soldiers, of whom 20,000 were killed or injured and a further
     20,000 were taken prisoner by the Russians. Dreifuss, *Relations*, 60.
5   *Wikipedia*, "History." Gutman, "Poland;" in, *Encyclopedia Judaica*, 752.
6   Zimmerman, *Polish*, 42.
7   Madajczyk, "Poland;" in, Gutman, *Encyclopedia of the Holocaust*, 1146.
     Lukas, *Forgotten*, 34.
8   Lukas, *Forgotten*, 25, 33.
9   Zimmerman, *Polish*, 379.
10   *Wikipedia*, "History."
11   Steinlauf, *Bondage*, 23.
12   Evans, *Third Reich*, 103-4.
13   Evans, *Third Reich*, 11.
14   Evans, *Third Reich* 14.
15   Evans, *Third Reich*, 102.
16   Evans, *Third Reich*, 28.
17   Evans, *Third Reich* 14.
18   Lukas, *Forgotten*, 5.
19   Despite the contrary assertion by Lukas, no conference or plans came
     forth, such as the Wannsee conference on Jews, to indicate a serious Nazi
     extermination decision, immediately or ultimately for the Polish popu-
     lation. The author also errs in stating that Poles were considered racially
     in the same category as Jews. To the Nazis, they were also Aryans, but of
     an inferior status. Their expulsion and enslavement was due, not to any
     ideological obsession, but the need to remove most of them to somewhere

in a subdued Russia, so as to create room for the colonization of Poland with German and kindred settlers, and making Poland over the years fully German. Lukas, *Forgotten*, 8, 24, 220.

20   Steinlauf, *Bondage*, x.

21   Madajczyk, "Poland;" in, Gutman, *Encyclopedia of the Holocaust*, 1146-7.

22   Davies, *God's*, 453-4. Lukas, *Forgotten*, 4.

23   Lukas, *Forgotten*, 32.

24   Lukas, *Forgotten*, 8.

25   Steinlauf, *Bondage*, 27. According to historian Richard Evans, at the onset of the German invasion, the Polish government arrested between ten and fifteen thousand ethnic Germans and marched them towards the eastern part of the country, beating laggards and shooting many of those who gave up walking through exhaustion. Altogether, around 2,000 ethnic Germans were killed in mass shootings or died from exhaustion on these marches. It fueled the hatred and resentment felt by the ethnic German minority in Poland against their former masters. I have not seen this mentioned elsewhere in the history of World War II. Evans, *Third Reich*, 8- 9.

26   Davies, *God's*, 445. Lukas, *Forgotten*, 24.

27   Madajczyk, "Poland;" in, Gutman, *Encyclopedia of the Holocaust*, 1145.

28   Evans, *Third Reich*, 102.

29   Bartoszewski, "Polish-Jewish;" in, Abramsky, *The Jews in Poland*, 149.

30   Evans, *Third Reich*, 29-30, 36-7. Davies, *God's*, 446.

31   Lukas, *Forgotten*, 21-2.

32   Joanna Beata Michlic. *Poland's Threatening Other: The Image of the Jew from 1880 to the Present*. Lincoln & London: University of Nebraska, 2006, 140. Madajczyk, "Poland;" in, Gutman, *Encyclopedia of the Holocaust*, 1145-6. Lukas states that children considered unfit for Germanization found their way to Auschwitz where, along with adults, they died, but does not provide sources for this. Lukas, *Forgotten*, 22.

33   Michlic, *Poland's*, 139. Zimmerman, *Polish*, 88-89. Madajczyk, "Poland;" in, Gutman, *Encyclopedia of the Holocaust*, 1145.

34   Madajczyk, "Poland;" in, Gutman, *Encyclopedia of the Holocaust*, 1149.

35   Gutman-Krakowski, *Unequal*, 253.

36   Steinlauf, *Bondage*, 25. Zimmerman, *Contested*, xi.

37   Lukas, *Forgotten*, 3, 9, 14-15. Evans, *Third Reich*, 20. Bartoszewski, "Polish-Jewish;" in, Abramsky, *The Jews in Poland*, 149.

38   Michlic, *Poland's*, 140l. Bartoszewski, "Polish-Jewish;" in, Abramsky, *The Jews in Poland*, 150.

39   Evans, *Third Reich*, 21. Davies, *God's*, 441, 455.

40   Lukas, *Forgotten*, 34-6.

41   Lukas, *Forgotten*, 34, 100.

42   Lukas, *Forgotten*, 8.

43   Evans, *Third Reich*, 16.

44   Lukas, *Forgotten*, 8-9.

45   Evans, *Third Reich*, 33-4. Witold Pilecki, *The Auschwitz Volunteer: Beyond Bravery*. Translated from Polish. Los Angeles, Cal.: Aquila Polonica, 2012. Zygmunt Klukowski. *Diary from the Years of Occupation, 1939-1944*. Urbana: University of Illinois, 1993, 106. Lukas, *Forgotten*, 1, who misrepresents the killing of intellectuals as a Holocaust. Zimmerman, *Polish*, 49. Michlic, *Poland's*, 172. Lukas, *Forgotten*, 9. Davies, *God's*, 447.

46   Lukas, *Forgotten*, 10.

47   Lukas, *Forgotten*, 10.

48   Lukas, *Forgotten*, 13.

49   Lukas, *Forgotten*, 13-4.

50   Davies, *God's*, 447. Evans, *Third Reich*, 75.

51   Evans, *Third Reich*, 76; Klukowski, *Diary*, 76.

52   Nechama Tec, *"Hiding and Passing on the Aryan Side: A Gendered Comparison;"* in, Zimmerman, *Contested*, 193-211; 194.

53   Lukas, *Forgotten*, 32. Evans, *Third Reich*, 21-22.

54   Evans, *Third Reich*, 22. Lukas, *Forgotten*, 33.

55   Klukowski, *Diary*, 166, 199.

56   Lukas, *Forgotten*, 24.

57   Davies, *God's*, 445-6.

58   Evans, *Third Reich*, 31.

59   Evans, *Third Reich*, 32. Poles who fought bravely against the German invaders, in September 1939, were believed by the Nazis to have a significant amount of Nordic blood which had enabled them to put up a good fight.

60   Evans, *Third Reich*, 23, 43. Lukas, *Forgotten*, 29.

61   Evans, *Third Reich*, 54. Lukas, *Forgotten*, 30.

62   Lukas, *Forgotten*, 30. Davies, *God's*, 445.

63   Lukas, *Forgotten*, 30, 42-43.

64   Lukas, *Forgotten*, 27.

65   Lukas, *Forgotten*, 27. Evans, *Third Reich*, 23.

66   Lukas, *Forgotten*, 29.

67   Lukas, *Forgotten*, 31, 42.

68   Lukas, *Forgotten*, 101.

69   Evans, *Third Reich*, 43-4.

70   *Klukowski, Diary*, 77.

71   *Klukowski, Diary*, 140.

72   Evans, *Third Reich*, 24-5.

73   Lukas, *Forgotten*, 113-4.
74   Lukas, *Forgotten*, 115.
75   Steinlauf, *Bondage*, 24.
76   Lukas, *Forgotten*, 111.
77   Lukas, *Forgotten*, 111-3.
78   Lukas, *Forgotten*, 115
79   Lukas, *Forgotten*, 116.
80   Lukas, *Forgotten*, 24, 117. Also, based on Ringelblum, *Polish-Jewish, 226.*
81   *Klukowski, Diary,* 255.
82   *Klukowski, Diary,* 290.
83   Evans, *Third Reich*, 44.
84   Evans, *Third Reich*, 45. Davies, *God's,* 448.
85   Davies, *God's,* 449.
86   Davies, *God's,* 451.
87   Davies, *God's,* 453. Lukas, *Forgotten,* ix.
88   Madajczyk, "Poland;" in, Gutman, *Encyclopedia of the Holocaust*, 1147-8. Lukas, *Forgotten*, 38-39.
89   Gutman, "Jews;" in, Gutman, *Encyclopedia of the Holocaust*, 1156; "Poland;" in, *Jewish Encyclopedia*, 763.
90   Gutman-Krakowski, *Unequal,* 98.
91   Gutman-Krakowski, *Unequal,* 29.
92   Michlic, *Poland's,* 140. Pawlikowski, "Polish;" in, Zimmerman, *Contested,* 108.
93   Steinlauf, *Bondage,* 28. Feliks Tych, "Jewish and Polish Perceptions of the Shoah as Reflected in Wartime Diaries and Memoirs;" in, Zimmerman, *Contested,* 134-141. Gutman-Krakowski, *Unequal,* v.
94   Evans, *Third Reich*, 51-52. Gutman, "Jews;" in, Gutman, *Encyclopedia of the Holocaust*, 1159; "Poland;" in, *Jewish Encyclopedia*, 753. Ringelblum, *Notes*, 17.
95   Gutman, "Poland;" in, *Jewish Encyclopedia*, 752.
96   Evans, *Third Reich*, 50.
97   Evans, *Third Reich*, 50-1. Gutman-Krakowski, *Unequal,* 30; Gutman, "Poland;" in, *Jewish Encyclopedia*, 752.
98   Evans, *Third Reich*, 50.
99   Evans, *Third Reich*, 25.
100   Michlic, *Poland's,* 141.
101   Gutman-Krakowski, *Unequal,* 30-1. Evans, *Third Reich*, 52.
102   Gutman, "Jews;" in Gutman, *Encyclopedia of the Holocaust*, 1158; "Poland;" in, *Jewish Encyclopedia*, 753.
103   *Wikipedia,* "History."

104   Gutman, "Jews;" in, Gutman, *Encyclopedia of the Holocaust*, 1158.

105   Jews needed by German economic interests were momentarily left in their work places.

106   Gutman, "Jews;" in, Gutman, *Encyclopedia of the Holocaust*, 1156.

107   Gutman, "Jews;" in, Gutman, *Encyclopedia of the Holocaust*, 1158. Evans, *Third Reich*, 59.

108   Michlic, *Poland's*, 141. Originally it was planned that over half a million Jews were to be deported from the annexedd territories along with the remaining 30,000 Gypsies and Jews from Prague and Vienna and other parts of the Reich and Protectorate, into a specially created reservation – known as the Nisko region, in Lublin province. After an initial transfer of several thousand Jews there by SS officer Adolf Eichmann, the Germans put a stop to the whole action, due to logistic difficulties and the strong opposition of adding more Jews under his control, by the Nazi German governor, Hans Frank. This original grandiose scheme by Eichmann came to nothing. Evans, *Third Reich*, 55-6.

109   Gutman, "Jews;" in, Gutman, *Encyclopedia of the Holocaust*, 1161.

110   Gutman, "Jews;" in, Gutman, *Encyclopedia of the Holocaust*, 1159.

111   Gutman, "Jews;" in, Gutman, *Encyclopedia of the Holocaust*, 1161.

112   Wikipedia, "History."

113   Evans, *Third Reich*, 62.

114   Gutman-Krakowski, *Unequal*, 184.

115   Gutman-Krakowski, *Unequal*, 185.

116   Steinlauf, *Bondage*, 28.

117   Gutman, "Jews;" in, *Gutman, Encyclopedia of the Holocaust*, 1157-8.

118   Gutman-Krakowski, *Unequal*, 190. Michlic, *Poland's*, 141.

119   Gutman-Krakowski, *Unequal*, v. Gutman, "Jews;" in, Gutman, *Encyclopedia of the Holocaust*, 1160.

120   Gutman, "Jews;" in, Gutman, *Encyclopedia of the Holocaust*, 1162.

121   Gutman-Krakowski, *Unequal*, 81-82, note 20, 182.

122   Evans, *Third Reich*, 59, 62.

123   Gutman-Krakowski, *Unequal*, 188.

124   Gutman, "Jews;" in, Gutman, *Encyclopedia of the Holocaust*, 1162. Ringelblum, *Notes*, 97. *Wikipedia*, "History."

125   Gutman-Krakowski, *Unequal*, 80, note 19.

126   Gutman-Krakowski, *Unequal*, 190.

127   Gutman, "Jews;" in, Gutman, *Encyclopedia of the Holocaust*, 1163-4.

128   Gutman-Krakowski, *Unequal*, 83, note 22.

129   Gutman, "Jews;" in, *Gutman, Encyclopedia of the Holocaust*, 1164.

130   Gutman-Krakowski, *Unequal*, 45, 186.

131   Ringelblum, *Polish-Jewish*, 77.

132   Ringelblum, *Polish-Jewish*, 64.

133   Ringelblum, *Polish-Jewish*, 65.

134   Ringelblum, *Polish-Jewish*, 75.

135   Ringelblum, *Polish-Jewish*, 76, 86, note 26.

136   Madajczyk, "Poland;" in, Gutman, *Encyclopedia of the Holocaust*, 1145, 1148, 1149.

137   Evans, *Third Reich*, 45-6.

138   Evans, *Third Reich*, 45.

139   Ringelblum, *Notes*, 93.

140   *Wikipedia*, "History."

141   Davies, *God's*, 451. Evans, *Third Reich*, 46. Menachem Begin, future Prime Minister of Israel, was one of those deported by the Soviets, after a long and severe interrogation, for his pre-war leadership role in the Zionist movement. Lukas claims that according to one report, some 75 percent of all the top administrative posts were in Jewish hands in some major cities during the Soviet occupation of eastern Poland, but fails to indicate the credible source of this exaggerated assertion. Lukas, *Forgotten*, 128.

142   *Wikipedia*, "Żydokomuna." *Wikipedia*, "History."

143   *Wikipedia*, "History."

144   Evans, *Third Reich*, 220-1.

145   Yehuda Bauer, *A History of the Holocaust*. New York: Franklin Watts, 2001; 227-47. Lukas, *Forgotten*, 38. Davies, *God's*, 456-7.

146   Bauer, *History*, 227.

147   Zygmunt Bauman, *Modernity and the Holocaust*. Ithaca, N.Y.: Cornell University, 1989, 232, note 1 to chapter 5.

148   Zimmerman, *Polish*, 167. Bartoszewski, "Polish-Jewish;" in, Abramsky, *The Jews in Poland*, 156.

149   Gutman-Krakowski, *Unequal*, 73-5, 108. Zimmerman, *Polish*, 168. Michlic, *Poland's*, 155. Pawlikowski, "Polish;" in, Zimmerman, *Contested*, 109.

150   Lukas, *Forgotten*, 156. Klukowski, *Diary*, 224. Gutman-Krakowski, *Unequal*, 70-1, 165. In August 1942, an article in the PPR's clandestine newspaper *Trybuna Chłopska* (The Farmers' Platform) called on people to help Jews, since if the Germans succeeded in destroying all Jews, this could be a stepping stone to do likewise to the Poles, by physically destroying them." Gutman, *The Jews of Warsaw, 1939-1943: Ghetto, Underground, Revolt*. Bloomington: Indiana University, 1982, 258-9.

Chapter 4

1 Daniel Blatman, "Poland and the Polish Nation as Reflected in the Jewish Underground Press." Zimmerman, ed., Contested, 123-133; 123-4.

2 Gutman-Krakowski, Unequal, 32.

3 Dreifuss, Relations, 221-222.

4 Dreifuss, Relations, 44.

5 Dreifuss, Relations, 118.

6 Dreifuss, Relations, 118, 120, 125, 137.

7 Gutman-Krakowski, Unequal, 32.

8 Dreifuss, Relations, 57.

9 Ringelblum, Polish-Jewish, 37.

10 Ringelblum, Polish-Jewish, 38, 42.

11 Gutman-Krakowski, Unequal, 36.

12 Dreifuss, Relations, 58.

13 Gutman, "Jews;" in, Encyclopedia Holocaust, 1165; "Poland;" in, Encyclopedia Judaica, 776.

14 Dreifuss, Relations, 49.

15 Dreifuss, Relations, 233-240, file 92 in the Oneg Shabbes archives.

16 Dreifuss, Relations, 79.

17 Dreifuss, Relations, 79, note 21.

18 Dreifuss, Relations, 81.

19 Barbara Engelking, "Psychological Distance between Poles and Jews in Nazi-Occupied Warsaw;" in, Zimmerman, Contested Memories, 47-53, 48.

20 Steinlauf, Bondage 31.

21 Gutman-Krakowski, Unequal, 194.

22 Gutman-Krakowski, Unequal, 177; Ringelblum, Polish-Jewish, 196. In 1928, the Endeks dropped the word "Democratic" from their party's name.

23 Ringelblum, Polish-Jewish, 197.

24 Dreifuss, Relations, 80, note 23.

25 Dreifuss, Relations, 130.

26 Kassow, "Ringelblum;" in, Gutman, Ringelblum, 198.

27 Ringelblum, Notes, 18.

28 Dreifuss, Relations, 86.

29 After the war, Władysław Bartoszewski, in his introduction to the book Righteous Among the Nations (p. lxxxiv) wrote: "The conditions of the German occupation led in general to a marked decline in antisemitic sentiments which had existed in pre-war Poland. The common fate of the persecuted, suffering, fighting people helped to awaken a sense of solidarity

and a will to help those who were dying." To which, Yisrael Gutman (active in the Warsaw ghetto) responded by disagreeing. "I cannot agree that the views and actions of the Polish people underwent a general process of modification born of the conditions and bitter experience of the times." Yisrael Gutman, "Polish and Jewish Historiography on the Question of Polish-Jewish Relations During World War II;" in, Abramsky, *The Jews*, 177-89, 179.

30 Dreifuss, *Relations*, 58-9.

31 Dreifuss, *Relations*, 60-1.

32 Lukas, *Forgotten*, 129.

33 Dreifuss, *Relations*, 80, 86.

34 Ringelblum, *Notes*, 17; Dreifuss, *Relations*, 88.

35 Ringelblum, *Notes*, 68.

36 Dreifuss, *Relations*, 49. Gutman-Krakowski, *Unequal*, 179.

37 Chaim A. Kaplan, *The Scroll of Agony*. New York: Macmillan 1965, 114.

38 Gutman-Krakowski, *Unequal*, 180.

39 Ringelblum, *Polish-Jewish*, 48.

40 Gutman-Krakowski, *Unequal*, 34.

41 Gutman-Krakowski, *Unequal*, 180.

42 Ringelblum, *Polish-Jewish*, 52.

43 Gutman-Krakowski, *Unequal*, 33.

44 Gutman-Krakowski, *Unequal*, 34.

45 Ringelblum, *Polish-Jewish*, 45.

46 Gutman-Krakowski, *Unequal*, 49.

47 Gutman-Krakowski, *Unequal*, 180.

48 Lukas, *Forgotten*, 130.

49 Ringelblum, *Polish-Jewish*, 51.

50 Dreifuss, *Relations*, 261-262. Yarden, a woman from Łódz, attributes the Poles' involvement in the persecution of Jews to the ethnic Germans among them: "On the street corner they are lurking in wait for us, our neighbors of yesterday and the day before. The German citizens of Lodz... stubbornly scrutinize every passerby... Armed with scissors... cutting off beards, pulling out hair until they see blood." There were also a few exceptions. Such as a Pole who stole his way in between the assembled Jews and gave a close acquaintance bread and money. Dreifuss, *Relations*, 93.

51 Ringelblum, *Polish-Jewish*, 53.

52 Kassow, "Polish-Jewish Relations;" in, Zimmerman, *Contested*, 142-157; 151.

53 Dreifuss, *Relations*, 253.

54 Evans, *Third Reich*, 102.

55   Lukas, *Forgotten*, 127.
56   Evans, *Third Reich*, 294.
57   Gutman-Krakowski, *Unequal*, 52-3.
58   Carla Tonini, "Zofia Kossak: the anti-Semite who Rescued Polish Jews." In, Arslan, Bibo, Boella et al., *There is Always an Option to say 'Yes' or 'No': The Righteous Against the Genocides of Armenians and Jews*. Padova, Cleup: 2001, 81.
59   Tec, *When Light*, 111-2.
60   Rachel Feldhay Brenner, "Polka-Katoliczka and the Holocaust: The Enigma of Zofia Kossak." In, Yad Vashem Studies 45:2 (2017), 125-158, 156.
61   Zofia Kossak-Szczucka, *Yad Vashem Archives*; henceforth, YVA, 31.2/577. Joseph Kermish, "Postcript." Ringelblum, *Polish-Jewish*, 292-3.
62   Lukas, *Forgotten*, 121.
63   Lukas, *Forgotten*, 127. These totally unfounded charges are perhaps merely an indication of the author's own penchant prejudices. Lukas also makes a faulty comparison between the fate of Jews and Poles in the period preceding the start of the mass extermination of Jews. However, there is some truth in the author's assertion that at first, Poles felt that their situation was far worse than the Jews who lived in ghettos. That, since the Germans wanted to destroy the Poles politically, they seemed to want only to cripple the Jews economically, since Jews as a group were not deported or executed as the Poles were in these early days of the German occupation. At the same time, most Poles were cognizant that Jews inside the ghettos were dying at an accelerated rate, due to starvation and various infectious illnesses – way above what the Polish population was experiencing. Lukas, *Forgotten*, 127.
64   Lukas, *Forgotten*, 126.
65   Lukas, *Forgotten*, 179.
66   Evans, *Third Reich*, 64.
67   Evans, *Third Reich*, 51.
68   Evans, *Third Reich*, 311.
69   Evans, *Third Reich*, 64.
70   Nechama Tec, *When Light Pierced the Darkness: Christian Rescue of Jews in Nazi-Occupied Poland*. New York: Oxford University Press, 1986, 99.
71   Zimmerman, *Polish*, 73.
72   Zimmerman, *Polish*, 74.
73   Michlic, *Poland's*, 185.
74   Michlic, *Poland's*, 185.
75   Zimmerman, *Polish*, 78.
76   Gutman-Krakowski, *Unequal*, 52.
77   Michlic, *Poland's*, 186.

78   Gutman, "Some Issues;" in, Zimmerman, *Contested*, 213.

79   Gutman, "Some Issues;" in, Zimmerman, *Contested*, 215.

80   Gutman, "Some Issues;" in, Zimmerman, *Contested*, 216.

81   Michlic, *Poland's*, 172.

82   Lukas, *Forgotten*, 22.

83   Kassow, "Ringelblum;" in, Gutman, *Emanuel Ringelblum*, 201.

84   Ringelblum, *Notes*, 199.

85   Ringelblum, *Notes*, 202-3.

86   Abraham Lewin, *A Cup of Tears*. Oxford: Blackwell, 1988, 124; Kassow, "Ringelblum;" in, Gutman, *Ringelblum*, 200.

87   Dreifuss, *Relations*, 79-80.

88   Dreifuss, *Relations*, 150.

89   Dreifuss, *Relations*, 151, 153. I find it necessary to differ with Dreifuss's assessment that this "cognitive dissonance" affected "most" Jews; when stating that "more Jews than before believed that these acts were signs of the beginning of the significant and far-reach change in Polish society." That may have been a viewpoint shared by some (mostly intellectual) Jews, but it is hardly substantiated in Dreifuss's own study, with what most Jews felt (Dreifuss, *Relations*, 76, 80, 91, 160). Havi Dreifuss maintains that even during the ghetto period such a positive image of Poles "raised it to mythical proportions" (Dreifuss, *Relations*, 117). In her defense of the "positive" image Jews had of Poles, Dreifuss adds that it is impossible to say that the negative image that developed toward the end of the war represented an accurate portrayal of Polish society as it was in reality (Dreifuss, *Relations*, 210). It should be pointed out that this is not a viewpoint shared by many other historians, such as Israel Gutman and Shmuel Krakowski.

Chapter 5

1   Engelking, "Psychological;" in, Zimmerman, *Contested*, 51-2.

2   Gunnar S. Paulsson, "Ringelblum Revisited: The Destruction of Polish Jewry and Polish Popular Opinion;" in, Zimmerman, *Contested*, 173-92; 177. Ringelblum, *Polish-Jewish*, 95.

3   Gutman, *Jews of Warsaw*, 265. It is impossible to estimate how many helped Jews, not out of merely goodwill, but in exchange for what amounted to ransom.

4   Gutman-Krakowski, *Unequal*, 102.

5   Ringelblum, *Polish-Jewish*, 96.

6   Ringelblum, *Polish-Jewish*, 97-98.

7   Paulsson, "Ringelblum;" in, Zimmerman, *Contested*, 178.

8   Paulsson, "Ringelblum;" in, Zimmerman, *Contested*, 179.

9   Kassow, "Polish-Jewish;" in, Gutman, *Emanuel*, 203.

10   Alina Skibińska & Jakub Petelewicz, "The Participation of Poles in Crimes Against Jews in the Świętokrzyskie Region." In, *Yad Vashem Studies* 35:1, Jerusalem, 2007, 5-48; 19.

11   Zimmerman, *Contested*, 9; Ringelblum, *Polish-Jewish*, 152.

12   Copies of these German promulgations are in the author's possession. The original posters may be found in the Yad Vashem archives, as well as in a multitude of Polish archives.

13   Engelking, "Psychological;" in, Zimmerman, *Contested*, 50.

14   Engelking, "Psychological;" in, Zimmerman, *Contested*, 52.

15   Gutman, "Jews;" in, Gutman, *Encyclopedia of the Holocaust*, 1171.

16   Gutman, "Jews;" in, Gutman, *Encyclopedia of the Holocaust*, 1171; *Wikipedia*, "History."

17   Zimmerman, *Polish*, 162. Gutman-Krakowski, *Unequal*, 195.

18   Gutman, *Jews of Warsaw*, 265. Historian Gunnar S. Paulsson goes so far as to argue that tens of thousands of Poles in German-occupied Warsaw stood by and waited for Jews to "choose" to escape the ghetto to the Aryan side. But, Paulsson continues, due to the Jewish negative image of the Poles, this prevented many thousands of them from taking advantage of the "safety net" that awaited them outside the ghetto. The record on hand, however, is far from supporting this imaginary reality. Dreifuss, *Relations*, 24.

19   Gutman-Krakowski, *Unequal*, 196.

20   Engelking, "Psychological;" in, Zimmerman, *Contested*, 50. Tec, "Hiding;" in, Zimmerman, *Contested*, 195. Wikipedia, "History."

21   Ringelblum, *Polish-Jewish*, 100.

22   Tec, "Hiding;" in, Zimmerman, *Contested*, 199.

23   Tec, "Hiding;" in, Zimmerman, *Contested*, 196.

24   Ringelblum, *Polish-Jewish*, 103.

25   Ringelblum, *Polish-Jewish*, 101. It was not a rare thing for people who had large beautifully furnished flats before the war, with many servants, to become servants themselves in order to save their lives. Ringelblum, *Relations*, 101, note 2.

26   Ringelblum, *Polish-Jewish*, 104.

27   Ringelblum, *Polish-Jewish*, 109. Bracha Karwasser, who came from a religious family in Brwinów and who survived the ghetto and then moved to Israel, wrote the following account: "When the displacement campaign started my father went to the Rabbi and asked for advice. Rabbi Shapiro told him: 'Send the children to the Aryan side, because this is of utmost

importance – maybe one of you will survive.' My father divided jewelry among us and said, 'children, this is the will of HaShem [God] – save yourselves as you can. At home you never ate non-Kosher food, I never let you do this, but now act in such manner as to save yourselves, survive and later tell people what we all experienced in the ghetto. Bracha Karwasser, "A Testimony," Yad Vashem Archives, Jerusalem, 03/3484. Engelking, "Psychological;" in, Zimmerman, *Contested,* 51.

28   Ringelblum, *Polish-Jewish,* 104.

29   Personal communication to the author. Also, Yanina Brandwajn-Ziemian, *Neurim Vetushiyah Bamilhamah* (Hebrew). Tel-Aviv: Yaron Golan, 1994. Available: New York Public Library, Fifth Avenue & 42nd Street, Dorot Room (PXK 95-595). Also by same author: *Młodość w cieniu śmierci.* Łódź: Oficyna Bibliofilów, 1995.

30   Ringelblum, *Polish-Jewish,* 119.

31   Tec, "Hiding;" in, Zimmerman, *Contested,* 197.

32   Tec, "Hiding;" in, Zimmerman, *Contested,* 197.

33   Gutman-Krakowski, *Unequal,* 198.

34   Ringelblum, *Polish-Jewish,* 104, 226.

35   Ringelblum, *Polish-Jewish,* 227.

36   Tec, "Hiding;" in, Zimmerman, *Contested,* 197-198.

37   Tec, "Hiding;" in, Zimmerman, *Contested,*198.

38   Ringelblum, *Polish-Jewish,* 102; Tec, "Hiding;" in Zimmerman, *Contested,* 203-4.

39   Ringelblum, *Polish-Jewish,* 149. Teresa Prekerowa. "The Relief Council for Jews in Poland, 1942-1945;" in, Abramsky, *The Jews,* 161-76, 169.

40   Ringelblum, *Polish-Jewish,* 141; Michlic, *Poland's,* 188.

41   Kermish, "Postscript;" in, Ringelblum, *Polish-Jewish,* 299.

42   Ringelblum, *Polish-Jewish,* 299

43   Mordecai Paldiel, *Saving One's Own.* Philadelphia: Jewish Publishing Society, 2017, 42-7. Also, Jozeph Ziemian, *The Cigarette Sellers of Three Crosses Square.* New York: Avon, 1975.

44   Tec, *When Light,* 54, 58; Zimmerman, *Contested,* 5.

45   Michlic, *Poland's,* 190.

46   *Yalkut Moreshet,* "Bogushia," No. 7, July 1967; Gutman-Krakowski, *Unequal,* 196.

47   Gutman-Krakowski, *Unequal,* 272.

48   Tych, "Jewish and Polish;" in, Zimmerman, *Contested,* 138. Those among the local population out in the hunt after Jews included the local Polish (Blue) police as well as miscellaneous units of railroad, forest, or industrial guards. In the countryside, the local population created local formations of

"Night Watch" (*Nachtschutz*), as well as fire brigades, which often carried out various public order and auxiliary duties, and they also too took part in the hunt of Jews. Skibinska-Petelewicz, "Participation;" in, *Yad Vashem*, 79.

49   Lukas, *Forgotten*, 117. Ringelblum, Polish-Jewish, 124.

50   Ringelblum, *Polish-Jewish*, 123.

51   Gutman-Krakowski, *Unequal*, 114.

52   Tec, "Hiding," 194.

53   Ringelblum, *Polish-Jewish*, 123-4. Gutman-Krakowski, *Unequal*, 201. The Berman couple describe how they were blackmailed three times on the very day they left the ghetto. Ringelblum, *Polish-Jewish*, 42, note 6.

54   Engelking, "Psychological," 50-51.

55   Tec, "Hiding;" in, Zimmerman, *Contested*, 196.

56   Tec, "Hiding;" in, Zimmerman, *Contested*, 197.

57   Ringelblum, *Polish-Jewish*, 126.

58   Yoseph Komem, *Courage and Grace*. Copyright Yoseph Komem. Middletown, Delaware, USA, 2017, 77-8.

59   Komem, *Courage*, 87.

60   Komem, *Courage*, 92.

61   Komem, *Courage*, 99.

62   Gutman, *Jews of Warsaw*, 265. Skibinska-Petelewicz, "Participation;" in, *Yad Vashem*, 20-1.

63   Tec, "Hiding;" in, Zimmerman, *Contested*, 194.

64   Ringelblum, *Polish-Jewish*, 137.

65   Gutman-Krakowski, *Unequal*, 200.

66   Paulsson, "Ringelblum;" in, Zimmerman, *Contested*, 188. Bund member Bernard Goldstein in his book, *Finf yor in varshever geto* (Five years in the Warsaw Ghetto), states: "[Extortions] was a terribly calamity for Jews who lived on the Aryan side... The Marranos of our time were threatened by an Inquisition run by Polish thugs who made traffic in Jewish lives a profitable venture. These scoundrels came from every level of society. Students would expose their Jewish friends, former classmates from school or university; neighbors identified Jews who had lived in the same building or with whom they shared the same courtyard; businessmen, merchants and shopkeepers identified Jews from whom they had received – as it were 'bought' – businesses and apartments when the latter were forced to move into the ghetto. Polish policemen and officials, armed with authority from their new masters and in the guise of their servants, could now 'rediscover' all of those Jews they had known so well in the past." Gutman-Krakowski, *Unequal*, 286.

67   Gutman-Krakowski, *Unequal*, 220.

68   Zimmerman, *Underground,* 228.

69   Zimmerman, *Underground,* 165.

70   Gutman-Krakowski, *Unequal,* 201.

71   Ringelblum, *Polish-Jewish,* 128.

72   Ringelblum, *Polish-Jewish,* 133.

73   Ringelblum, *Polish-Jewish,* 42, note 7.

74   Ringelblum, *Polish-Jewish,* 134.

75   Klukowski, 289-295. Ringelblum, *Relations,* 134, note 23. Gutman, "Poland;" in, *Encyclopedia Judaica,"* 777.

76   Skibinska-Petelewicz, "Participation;" in, *Yad Vashem,* 31.

77   Paulsson, "Ringelblum;" in, Zimmerman, *Contested,* 183.

78   Paulsson, "Ringelblum;" in, Zimmerman, *Contested,* 182.

79   Shmuel Krakowski, "The Attitude of the Polish Underground to the Jewish Question During the Second World War;" in, Zimmerman, *Contested,* 97-106.

80   Gutman-Krakowski, *Unequal,* 103.

81   Gutman-Krakowski, *Unequal,* 210.

82   Gutman-Krakowski, *Unequal,* 238.

83   Dreifuss, *Relations,* 144.

84   Kermish, "Postscript;" in, Ringelblum, *Polish-Jewish.* 312-3.

85   Steinlauf, *Bondage,* 55-56; 157, notes 33, 34 157. Based on, David Engel, "The Situation of Polish Jewry as Reflected in United States Diplomatic Documents, Dec. 1945-July 1946," *Gal-Ed: On the History of the Jews in Poland* 14 (1995), 120. The author of the memorandum was Samuel Margoshes, a former editor of the New York Yiddish daily, *Der Tog.*

86   *Wikipedia,* "History." The German plans for Russia, when they invaded in June 1941 was even worse than what they had in mind for Poland, since the Nazis viewed the communist regime in Russia as nothing less than a Jewish-led cabal to subdue and destroy the Russian people, as a first step to extend Jewish rule over all of Europe. In his speech to the *Reichstag* justifying the invasion of Russia, Hitler said: "For more than two decades the Jewish Bolshevik regime in Moscow had tried to set fire not merely to Germany but to all of Europe." Now, the time had come to destroy the Jewish center in Moscow. Andreas Hillgruber, "War in the East and the Extermination of the Jews." *Yad Vashem Studies 18 (1987),103–132.* Field-Marshal Wilhelm Keitel gave an order to the German army on 12 September 1941 which declared, "the struggle against Bolshevism demands ruthless and energetic, rigorous action above all against the Jews, the main carriers of Bolshevism. Kershaw, *Hitler,* 465. German army officers explained to the troops that the war against the Soviet Union was a war to

wipe out what were variously described as "Jewish Bolshevik sub-humans", the "Mongol hordes," the "Asiatic flood" and the "red beast." Richard J. Evans, *In Hitler's Shadow: West German Historians and the Attempt to Escape the Nazi Past.* New York: Pantheon, 1989, 59-60.

87   Skibinska-Petelewicz, "Participation;" in, *Yad Vashem*, 21-2, 33.

88   Skibinska-Petelewicz, "Participation;" in, *Yad Vashem*, 34, note 88.

89   Gutman-Krakowski, *Unequal*, 243-4.

90   Zimmerman, *Underground* 94. *Wikipedia*, "Żydokomuna." Jan T. Gross, *Neighbors: The Destruction of the Jewish Community in Jedwabne, Poland.* Princeton, N.J.: Princeton University Press, 2001.

91   Zimmerman, *Underground*, 96.

92   Zimmerman, *Underground*, 162.

93   Zimmerman, *Underground*, 164.

94   Skibinska-Petelewicz, "Participation;" in, *Yad Vashem*, 47-8.

95   Ben Cion Pinchuk, "On the Subject of Jewish 'Collaboration' in Soviet-Occupied Eastern Poland, 1939-1941;" in, Zimmerman, *Contested*, 61-8; 67. Historian Jan T. Gross wrote that his research did not demonstrate any evidence of outward collaboration between the Jews and the Soviets when they held that town. Besides, it was not specifically those who were suspected of collaboration who were murdered, but every Jewish person. Michlic, *Poland's*, 180.

96   Jan T. Gross, "Jews and their Polish Neighbors: The Case of Jedwabne in the Summer of 1941." In, Zimmerman, *Contested*, 69-82; 69.

97   Gross, "Jews;" in, Zimmerman, *Contested*, 70.

98   Skibinska-Petelewicz, "Participation;" in, *Yad Vashem*, 23-4. B. Hamerman, Yad Vashem Archives, M-1/E-2492. Gutman-Krakowski, *Unequal*, 222-3.

99   Skibinska-Petelewicz, "Participation;" in, *Yad Vashem*, 21. 27.

100   Skibinska-Petelewicz, "Participation;" in, *Yad Vashem*, 40, 42.

101   Skibinska-Petelewicz, "Participation;" in, *Yad Vashem*, 22.

102   Grabowski-Libionka, "Participation;" in, *Yad Vashem*, 55-56. Jan and Maria Wiglusz are on Yad Vashem's list of Righteous Among the Nations. YVA M31.2/2340.

103   Dreifuss, *Relations*, 266-273. Historians, Jan Tomasz Gross, Barbara Engelking and Jan Grabowski have researched cases of local collusion in the hunt after Jews. See, some of their writings in the Bibliography.

104   Paulsson, "Ringelblum;" in, Zimmerman, *Contested*, 173.

105   Paulsson, "Ringelblum;" in, Zimmerman, *Contested*, 174.

106   Paulsson, "Ringelblum;" in, Zimmerman, *Contested*, 174.

107   Paulsson, "Ringelblum;" in, Zimmerman, *Contested*, 189.

108   Kermish, "Introduction;" in, Ringelblum, *Polish-Jewish*, xxix-xxx.

109   Michlic, *Poland's*, 189.
110   Michlic, *Poland's*, 190.
111   Steinlauf, *Bondage*, 41-42.
112   Paulsson, "Ringelblum;" in, Zimmerman, *Contested*, 183.
113   Steinlauf, *Bondage*, x.
114   Zimmerman, *Contested*, 8.
115   Zimmerman, *Underground*, 364.

Chapter 6

1   Ringelblum, *Polish-Jewish*, 245. Gutman-Krakowski, *Unequal*, 202, 204.
2   Kermish, "Introduction;" in, Ringelblum, *Polish-Jewish*, xxx. Teodor [Pajewski], is one such "idealist" mentioned by Ringelblum; a Polish railway man, and member of the underground who got Ringelblum out of Trawniki labor camp with the help of the Jewish Shoshana (Emilka) Kosower, a liaison officer of the Jewish underground, and brought him to Warsaw, for further hiding. Ringelblum, *Polish-Jewish*, 227, note 1. Teodor had a ground floor flat in Warsaw, and also a hide-out where a Jewish family lived. Ringelblum, *Polish-Jewish*, 228.
3   Ringelblum, *Polish-Jewish*, 245.
4   Paulsson, "Ringelblum;" in, Zimmerman, *Contested*, 177.
5   Gutman-Krakowski, *Unequal*, 197.
6   Michlic, *Poland's*, 137-8.
7   Lukas, *Forgotten*, 144.
8   Gutman-Krakowski, *Unequal*, 242. Krakowski, "Attitude;" in, Zimmerman, *Contested*,101.
9   Gutman-Krakowski, *Unequal*, 228.
10   Gutman-Krakowski, *Unequal*, 229.
11   Lukas, *Forgotten*, 146.
12   Lukas, *Forgotten*, 145.
13   Antonina Gacz plus, YVA 31.2/4733.
14   Stean Marcyniuk, YVA 31.2/4640.
15   Ignacy Ustjanowsky, YVA 31.2/135.
16   Mieczysław Gosk, YVA 31/2/50.
17   Jan Mikulski, YVA 31.2/206; Józef Fink, YVA 31.2/555; Stanisław Stańczyk, YVA 31.2/443.
18   Wawrzyiec Bruniany, YVA 31.3/1020; Jan Puchalski, YVA 31.2/3466.
19   Wacław Golowacz, YVA 31.2/673; Maria Szczecinska, YVA 31.2/2126.
20   Franciszek Zalwowski, YVA 31.2/1151.

21   Stanisław Krzemienski, YVA 31.2/293.
22   Rozalia Paszkiewicz, YVA 31.2/44 and 3663.
23   Franciszka Halamajowa, YVA 31.2/2864.
24   Stanisław Jacków, YVA 31.2/277.
25   Aleksander Mikołajków, YVA 31.2/90.
26   Jan Żabiński, YVA 31.2/170.
27   Władysław Kołodziejek, YVA 31.2/2611; Jan Joniuk, YVA 31.2/2630.
28   Wiktoria Struszinska, YVA 31.2/274.
29   Adam Suchodolski, YVA 31.2/953.
30   Tadeusz Soroka, YVA 31.2/2695.
31   Andrzej Kostrz, YVA 31.2/809.
32   Jerzy Bielecki, YVA 31.2/3245.
33   Szymon Calka, YVA 31.2/467. Similarly, Julian and Stanisława
      Serafinowicz, in Mostówka village, sheltered on their farm home two es-
      capees from the Treblinka death camp, from August 1943 until the area's
      liberation on August 29, 1944. Julian Serafinowicz, YVA 31.2/1706.
34   Konrad Zimon, YVA 31.2/4530. Likewise, for Anna Dafner and her sister
      Malka, who escaped from the Auschwitz death march, of January 18,
      1945 while passing through Jastrzębie-Zdrój, and were sheltered by the
      farming couple, Erwin and Gertruda Moldrzyk. "They never asked us to
      leave and told the neighbors and their friends that we were cousins but we
      had run away from the front line where the Russians were advancing." The
      two stayed with the family until the arrival of the Russians in April 1945.
      Erwin Moldrzyk, YVA 31.2/5657.
35   Stanisław Nowosielski, YVA 31.2/4995.
36   Władysław Jeziorski, YVA 31.2/366.
37   Józef Job, YVA 31.2/1828.
38   Jadwiga Kieloch, YVA 31.2/3274.
39   Władysław Kowalski, YVA 31.2/4.
40   Jan Mirek, YVA 31.2/587.
41   Jan Charuk, YVA 31.2/1971.
42   Leonard Gliński, YVA 31.2/2826. x
43   *Prawda Młodych*, the youth organ of the moderate Catholic grouping FOP
      (Front for the Rebirth of Poland), edited by Władysław Bartoszewski and
      with most of the programmatic material contributed by Zofia Kossak-
      Szczucka – both of them recognized by Yad Vashem as Righteous Among
      the Nations, and heavily involved in helping Jews during the German oc-
      cupation – that journal, nevertheless, continued to publish anti-Jewish di-
      atribes, dubbing Jews as "parasites," and the cause of Europe's misfortunes.
44   Paulsson, "Ringelblum;" in, Zimmerman, *Contested*, 184.

45 Pawlikowski, "Polish Catholics;" in, Zimmerman, *Contested,* 109. Ringelblum, *Polish-Jewish,* 211. In Warsaw, over 200 Jews converted between November 1939 and March 1940, mainly members of the liberal professions, in the vain hope that the antisemitic laws and restrictions would not apply to them. Ringelblum, Polish-Jewish, 210, note 26.

46 Marceli Godlewski, YVA 31.2/9841. There are striking similarities between his story and that of Zofia Kossak-Szczucka with regard to their antisemitic views coupled with their rescue of Jews.

47 Stanisław Falkowski, YVA 31.2/1175.

48 Michał Kubacki, YVA 31.2/7482.

49 Dr. Olga Goldfein left for Israel where she was a physician in a hospital. Before dying in 1974, she turned over to the Beit Lohamei Hagetaot Museum, outside Haifa, for permanent safekeeping, a photograph of herself and her benefactress, both in nun's habits. Genowefa Czubak, YVA 31.2/1851.

50 Matylda Getter, YVA 31.2/3097.

51 Gertruda Babilińska, YVA 31.2/11. Similarly, Helena Szemet, a nursemaid with Jewish families in Wilno-Vilna, saved the two children Haviva and Gerson Minikes children, after successfully snatching them out from the Vilna ghetto, while supporting herself by selling haberdashery on the market. After the war, she took the children with her to Israel, where the three settled on a kibbutz. Helena Szemet, YVA 31.2/270.

52 Aniela Krzysztonek & Maryna Falska, YVA 31.2/638, 3175.

53 Apolonia Oldak, YVA 31.2/272.

54 After liberation, Lilian's parents, who survived, came to fetch their child, but Irena, herself childless, hedged as she had become emotionally tied to the child. She consulted her parish priest, and was told in no uncertain terms that she must return the child to its natural parents. Both sides parted amicably and continued a close relationship. Irena Ogniewska-Jorasz, YVA 31.2/2019.

55 Wiktoria Rodziewicz, YVA 31.2/1178.

56 Genowefa Pająk, YVA 31.2/2349.

57 Pawel Dyrda, YVA 31.2/3784.

58 Aleksander Roslan, YVA 31.2/427.

59 Maria Maciarz, YVA 31.2/2960.

60 Józef Zwonarz, YVA 31.2/331.

61 Irena Sendlerowa, YVA 31.2/153. Also, Anna Mieszczkowska, *Irena Sendler: Mother of the Children of the Holocaust.* Santa Barbara, California: Praeger, 2011, 74-81.

62 Wacław Nowiński YVA 31.2/611.

63 Władysław Misiuna, YVA 31.2/231.

64 Feliks Kanabus, YVA 31.2/87. Also, Jacob Glatstein, *Anthology of Holocaust Literature*. Philadelphia, JPS, 1969; 392-395.

65 Jan Karski, YVA 31.2/934. Also, Jan Karski, *Story of a Secret State*. Boston: Houghton Mifflin, 1944; chapter 29.

66 Jan Kurdziel, YVA 31.2/5143.

67 Jan Grabowski and Dariusz Libionka, "Distorting and Rewriting the History of the Holocaust in Poland. The Case of the Ulma Family Museum of Poles Saving Jews During World War II in Markowa." In, *Yad Vashem Studies* 45:1, Jerusalem 2017, 29-60.

68 Jadwiga Deneko, YVA 31.2/3575; Zimmerman, *Underground*, 311.

69 Adam Sztark, YVA 31.2/9178; Gutman-Krakowski, *Unequal*, 236-7.

70 Franciszek Antczak, YVA 31.2/10081.

71 Jakuk Gargasz, YVA M31.2/1622.

72 Anna Bogdanowicz, YVA 31.2/*2685*. Sara Diller miraculously escaped arrest and made her way to Warsaw, via Kraków; then, under a new identity, she was sent to Germany for labor, from where she fled to Switzerland, via the microstate principality of Lichtenstein. She eventually moved to Israel. Natalia Abramowicz, YVA 31.2/*533*.

73 Some of the rescuers in west Europe countries who also paid with their lives for help to Jews, include: Father Jacques (Lucien Bunel), in France; Heinrich List, in Germany; Odile and Remy Ovart, in Belgium; Johannes (Joop) Westerweel, in the Netherlands; and Henry Thomsen, in Denmark – all recognized by Yad Vashem as Righteous.

74 Czesław Kubik, YVA 31.2/4094.

75 Antoni Duda and Franciszka Ognowska, YVA 31.2/141.

76 Konstanty Celuch, YVA 31.2/8552.

77 Jan Sosnowy, YVA 31.2/5950.

78 Wlodzimierz Daniluk, YVA 31.2/9984.

79 Lukas, *Forgotten*, 144; Prekerowa, "The Relief;" in, Abramsky, *Jews*, 168.

80 Nechama Tec, *Dry Tears: The Story of a Lost Childhood*. New York: Oxford University Press, 1982. Samuel and Pearl Oliner, The Altruistic Personality: Rescuers of Jews in Nazi Europe. New York: Free Press, 1988.

81 Eva Fogelman, *Conscience and Courage: Rescuers of Jews During the Holocaust*. New York: Anchor Books, 1994.

82 Bauman, *Modernity*, 182-3. For more on Levinas, see Emmanuel Levinas, *Total and Infinity*. Pittsburgh: Duquesne University, 1969. Also, *Alterity and Transcendence*. London: Athlone, and New York: Columbia University, 1999. See also: Mordecai Paldiel, "The Face of the Other: Reflections on the Motivations of Gentile Rescuers of Jews." In, John K. Roth & Elisabeth

Maxwell (eds.), *Remembering for the Future: The Holocaust in an Age of Genocide.* Vol. 2. London: Palgrave, 2001, 334-6.

83 Kristen Renwick Monroe, "John Donne's People: Explaining Differences Between Rational Actors and Altruists Through Cognitive Frameworks." *The Journal of Politics* 53 (May 1991), No. 2, 394-433, 401.

84 Monroe, "John Donne's;" in, *Journal,* 404-5, 424, 428.

85 Monroe, "John Donne's;" in, *Journal,* 426-417, 420.

Chapter 7

1   Gutman-Krakowski, *Unequal,* 75, 252.

2   Gutman-Krakowski, *Unequal,* 254-5.

3   Gutman-Krakowski, *Unequal,* 255, 257, 262.

4   Zimmerman, *Underground,* 177. Prekerowa, "The Relief;" in, Abramsky, *Jews,* 162.

5   Gutman-Krakowski, *Unequal,* 265.

6   Gutman-Krakowski, *Unequal,* 259. Gutman, "Jews;" in, Gutman, *Encyclopedia of the Holocaust,* 1171.

7   Zimmerman, *Underground,* 178.

8   Gutman-Krakowski, *Unequal,* 259.

9   Gutman-Krakowski, *Unequal,* 261.

10 Gutman-Krakowski, *Unequal,* 261. Prekerowa, "The Relief;" in, Abramsky, *Jews,* 162.

11 Gutman-Krakowski, *Unequal,* 258.

12 Gutman-Krakowski, *Unequal,* 276 255. Steinlauf, *Bondage,* 39.

13 Gutman-Krakowski, *Unequal,* 266.

14 Prekerowa, "The Relief;" in, Abramsky, *Jews,* 165.

15 Gutman-Krakowski, *Unequal,* 264, 276.

16 Gutman-Krakowski, *Unequal,* 264.

17 Gutman-Krakowski, *Unequal,* 271. Prekerowa, "The Relief;" in, Abramsky, *Jews,* 166.

18 Gutman-Krakowski, *Unequal,* 273. The number of documents supplied totaled some 50,000, according to the estimates by Ferdinand Arczyński, Żegota's officer responsible for that line of activity. Prekerowa, "The Relief;" in, Abramsky, *Jews,* 166.

19 Gutman-Krakowski, *Unequal,* 275.

20 Kermish, "Postscript;" in, Ringelblum, *Polish-Jewish,* 300.

21 Prekerowa, "The Relief;" in, Abramsky, *Jews,* 171.

22   Gutman-Krakowski, *Unequal,* 278. Kermish, "Postscript," in, Ringelblum, *Polish-Jewish,* 299.

23   Prekerowa, "The Relief;" in, Abramsky, *Jews,* 169-70.

24   Prekerowa, "The Relief;" in, Abramsky, *Jews,* 172-3.

25   Gutman-Krakowski, *Unequal,* 290.

26   Krakowski, "Attitude," 99; Gutman-Krakowski, *Unequal* 264.

27   Prekerowa, "The Relief;" in, Abramsky, *Jews,* 164-5.

28   Prekerowa, "The Relief;" in, Abramsky, *Jews,* 165.

29   Gutman-Krakowski, *Unequal,* 283.

30   Ringelblum, *Polish-Jewish,* 312.

31   Gutman-Krakowski, *Unequal, 284.*

32   Gutman-Krakowski, *Unequal,* 284.

33   Zimmerman, *Underground,* 196.

34   Prekerowa, "The Relief;" in, Abramsky, *Jews,* 174.

35   Gutman, "Some Issues;" in, Zimmerman, *Contested,* 216. A month later, in April 1943, Żegota wrote again to the Delegate Office pleading to fight against the plague of the blackmailing *Szmaltsowniks,* stating that this phenomenon "is on the increase at an appalling rate... Not a day passes without many cases of blackmail, of victims being robbed of their last money and belongings. There is hardly a single family or individual who has not been subjected to this vile proceeding... and often... two, three or many more times. It is not infrequent for these cases to end with death-by suicide or through the liquidation of the victims by the authorities into whose hands they are delivered by the blackmailers.... [This] haunting our streets day by day cancels out the Council's attempts to assistance; in fact renders them impossible." Ringelblum, *Polish-Jewish,* 123, note 17. Gutman-Krakowski, *Unequal,* 285.

36   Lukas, *Forgotten,* 119. Zimmerman, *Polish,* 229. Prekerowa, "The Relief;" in, Abramsky, *Jews,* 173-4.

37   Gutman-Krakowski, *Unequal,* 285.

38   Gutman-Krakowski, *Unequal,* 286.

39   Prekerowa makes the astounding statement, not supported by other sources, that although punishments for extortionists did not wipe out the plague of blackmailing, they reduced it so much that it ceased to be of primary importance to the council. She attributes the *Szmaltsowniks* to "the scum of society." Prekerowa, "The Relief;" in, Abramsky, *Jews,* 175.

40   Ringelblum, *Polish-Jewish,* 216-217, note 32.

41   Prekerowa, "The Relief;" in, Abramsky, *Jews,* 175.

42   Gutman-Krakowski, *Unequal,* 286. Zimmerman, *Underground,* 300-1.

43   Gutman-Krakowski, *Unequal,* 268.

44   Gutman-Krakowski, *Unequal,* 267.

45   Pawlikowski, "Polish Catholics;" in, Zimmerman, *Contested,* 110.

46   Lukas, *Forgotten,* 150.

47   Gutman-Krakowski, *Unequal,* 265. Yad Vashem historian Joseph Kermish claims that former leading members of Żegota give inflated figures of the numbers of Jews covered by the Council. Tadeusz Rek quotes 40,000 Jews; Arczynski, over 50,000. Kermish, "Postscript," Ringelblum, *Polish-Jewish,* 301.

48   Kermish, "Postscript;" in, Ringelblum, *Polish-Jewish.* 297. Gutman and Krakowski wrote that the numbers given by the Jewish organizations of persons aided, also seems to be somewhat inflated. Gutman-Krakowski, *Unequal,* 266-267.

49   Prekerowa, "The Relief;" in, Abramsky, *Jews,* 176.

50   Lukas, *Forgotten,* 143.

51   Ringelblum, *Polish-Jewish,* xxx.

52   Krakowski, "Attitude;" in, Zimmerman, *Contested,* 104.

53   Gutman-Krakowski, *Unequal,* 256.

54   Lukas, *Forgotten,* 150, 260.

55   Zimmerman, *Contested,* 5. Based on Teresa Prekerowa, "The 'Just' and the 'Passive.'" In, Antony Polonsky, *My Brother's Keeper?* London: Routledge, 1990, 72-80, 73.

56   Gutman-Krakowski, *Unequal,* 207.

57   Ringelblum, *Polish-Jewish,* 247.

58   Paulsson, "Ringelblum;" in, Zimmerman, *Contested,* 175-6. The Hotel Polski Affair refers to a German bait to entrap Jews in hiding in Warsaw, after the destruction of the Warsaw ghetto, by inviting them to come out in the open, and buy foreign Latin American passports, and thus leave territories occupied by Nazi Germany. Approximately 2,500 Jews fell for this bait, and were initially accommodated in the Polski hotel, entrapped in one building; then, they were sent to concentration camps and most were killed. For more on this bizarre story, see: Abraham Shulman, *The Case of Hotel Polski.* New York: Holocaust Library, 1982.

59   Paulsson, "Ringelblum;" in, Zimmerman, *Contested,* 186-187.

60   For a critical appraisal of Gunnar Paulsson's position, see Joanna B. Michlic, "Secret City: The Hidden Jews of Warsaw 1940-1945." *Holocaust and Genocide Studies* 19, no. 3, 2005, 538-540.

61   The following section is based principally on archives received through the Polish embassy, in Bern, Switzerland, with special thanks to ambassador Jakub Kumoch, and Jedrzej Uszyński. Also available are the Abraham Silberschein documents in the Yad Vashem Archives, and the Israel Eiss

documents, in the Auschwitz Museum Archives. See, Jakub Kumoch, Monika Maniewska, Jędrzej Uszyński, and Zygmunt Bartłomiej, *The Ładoś List*. Warsaw: Pilecki Institute, 2020.

62   Walter Laqueur, *The Terrible Secret*. New York: H. Holt, 1998, 83-84.

63   Isaac Lewin and Ludwik Krzyzanowski, "Attempts at Rescuing European Jews with the Help of Polish Missions During World War II." *The Polish Review*, Vol. 22, No. 4 (1977), 3-23; Vol. 24, No. 1 (1979), 46-61; Vol. 27, No. 1/2, 99-111.

64   "Document 18," Mordecai Paldiel, *Ładoś Report to Yad Vashem*; January 15, 2020.

65   Konstanty Rokicki file, Department for the Righteous Among the Nations, Yad Vashem.

66   I am thankful to Kühl's grandson, Elie Singer, for making available to me these passages from his grandfather's memoirs.

67   Leviticus 19:16.

Chapter 8

1   Lukas, *Forgotten*, 41, 44. The Polish Socialists, like most Polish political groups, were badly split. Left wing socialists gravitated toward Moscow and at the end of the war cooperated with the Communists in establishing the Lublin regime, which became the cornerstone of Poland's postwar government. Lukas, *Forgotten*, 45.

2   Dariusz Stola, "The Polish Government-in-Exile and the Final Solution: What Conditioned its Actions and Inactions?;" in, Zimmerman, *Contested*, 85-96; 91; Zimmerman, *Polish*, 44. Lukas, *Forgotten*, 45.

3   Lukas, *Forgotten*, 55. Sikorski died in an airplane crash on July 4, 1943. Lukas, *Forgotten*, 73.

4   Stola, "Polish;" in, Zimmerman, *Contested*, 86.

5   Stola, "Polish;" in, Zimmerman, *Contested*, 86-7.

6   Lukas, *Forgotten*, 56. Cyryl Ratajski was the first government delegate, in 1940, followed with Jan Piekałkiewicz, in September 1942. Lukas, *Forgotten*, 59-60. Arrested by the Germans in February 1943 (tortured and killed), Piekałkiewicz was succeeded by Jan Stanisław Jankowski. In summer 1944 Jankowski criticized the "overtly philosemitic" policies of the London-based Polish government, stating that the government should "bear in mind that inside the country Jews are disliked." Arrested by the Soviets in March 1945, he was taken to Moscow, where he either died in jail or was murdered, in 1953. Michlic, *Poland's*, 154.

7   Steinlauf, *Bondage*, 26. Gutman-Krakowski, *Unequal*, 143.

8   Zimmerman, *Polish*, 68-9.

9   Stola, "Polish;" in, Zimmerman, *Contested*, 91.

10   Lukas, *Forgotten*, 46, 69; Davies, *God's*, 484.

11   Lukas, *Forgotten*, 70, 72.

12   Stola, "Polish;" in, Zimmerman, *Contested*, 86.

13   Michlic, *Poland's*, 147.

14   Zimmerman, *Polish*, 85.

15   Michlic, *Poland's*, 149-150.

16   Zimmerman, *Polish*, 166.

17   Zimmerman, *Polish*, 167.

18   Stola, "Polish Government," in, Zimmerman, *Contested*, 92.

19   Stola, "Polish Government," in, Zimmerman, *Contested*, 88.

20   Zimmerman, *Polish*, 80-81.

21   Stola, "Polish Government," in, Zimmerman, *Contested*, 89.

22   Gutman, *Jews of Warsaw*, 266.

23   Zimmerman, *Polish*, 112.

24   Lukas, *Forgotten*, 45.

25   Gutman, *Jews of Warsaw*, 410-411.

26   Lukas, *Forgotten*, 85, 88-90.

27   Lukas, *Forgotten*, 153.

28   Dariusz Stola. "Early News of the Holocaust from Poland." In, *Holocaust and Genocide Studies*, Vol. 11, No. 1, Spring 1997, 1-27; 4.

29   Stola, "Early News;" in, *Holocaust*, 4. Sikorski and Schwarzbart talked about "the horrible situation of Polish Jews," but as an example Sikorski gave a German order not to give medicine to Jews above 40 and below 3 years of age. It is difficult to imagine any other reason why neither Schwarzbart nor Sikorski mentioned the news of the massacres than that neither the two found it reliable. The SS burning down a whole Jewish quarter together with all its inhabitants, or taking a break during the slaughter to eat lunch, was seen as a fanciful addition to what really happened, and not accepted as credible. Stola, "Early News;" in, *Holocaust*, 5.

30   Stola, "Early News;" in, *Holocaust*, 5.

31   Stola, "Early News;" in, *Holocaust*, 6.

32   Lukas, *Forgotten*, 154.

33   Stola, "Early News;" in, *Holocaust*, 8.

34   Stola, "Early News;" in, *Holocaust*, 7.

35   Stola, "Early News;" in, *Holocaust*, 8.

36   Stola, "Early News;" in, *Holocaust*, 6.

37   Lukas, *Forgotten*, 155.

38   Lukas, *Forgotten*, 158. Gerhart Riegner, the World Jewish Congress (WJC) representative, in Geneva, Switzerland, received news from German industrialist, Eduard Schulte, about a German government decision to exterminate all of Europe's Jews, by end 1942, in the swiftest way possible. Riegner passed on this information to WJC head, Stephen Wise, on August 8, 1942, via the US State Department (who did not deliver it to Wise), as well as to Sydney Silverman, the WJC representative in England, as well as a member of the British parliament, who then forwarded it to Wise.

39   Lukas, *Forgotten*, 156.

40   Lukas, *Forgotten*, 157; Stola, "Early News;" in, *Holocaust*, 8.

41   Stola, "Early News;" in, *Holocaust*, 12, note 60. Rowecki's dispatch, though the longest and most detailed of the three, was known to neither Schwarzbart nor Zygielbojm, and it is not known who, besides some officers in the government actually read the dispatch. Who decided not to reveal it, and why? Some historians believe it was deliberately suppressed by the government as a part of a broader policy of downplaying Jewish sufferings, or combine it with the suffering of the larger non-Jewish population.

42   Stola, "Early News;" in, *Holocaust*, 15.

43   Karski, *Story*, 158-159.

44   Lukas, *Forgotten*, 165.

45   Lukas, *Forgotten*, 161.

46   Gutman-Krakowski, *Unequal*, 92.

47   Evans, *Third Reich*, 559.

48   Stola, "Early News;" in, *Holocaust*, 16. Polish Ministry of Foreign Affairs, *The Mass Extermination of Jews in German-Occupied Poland: Note addressed to the Governments of the United Nations, on December 10, 1942*. London: Hutchinson, 2019 reprint.

49   Stola, "Early News;" in, *Holocaust*, 16.

50   Evans, *Third Reich*, 560.

51   Zofia Nałkowska, *Diaries 1939-1945*. Warsaw, 1996, 10. In the estimation of Lukas, one of the obstacles preventing the establishment of a relationship of confidence between the Polish government-in-exile and Jewish organizations abroad was the antisemitic orientation of prewar Polish governments. The past prevented genuine cooperation by most Jewish groups with the Sikorski and later the Mikołajczyk governments. Lukas, *Forgotten*, 1968.

52   Michlic, *Poland's*, 150; Gutman-Krakowski, *Unequal*, 301.

53   Gutman, *Jews of Warsaw*, 258, 411.

54   Gutman-Krakowski, *Unequal*, 306-7.

55   Zimmerman, *Polish*, 301.

56   Gutman-Krakowski, *Unequal*, 301.

57   Gutman-Krakowski, *Unequal,* 302.

58   Michlic, *Poland's,* 148-9.

59   Michlic, *Poland's,* 149.

60   Zimmerman, *Polish,* 47.

61   Kaczynski, a priest with the rank of colonel and the Polish army's chief chaplain, told Schwarzbart: "For me, the best solution is to settle the Polish Jews in Bessarabia... A part of Bukovina where they live would be annexed to Poland, with the local Jews being permitted to reside... I presented to [Soviet ambassador to the USA] Litvinov my plans of settling the Polish Jews in Bessarabia. Litvinov was taken by surprise... I stressed that Bessarabia, although a part of Russia, would be administered by Poland and Russia jointly for the benefit of the colonization of those Jews who would opt for settlement there." Gutman-Krakowski, *Unequal,* 84-85.

62   Blatman, "Poland;" in, Zimmerman, *Contested,* 131.

63   Blatman, "Poland;" in, Zimmerman, *Contested,* 132.

64   Gutman-Krakowski, *Unequal,* 340, 345. Madajczyk, "Poland;" in, Gutman, *Encyclopedia of the Holocaust,* 1149.

65   Gutman-Krakowski, *Unequal,* 330.

66   Lukas, *Forgotten,* 132.

67   Gutman-Krakowski, *Unequal,* 333-5, 337, note 90, 349. Michlic, *Poland's,* 144.

68   Lukas, *Forgotten,* 132.

69   Zimmerman, *Polish,* 367. Gutman-Krakowski, *Unequal,* 359-60.

70   Zimmerman, *Polish,* 367. Gutman, "Jews;" in, *Encyclopedia of the Holocaust,* 1151.

71   Zimmerman, *Polish,* 367. Steinlauf, *Bondage,* 27. Michlic, *Poland's,* 142. Lukas, *Forgotten,* 43, 50.

72   Lukas, *Forgotten,* 61

73   Lukas, *Forgotten,* 73-5.

74   Lukas, *Forgotten* 50-3, 62

75   Steinlauf, *Bondage,* 26-7; Krakowski, "Attitude;" in Zimmerman, *Contested,* 97; Madajczyk, "Poland; in, Gutman, *Encyclopedia of the Holocaust,* 1149-1150.

76   Gutman, "Poland; in, *Encyclopedia Judaica,* 777.

77   Zimmerman, *Polish,* 81.

78   Zimmerman, *Polish,* 240. Lukas gives the slightly higher number of 380,175 Home Army men by early 1944. Lukas, *Forgotten,* 62.

79   Gutman, *Jews of Warsaw,* 251.

80   Lukas, *Forgotten,* 91. Such as the following message sent to London: "June 21, 1944 – In the period of June 2-19, ... 136 Gestapo agents and spies,

including Willie Holtze, August Gering, and Kammertentz, were executed in the provinces of Warsaw, Lublin, and Kielce." Lukas, *Forgotten*, 91.

81   Lukas, *Forgotten*, 92-93 The underground also dealt in non-combatant activities, such as clandestine secondary and higher education; cultural events, especially theater; and an underground press. It was the most extensive in occupied Europe, and made its voice known in numerous publications and millions of copies.

82   Lukas, *Forgotten*, 61.

83   Lukas, *Forgotten*, 64-5.

84   Lukas, *Forgotten*, 66.

85   Lukas, *Forgotten*, 64.

86   Lukas gives a higher toll of this operation by the AK – 60 different sabotage and diversionary operations in the Zamość area, destroying four bridges and two trains. Lukas, *Forgotten*, 23.

87   Klukowski, *Diary*, 235-6.

88   Klukowski, *Diary*, 248, 250, 253.

89   Klukowski, *Diary*, 257.

90   Lukas, *Forgotten*, 23.

91   Lukas, *Forgotten*, 67.

92   Lukas, *Forgotten*, 165-166.

93   Gutman, "Jews;" in, Gutman, *Encyclopedia of the Holocaust*, 1171. Gutman, *Jews of Warsaw*, 257.

94   Steinlauf, *Bondage*, 37.

95   Krakowski, "Attitude;" in, Zimmerman, *Contested*, 102.

96   Michlic, *Poland's*, 178.

97   Zimmerman, *Polish*, 345-6.

98   Michlic, *Poland's*, 153.

99   Kazimierz Iranek-Osmecki, *He Who Saves One Life*. New York: Crown, 1971, 109-10.

100   Gutman-Krakowski, *Unequal*, 41.

101   Gutman-Krakowski, *Unequal*, 144. Henryk Woliński, of the Jewish section in the Delegate's Office, had essentially only one function during the period under discussion: coordinating and transmitting to London intelligence that was gathered concerning the Jews. Lukas, *Forgotten*, 79.

102   Michlic, *Poland's*, 176-177.

103   Zimmerman, *Polish*, 140.

104   Zimmerman, *Polish*, 353. Michlic, *Poland's*, 181.

105   Lukas, *Forgotten*, 78-9.

106   Zimmerman, *Polish*, 135.

107   Gutman-Krakowski, *Unequal,* 133. Gutman, "Some Issues;" in, Zimmerman, *Contested,* 216. Ringelblum, *Jewish-Polish,* 7, note 14. Michlic, *Poland's,* 153.

108   Gutman-Krakowski, *Unequal,* 116. Zimmerman, *Polish,* 247.

109   Zimmerman, *Polish,* 366. Ber Mark writes that Bór-Komorowski, the AK head in 1943-44, was linked with the "reactionary anti-Semitic camp." Ber Mark, *Uprising in the Warsaw Ghetto.* New York: Schocken, 1975, 164. Ainsztein also mentions the man's "connections with the antisemitic National Party." Reuben Ainsztein, *Jewish Resistance in Nazi-Occupied Poland.* New York: Harper & Row, 1974, 672. Lukas, *Forgotten,* 241.

110   Gutman-Krakowski, *Unequal,* 114-5, 135.

111   Gutman-Krakowski, *Unequal,* 135.

112   Michlic, *Poland's,* 163. Bartoszewski, "Polish-Jewish;" in, Abramsky, *Jews,* 159.

113   Zimmerman, *Polish,* 103.

114   Michlic, *Poland's,* 154. Zimmerman, *Polish,* 87, 110, 136.

115   Gutman-Krakowski, *Unequal,* 107. Gutman, "Poland;" in, *Encyclopedia Judaica,* 776.

116   Michlic, *Poland's,* 154.

117   Gutman-Krakowski, *Unequal,* 55.

118   Gutman-Krakowski, *Unequal,* 56-7.

119   Gutman-Krakowski, *Unequal,* 193.

120   Gutman-Krakowski, *Unequal,* 119, 187, 193. Gutman, "Polish;" in, Abramsky, *Jews,* 182. Michlic, *Poland's,* 183. Zimmerman, *Polish,* 253. Ringelblum, *Polish-Jewish,* 257-8.

121   Michlic, *Poland's,* 157.

122   Michlic, *Poland's,* 158.

123   Steinlauf, *Bondage,* 38.

124   Gutman, *Jews of Warsaw,* 254.

125   Lukas, *Forgotten,* 173. Gutman, *Jews of Warsaw,* 255.

126   Gutman, *Jews of Warsaw,* 255. Gutman-Krakowski, *Unequal,* 154. Stefan Rowecki was captured by the Germans on June 30, 1943, and was succeeded by Tadeusz Komorowski-Bór.

127   Gutman, *Jews of Warsaw,* 256-7.

128   Gutman, *Jews of Warsaw,* 257.

129   Gutman-Krakowski, *Unequal,* 153.

130   Gutman-Krakowski, *Unequal,* 155.

131   Gutman-Krakowski, *Unequal,* 156.

132   Zimmerman, *Polish,* 172, 207. Lukas, *Forgotten,* 173.

133   Zimmerman, *Polish,* 171.

134   Lukas, *Forgotten*, 174.

135   Gutman-Krakowski, *Unequal*, 159.

136   Zimmerman, *Polish*, 198, 202. Gutman-Krakowski, *Unequal*, 161.

137   Lukas, *Forgotten*, 175. However, in a message believed sent by ŻOB commander Mordechai Anielewicz to the Home army commander, in March 1943, he complained that of the 49 weapons that have been allocated only 36 can be used for lack of ammunition, since there were no more than ten bullets for each weapon. "This is a catastrophic situation…. The allocation of weapons without ammunition is a cynical mockery of our fate, and confirms the assumption that the poison of antisemitism continues to pervade the leading circles in Poland… Please send at least 100 grenades, 50 pistols, 10 machine guns, and several thousand rounds of ammunition of all calibers." Zimmerman, *Polish*, 203-204, 206; Gutman-Krakowski, *Unequal*, 162. Henryk Iwański, who belonged to the KB (Security Corps), which was part of the AK, related that the Zionist Revisionist underground in the Warsaw ghetto (initials, ZZW) were handed over 2 heavy machine guns, 4 light machine guns, 21 submachine guns, 20 rifles, 50 pistols, and over 400 grenades. Lukas, *Forgotten*, 175.

138   According to a credible Polish source, the Home Army possessed in the Warsaw region alone since 1939: 135 heavy machine guns with 16,800 rounds of ammunition; 190 light machine guns with 54,000 rounds; 6,045 rifles with 794,00 rounds; 1,070 pistols and revolvers with 8,708 rounds; 7,561 grenades; and seven small anti-tank guns with 2,174 rounds. See also on this in, *Polskie Siły Zbrojne*, Vol. 3, 234; Gutman-Krakowski, *Unequal*, 159. Lukas gives a slightly different account. According to him, in Warsaw, the AK had immediately prior to the ghetto uprising 25 heavy machine guns, 62 light machine guns, 1,182 riles, 1,099 pistols, and 51 submachine guns. Lukas, *Forgotten*, 175.

139   Lukas, *Forgotten*, 178.

140   On March 6, 1943, Aryeh Wilner was arrested while outside the ghetto but with the help of Polish underground activist Henryk Grabowski, he managed to escape from detention and made it back to the ghetto. In the meantime, he was replaced by Antek Yitzhak (Antek) Zuckerman. Gutman-Krakowski, *Unequal*, 163-5. Zimmerman, *Polish*, 204. Gutman-Krakowski, *Unequal*, 163-165. Henryk Grabowski, YVA 31.2/2653.

141   Lukas, *Forgotten*, 178.

142   Lukas, *Forgotten*, 176.

143   Zimmerman, *Polish*, 205, 214-215. Gutman-Krakowski, *Unequal*, 167.

144   Zimmerman, *Polish*, 217. After the war, SS commander Jürgen Stroop, in charge of suppressing the ghetto uprising, wrote: "There is no doubt that

there was a connection with the Polish resistance movement, [but] I don't think it extended any real aid." Gutman, *Jews of Warsaw*, 402.

145 Gutman, *Jews of Warsaw*, 417. Lukas, *Forgotten*, 178.

146 In November 1941, a group of Poles and some Jewish communists, sent by Moscow, parachuted near Warsaw and, together with another group which landed later, established the Polish Workers Party on January 5, 1942, thus reviving the communist party that had been dissolved before the war. Lukas, *Forgotten*, 77. Ainsztein, *Jewish*, 572. Based mostly on apologetic sources, and failing to differentiate between strictly communist and various Marxist Jewish (mostly Zionist) organizations – Lukas claims that there were several Jewish communists on the staff of the organizers of the Warsaw ghetto uprising, thus lending support to the pre-war *Żydokomuna* myth, prevalent among many Polish circles. Lukas, *Forgotten*, 172. Ainsztein, *Jewish*, 602.

147 Ringelblum, *Polish-Jewish*, 186-187, note 27. Gutman-Krakowski, *Unequal*, 114.

148 Gutman, *Jews of Warsaw*, 403-7.

149 Gutman-Krakowski, *Unequal*, 216. Some 50 Jewish prisoners-of-war, originally taken to a POW camp in Lublin, at 7, Lipowa Street, escaped, and were treacherously murdered by members of the Polish underground who had promised to help them join the partisans. Ringelblum, *Polish-Jewish*, 53, 56-7, note 16.

150 Krakowski, "Attitude;" in, Zimmerman, *Contested*, 103. Zimmerman, *Polish*, 267, 377. Gutman-Krakowski, *Unequal*, 135. Kermish, "Postscript;" in, Ringelblum, *Polish-Jewish*, 310. On March 7, 1944, the NSZ was officially incorporated into the Home Army.

151 Lukas, *Forgotten*, 54.

152 Lukas, *Forgotten*, 81.

153 Klukowski, *Diary*, 197-8.

154 Particularly, in Nowogródek and Vilna-Vilnius. Ainsztein, *Jewish*, 305. Lukas, *Forgotten*, 82.

155 Zimmerman, *Polish*, 254-5.

156 Lukas, *Forgotten*, 82-3.

157 Zimmerman, *Polish*, 255.

158 Zimmerman, *Polish*, 255.

159 Michlic, *Poland's*, 178.

160 Kermish, "Postscript;" in, Ringelblum, *Polish-Jewish*, 303.

161 Kermish, "Postscript;" in, Ringelblum, *Polish-Jewish*, 304.

162 Zimmerman, *Polish*, 284.

163 Gutman-Krakowski, *Unequal*, 126.

164 Gutman-Krakowski, *Unequal,* 127-8.

165 Gutman-Krakowski, *Unequal,* 129.

166 Gutman-Krakowski, *Unequal,* 130.

167 Zimmerman, *Polish,* 289-90.

168 Zimmerman, *Polish,* 296-97.

169 Gutman-Krakowski, *Unequal,* 130-1.

170 Gutman-Krakowski, *Unequal,* 289.

171 Gutman-Krakowski, *Unequal,* 132-3.

172 Zimmerman, *Polish,* 314.

173 Zimmerman, *Polish,* 317; Kermish, "Postscript;" in, Ringelblum, *Jewish-Polish,* 304, 313. Lukas, *Forgotten,* 241. Ainsztein, *Jewish,* 457. Historian Joshua Zimmerman, in his conclusion on the Polish underground and the Jews, states that the same organization both helped and harmed Jews – that the Polish underground was an umbrella organization representing Polish society as a whole. He then adds that the preponderance of evidence nonetheless suggests that the Home Army saved many more Jews than it harmed. But this is not borne out in the examples provided by the author's own very comprehensive research in this matter. The evidence, sadly, points in the opposite direction. Zimmerman, *Polish,* 413-4.

174 Gutman-Krakowski, *Unequal,* 138.

175 Krakowski, "Attitude;" in, Zimmerman, *Contested,* 102.

176 Gutman-Krakowski, *Unequal,* 216.

177 Gutman-Krakowski, *Unequal,* 217.

178 Zimmerman, *Polish,* 293-4.

179 Zimmerman, *Polish,* 295-6.

180 Stefan Sawa, YVA 31.2/5013.

181 Davies, *God's,* 472.

182 Lukas, *Forgotten,* 68.

183 Lukas, *Forgotten,* 62, 176.

184 This division was commanded by a former Soviet officer of Polish origin, Mieczysław Kamiński, who was later shot by the Germans for insubordination. Davies, *God's,* 475-6.

185 Lukas, *Forgotten,* 213, 215.

186 Lukas, *Forgotten,* 213-4.

187 Lukas, *Forgotten,* 116, 218. Zimmerman, *Polish,* 408-9. Davies, *God's,* 477.

188 Davies, *God's* 477. Evans, *The Third,* 622.

189 Davies, *God's,* 477.

190 Zimmerman, *Polish,* 411. Davies, *God's,* 479-80.

191 Zimmerman, *Polish,* 385.

192   Zimmerman, *Polish*, 406. Paulsson, "Ringelblum;" in, Zimmerman, *Contested*, 181.
193   Zimmerman, *Polish*, 389-92.
194   Zimmerman, *Polish*, 393.
195   Zimmerman, *Polish*, 387.
196   Those killed included Ignacy Bursztyn and wife Esther and their 11-year-old daughter, Noemi; Esther's sister, Anka; Ignacy's sister, and her 17-year-old daughter, Esther. Zimmerman, *Underground*, 405-6.
197   Zimmerman, *Polish*, 406.
198   Zimmerman, *Polish*, 407.
199   Zimmerman, *Polish*, 402.
200   Zimmerman, *Polish*, 403-4.
201   Zimmerman, *Polish*, 401.
202   Zimmerman, *Polish*, 336, 339.
203   Zimmerman, *Polish*, 341.
204   Zimmerman, *Polish*, 342.
205   Zimmerman, *Polish*, 343.
206   Zimmerman, *Polish*, 344. See also, Halina Zawadzka's dramatic story; in, Halina Zawadzka, *Living in Fear on the Aryan Side*. Bowie, Maryland: Heritage Books, 2004.
207   Zimmerman, *Contested*, 2. Gutman-Krakowski, *Unequal*, 246-7.

Chapter 9

1   Steinlauf, *Bondage*, 66.
2   Madajczyk, "Poland," in, Gutman, *Encyclopedia Holocaust*, 1151.
3   Madajczyk, "Poland," in, Gutman, *Encyclopedia Holocaust*, 1149.
4   Davies, *God's*, 489.
5   Davies, *God's*, 489, 491. Steinlauf, *Bondage*, 34-5. Zimmerman, *Polish*, 352.
6   Steinlauf, *Bondage*, 35.
7   Steinlauf, *Bondage*, 45.
8   Steinlauf, *Bondage*, 63-64.
9   Gutman-Krakowski, *Unequal*, 351. Bożena Szaynok, "The Impact of the Holocaust on Jewish Attitudes in Postwar Poland," In, Zimmerman, *Contested*, 239-46; 244.
10   Stanislaw Krajewski, "The Impact of the Shoah on the Thinking of Contemporary Polish Jewry: A Personal Account;" in, Zimmerman, *Contested*, 291-303; 293. Natalia Aleksiun, "Jewish Responses to Antisemitism in Poland, 1944-1947;" in, Zimmerman, *Contested*,

247-61; 248. Steinlauf, *Bondage*, 46. Gutman-Krakowski, *Unequal*, 365. Anna Cichopek, "The Kraków Pogrom of August 1945: A Narrative Reconstruction;" in, Zimmerman, *Contested*, 221-38; 223.

11   Gutman-Krakowski, *Unequal*, 364. Gutman, "Poland;" in, *Encyclopedia Judaica*, 771, 778-9, 784; Wikipedia, "History."

12   Gutman-Krakowski, *Unequal*, 370.

13   Krajewski, "Impact;" in, Zimmerman, *Contested*, 293.

14   Steinlauf, *Bondage*, 47.

15   Gutman, "Poland;" in, *Encyclopedia Judaica*, 778.

16   *Wikipedia*, "History."

17   Tych, "Jewish;" in, Zimmerman, *Contested*, 139.

18   Gitelman, "Collective Memory;" in, Zimmerman, *Contested*, 271-90, 274. Michal Borwicz, "Polish-Jewish Relations, 1944-1947;" in, Abramsky, *The Jews*, 190-8, 192.

19   Gutman-Krakowski, *Unequal*, 367; Steinlauf, *Bondage*, 50.

20   Krajewski, "Impact;" in, Zimmerman, *Contested*, 299.

21   Steinlauf, *Bondage*, 50-1.

22   Gutman-Krakowski, *Unequal*, 368-9.

23   Tych, "Jewish;" in, Zimmerman, *Contested*, 140.

24   Kermish, "Postscript;" in, Ringelblum, *Relations*, 315; Borwicz, "Polish-Jewish;" in Abramsky, *Jews*, 193.

25   Gutman, "Poland;" in, *Encyclopedia Judaica*, 783.

26   Steinlauf, *Bondage*, 51-52.

27   Cichopek, "Kraków;" in, Zimmerman, *Contested*, 222.

28   Cichopek, "Kraków;" in, Zimmerman, *Contested*, 222-3.

29   Gutman, "Poland;" in, *Encyclopedia Judaica*, 783.

30   Cichopek, "Kraków;" in, Zimmerman, *Contested*, 223-35. Steinlauf, *Bondage*, 52.

31   Gutman-Krakowski, *Unequal*, 372; Steinlauf, *Bondage*, 52.

32   Krajewski, "Impact;" in, Zimmerman, *Contested*, 296-7.

33   Gutman-Krakowski, *Unequal*, 352.

34   Aleksiun, "Jewish;" in, Zimmerman, *Contested*, 252.

35   Aleksiun, "Jewish;" in, Zimmerman, *Contested*, 250.

36   Aleksiun, "Jewish;" in, Zimmerman, *Contested*, 252.

37   Borwicz, "Polish-Jewish;" in, Zimmerman, *Contested*, 196. Gutman-Krakowski, *Unequal*, 373-374. In May 1946, two months before the Kielce pogram, Rabbi Dr. David Kahane and the Secretary General of the Jewish religious associations, Professor Michal Silberberg, went to the residence of Primate Hlond (then still in Poznań), in order to gain an audience and request that a pastoral letter be issued on the subject of the murders which

occurred almost daily. Cardinal Hlond declined to receive these delegates of religious organizations. Borwicz, "Polish-Jewish;" in, Zimmerman, *Contested*, 195.

38   Steinlauf, *Bondage*, 95.
39   Steinlauf, *Bondage*, 96.
40   Gutman, "Poland;" in, *Encyclopedia Judaica*, 323.
41   Steinlauf, *Bondage*, 48.
42   Krajewski, "Impact;" in, Zimmerman, *Contested*, 293.
43   Krajewski, "Impact;" in, Zimmerman, *Contested*, 293.
44   Steinlauf, *Bondage*, 67-8.
45   Steinlauf, *Contested*, 264.
46   Michael Steinlauf, "Teaching about the Holocaust in Poland." Zimmerman, *Contested*, 262-270, 265.
47   Steinlauf, *Bondage*, 76.
48   Until 1968 most of this de-Judaized group believed, to varying degrees, that the new regime in Poland would liberate them completely from their Jewish predicament and facilitate their full assimilation into Polish society. Lukasz Hirszowicz, "The Jewish Issue in Post-War Communist Politics;" in, Abramsky, *The Jews*, 199-208, 200.
49   Steinlauf, *Bondage*, 88.
50   Steinlauf, *Bondage*, 93. Szaynok, "Impact;" in, Zimmerman, *Contested*, 242, 294.
51   Steinlauf, *Bondage*, 110-1.
52   Steinlauf, *Bondage*, 111.
53   Steinlauf, *Bondage*, 112.
54   Steinlauf, *Bondage*, 113-4.
55   Steinlauf, *Bondage*, 114.
56   Jan Błoński, "The Poor Poles Look at the Ghetto;" in, Polonsky, '*My Brother's*, 34-48, 44-45. Steinlauf, *Bondage*, 114-5.
57   Błoński, "The Poor;" in, Polonsky, *My Brother*, 6-7.
58   Błoński, "The Poor;" in, Polonsky, *My Brother*, 115.
59   Steinlauf, *Bondage*, 115.
60   Steinlauf, *Bondage*, 115-6.
61   According to Jan T. Gross, in the Jewish Historical Institute in Warsaw alone, one can find over seven thousand depositions collected from the survivors of the Holocaust immediately after the war. These, according to Gross, provide voluminous evidence of collusion by persons in the destruction of their Jewish neighbors. Gross, "Jews;" in, Zimmerman, *Contested*, 77-9.
62   Gross, "Jews;" in, Zimmerman, *Contested*, 78.

63   Zimmerman, *Contested*, 10-1.

64   Zimmerman, *Contested*, 11.

65   Zimmerman, *Contested*, 11.

66   Krajewski, "Impact;" in, Zimmerman, *Contested*, 292. According to some speculative sources, there are 100,000 Jews living in Poland who don't actively practice Judaism and do not list "Jewish" as their nationality. The American Jewish Joint Distribution Committee and Jewish Agency for Israel estimate that there are between 25,000 and 100,000 Jews living in Poland, and a similar number to that estimated by Jonathan Ornstein, head of the Jewish Community Center in Kraków – between 20,000 and 100,000. The real number may never be known, for Jews in Poland (a tiny fraction from the larger prewar community) still fear or worry the possibility of a recurrence of widespread open antisemitism, and prefer to keep their identity unknown. Wikipedia, "History."

67   Steinlauf, *Bondage*, 127-8.

68   Gutman, "Poland;" in, *Encyclopedia Judaica*, 322.

69   Krajewski "Impact;" in, Zimmerman, *Contested*, 296. *Wikipedia*, "History;" Gutman, "Poland;" in, *Encyclopedia Judaica*, 322-3.

70   Steinlauf, *Bondage*, 126-7.

71   Krajewski, "Impact;" in, Zimmerman, *Contested*, 302.

72   Krajewski, "Impact;" in, Zimmerman, *Contested*, 297-299.

73   Steinlauf, *Bondage*, 53.

74   Michlic, *Poland's*, 131.

75   Gitelman, "Collective;" in, Zimmerman, *Contested*, 276.

76   Steinlauf, *Bondage*, 55.

77   Gitelman, "Collective;" in, Zimmerman, *Contested*, 273.

78   Gitelman, "Collective;" in, Zimmerman, *Contested*, 273-4.

79   Steinlauf, *Bondage*, 58.

80   Steinlauf, *Bondage*, 59.

81   Steinlauf, *Bondage*, 131, 133.

Conclusion

1   Engelking, "Psychological." In, Zimmerman, *Contested*, 52.

BIBLIOGRAPHY

a) Books and Journals

Abramsky, Chimen, Maciej Jachimczyk and Antony Polonsky, eds. *The Jews in Poland*. Oxford, UK: Basil Blackwell, 1987.

Ainsztein, Reuben. *Jewish Resistance in Nazi-Occupied Poland*. New York: Harper & Row, 1974.

Aleksiun, Natalia. "Jewish Responses to Antisemitism in Poland, 1944-1947." In, Joshua D. Zimmerman, ed., *Contested Memories: Poles and Jews during the Holocaust and its Aftermath*. New Brunswick, New Jersey & London: Rutgers University, 2003, 247-61.

Arslan, Bibo, Boella et al., *There is Always an Option to say 'Yes' or 'No': The Righteous Against the Genocides of Armenians and Jews*. Padova, Cleup: 2001.

Bartal, Israel. "The *Pinkas* of the Council of the Four Lands." In, A. Polonsky, J. Basista and A. Link-Lenczowski, eds., *The Jews in Old Poland 1000-1795*. London, New York: I.B. Tauris & Co, 1993, 110-8.

Bartoszewski, Władysław and Zofia Lewin. *Righteous among Nations: How Poles Helped the Jews, 1939-1945*. London: Earlscourt Publications, 1969.

Bartoszewski, Władysław. "Polish-Jewish Relations in Occupied Poland, 1939-1945. In, Chimen Abramsky, Maciej Jachimczyk and Antony Polonsky, eds. *The Jews in Poland*. Oxford, UK: Basil Blackwell, 1987, 147-60.

Bartoszewski, Władysław. *The Blood Shed Unites Us: Pages from the History of Help to the Jews in Occupied Poland.* Warsaw: Interpress Publishers, 1970.

Bauer, Yehuda. *A History of the Holocaust.* New York: Franklin Watts, 2001.

Bauer, Yehuda. *The Holocaust in Historical Perspective.* Seattle: University of Washington, 1978.

Bauman, Zygmunt. *Modernity and the Holocaust.* Ithaca, N.Y.: Cornell University, 1989.

Beauvois, Daniel. "Polish-Jewish Relations in the Territories Annexed by the Russian Empire in the First Half of the Nineteenth Century." In, Chimen Abramsky, Maciej Jachimczyk and Antony Polonsky, eds. *The Jews in Poland.* Oxford, UK: Basil Blackwell, 1987, 78-90.

Bender, Ryszard. "Jews in the Lublin Region Prior to the January Uprising, 1861-1862." In, Chimen Abramsky, Maciej Jachimczyk and Antony Polonsky, eds. *The Jews in Poland.* Oxford, UK: Basil Blackwell, 1987, 91-6.

Ben Sasson, Haim Hillel. "Poland." *Encyclopaedia Judaica,* Jerusalem: Keter, 1971, 709-89.

Blatman, Daniel. "Poland and the Polish Nation as Reflected in the Jewish Underground Press." In, Joshua D. Zimmerman, ed., *Contested Memories: Poles and Jews during the Holocaust and its Aftermath.* New Brunswick, New Jersey & London: Rutgers University, 2003, 123-33.

Błoński, Jan. "Polish-Catholics and Catholic Poles: The Gospel, National Interest, Civic Solidarity and the Destruction of the Warsaw Ghetto." *Yad Vashem Studies* 25 (1996), 181-195.

Błoński, Jan. "The Poor Poles Look at the Ghetto." In, Antony Polonsky, *'My Brother's Keeper?': Recent Polish Debates on the Holocaust.* London: Routledge, 1990, 34-48.

Bogucka, Maria. "The Jews in the Polish Cities in the 16th-18th Centuries." In, Adam Teller, ed., *Studies in the History of the Jews in Old Poland.* Jerusalem: The Magnes Press, 1998, 51-66.

Borwicz, Michal. "Polish-Jewish Relations, 1944-1947." In, Chimen Abramsky, Maciej Jachimczyk and Antony Polonsky, eds. *The Jews in Poland*. Oxford, UK: Basil Blackwell, 1987, 190-98.

Brandwajn-Ziemian, Yanina. *Neurim Vetushiyah Bamilhamah* (Hebrew). Tel-Aviv: Yaron Golan, 1994.

Bullen, R.J., H. Pogge von Strandman, A.B. Polonsky, *Ideas into Politics: Aspects of Human Historv 1880-1950*. London & Sydney: Croom Helm, 130-46.

Cala, Alina. *The Image of the Jew in Polish Folk Culture*. Jerusalem: Magnus Press, 1995.

Cichopek, Anna. "The Kraków Pogrom of August 1945: A Narrative Reconstruction." In, Joshua D. Zimmerman, ed., *Contested Memories: Poles and Jews during the Holocaust and its Aftermath*. New Brunswick, New Jersey & London: Rutgers University, 2003, 221-38.

Churchill, Winston. "Zionism versus Bolshevism;" in, *Illustrated Sunday Herald*, February 8, 1920.

Davies, Norman. *God's Playground: A History of Poland*. Volume 2. Oxford: Clarendon Press, 1982.

Dawidowicz, Lucy. *Holocaust and the Historians*, Cambridge, Mass.: Harvard University, 1981.

Dobroszycki, Lucjan. *Survivors of the Holocaust in Poland*. Armonk. N.Y: M. E. Sharpe, 1994.

Donat, Alexander. *The Holocaust Kingdom*. New York: Holt, Rinehart, 1965.

Dreifuss (Ben-Sasson), Havi. *Relations Between Jews and Poles During the Holocaust: the Jewish Perspective*. Jerusalem: Yad Vashem, 2017.

Eck, Nathan. "The Rescue of Jews with Aid of Passports and Citizenship Papers of Latin American States." *Yad Vashem Studies* 1 (1957), 125-52.

Eisenbach, Artur. "The Four Years' Sejm and the Jews." In, A. Polonsky, J. Basista and A. Link-Lenczowski, eds., *The Jews in Old Poland 1000-1795*. London, New York: I.B. Tauris & Co, 1993, 73-89.

Engel, David. "Patterns of Anti-Jewish Violence in Poland." In, *Yad Vashem Studies* (1998), 69-70.

Engel, David, "The Reconstruction of Jewish Communal Institutions in Postwar Poland: Central Committee of Polish Jews. 1944-1946." In, *East European Politics and Societies* 10. no. 1 (1996), 85-107.

Engel, David. "The Situation of Polish Jewry as Reflected in United States Diplomatic Documents, Dec. 1945-July 1946." In, *Gal-Ed: On the History of the Jews in Poland* 14 (1995).

Engel, David. "An Early Account of Polish Jewry under Nazi and Soviet Occupation Presented to the Polish Government-in-Exile, February 1940." In, *Jewish Social Studies* 45 (1983), 1-16.

Engel, David. *Facing a Holocaust: The Polish Government-in-Exile and the Jews, 1943-1945.* Chapel Hill & London: University of North Carolina Press, 1993.

Engelking, Barbara. "Moral Issues in Emanuel Ringelblum's Writings from World War II." In, Israel Gutman (ed.), *Emanuel Ringelblum: The Man and the Historian.* Jerusalem: Yad Vashem, 2010, 207-27.

Engelking, Barbara. "Psychological Distance between Poles and Jews in Nazi-Occupied Warsaw." In, Joshua D. Zimmerman, ed., *Contested Memories: Poles and Jews during the Holocaust and its Aftermath.* New Brunswick, New Jersey & London: Rutgers University, 2003, 47-53.

Engelking, Barbara. *Such a Beautiful Sunny Day...: Jews Seeking Refuge in the Polish Countryside 1942-1945.* Jerusalem: Yad Vashem, 2016.

Ettinger, Shmul. "The Council of the Four Lands." In, A. Polonsky, J. Basista and A. Link-Lenczowski, eds., *The Jews in Old Poland 1000-1795.* London, New York: I.B. Tauris & Co, 1993, 93-109.

Evans, Richard J. *In Hitler's Shadow West German Historians and the Attempt to Escape the Nazi Past.* New York: Pantheon, 1989.

Evans, Richard J. *The Third Reich at War.* New York: Penguin, 2014.

Feldhay Brenner, Rachel. "Polka-Katoliczka and the Holocaust: The Enigma of Zofia Kossak." In, Yad Vashem Studies 45:2 (2017), 125-158.

Fogelman, Eva. *Conscience and Courage: Rescuers of Jews During the Holocaust.* New York: Anchor Books, 1994.

Gieysztor, Aleksander. "The Beginnings of Jewish Settlement in the Polish Lands." In, Chimen Abramsky, Maciej Jachimczyk and Antony Polonsky, eds. *The Jews in Poland*. Oxford, UK: Basil Blackwell, 1987, 16-21.

Gitelman, Zvi. "Collective Memory and Contemporary Polish-Jewish Relations." In, Joshua D. Zimmerman, ed., *Contested Memories: Poles and Jews during the Holocaust and its Aftermath*. New Brunswick, New Jersey & London: Rutgers University, 2003, 271-90.

Glatstein, Jacob. *Anthology of Holocaust Literature*, Philadelphia: JPS, 1969.

Goldberg-Mulkiewicz, Olga, "The Stereotype of the Jew in Polish Folklore." In, Issachar Ben-Ami and Joseph Dan, eds. *Studies in Aggadah and Jewish Folklore*, Jerusalem: Magnes Press, 1983, 83-94.

Goldberg, Jacob. "On the Study of Polish-Jewish History." In, Adam Teller, ed., *Studies in the History of the Jews in Old Poland*. Jerusalem: The Magnes Press, 1998, 9-13.

Goldberg, Jacob. "The Jewish Sejm: Its Origins and Functions." In, A. Polonsky, J. Basista and A. Link-Lenczowski, eds., *The Jews in Old Poland 1000-1795*. London, New York: I.B. Tauris & Co., 1993, 147-65.

Goldberg, Jacob. "The Privileges Granted to Jewish Communities of the Polish Commonwealth as a Stabilizing Factor in Jewish Support." In, Chimen Abramsky, Maciej Jachimczyk and Antony Polonsky, eds. *The Jews in Poland*. Oxford, UK: Basil Blackwell, 1987, 32-54.

Goldstein, Bernard, *The Stars Bear Witness*. New York, Viking Press, 1949.

Grabowski, Jan and Dariusz Libionka, "Distorting and Rewriting the History of the Holocaust in Poland. The Case of the Ulma Family Museum of Poles Saving Jews During World War II in Markowa." In, *Yad Vashem Studies* 45:1, Jerusalem 2017, 29-60.

Grabowski, Jan. *Hunt for the Jews: Betrayal and Murder in German-Occupied Poland*. Bloomington: Indiana University, 2013.

Graetz, Heinrich, *History of the Jews*. Vol IV. Philadelphia: JPS, 1949; Vol V. Philadelphia: JPS, 1956.

Gross, Jan T. "Jews and their Polish Neighbors: The Case of Jedwabne in the Summer of 1941." In, Joshua D. Zimmerman, ed., *Contested Memories: Poles and Jews during the Holocaust and its Aftermath.* New Brunswick, New Jersey & London: Rutgers University, 2003, 69-82.

Gross, Jan T. *Neighbors: The Destruction of the Jewish Community in Jedwabne, Poland.* Princeton, N.J.: Princeton University Press, 2001.

Gross, Jan T. *Polish Society under German Occupation: The Generalgouvernment, 1939-1944.* Princeton, N.J.: Princeton University Press, 1979.

Guldon, Zenon and Karol Krzystanek, "The Jewish Population in the Towns on the West Bank of the Vistula in Sandomierz Province from the Sixteenth to the Eighteenth Centuries." In, A. Polonsky, J. Basista and A. Link-Lenczowski, eds., *The Jews in Old Poland 1000-1795.* London, New York: I.B. Tauris & Co, 1993, 322-39.

Gumkowski, J. and K. Kleszczynski, *Poland under Nazi Occupation.* Warsaw, Polonia Publishing House, 1961.

Gutman, Israel (ed.), *Emanuel Ringelblum: The Man and the Historian.* Jerusalem: Yad Vashem, 2010.

Gutman, Israel (ed.), *Encyclopedia of the Holocaust.* New York: Macmillan, 1990.

Gutman, Israel, "The Jews in Poland." In, Israel Gutman, ed. *Encyclopedia of the Holocaust,* Vol. 3. New York: Macmillan 1990, 1143-76.

Gutman, Israel, "Poland," *Encyclopedia Judaica.* Vol. 13. Jerusalem: Keter, 1971, 709-89.

Gutman, Israel, ed. *Encyclopedia of Righteous Among the Nations.* Vol. 1, Poland. Yad Vashem: Jerusalem, 2004.

Gutman, Israel. "Some Issues in Jewish-Polish Relations During the Second World War." In, Joshua D. Zimmerman, ed., *Contested Memories: Poles and Jews during the Holocaust and its Aftermath.* New Brunswick, New Jersey & London: Rutgers University, 2003, 212-17.

Gutman, Israel. *The Jews of Warsaw 1939-1943: Ghetto, Underground, Revolt.* Bloomington: Indiana University, 1982.

Gutman, Yisrael and Krakowski Shmuel, *Unequal Victims: Poles and Jews During World War Two.* New York: Holocaust Library, 1986.

Gutman, Yisrael, "Polish and Jewish Historiography on the Question of Polish-Jewish Relations During World War II." In, Chimen Abramsky, Maciej Jachimczyk and Antony Polonsky, eds. *The Jews in Poland.* Oxford, UK: Basil Blackwell, 1987, 177-89.

Gutman, Yisrael, E. Mendelsohn, J. Reinharz & C. Shmeruk, ed., *The Jews of Poland between Two World Wars.* Waltham, Mass.: Brandeis University Press, 1989.

Heller, Celia S. *On the Edge of Destruction: Jews of Poland Between the Two World Wars.* New York: Columbia University, 1977.

Hillgruber, Andreas, "War in the East and the Extermination of the Jews." In, *Yad Vashem Studies 18 (1987), 103–32.*

Hirszowicz, Lukasz. "The Jewish Issue in Post-War Communist Politics." In, Chimen Abramsky, Maciej Jachimczyk and Antony Polonsky, eds. *The Jews in Poland.* Oxford, UK: Basil Blackwell, 1987, 199-208.

Holzer, Jerzy. "Relations Between Polish and Jewish Left-Wing Groups in Interwar Poland." In, Chimen Abramsky, Maciej Jachimczyk and Antony Polonsky, eds. *The Jews in Poland.* Oxford, UK: Basil Blackwell, 1987, 140-46.

Horn, Maurycy, "The Chronology and Distribution of Jewish Craft Guilds in Old Poland, 1613-1795." In, A. Polonsky, J. Basista and A. Link-Lenczowski, eds., *The Jews in Old Poland 1000-1795.* London, New York: I.B. Tauris & Co, 1993, 249-66.

Hundert, Gershon D. "On the Problem of Agency in 18th Century Jewish Society." In, Adam Teller, ed., *Studies in the History of the Jews in Old Poland.* Jerusalem: The Magnes Press, 1998, 82-9.

Hundert, Gershon. "The Implications of Jewish Economic Activities for Christian-Jewish Relations in the Polish Commonwealth." In, Chimen Abramsky, Maciej Jachimczyk and Antony Polonsky, eds. *The Jews in Poland.* Oxford, UK: Basil Blackwell, 1987, 55-63.

Iranek-Osmiecki, Kazimierz. *He Who Saves One Life.* New York: Crown Publishers 1971.

Irwin-Zarecka, Iwona, *Neutralizing Memory: The Jew in Contemporary Poland.* New Brunswick, N.J.: Transaction Publishers, 1989.

Jaromirska, Leokadia. "Bogushia." (Hebrew). *Yalkut Moreshet,* No. 7, July 1967, 7-32.

Kalik, Judith. "Patterns of Contacts Between the Catholic Church and the Jews in the Polish-Lithuanian Commonwealth: the Jewish Debts." In, Adam Teller, ed., *Studies in the History of the Jews in Old Poland.* Jerusalem: The Magnes Press, 1998, 102-22.

Kaplan, Chaim A. *The Scroll of Agony.* New York: Macmillan 1965.

Karski, Jan. *Story of a Secret State.* Boston: Houghton Mifflin, 1944; especially, chapter 29.

Karwasser, Bracha. "A Testimony," *Yad Vashem Archives,* Jerusalem, 03/3484.

Kassow, Samuel. "Polish-Jewish Relations in the Writings of Emmanuel Ringelblum." In, Joshua D. Zimmerman, ed., *Contested Memories: Poles and Jews during the Holocaust and its Aftermath.* New Brunswick, New Jersey & London: Rutgers University, 2003, 142-57.

Kassow, Samuel. "Polish-Jewish Relations in Emanuel Ringelblum's Writings." In, Israel Gutman, ed., *Emanuel Ringelblum: The Man and the Historian.* Jerusalem: Yad Vashem, 2010, 189-205.

Kershaw, Ian. Hitler: 1889-1936. New York: W.W. Norton, 1998.

Kieniewicz, Stefan. "Polish Society and the Jewish Problem in the Nineteenth Century." In, Chimen Abramsky, Maciej Jachimczyk and Antony Polonsky, eds. *The Jews in Poland.* Oxford, UK: Basil Blackwell, 1987, 70-7.

Kloczkowski, Jerzy, *A History of Polish Christianity.* Cambridge: Cambridge University Press, 2000.

Klukowski, Zygmunt. *Diary from the Years of Occupation, 1939-1944.* Urbana: University of Illinois, 1993.

Koestler, Arthur. *The Thirteenth Tribe.* New York: Random House, 1976.

Komem, Yoseph. *Courage and Grace.* Copyright Yoseph Komem. Middletown, Delaware, USA, 2017.

Krajewski, Stanislaw. "The Impact of the Shoah on the Thinking of Contemporary Polish Jewry: A Personal Account." In, Joshua D. Zimmerman, ed., *Contested Memories: Poles and Jews during the Holocaust and its Aftermath.* New Brunswick, New Jersey & London: Rutgers University, 2003, 291-303.

Krakowski, Shmuel. "The Holocaust in the Polish Underground Press," *Yad Vashem Studies* 16 (1984), 241-70.

Krakowski, Shmuel. "The Attitude of the Polish Underground to the Jewish Question During the Second World War." In, Joshua D. Zimmerman, ed., *Contested Memories: Poles and Jews during the Holocaust and its Aftermath.* New Brunswick, New Jersey & London: Rutgers University, 2003, 97-106.

Krakowski, Shmuel. The Polish Underground and the Extermination of the Jews," *Polin* 9 (1996), 138-47.

Kubar, Sofia S., *Double Identity.* New York: Hill and Wang, 1989.

Kumoch, Jakub; Monika Maniewska, Jędrzej Uszyński and Zygmunt Bartłomiej. *The Ładoś List.* Warsaw: Pilecki Institute, 2020.

Kurek, Ewa, *Your Life Is Worth Mine: The Story Never Told Before of How Polish Nuns Saved Hundreds of Jewish Children.* New York: Hippocrene, 1996.

Landau-Czajka, Anna. "The Jewish Question in Poland: Views Expressed in the Catholic Press between the Two World Wars," *Polin* 11 (1998), 263-80.

Langbein, Hermann. *People in Auschwitz;* Chapel Hill & London: University of North Carolina, 2004.

Laqueur, Walter. *The Terrible Secret.* New York: H. Holt, 1998.

Lendvai, Paul, *Antisemitism without Jews.* Garden City, N.Y.: Doubleday, 1971.

Leszczyński, Anatol. "The Terminology of the Bodies of Jewish Self-Government." In, A. Polonsky, J. Basista and A. Link-Lenczowski, eds., *The Jews in Old Poland 1000-1795.* London, New York: I.B. Tauris & Co, 1993, 132-46.

Levinas, Emmanuel. *Total and Infinity.* Pittsburgh: Duquesne University, 1969.

Levinas, Emmanuel *Alterity and Transcendence.* London: Athlone, and New York: Columbia University, 1999.

Lewin, Abraham. *A Cup of Tears.* Oxford: Blackwell, 1988, 124.

Lewin, Isaac and Ludwik Krzyzanowski, "Attempts at Rescuing European Jews with the Help of Polish Missions During World War II." In, *The Polish Review,* Vol. 22, No. 4 (1977), 3-23; Vol. 24, No. 1 (1979), 46-61; Vol. 27, No. 1/2, 99-111.

Lichten, Joseph. "Notes on the Assimilation and Acculturation of Jews in Poland, 1863-1943." In, Chimen Abramsky, Maciej Jachimczyk and Antony Polonsky, eds. *The Jews in Poland.* Oxford, UK: Basil Blackwell, 1987, 106-29.

Link-Lenczowski, Andrzej. "The Jewish Population in the Light of the Dietines of the Sixteenth to Eighteenth Centuries." In, A. Polonsky, J. Basista and A. Link-Lenczowski, eds., *The Jews in Old Poland 1000-1795.* London, New York: I.B. Tauris & Co, 1993, 36-44.

Lukas, Richard C. *The Forgotten Holocaust: The Poles under German Occupation, 1939-1944.* Lexington: University Press of Kentucky, 1986.

Madajczyk, Czesław. "Poland: General Survey." In, Israel Gutman, ed., *Encyclopedia of the Holocaust.* Volume 3. New York: Macmillan, 1990, 1143-51.

Małecki, Jan M. "Jewish Trade at the End of the Sixteenth Century and in the First half of the Seventeenth Century." In, A. Polonsky, J. Basista and A. Link-Lenczowski, eds., *The Jews in Old Poland 1000-1795.* London, New York: I.B. Tauris & Co, 1993, 267-81.

Maltz, Moshe, *Years of Horror—Glimpse of Hope: The Diary of a Family in Hiding.* New York: Shengold, 1993.

Marcus, Joseph. *Social and Political History of the Jews in Poland, 1919-1939.* Berlin, New York, Amsterdam: Mouton Publishers, 1983.

Mark, Ber. *Uprising in the Warsaw Ghetto.* New York: Schocken, 1975.

Meed, Vladka, *On Both Sides of the Wall.* Washington, D.C.: The Holocaust Library, 1999.

Melzer, Emanuel. "Emigration versus Emigrationism: Zionism in Poland and the Territorialist Projects of the Polish Authorities, 1936-1939."

In, Joshua D. Zimmerman, ed., *Contested Memories: Poles and Jews during the Holocaust and its Aftermath.* New Brunswick, New Jersey & London: Rutgers University, 2003, 19-31.

Melzer, Emanuel. *No Way Out: The Politics of Polish Jewry, 1935-1939.* Cincinnati: Hebrew Union College Press, 1997.

Mendelsohn, Ezra. "Interwar Poland: Good for the Jews or Bad for the Jews?" In, Chimen Abramsky, Maciej Jachimczyk and Antony Polonsky, eds. *The Jews in Poland.* Oxford, UK: Basil Blackwell, 1987, 130-46.

Michalski, Jerzy. "The Jewish Question in Polish Public Opinion During the First Two Decades of Stanisław August Poniatowski's Reign." In, Adam Teller, ed., *Studies in the History of the Jews In Old Poland.* Jerusalem: The Magnes Press, 1998, 123-46.

Michlic-Coren, Joanna. "Anti-Jewish Violence in Poland, 1918-1939 and 1945-1947." In, *Polin* 13 (2000), 34-61.

Michlic-Coren, Joanna. "The Troubling Past: The Polish Collective Memory of the Holocaust." In, *East European Jewish Affairs* 29, nos. 1-2 (1999), 75-84.

Michlic, Joanna Beata. *Poland's Threatening Other: The Image of the Jew from 1880 to the Present.* Lincoln & London: University of Nebraska, 2006.

Michlic, Joanna B. "Secret City: The Hidden Jews of Warsaw 1940-1945." *Holocaust and Genocide Studies* 19, no. 3, 2005, 538-40.

Mieszkowska, Anna. *Irena Sendler: Mother of the Children of the Holocaust.* Santa Barbara, California: Praeger, 2011.

Modras, Ronald, *The Catholic Church and Antisemitism: Poland, 1933-1939.* Chur, Switzerland: Hardwood, 1994.

Monroe, Kristen Renwick. "John Donne's People: Explaining Differences Between Rational Actors and Altruists Through Cognitive Frameworks." In, *The Journal of Politics* 53 (May 1991), No. 2, 394-433.

Oliner, Samuel & Pearl. *The Altruistic Personality: Rescuers of Jews in Nazi Europe.* New York: Free Press, 1988.

Oliner, Samuel. *Restless Memories: Recollections of the Holocaust Years.* Berkeley. Calif.: Judah L. Magnes Museum, 1986.

Paldiel, Mordecai. "Fear and Comfort: The Plight of Hidden Jewish Children in Wartime-Poland." In, *Holocaust and Genocide Studies* 6/4, 1991, 397-413.

Paldiel, Mordecai. "The Face of the Other: Reflections on the Motivations of Gentile Rescuers of Jews." In, John K. Roth & Elisabeth Maxwell (eds.), *Remembering for the Future: The Holocaust in an Age of Genocide.* Vol. 2. London: Palgrave, 2001, 334-46.

Paldiel, Mordecai. *Righteous Among the Nations.* New York: HarperCollins, 2007.

Paldiel, Mordecai. *Saving the Jews: Amazing Stories of Men and Women Who Defied the Final Solution.* Rockville, MD: Schreiber Publishing, 2000.

Paldiel, Mordecai. *The Path of the Righteous: Gentile Rescuers of Jews During the Holocaust.* Hoboken, New Jersey, 1993; especially, "Poland," 176-276.

Paldiel, Mordecai. *Saving One's Own.* Philadelphia: Jewish Publishing Society, 2017.

Paulsson, Gunnar S. "Ringelblum Revisited: The Destruction of Polish Jewry and Polish Popular Opinion." In, Joshua D. Zimmerman, ed., *Contested Memories: Poles and Jews during the Holocaust and its Aftermath.* New Brunswick, New Jersey, & London: Rutgers University, 2003, 173-92.

Paulsson, Gunnar S., "The Demography of Jews in Hiding in Warsaw, 1943-1945." In, *Polin* 13 (2000), 78-103.

Pawlikowski, John T. "The Vatican and the Holocaust: Putting *We Remember* in Context." In, *Dimensions* 12. no. 2 (1998), 11-6.

Pawlikowski, John T. "Polish Catholics and the Jews during the Holocaust: Heroism, Timidity, and Collaboration." In, Joshua D. Zimmerman, ed., *Contested Memories: Poles and Jews during the Holocaust and Its Aftermath.* New Brunswick, New Jersey & London: Rutgers University, 2003, 107-19.

Pilecki, Witold. *The Auschwitz Volunteer: Beyond Bravery.* Translated from Polish. Los Angeles, Cal.: Aquila Polonica, 2012.

Pinchuk, Ben Cion. "On the Subject of Jewish 'Collaboration' in Soviet-Occupied Eastern Poland, 1939-1941." In, Joshua D. Zimmerman, ed., *Contested Memories: Poles and Jews during the Holocaust and its Aftermath.* New Brunswick, New Jersey & London: Rutgers University, 2003, 61-8.

Podraza, Antony. "Jews and the Village in the Polish Commonwealth." In, A. Polonsky, J. Basista and A. Link-Lenczowski, eds., *The Jews in Old Poland 1000-1795.* London, New York: I.B. Tauris & Co, 1993, 299-321.

Polish Ministry of Foreign Affairs. *The Mass Extermination of Jews in German-Occupied Poland.* London: Hutchinson & Co., reprinted 2019.

Polonsky, Antony. "Roman Dmowski and Italian Fascism." In, R.J. Bullen, H. Pogge von Strandman, A.B. Polonsky, *Ideas into Politics: Aspects of Human History 1880-1950.* London & Sydney: Croom Helm, 130-46.

Polonsky, Antony. "'Loving and Hating the Dead': Present-Day Polish Attitudes to the Jews." In, *Religion, State and Society* 20, no. 1 (1992), 69-79.

Polonsky, Antony. *'My Brother's Keeper?': Recent Polish Debates on the Holocaust.* London: Routledge, 1990.

Polonsky, Antony. "Beyond Condemnation, Apologetics and Apologies: On the Complexity of Polish Behavior toward the Jews during the Second World War." In, Jonathan Frankel, ed., *Studies in Contemporary Jewry 13.* Jerusalem, 1998, 190-224.

Polonsky, Antony. "Introduction." In, A. Polonsky, J. Basista and A. Link-Lenczowski, eds., *The Jews in Old Poland 1000-1795.* London, New York: I.B. Tauris & Co, 1993, 1-9.

Prekerowa, Teresa. "The Relief Council for Jews in Poland, 1942-1945." In, Chimen Abramsky, Maciej Jachimczyk and Antony Polonsky, eds. *The Jews in Poland.* Oxford, UK: Basil Blackwell, 1987, 161-76.

Prekerowa, Teresa. "The 'Just' and the 'Passive.'" In, 0Antony Polonsky, *My Brother's Keeper?* London: Routledge, 1990, 72-80.

Radziwiłł, Anna, "The Teaching of the History of the Jews in Secondary Schools in the Polish Peoples Republic, 1949-88."*Polin* 4 (1989), 402-24.

Ringelblum, Emanuel. *Notes from the Warsaw Ghetto: The Journal of Emanuel Ringelblum.* New York: Schocken Books, 1974.

Ringelblum, Emanuel. *Polish-Jewish Relations During the Second World War.* Jerusalem: Yad Vashem, 1974. Footnotes by Joseph Kermish and Shmuel Krakowski.

Rosman, Moshe. "The Indebtedness of the Lublin Kahal in the 18th Century." In, Adam Teller, ed., *Studies in the History of the Jews in Old Poland.* Jerusalem: The Magnes Press, 1998, 161-88.

Segel, Harold. *Stranger in Our Midst: Images of the Jew in Polish Literature.* Ithaca. N.Y.: Cornell University Press, 1996.

Shulman, Abraham, *The Case of Hotel Polski.* New York: Holocaust Library, 1982.

Skibińska, Alina and Jakub Petelewicz, "The Participation of Poles in Crimes Against Jews in the Świętokrzyskie Region." In, *Yad Vashem Studies* 35:1, Jerusalem, 2007, 5-48.

Staszewski, Jacek. "*Votum Separatum* to Research on the history of the Jews in Pre-Partition Poland." In, Adam Teller, ed., *Studies in the History of the Jews in Old Poland.* Jerusalem: Magnes Press, 1998, 224-32.

Steinlauf Michael C. *Bondage to the Dead: Poland and the Memory of the Holocaust.* Syracuse, N.Y.: Syracuse University, 1997.

Steinlauf, Michael C. "Teaching about the Holocaust in Poland." In, Joshua D. Zimmerman, ed., *Contested Memories: Poles and Jews during the Holocaust and its Aftermath.* New Brunswick, New Jersey & London: Rutgers University 2003, 262-70.

Stola, Dariusz. "Early News of the Holocaust from Poland." In, *Holocaust and Genocide Studies,* Vol. 11, No. 1, Spring 1997, 1-27.

Stola, Dariusz. "The Polish Government-in-Exile and the Final Solution: What Conditioned its Actions and Inactions?" In, Joshua D.

Zimmerman, ed., *Contested Memories: Poles and Jews during the Holocaust and its Aftermath*. New Brunswick, New Jersey & London: Rutgers University, 2003, 85-96.

Szaynok, Bożena. "The Impact of the Holocaust on Jewish Attitudes in Postwar Poland." In, Joshua D. Zimmerman, ed., *Contested Memories: Poles and Jews during the Holocaust and its Aftermath*. New Brunswick, New Jersey & London: Rutgers University, 2003, 239-46.

Szereszewska, Helena, *Memoirs from Occupied Warsaw, 1940-1945*. London: Vallentinc Mitchell, 1997.

Tazbir, Janusz. "Anti-Jewish Trials in Old Poland." In, Adam Teller, ed., *Studies in the History of the Jews in Old Poland*. Jerusalem: The Magnes Press, 1998, 233-45.

Tec, Nechama, "Sex Distinctions and Passing as Christians during the Holocaust." In, *East European Quarterly* 18, no. 1 (March 1984), 113-23.

Tec, Nechama, *Dry Tears: The Story of a Lost Childhood*. New York: Oxford University Press, 1982.

Tec, Nechama. "Hiding and Passing on the Aryan Side: A Gendered Comparison." In, Joshua D. Zimmerman, ed., *Contested Memories: Poles and Jews during the Holocaust and its Aftermath*. New Brunswick, New Jersey & London: Rutgers University, 2003, 193-211.

Tec, Nechama. *When Light Pierced the Darkness: Christian Rescue of Jews in Nazi-Occupied Poland*. Oxford: Oxford University Press, 1986.

Teller, Adam, ed., *Studies in the History of the Jews in Old Poland*. Jerusalem: The Magnes Press, 1998.

Teller, Adam. "Radziwiłł, Rabinowicz, and the Rabbi of Świerz: The Magnates' Attitude to Jewish Regional Autonomy in the 18th Century." In, Adam Teller, ed., *Studies in the History of the Jews in Old Poland*. Jerusalem: The Magnes Press, 1998, 246-69.

Teter, Magda. *Jews and Heretics in Catholic Poland: A Beleaguered Church in the Post-Reformation Era*. Cambridge, UK: Cambridge University, 2006.

Tollet, Daniel, "La législation commerciale régissant les Juifs des grandes villes royales de Pologne sous les règnes de Wasa." In, Adam Teller, ed., *Studies in the History of the Jews in Old Poland*. Jerusalem: The Magnes Press, 1998, 277-302.

Tollet, Daniel. "Merchants and Businessmen in Poznań and Cracow, 1588-1688." In, Chimen Abramsky, Maciej Jachimczyk and Antony Polonsky, eds. *The Jews in Poland*. Oxford, UK: Basil Blackwell, 1987, 22-30.

Tollet, Daniel. "The Private Life of Polish Jews in the Vasa Period." In, A. Polonsky, J. Basista and A. Link-Lenczowski, eds., *The Jews in Old Poland 1000-1795*. London, New York: I.B. Tauris & Co., 1993, 45-62.

Tomaszewski, Irene and Tecia Werbowski, *Zegota: The Rescue of Jews in Wartime Poland*. Montreal: Price-Patterson, 1994.

Tonini, Carla. "Zofia Kossak: the anti-Semite who Rescued Polish Jews." In, Arslan, Bibo, Boella et al., *There is Always an Option to say 'Yes' or 'No': The Righteous Against the Genocides of Armenians and Jews*. Padova, Cleup: 2001.

Tych, Feliks. "Witnessing the Holocaust: Polish Diaries, Memoirs and Reminiscences." In, David Bankier and Israel Gutman, *Nazi Europe and the Final Solution*. Jerusalem: Yad Vashem, 2003, 175-98.

Tych, Feliks. "Jewish and Polish Perceptions of the Shoah as Reflected in Wartime Diaries and Memoirs." In, Joshua D. Zimmerman, ed., *Contested Memories: Poles and Jews during the Holocaust and its Aftermath*. New Brunswick, New Jersey & London: Rutgers University, 2003, 134-41.

Weeks, Theodore R. *Assimilation to Antisemitism: The 'Jewish Question' in Poland. 1850-1914*. DeKalb, Illinois: Northern Illinois University Press, 2006.

Wegrzynek, Hanna, *The Treatment of Jewish Themes in Polish Schools*. New York: American Jewish Committee, 1998.

Weinbaum, Laurence. *A Marriage of Convenience: The New Zionist Organization and the Polish Government, 1936-1939*. Boulder: East European Monographs, 1993.

Wikipedia, "History of the Jews in Poland," March 2019.
Wikipedia, "Jewish Bolshevism," May 2019.
Wikipedia, "The Council of Four Lands," November 2018.
Wikipedia, "*Żydokomuna*," June 2019.
Wrobel, Piotr. *"Neighbors* Reconsidered." In, *Polish Review* 4 (2001), 419-429.
Wyrozumski, Jerzy. "Jews in Medieval Poland." In, A. Polonsky, J. Basista and A. Link-Lenczowski, eds., *The Jews in Old Poland 1000-1795.* London, New York: I.B. Tauris & Co, 1993, 13-22.
Yahil, Leni. "Madagascar – Phantom of a Solution for the Jewish Question." In, Bela Vago and Georg L. Mosse, eds. *Jews and Non-Jews in Eastern Europe.* New York: Wiley, 1974, 316-18.
Zawadzka, Halina. *Living in Fear on the Aryan Side.* Bowie, Maryland: Heritage Books, 2004.
Żbikowski, Andrzej. "Polish Jews under Soviet Occupation, 1939-1941: Specific Strategies of Survival." In, Joshua D. Zimmerman, ed., *Contested Memories: Poles and Jews during the Holocaust and its Aftermath.* New Brunswick, New Jersey & London: Rutgers University, 2003, 54-60.
Ziemian, Joseph. *The Cigarette Sellers.* Minneapolis, Minn.: Lerner Publications Company, 1975.
Zimmerman, Joshua D. *The Polish Underground and the Jews, 1939-1945.* New York: Cambridge University, 2015.
Zimmerman, Joshua D., ed. *Contested Memories: Poles and Jews during the Holocaust and its Aftermath.* New Brunswick, New Jersey & London: Rutgers University, 2003.

* * *

b) Polish Righteous Among the Nations honored by Yad Vashem, appearing in the book. Each name is followed with YVA (Yad Vashem Archives), and the case file number.

Abramowicz, Natalia. YVA 31.2/533.
Antczak, Franciszek. YVA 31.2/10081.

Babilińska, Gertruda. YVA 31.2/11.

Bielecki, Jerzy. YVA 31.2/3245.

Bogdanowicz, Anna. YVA 31.2/2685.

Bruniany, Wawrzyniec. YVA 31.2/1020.

Calka, Szymon & Helena. YVA 31.2/467.

Celuch, Konstanty & Justyna; son Tadeusz. YVA 31.2/8552.

Charuk, Jan & Rozalia. YVA 31.2/1971.

Czubak, Genowefa. YVA 31.2/1851.

Daniluk, Włodzimierz & Anna; daughters Luba & Rajsa. YVA
31.2/9984.

Deneko, Jadwiga. YVA 31.2/3575.

Dobraczyński, Jan. YVA 31.2/5618.

Duda, Antoni & Helena; children Zygmunt & Marianna. YVA 31.2/141.

Dyrda, Pawel & Maria; son Pawel. YVA 31.2/3784.

Falkowski, Stanisław. YVA 31.2/1175.

Falska, Maryna. YVA 31.2/3175.

Fink, Józef & Lucyna. YVA 31.2/555.

Gacz, Antonina, YVA 31.2/4733.

Gargasz, Jakub & Zofia. YVA M31.2/1622.

Getter, Matylda. YssVA 31.2/3097.

Gliński, Leonard, YVA 31.2/2826.

Godlewski, Marceli. YVA 31.2/9841.

Golowacz, Wacław & Jadwiga. YVA 31.2/673.

Gosk, Mieczyslaw & Helena; his father Stanisław. YVA 31.2/50.

Grabowski, Henryk. YVA 31.2/2653.

Halamajowa, Franciszka; daughter Helena. YVA 31.2/2864.

Iwański, Henryk, YVA 31.2/54.

Jacków, Stanislaw. YVA 31.2/277.

Jeziorski, Władysław & Anna; sons Władysław & Marian. YVA
31.2/366.

Job, Józef & Wiktoria; son Edward. YVA 31.2/1828.

Joniuk, Jan; daughters, Leokadia, Eugenia & Zofia. YVA 31.2/2630.

Kanabus, Feliks. YVA 31.2/87.

Kann, Maria, YVA 31.2/30.

Karski, Jan. YVA 31.2/934.

Kieloch, Jadwiga & five daughters. YVA 31.2/3274.

Kołodziejek, Władysław & Zofia. YVA 31.2/2611.

Kostrz, Andrzej. YVA 31.2/809.

Kossak-Szczucka, Zofia, YVA 31.2/577.

Kowalski, Władysław, YVA 31.2/4.

Krzemienski, Stanisław & Anna. YVA 31.2/293.

Krzysztonek, Aniela. YVA 31.2/638.

Kubacki, Michał. YVA 31.2/7482.

Kubik, Czesław. YVA 31.2/4094.

Kurdziel, Jan. YVA 31.2/5143.

Kuropieska, Leopolda. YVA 31.2/355.

Łoza, Stefania and son Eugeniusz. YVA 31.2/2508.

Maciarz, Maria. YVA 31.2/2960.

Marcyniuk, Stefan & Teresa; sons Jan & Piotr. YVA 31.2/4640.

Mikołajków, Aleksander & Leokadia; sons Andrzej & Leszek. YVA 31.2/90.

Mikulski, Jan & Melania; and four children. YVA 31.2/206.

Mirek, Jan. YVA 31.2/587.

Misiuna, Władysław. YVA 31.2/231.

Moldrzyk, Erwin & Gertruda. YVA 31.2/5657.

Nowiński, Wacław & Janina; son Wacław. YVA 31.2/611.

Nowak, Irena. YVA 31.2/2508.

Nowosielski, Stanisław. YVA 31.2/4995.

Ogniewska-Jorasz Irena & Bogdan. YVA 31.2/2019.

Ogonowska, Franciszka; children Władysław, Stefan & Irena. YVA 31.2/141.

Oldak, Apolonia & Aleksander. YVA 31.2/272.

Pająk, Genowefa. YVA 31.2/2349.

Pajewski, Teodor, YVA 31.2/1270

Paszkiewicz, Rozalia & Władysław. YVA 31.2/44 & 3663.

Piotrowska, Jadwiga. YVA 31.2/3742.

Puchalski, Jan & Anna. YVA 31.2/3466.

Rodziewicz, Wiktoria. YVA 31.2/1178.

Roslan, Aleksander & Amelia. YVA 31.2/427.

Sawa, Stefan, YVI 31.2/5013.

Sendlerowa, Irena. YVA 31.2/153.

Serafinowicz, Stanislawa & Julian. YVA 31.2/1706.

Słowik, Karolina & daughter Olga. YVA 31.2/7812.

Soroka, Tadeusz. YVA 31.2/2695.

Sosnowy, Jan & Stefania. YVA 31.2/5950.

Stańczyk, Stanisław & Wiktoria. YVA 31.2/443.

Struszinska, Wiktoria & Zygmunt. YVA 31.2/274.

Suchodolski, Adam & Stanisława; children Jadwiga & Stanisław. YVA 31.2/953.

Szczecinska, Maria & son Jerzy. YVA 31.2/2126.

Szemet, Helena, YVA 31.2/270.

Sztark, Adam. YVA 31.2/9178.

Ustjanowsky, Ignacy & Bronislawa; children Czesław & Urszula. YVA 31.2/135.

Wiglusz, Jan & Maria; sons Stanisław & Józef. YVA M31.2/2340.

Woliński, Heryk. YVA 31.2/511.

Wolski, Mieczysław, YVA 31.2/4252.

Żabiński, Jan & Antonina. YVA 31.2/170.

Zalwowski, Franciszek & Tekla; and four sons. YVA 31.2/1151.

Zimon, Konrad & Regina; daughter Stefania. YVA 31.2/4530.

Zwonarz, Józef and Franciszka. YVA 31.2/331.

INDEX

"Above ground," 123-6.

A Poor Christian Looks at the Ghetto, 248.

Abramowicz, Natalia, 172-3.

Adamczyk, Józef, 139.

Agudat Israel, 29, 48, 57, 192, 194, 198, 276n108.

Ainsztein, Reuben, 227, 306n109.

Alcohol & taverns, 18-9.

Alexander I, 24.

Alexander II, 30.

Aliens-Other, xii, 32, 34, 46-7, 60, 63, 113-4, 177, 219, 221, 242, 258, 298n82.

Alter, Wiktor, 273n53.

Amendment Act (2018), 259.

Anders, Władysław, 203, 212-3.

Andrzejewski, Jerzy, 252.

Angola plan, 56.

Anielewicz, Mordechai, 307n137.

Ansbacher, Hanan, 156.

Antczak, Franciszek, 171-2.

Anti-Jewish violence, 30-1, 55, 84, 102-3, 139, 238, 240, 242-6, 269n139.

Arczynski, Ferdynand, 180, 298n18, 300n47.

Armia Krajowa (AK-Home Army), 202, 208, 213-20, 222-33, 233, 304n78, 307n138, 309n173.

Armia Ludowa (AL-People's Army), 213-4, 226, 230, 234.

Ashenberg, Eli, 174-5.

Association of Hidden Children, 252.

Association of Poles of Mosaic Faith, 45.

Association of Polish Jews (Torch), 45.

Auschwitz-Birkenau, 65, 71, 83, 93, 155, 245

Baal Shem Tov, Israel, 23.

Babi Yar, 92.

Babilińska, Gertruda, 163.

Bartoszewski, Władysław, 44, 180, 277n139, 285n29, 295n43.

Barwy Biale (White Colors), 228.

Bathory, Stefan, 3.

Beck, Józef, 42, 56-7.

Będzin, 84, 165.

Begin, Menachem, vii, 212, 275n96, 284n141.

Beit Lohamei Hagetaot Museum, 296n49.

Bełżec camp, ix, 83, 93, 188, 208-9.

Berg, Mary, 103.

Berling, Zygmunt, 213, 231.

Berman, Adolf & Batya (Temkin), 125, 180, 182, 186, 291n53.
Bernarda, Sister, 161-2.
Bielecki, Jerzy, 155-6.
Bienkowski, Władysław, 180.
Bienkowski, Witold, 185.
Biuletyn Infomacyjny, 139, 185.
Blaskowitz, Johannes, 78.
Bloc of Polish Jews of All Classes, 45.
Blond, Shlomo, 152.
Błoński, Jan, 247-50, 253.
Blood libel 4, 16-7, 52, 277-8n139.
Blum, Léon, 56, 276n112.
Bogdanowicz, Anna, 172.
Bogucka, Maria, 13.
Bolesław III, 2.
Bolesław V (the Pious), 4.
Bór-Komorowski, Tadeusz, 208, 222, 227, 231, 306n109,126.
Bortnowska, Halina, 250.
Boruchewicz, Maksymilian (Borwicz, Michel), 183.
Brauchitsch, Walther von, 78.
Brenner, Lilian, 164.
Brik, Samuel, 150.
Brodetsky, Selig, 211.
Bronowski, Aleksander, 168-9.
Bruniany, Wawrzyniec, 150-1.
Brunner, Alois, 196-7.
Bund (General Workers' Union), vii, 27-9, 48- 9, 55, 91, 98, 180-1, 184, 186, 201-2, 206-7, 212, 221, 239, 273n53, 291n66.
Bunel, Lucien (Father Jacques), 297n73.
Burg, Joseph, 193.
Burghers, 2-5, 11-3, 310n196.
Bursztyn, Ignacy & Esther, 310n196.
Calka, Szymon, 156.
Campo dei Fiori, 248.

Capistrano, John, 30.
Casimir-Kazimierz III (the Great), 4.
Catherine II, 24.
Cejlon, Chil-Hillel, 218.
Celemenski, Jacob, 233-4.
Celuch, Konstanty & Justyna, 174.
Chamberlain, Houston, xi.
Charuk, Jan, 159.
Chełmno camp, ix, 93.f
Children-Jewish, x, 26, 83, 88, 105, 114-5, 128-9, 138, 162-8, 171, 181-3, 227, 230, 240-1, 244, 252, 289n27, 296n51.
Chodźko, Jan, 31.
Christian Democratic Party, 49.
Church loans, 19-21.
Churchill, Winston, 274n73.
Cognitive dissonance, 114-6, 288n89.
Cossacks, 13-4.
Council of Four Lands, 5-7, 19.
Curzon line, 203, 238.
Cygler, Tamar, 165.
Cymerman, Chawa, 151.
Czack, Tadeusz, 22-3.
Czarny, Josef & Helena, 156.
Czerniaków, Adam, 103, 208.
Czubak, Genowefa (Sr. Dolorosa), 162.
Dafner, Anna & sister Malka, 295n34.
Daniluk, Włodzimierz & Anna, 175.
Davies, Nathan, 58, 61, 271n15.
Death marches, 82, 94, 156, 295n34.
December 17, 1942 declaration, 209-10.
Delegatura (Delegate Office), 113, 135, 139, 179, 184-7, 202, 204, 206, 208, 218-21, 229, 299n35, 301n6.
Deneko, Jadwiga, 171.

Dereczynski, Aron, 155.
Diamant, Ita, 132.
Diller, Sara, 172, 297n72.
Dmowski, Roman, 27, 32, 40, 49,
    59-60.
Dobraczyński, Jan, 128.
Domagała, Kazimierz, 140
Drang nach Osten (expansion east-
    ward), 64.
Dreifuss, Havi, 101, 115-6, 142,
    279n4m, 288n89.
Drumont, Edouard, xii
Duda, Antoni & Helena, 174
Dusza, Władysław, 138-9.
Dyrda, Maria & Pawel, 165.
Dziennik Polski, 206.
Ehrlich, Henryk, 273n53
Ehrlich, Yehuda, 141.
Eichmann, Adolf, 94, 196, 283n108.
Einsatzgruppen, ix, 82, 92, 138, 194.
Eisenbach, Artur, 26, 29.
Eiss, Chaim Israel, 192, 198.
Eitel, Leon, 147-8.
Elbojm-Dorembus, Chaya-Helena,
    145-6.
Elimination of elites, 72-3.
Elongatio Preputii, 169.
Emden, Jacob, 264n33.
Engelhard, Halina, 161-2.
Engelking-Boni, Barbara, 259-60.
Epistle to the Galatians, 16.
Esther (Esterka), 263n17.
Ettinger, Shmul, 6, 13.
Evans, Richard, 111, 280n25, 281n59.
Eybeschutz, Jonathan, 264n33.
Falkowski, Stanisław, 161.
Falska, Maryna, 164.
Feiner, Leon, 180, 186.
Figowicz, Herman, 174.
Fink, Józef, 150.

Fischer, Ludwig, 120.
Fiszgrund, Hanna, 163-4.
Flakowicz-Komem, Josef, 133-4.
Folks-Shtime (People's Voice), 241.
Folkspartei (People's Party), 29.
Fontaine, J.L. de la, 8-9.
Forced labor in Germany, 74-5, 181.
Four-year *Sejm*, 22-3,
Frank, Hans, 69, 72-3, 78, 86, 88,
    172, 276n110, 283n108.
Frank, Jacob, 28.
Friedman, Lutek, 233.
Frydman, Margareta, 162.
Gacz, Antonina, 147-8.
Gardzielowa, Feliksa, 133.
Gargasz, Sophie & Jakob, 172.
Gebirtig, Mordechai, 63.
General Government, 65-6, 69-73, 76,
    80, 86, 215.
Generalplan-Ost, 69.
German warnings, 119-21.
Getter, Matylda, 162.
Głębicka, Maria, 148.
Gliński, Leonard, 159-60.
Główna Komisja, 240.
Godlewski, Marceli, 160-1.
Goebbels, Joseph, 68, 84.
Goldberg, Jacob, vii, 7, 37, 261n1.
Golden Age, 5.
Goldfein, Olga, 162, 296n49.
Goldman, Golda & Layka, 171.
Goldman, Michael, 156.
Goldstein, Bernard, 291n66.
Goldstein, Chaim, 233.
Goldstein, Tatiana, 154.
Gołowacz, Wacław & Jadwiga, 151.
Gołuchówski, Jozef, 31.
Goodman, H.A., 198.
Górski, Stanisław, 20.
Gosk, Stanisław, 149-50.

Government-in-Exile, 170, 179, 190-
1, 201-2, 209-10, 221, 238,
303n51.
Grabiec, Jan, 185.
Grabowski, Henryk, 307n140.
Grabowski, Ignacy, 37.
Grabski, Władysław, 53.
Graetz, Heinrich, 262n8, 263n17.
Grobelny, Julian, 180.
Gross, Jan T., 143, 250, 293n95,
312n61.
Gruszniewski, Pinchas, 244.
Guilds, 2-3, 11-2.
Gumplowicz, Ludwik, 12-3.
Gutman, Israel, 113, 137, 144, 185-6,
188, 210, 222, 230, 235, 285-
6n29, 299n48, 304n61.
Gutter, Alexandra, 124, 132-3.
Guzik, Joseph, 142.
Hadziewicz, Piotr, 265n53.
Haganah, 57.
Halamajowa, Franciszka, 152.
Halevi, Judah, 262n3.
Halperin, Jozeph, 218.
Hanaczów, 229.
Harvest Festival (*Erntefest*), 93.
Hasidism, vii, 23, 43.
Haskalah, 24.
Heller, Celia, 52, 60-1.
Herman, Eli, 156.
Herzig, Jakub, 104-5.
Heydrich, Reinhard, 85-6.
Himmler, Heinrich, 68, 75.
Hirszfeld, Ludwik, 46, 87.
Hitler, Adolf, 60, 68, 78, 99, 222,
234, 248, 274n72, 292n86.
Hlond, August, 52-3, 107, 245,
311n37.
Hochberg Miriam (Mariańska,
Maria), 180.

Holocaust by Bullets, ix, 83.
Home Army; see, Armia Krajowa.
Hotel Polski affair, 189, 300n58.
Hügli, Rudolf, 191-3, 197.
Igran, Marian, 233.
Irgun Zva Leumi (Etzel), 57.
Isserles, Moses (Remah), 8-9.
Iwański, Henryk, 307n137.
Izraelita, 19, 26-7.
Jabotinsky, Vladimir-Zeev, 63-4,
277n117.
Jacków, Stanisław, 152-3.
Jagiellonian university, 72, 248.
Jaki, Patryk, 259.
Jankiel, 25, 62.
Jankowski, Jan Stanisław, 301n6.
Jastrębski, Wincenty, 79.
Jedwabne massacre, 92, 139-41,
250-1.
Jeleński, Jan, 31-2.
Jewish Colonization Committee,
276n108.
Jewish National Council, 180-1,
184, 186.
Jewish population, vii, 10, 13-4, 15,
29-30, 40, 43-4, 46, 53-4, 58,
82, 87, 188, 195, 209, 239-40,
246, 251, 271n32, 313n66.
Jewish Religious Council, 241.
Jewish soldiers, 66, 102, 212-3,
279n4.
Jeziorski, Władysław, 157.
Job, Józef & Wiktoria & d. Stefania,
157-8.
John Donne's People, 177, 255.
John of Swisłocz the Peddler, 31.
Joint Distribution Committee, 42, 88,
241, 313n66.
Joniuk, Jan, 154.
Joselewicz, Dov Ber (Berek), 21.

Józefów town, 71.
Judenrat (Jewish Council), 86-7.
Kaczyński, Zygmunt, 207.
Kahane, David, 311n37.
Kalek, Weronika, 172-3.
Kalisz Statute, 4.
Kamiński, Mieczysław, 309n184.
Kanabus, Feliks, 169.
Kann, Maria, 144.
Kaplan, Chaim Aron, 97-8, 101, 103, 105, 115.
Karp, Josaphat Michał, 15, 20.
Karski, Jan, 112, 170, 208-10, 223, 247.
Karwasser, Bracha, 289n27.
Kassow, Samuel, 114, 278n153.
Katyn massacre, 81, 91, 203
Katz, Heni, 172.
KB (Security Corps), 307n137.
Kehillah, kehilot, 5.
Keitel, Wilhelm, 292n86.
Kelley, David, 194.
Kennkarte ID, 126, 181-2.
Kermish, Joseph 300n47.
Khazar, 1, 262n3.
Khmelnytsky, Bohdan, xi, 13-4.
Kielce pogrom (1946), 243. 245-6.
Kieloch, Jadwiga, 158.
Kleinman, Josef, 150-1.
Klukowski, Zygmunt, 74-5, 77, 80, 136, 215-6, 226, 229.
Knoll, Roman, 221.
Kocborowo (Conradstein), 73.
Koestler, Arthur, 262n3.
Kołodziejek, Władysław, 153-4.
Konrad Żegota, 180.
Koordynacia (Coordination), 241.
Korboński, Stefan, 77, 208.
Kościuszko, Tadeusz, 21.
Kosher meat law, 42.

Kosower, Shoshana-Emilka, 294n2.
Kossak-Szczucka, Zofia, 108-10, 179-80, 253, 295n43, 296n46.
Kostrz, Andrzej, 155.
Kot, Stanisław, 205, 211.
Kowalski, Adam, 147.
Kowalski, Władyslaw, 158.
Kozłowski, Leon, 79.
KPP—Communist party, 41, 50
Krahelska-Filipowiczowa, Wanda, 180.
Kraków pogrom (1945), 243, 245.
Krakowski, Shmuel, 137, 185-8, 210, 230, 235, 300n48, 304n61, 307n138/140.
Krasiński, Wincety, 31.
Kruszyński, Józef, 52, 274n79.
Kryski, Rachela, 164-5.
Krzemienski, Stanisław, 152.
Krzysztonek, Aniela, 163-4.
Kubacki, Michał, 161.
Kubik, Czesław, 173.
Kubina Teodor, 245.
Küchler, Georg von, 84-5.
Kühl, Julius, 190-2, 197-8, 301n66.
Kukieł, Marian, 205.
Kula, Alfons, 276n112.
Kumoch, Jakub, 197, 300n61.
Kuperman, Moshe, 171-2.
Kurdziel, Stanisław & Jan, 170.
Kuropieska, Leopolda, 133-4.
Kutrzeba, Joseph, 161.
Ładoś, Aleksander, 190-9.
Landau, Ludwik, 100-1.
Lanzmann, Claude, 247.
Laqueur, Walter, 194.
Latifundia, 10.
Lebensborn (Fountain of Life)
Lebensraum (living space), 75.
Lehman, Mindla, 174.

Lemkin, Raphael, 272-3n44.
Levinas, Emmanuel, 177.
Lewandowski, Zbigniew, 223-4.
Lewin, Abraham, 115.
Lewin, Isaac, 194.
Lewin, Józef, 171-2.
Lewin, Yitshak Meir, 276n108.
Lewinski, Jerzy, 224.
Liberman, Eliahu, 227-8.
Lichten, Joseph, 60
List, Heinrich, 297n73.
Lizhensk, Elimelech of, 23.
Łódź ghetto, 86-9, 93.
Łoza, Stefania & son Eugeniuz, 134.
Lublin *kahal*, 20-1.
Lukas, Richard, 111, 209, 214-5,
    219, 270n11, 279n19, 280n32,
    284n141, 287n63, 303n51,
    304n78, 307n138, 308n146.
Lumpenproletariat, 100.
Luria, Solomon (Maharshal), 8.
Lustgarten, Arieh, 157.
Maciarz, Maria, 166.
Madagascar plan, 56, 82, 276n110
Majdanek camp, ix, 93, 183.
Makson, Antoni, 174.
Maltz, Moshe, 152.
Marcus, Joseph, 60-1.
Marcyniuk, Stefan, 149.
Margoshes, Samuel, 292n85.
Mark, Ber, 306n109.
Markowitz, Benjamin & Zlata, 156-7.
Marr, Wilhelm, xii.
Masiukiewicz, Pawel, 265n50.
Mazur, Feliks, 104.
Meisels, Dov Ber, 9, 21-2.
Mendelsohn, Ezra, 59, 61-2.
Mendès-France, Pierre, 193-4.
Mickiewicz, Adam, 21, 25, 62.
Micuta, Wacław, 232.

Mikołajczyk, Stanisław, 201, 206,
    299, 303n51.
Mikołajków, Aleksander &
    Leokadia, 153.
Mikulski, Jan, 150.
Miłosz, Czesław, 248.
Minikes, Haviva and Gerson, 296n51.
Mintz, Yitzhak, 174.
Mirek, Jan, 158-9.
Misiuna, Władysław, 169.
Mitzenmacher, Rachela, 169.
Mława, 84-5.
Mlynarczyk, Natalia, 166.
Moczar, Mieczysław, 246-7.
Moldrzyk, Erwin & Gertruda,
    295n34.
Monroe, Kristen, 177-8, 254-5.
Morgenthau, Henry Sr., 41.
Moszczeńska, Iza, 33.
Mularski, Józef, 228.
Musial, Stanisław, 250.
Nasz Dom (Our Home), 164.
Natanson, Jakub, 46.
National Democratic Party (Endecja),
    27, 32-3, 40-1, 49, 55, 59, 98,
    101, 201, 205, 220, 285n22.
Neighbors?, 250.
Ney, Julian, 172.
Nicholas I, 24.
Night Watch (*Nachtschutz*), 290-1n48.
Nisko region, 283n108.
Nowak, Irena, 134.
Nowak, Juliana, 148.
Nowiński, Wacław, 168-9.
Nowodworski, Leon, 101.
Nowosielski, Stanisław, 157.
NSZ (National Armed Forces), 174,
    214, 218, 226, 229-30, 233,
    235, 308n150.
Numerus clausus, 54, 60-1.

Nussbaum, Lisa, 155.
Nussenblat, Yitzhak, 152.
NZO (New Zionist Organization), 277n117.
Ogniewska-Jorasz, Irena, 164, 296n54.
Ognowska, Franciszka, 174.
Oldak, Apolonia & Aleksander, 164.
Oliner, Samuel & Pearl, 176.
Oneg Shabbes archives, 89, 99-100, 106, 115, 240.
ONR-Falanga (National Radical Camp), 49, 55, 80.
Orbach, Sonia, 146.
Orzeszkowa, Eliza, 25-6.
Ovart, Odile & Remy, 297n73.
Owińska (Treskau), 74
Paderewski, Ignacy, 41.
Pająk, Genowefa, 165.
Pajewski, Teodor, 183, 294n2.
Pale of Settlement, xi, 24, 268n113.
Pan Tadeusz, 25, 62.
Paraguayan passports, 190-3, 195, 197.
Parnasim, 7.
Partition of Poland, 21-3, 257.
Passover Warsaw pogrom, 105.
Paszkiewicz, Rozalia, 152.
Paulsson, Gunnar, 189, 289n18.
Pawlikowski, John, 53.
Pawlikowski, Józef, 22.
Pechter, Esther, 159.
Peltel, Feigele (Vladka), 142-3, 233.
Peltyn, Samuel H., 26-7.
Pielkałkiewicz, Jan, 301n6.
Pieńkowski, Wincenty, 22.
Pilecki, Witold, 72, 197.
Pilet-Golaz, Marcel, 196.
Piller, Hanna, 158.
Pilnik, Jan, 185.

Piłsudski, Józef, 39-42, 54-5, 59-60, 258.
Piotrków Trybunalski, 86, 139, 163.
Piotrowska, Jadwiga, 128.
Piszczkowski, Tadeusz, 276.
Pius XII, 210.
Poalei Zion Left, 278.
Pogroms, viii, xi, 17, 29-30, 41, 102, 104-5, 139, 243, 261n2.
Poincaré, Raymond, 54.
Polin-Polania, 9.
Polish "Blue" Police, 74, 136, 138, 214, 290n48, 291n66.
Polish army, 66, 91, 102, 203, 212-3, 231.
Polish National Council, 201, 204, 207, 209, 211, 220.
Polish-Lithuanian Commonwealth, 3-5, 12-4, 23, 39-40.
Polonsky, Antony, 13, 227.
Ponary massacre, 92, 206.
Poniatowski, Stanislaus August, 7.
Potocki, Jerzy, 56.
Potok, Alina, 160.
PPR-New Communist party, 213, 239, 284n150.
PPS—Polish Socialist Party, 28, 40-1, 48-9, 180, 220.
Pragier, Adam, 207.
Prekerowa, Teresa, 181, 183-4, 188, 299n39.
Promesas, 193.
Protocols of the Elders of Zion, 51.
Prus, Bolesław, 35.
Przytyk pogrom (1936), 275n102.
Pszenny, Józef, 224.
Puchalski, Jan & Anna, 151.
Racial Register, 69, 75, 279n19.
Raczki, Robert, 155.
Raczkiewicz, Władysław, 201, 210.

Raczyński, Edward, 57, 209-11.
Radziwiłł, Janusz, 79.
Rafaelowitz, Pinhas, 150.
Rappaport, Natan, 241.
Ratajski, Cyryl, 301n6.
Rechtman-Schwarz, Zwia, 128.
Reich, Chaskiel, 153.
Rek, Tadeusz, 180, 300n47.
Rembiszewski, Dora, 165.
Ribbentrop-Molotov Pact, 81.
Riegner, Gerhart, 208, 303n38.
Riga treaty (1921), 203.
Righteous Among the Nations, x, 134,
    144, 148, 156, 160, 198, 229,
    231, 254-5.
Ringelblum, Emanuel, 62-3, 80, 89-
    90, 98-9, 102-6, 113, 115, 119,
    122, 125, 131, 133, 136, 142,
    145, 175-6, 181, 183, 187, 224,
    240, 278n153, 294n1.
Ritual murder charge, 17, 51,
    243, 253.
Rodziewicz, Wiktoria, 165.
Rokicki, Konstanty, 190, 192, 197-8.
Rolan journal, 31.
Ronald Lauder Foundation, 251.
Roosevelt, Franklin D., 56, 170,
    195, 207.
Rosenbaum, Benzion, 150.
Rosenheim, Yaakov, 194.
Roslan, Aleksander & Amelia, 166.
Rostkowski, Ludwik, 182.
Rowecki, Stefan, 95, 206, 208, 220,
    222-3, 303n41, 306n126.
Ryniewicz, Stefan, 190, 192, 197-8.
Rzewuski, Stanisław Mateusz, 34.
Saginur, Max, 152-3.
Sanacja, 42.
Sawa, Stefan, 230-1.
Schaft, Michal, 154.

Schulte, Eduard, 303n38.
Schwarzbart, Yitzhak-Ignacy, 201,
    204, 206-7, 302n29, 303n41,
    304n61.
Segal, Roman, 151.
Sendlerowa, Irena, 128, 160, 167-8,
    173, 182, 260.
Serafinowicz, Julian & Stanisława,
    295n33.
Shachna, Shalom, 8.
Shatzky (Szacki), Jacob, 26, 28.
Shikler, Mordechai, 149.
Shoah film, 247.
Shorr, Moshe, 276n108.
Shtetel, 2.
Shulchan Aruch (Code of Jewish
    Law), 8.
Shumowitz, Yitzhak, 150.
Sigismund I, 18.
Sigismund III, 3.
Sikorski, Władysław, 66, 91, 201,
    203-4, 207-8, 210-1, 212, 220,
    301n3, 302n29.
Silberberg, Michal, 311n37.
Silberschein, Avraham, 192, 195, 197-
    8. 300n61.
Silverman, Sydney, 303n38.
Sinai peninsula plan, 276n112.
Singer, Elie, 301n66.
Sławoj-Skladkowski, Felicjan, 54.
Słowik, Karolina & daughter Olga,
    234-5.
Śmigły-Rydz, Edward, 42.
Sneh-Kleinbaum, Moshe, 211.
Sobibór camp, ix, 83, 93, 149, 209.
Solomon, Yeshieh, 233.
Soltysiak, Marian (Barabasz), 230-1.
Soroka, Tadeusz, 155.
Sosnowy, Jan & Stefania, 174-5.
Środa, Jan, 141.

Stańczyk, Jan, 203-4.
Stańczyk, Stanisław & d.
  Klementyna, 150
Starowolski, Szymon, 5.
Stawiska-Cebulska, Cyla, 155-6.
Steinlauf, Michael, 172-3.
Sternbuch, Yitzhak & Recha, 192,
  194, 198-9.
Sternik, Edward, 228-9.
Stolowicka Lidia & son Michael, 163.
Stroop, Jürgen, 111, 307n144.
Struszinska, Wiktoria &
  Zygmunt, 154.
Strzelec, Stanisława, 151.
Studnicki, Władysław, 79.
Stykowski, Wacław, 233.
Suchodolski, Adam &
  Stanisława, 154.
Sunday Rest Law, 54, 61.
Świętochowski, Aleksander, 25.
Szajner, Abraham, 157.
Szczebrezeszyn (Zamość region), 74,
  136, 215.
Szczecinska, Maria, 151.
Szembek, Krzysztof, 16, 18.
Szemet, Helena, 296n51.
Szlachta (nobility), 3, 9, 41.
Szmaltsowniks—blackmailers, 131-2,
  186, 210, 250, 299n35,39.
Sztark, Adam, 171.
Sztok, Zofia & son Kazimierz, 171-2.
Szturm, Berl & daughter Helen, 157-8.
Szumielewicz, Władysław, 230-1.
Tanay, Emanuel, 130.
Tartakower, Aryeh, 46.
Taube Foundation for Jewish
  Life, 251.
Tec, Nechama, 112, 127, 129,
  131, 176.
Tehran Conference (1943), 238.

Ten-Year Evacuation Plan, 277n117.
Terner, Esther, 149.
Thomsen, Henry, 297n73.
Three Crosses Square, 129.
Train derailments, 215-7.
Trawniki labor camp, 119, 183, 216,
  294n2.
Treblinka camp, ix, 83, 93, 107, 129,
  147, 156, 161, 208-9, 217, 233,
  295n33.
Trustees Head Office of East, 76.
Turkow, Yonas, 244.
Turowicz, Jerzy, 249-50.
Tuwim, Julian, 47, 272n42.
Twersky, Natalia; son Jack, 166.
Ulma, Józef & Wiktoria, 171.
Ustjanowsky, Ignacy &
  Bronisława, 149.
Uszyński, Jedrzej, 300n61.
Vaad Arba Aratsot, (Sejm Żydowski);
  see, Council of Four Lands
Vaad Hatzalah, 192.
Vatican II (Nostra Aetate), 245, 253-4.
Versailles Treaty, 41.
Verstandig, Marek, 173-4.
Volksdeutsche, 69, 80, 136, 173.
Wagner, Richard, xii
Walas, Marcin, 174.
Wallach, Nathan, 166.
Wannsee conference, 92-3, 279n19.
Warsaw ghetto, 86-9, 93, 102, 105,
  115, 118-9, 128-9, 133, 160,
  170, 173, 181-2, 195, 205, 208-
  9, 219-20, 222-5, 241, 248,
  289n18,307n137.
Warsaw Great Action, 93, 208.
Warsaw Rabbinical School, 26.
Warsaw uprising (1944), 231-4.
Wartheland, 65, 73-4.
Wasilewski, Zygmunt, 47.

Wasser, Hersh, 99-100.
Weeks, Theodore, 4, 34.
Weinryb, Bernard, 30.
Weizmann, Chaim, 57, 276n112.
Welles, Sumner, 195.
Westerweel, Johannes (Joop), 297n73.
Wiglusz, Jan & Maria, 141, 293n102.
Wilner, Aryeh, 222-4, 307n140.
Windenstreich, Isaac & Hanna, 159.
Wise, Stephen, 195, 303n38
Wiśniewski, Zygmunt, 139-40.
Wittenberg, Samuel, 233.
Wojtowicz, Alojzy, Kazimierz &
    Antony, 229.
Wojtyla, Karol (John Paul II), 245.
Wolfgang, Adolf, 227.
Woliński, Henryk, 219, 223-4,
    305n101.
Wolman, Halina, 147-8.
Wolski, Mieczysław, 175-6.
World Jewish Congress (WJC), 192,
    208, 303n38.
World War I, viii, xii, 39, 189, 257.
World War II, viii, 43, 65-7, 234, 237,
    259, 280n25, 287b73.
Yad Vashem, x, 137, 144, 148, 260,
    295n43, 229, 231, 254-5,
    300n61.
Yalta Conference (1945), 238.
Yeshiva, yeshivot, 8, 58, 261n3,
Yiddish, xii, 1-2, 22, 26-9, 32-4, 44,
    46-7, 49, 57-8, 131, 239-40,
    241-2, 244, 252, 272n37.
YIVO institute, 58, 61.
Yom-Tov, Abraham, 154.
Żabiński, Jan, 153.
Zaderecki, Tadeusz, 274n79.
Załuski, Andrzej Stanisław, 19

Załuski, Józef Andrzej, 16-7.
Zalwowski, Franciszek & Tekla, 151.
Zamość region, 70, 74-6, 80, 114, 174,
    209, 215, 305.
Zandman, Alex, 151.
Ząnkiewicz, Feliks, 146-7.
Zawadzka, Halina, 234-5.
Żegota, 108, 110, 167-8, 171, 179-
    87, 202, 221-2, 229, 298n18,
    299n35, 300n47.
Zemora, Michael, 151.
Ziemian, Janina, 125-6.
ŻIH (Jewish Historical
    Institute), 240.
Zimmerman, Joshua, 139, 309n173.
Zimon, Konrad & Regina & d.
    Stefania, 156.
Zionism-Zionists, vii, 29, 44, 47-8,
    55, 57-9, 91, 193, 201, 212,
    241, 246, 274n73, 276n112,
    277n117, 278n153, 284n141,
    307n137.
Zissman, Sima & Nechama, 153.
ŻOB (Jewish Fighting Organization),
    223-4, 241, 307.
Zośka battalion, 232.
Żuchowski, Stefan, 16.
Zuchvinkel fun Kroyvim, 244.
Zuckerman, Yitzhak, 224, 244,
    307n140.
Związek Odwetu (Revenge
    Union), 228.
Zwonarz, Józef, 166.
Żydokomuna myth, 50-1, 92, 226,
    237, 308n146.
Zygielbojm, Szmuel, 201, 207.
Zygmunt, August, 12.
Zysman, Józef, 129.

Printed in the United States
by Baker & Taylor Publisher Services

Printed in the United States
by Baker & Taylor Publisher Services